PERFECT VEGETABLES

A BEST RECIPE CLASSIC

A BEST RECIPE CLASSIC

Perfect Vegetables

BY THE EDITORS OF

COOK'S ILLUSTRATED

PHOTOGRAPHY BY CARL TREMBLAY AND DANIEL J. VAN ACKERE

ILLUSTRATIONS BY JOHN BURGOYNE

FRONT COVER PHOTOGRAPH BY DANIEL J. VAN ACKERE

America's
TEST KITCHEN

BROOKLINE, MASSACHUSETTS

Copyright © 2003 by the Editors of *Cook's Illustrated*

America's Test Kitchen
17 Station Street
Brookline, MA 02445

ISBN-13: 978-0-936184-69-2
ISBN-10: 0-936184-69-8
Library of Congress Cataloging-in-Publication Data
The Editors of *Cook's Illustrated*

Perfect Vegetables—Would you make 23 batches of oven fries to find the best version? We did.
Here are 350 exhaustively tested recipes using our 53 favorite vegetables.
1st Edition

ISBN-13: 978-0-936184-69-2
ISBN-10: 0-936184-69-8
(hardback): $29.95
I. Cooking. I. Title
2003

Manufactured in the United States of America

Distributed by America's Test Kitchen, 17 Station Street, Brookline, MA 02445.

10 9 8 7 6 5 4 3 2

Pictured on front of jacket: Oven Fries (page 229)
Pictured on back of jacket: Oven Fries (page 229), Coleslaw with Bacon and Buttermilk Dressing (page 59),
Stuffed Bell Peppers (page 193), Mashed Potatoes (page 248)

CONTENTS

PREFACE

IN THE SMALL VERMONT TOWN WHERE I grew up, there was only one vegetable of note: the potato. It was either baked or mashed (never fried or steamed) or perhaps sliced and used in a casserole. The old farmers had a trick of popping open a piping hot baked potato using just their fingers, a bit of front-parlor wizardry that made an impression on a seven-year-old. They goaded me to try it and witnessed the predictable result: slightly burnt fingertips. Of course, luring the unsuspecting into embarrassing situations was the bread and butter of country living, holding out one's hand to a newcomer (while the other had a firm hold on an electric fence) being the epitome of a good laugh.

The spud aside, American cooking has not been kind to the vegetable. In the days when most of our vegetables came from the garden, simple preparation was satisfactory. As the quality of our produce dropped dramatically in terms of taste, Americans turned increasingly to casseroles. Green beans were slathered in a heavy white sauce, fresh corn on the cob was turned into an eggy corn pudding, and many vegetables—fennel, parsnips, radishes—were ignored altogether. These days, the french fry is the American vegetable of choice. Potatoes (mostly processed, by the way) are the number one seller (135 pounds per year per person). The number of parsnips (0.11 pounds) and endives (0.2 pounds) Americans consume in one year could probably fit in the back of my pickup.

This book is our attempt to bring vegetables back into the mainstream. These are not fancy preparations, and we have not attempted to reinvent the wheel. Our goal was to free vegetables from the culinary flotsam and jetsam of the last half-century so that we could once again bring them to the table with pride and enthusiasm. In short, we wanted to elevate the status of the vegetable from boring side dish, using every flavor-enhancing technique we could find.

We tested these recipes with run-of-the-mill supermarket vegetables and used the America's Test Kitchen recipe development process. Each recipe was tasted by a crew of test cooks until consensus on taste and texture was achieved.

We hope that this book will give you the opportunity to rediscover vegetables at home. As for myself, I now serve fewer potatoes and more of everything else, being more confident that I will deliver big flavors and winning dishes. As for my wife, Adrienne, she is quite happy about all of this. She may be the only person in Vermont who cannot abide the taste of potatoes.

Christopher Kimball
Founder and Editor
Cook's Illustrated and *Cook's Country*
Host, *America's Test Kitchen* and
Cook's Country from America's Test Kitchen

ACKNOWLEDGMENTS

ALL OF THE PROJECTS UNDERTAKEN at *Cook's Illustrated* are collective efforts, the combined experience and work of editors, test cooks, and writers, all joining in the search for the best cooking methods. Editor Jack Bishop spearheaded this project, Meg Suzuki was the chief recipe developer and writer for the book, and Julia Collin organized the photography shoots.

Amy Klee created the design for the Best Recipe series and Robin Gilmore-Barnes was responsible for the art direction of this book. Daniel J. van Ackere photographed the front-cover image. Carl Tremblay captured the images that appear throughout the book as well as on the back cover. Daniel J. van Ackere took photographs of the equipment and ingredients, and John Burgoyne drew all of the illustrations.

The following individuals on the editorial, production, circulation, customer service, and office staffs also worked on the book: Melissa Baldino, Ron Bilodeau, Barbara Bourassa, Erika Bruce, Matthew Card, Richard Cassidy, Sharyn Chabot, Garth Clingingsmith, Mary Connolly, Judy Davis, Cathy Dorsey, Keith Dresser, Keri Fisher, Lori Galvin-Frost, Elizabeth Germain, Rebecca Hays, India Koopman, Bridget Lancaster, Sean Lawler, Susan Light, Diane Mahoney, Jim McCormack, Jennifer McCreary, Erin McMurrer, Amy Monaghan, Nicole Morris, Henrietta Murray, John Olson, Jessica Lindheimer Quirk, Adam Ried, Jean Rogers, Mandy Shito, Tadashi Tezuka, Sonja Toulouse, Nina West, Lisa Wolff, Elizabeth Wray, and Dawn Yanagihara. And without help from members of the marketing staff, readers might never find our books. Special thanks to Deborah Broide, Steven Browall, Hugh Buchan, Shekinah Cohn, Connie Forbes, Julie Gardner, Jason Geller, Larisa Greiner, David Mack, Adam Perry, Laura Phillips, Steven Sussman, Jacqueline Valerio, and Jonathan Venier.

VEGETABLES

A TO Z

ARTICHOKES

ARTICHOKES ARE A PERENNIAL BELONGING TO THE SUNFLOWER FAMILY, with the edible portion of the plant being an immature thistle. The plants grow quite large, reaching up to 6 feet in diameter and 3 to 4 feet in height. While artichokes are sporadically available throughout the year, the spring months are high season. Then, artichokes are widely available, and their price is generally low.

Artichokes are commonly marketed in three sizes: small (2 to 4 ounces each), medium (8 to 10 ounces each), and large (12 ounces or more each). Surprisingly, different-size artichokes simultaneously bud on the same plant; the artichokes that grow on the plant's center stalk are the largest, and the smallest grow at the

juncture between the plant's leaves and the stem. After preparing, cooking, and eating all three sizes, we found that we preferred the small and medium artichokes to the large, which can be tough and fibrous.

When selecting fresh artichokes at the market, follow these rules of thumb. The artichokes should be tight and compact, like a flower blossom (which they are), as well as an unblemished bright green. They should "squeak" when you rub the leaves together—evidence that the artichoke still retains much of its moisture. If you tug at a leaf, it should cleanly snap off; if it bends, it's old. Also be on guard for leaves that look dried out and feathery about the edges—a sure sign of an over-the-hill artichoke.

There are two basic approaches to artichokes: Leave them whole (with minimal trimming before cooking) and let your dinner guests eat them leaf by leaf, or trim them to the heart before cooking (removing

all inedible portions) and let your guests reap the benefit of your labor. Medium artichokes can be left whole or trimmed to the heart. Because of their size, small artichokes are best trimmed to the heart.

Whether you are working with small or medium artichokes and leaving them whole or trimming them to the heart, artichokes will turn brown almost as soon as they are cut. It is crucial to submerge them in acidulated water, which neutralizes the enzymes responsible for oxidation. We tried a variety of acids to prevent oxidation, including white wine vinegar, apple cider vinegar, and lemon juice, and were most pleased with lemon juice because of its bright yet neutral flavor. Simply add the juice of half a lemon per quart of water and use the juiced lemon half to rub the cut portions of the artichoke to prevent them from browning as you trim them. Once they're cleaned, drop the artichokes into the bowl of acidulated water.

Medium artichokes are our favorite for serving whole, because they are easy to prepare and each artichoke conveniently serves one person. After experimenting with a variety of methods for cooking whole artichokes, including boiling, steaming, and microwaving, we concluded that steaming is the best choice. Steamed artichokes had the deepest, most pronounced flavor. We discovered that artichokes steam nicely when set on top of thick-sliced onion rings, which protect them from becoming waterlogged. A steaming rack also works. After steaming, allow the artichokes to cool down for at least 15 minutes before serving—it is easy to burn your fingers on them, as the dense artichokes retain a lot of heat. Steamed artichokes can also be chilled and eaten cool.

Braising is an option for medium artichokes that have been trimmed of all inedible portions before cooking. The artichokes become tender, and the braising liquid turns into a rich, flavorful sauce. To find the best braising method, we first looked at the braising liquid. We tested three obvious choices: wine, broth, and water. It was no surprise to discover that water diluted the artichoke flavor, making a dull, flat-tasting sauce. Using either wine or broth alone was better, but neither had the balance we were looking for. (For more on wine and artichokes, see page 8.) The solution was to use a combination of white wine and broth. The acidity of the wine gave the artichokes a bright flavor, and the broth added depth and richness.

As for herbs, we found the pungency of rosemary to be too strong for the master recipe (but quite promising for a variation), and parsley contributed little. We liked the subtle yet earthy flavors of thyme the best.

In the test kitchen, we find that small artichokes are best roasted, in part because there's no choke to remove. Roasting concentrates the delicate artichoke flavor and lightly crisps their exterior. This cooking method also intensifies the nuttiness of artichokes. The inedible outer portions must be trimmed, but otherwise, small artichokes can be roasted as is. To promote browning (and prevent the edges from burning), we found it best to coat the trimmed baby artichokes with olive oil. A 400-degree oven promotes maximum browning but does not run the risk of charring the artichokes, which can happen at higher temperatures.

INGREDIENTS:
What's Edible and What's Not

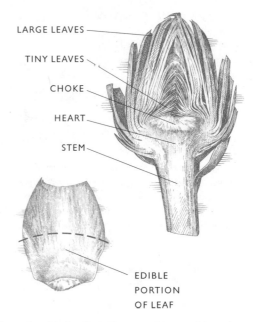

LARGE LEAVES
TINY LEAVES
CHOKE
HEART
STEM

EDIBLE
PORTION
OF LEAF

The entire exterior (including several layers of leaves), as well as the fuzzy choke and tiny leaves in the center, cannot be eaten. Only the heart and the bottom portions of the inner leaves become meaty and tender when cooked. The cooked heart can be eaten with a knife and fork. The edible portion at the bottom of the leaves is best scraped off with your teeth.

Master Recipe for Steamed Artichokes

SERVES 4

Artichokes steam nicely when set on top of thickly sliced onion rings, which keep the artichokes from becoming waterlogged. A steaming rack also works.

1   lemon, cut in half
4   medium artichokes (8 to 10 ounces each)
2   medium onions

1. Squeeze the lemon juice into a large bowl filled with cold water. Drop the spent lemon halves into the water.

2. Prepare the artichokes according to illustrations 1 through 3 below. Drop the trimmed artichokes into the acidulated water. Cut two 1½-inch-thick slices from the middle of each onion; using your fingers, pop out the outer three or four rings from the rest of the slice. Space the onion rings evenly across the bottom of a large

PREPARING ARTICHOKES FOR STEAMING

Medium artichokes (each weighing 8 to 10 ounces) are the best choice for steaming.

1. Removing the pin-sharp thorns from the tips of the leaves makes for easier handling and a more attractive presentation. Grasp the artichoke by the stem and hold it horizontal to the work surface. Use kitchen shears to trim the tips off the leaves row by row, skipping the top two rows.

2. Rest the artichoke on a cutting board. Holding the stem in one hand, cut off the top quarter (the top two rows) of the artichoke with a sharp chef's knife.

3. With the sharp thorns and leaf tips removed, the stem can now be cut flush with the base of the bulb. Drop the trimmed artichoke into the bowl of acidulated water.

4. Set a trimmed artichoke in each thick onion ring.

pot or Dutch oven and set one trimmed artichoke on top of each ring (see illustration 4 on page 4).

3. Fill the pot with water to ½ inch below the top of the onion rings. Bring the water to a boil over medium-high heat. Cover and cook until the outer artichoke leaves release easily when pulled, about 30 minutes. Check the pot periodically to make sure the water has not boiled dry; add more water as needed.

4. With tongs, carefully remove the artichokes from the pot and cool for at least 15 minutes before serving. Steamed artichokes can also be chilled and eaten cool. Serve with one of the following vinaigrettes.

Mustard Tarragon Vinaigrette
MAKES ABOUT ½ CUP

Both this and the Lemon Mint Vinaigrette that follows can be made ahead. However, in order to preserve their fresh flavor, the herbs should be added just before serving.

    6   tablespoons extra-virgin olive oil
    1   tablespoon red wine vinegar
    1   tablespoon Dijon mustard
    1   tablespoon minced fresh
        tarragon leaves
    1   medium clove garlic, minced or
        pressed through a garlic press
        Salt and ground black pepper

Whisk all the ingredients, including salt and pepper to taste, together in a medium bowl until thoroughly blended. Serve with steamed artichokes.

Lemon Mint Vinaigrette
MAKES ABOUT ½ CUP

Basil can be substituted for the mint. Depending on personal taste, you may want to increase the amount of honey.

    6   tablespoons extra-virgin olive oil
    1   teaspoon grated zest and 2
        tablespoons juice from 1 lemon
    1   tablespoon minced fresh mint leaves
    1   medium shallot, minced
    ½   teaspoon honey
        Salt and ground black pepper

Whisk all ingredients, including salt and pepper to taste, together in a medium bowl until thoroughly blended. Serve with steamed artichokes.

Master Recipe for Roasted Baby Artichokes
SERVES 4

Plan on roughly 4 small (or baby) artichokes per serving.

    1   lemon, cut in half
   16   small artichokes (2 to 4 ounces each)
    2   tablespoons extra-virgin olive oil
        Salt and ground black pepper

1. Adjust the oven racks to the upper-middle and lower-middle positions and heat the oven to 400 degrees.

2. Squeeze the lemon juice into a large bowl filled with cold water. Drop the spent lemon halves into the water.

3. Cut off the top quarter of each artichoke and snap off the fibrous outer leaves until you reach the inner leaves (see illustration 1 on page 6). With a paring knife, trim the dark

green exterior from the base of the artichoke as well as the exterior of the stem. Trim a thin slice from the end of the stem and cut the artichoke in half, slicing from tip to stem (see illustration 2 below). Drop the trimmed artichoke into the bowl of acidulated water until ready to cook.

4. Drain the artichokes and place them in a large bowl with the oil; toss to coat. Place the artichokes, cut-side down, on two rimmed baking sheets. Season lightly with salt and pepper to taste. Roast in the oven for 15 minutes. Using tongs, turn

PREPARING ARTICHOKES FOR ROASTING

Small artichokes (each weighing 2 to 4 ounces) are the best choice for roasting.

1. After cutting off the top quarter from the artichoke, snap off the fibrous outer leaves until you reach the yellow leaves.

2. With a paring knife, trim the dark green exterior from the base of the artichoke as well as the exterior of the stem. Trim a thin slice from the end of the stem and cut the artichoke in half, slicing from tip to stem. Drop the trimmed artichoke into a bowl of acidulated water.

the artichokes. Reverse the positions of the baking sheets, from top to bottom and front to back. Roast until the artichokes can be pierced easily with a skewer, about 10 minutes longer. Season to taste with additional salt and pepper, if desired, and serve.

➤ VARIATION

Roasted Baby Artichokes with Roasted Garlic Aïoli

Aïoli is a garlicky mayonnaise, and this version uses garlic that has been roasted along with the artichokes.

I	lemon, cut in half
16	small artichokes (2 to 4 ounces each)
I	head garlic, cloves separated from the bulb but with skins left on
I	cup extra-virgin olive oil
	Salt and ground black pepper
1/2	teaspoon dry mustard
	Pinch cayenne pepper
I	large egg yolk

1. Adjust the oven racks to the upper-middle and lower-middle positions and heat the oven to 400 degrees.

2. Reserve 1½ teaspoons of the juice from the lemon and set aside for the aïoli. Squeeze the rest of the lemon juice into a large bowl filled with cold water. Drop the spent lemon halves into the water. Set aside.

3. Cut off the top quarter of each artichoke and snap off the fibrous outer leaves until you reach the inner leaves (see illustration 1 at left). With a paring knife, trim the dark green exterior from the base of the artichoke as well as the exterior of the stem. Trim a thin slice from the end of the stem and cut the artichoke in half, slicing from tip to stem (see illustration 2 at left). Drop the trimmed artichoke into the bowl of acidulated water until ready to cook.

4. Drizzle the garlic cloves with 1 tablespoon of the oil and wrap the oiled cloves in aluminum foil. Drain the artichokes and place them in a large bowl with 3 tablespoons of the oil; toss to coat. Place the foil-wrapped garlic and the oiled artichokes, cut-side down, onto two rimmed baking sheets. Season the artichokes lightly with salt and pepper to taste. Roast in the oven for 15 minutes. Using tongs, turn the artichokes. Reverse the positions of the baking sheets, from top to bottom and front to back. Roast until the artichokes can be pierced easily with a skewer and the garlic cloves are soft, about 10 minutes longer.

5. When the garlic is cool enough to handle, squeeze the cloves from the skins into a small nonreactive bowl and press or mince the cloves finely. Add the dry mustard, cayenne, egg yolk, and reserved lemon juice and whisk together thoroughly. Add the remaining ¾ cup oil in a thin, steady stream while whisking constantly until a thick emulsion forms. Season with salt and pepper to taste and serve with the roasted artichokes.

Master Recipe for Braised Artichokes
SERVES 4 TO 6

Make sure to use a nonreactive pan; the acid in the wine will react with aluminum and cast-iron pans and will impart a metallic flavor to the sauce. The artichokes must be drained well before they are

PREPARING ARTICHOKES FOR BRAISING

1. Holding the artichoke by the stem, bend back and snap off the thick outer leaves, leaving the bottom portion of each leaf attached. Continue snapping off the leaves until you reach the light yellow cone at the center.

2. With a paring knife, trim off the dark outer layer from the bottom—this is the base of the leaves you've already snapped off.

3. Cut off the dark, purplish tip from the yellow cone of artichoke leaves.

4. With a vegetable peeler, peel off the fibrous, dark green exterior of the stem. Once peeled, cut off the bottom ½ inch of the stem.

5. Cut the artichoke in half, slicing from tip to stem.

6. Scrape out the small purple leaves and the fuzzy choke with a grapefruit spoon or tomato corer. Cut the artichoke into 1-inch wedges.

added to the pan; any additional water will dilute the braising liquid. Serve with fish or chicken.

1	lemon, cut in half
4	medium artichokes (8 to 10 ounces each)
3	tablespoons extra-virgin olive oil
2	small shallots, finely minced (about 1/4 cup)
3/4	cup dry white wine
3/4	cup low-sodium chicken broth
2	sprigs fresh thyme
	Salt
1/8	teaspoon ground black pepper

1. Squeeze the lemon juice into a large bowl filled with cold water. Drop the spent lemon halves into the water. Prepare the artichokes according to the illustrations on page

---

SCIENCE: Wine and Artichokes

Many sources warn against serving wine with artichokes, claiming that this vegetable can make an expensive Chardonnay taste like Welch's grape juice. In fact, artichokes contain a unique acid called cynarin that can stimulate sweetness receptors in the mouth and make anything consumed immediately afterward taste sweet. Does this mean you should not serve wine with artichokes? And what about braising artichokes in a mixture of wine and stock?

To find out if this problem really exists (and how widespread it is), 18 members of the test kitchen staff tasted steamed artichokes followed by plain water. Two tasters (or about 11 percent) reported that the water tasted distinctly sweet after sampling artichokes. It seems that sensitivity to cynarin is genetically determined, and the best way to find out if you have this sensitivity is to run a test at your leisure.

As for using wine as a braising liquid, no one in the test kitchen (including the two tasters who demonstrated some sensitivity to cynarin) objected.

---

7. Drop the artichoke wedges into the bowl of acidulated water until ready to cook.

2. Heat the oil in a large sauté pan or deep skillet over medium-high heat until shimmering. Add the shallots and cook until they start to turn golden, about 3 minutes. Drain the artichokes and add them to the pan along with the wine, broth, thyme, 1/4 teaspoon salt, and pepper. Bring to a simmer, cover the pan, turn the heat down to medium, and simmer until the artichokes are tender when pierced with a fork, about 30 minutes. Add more salt, if necessary, to taste. Serve.

➤ VARIATION
Braised Artichokes with Tomatoes and Rosemary

Canned tomatoes (and their juices) take the place of the chicken broth in this recipe. To turn this dish into an entrée, toss it with 1 pound of cooked pasta and serve it with freshly grated Parmesan cheese.

1	lemon, cut in half
4	medium artichokes (8 to 10 ounces each)
3	tablespoons extra-virgin olive oil
4	medium cloves garlic, minced or pressed through a garlic press
1	(14.5-ounce) can diced tomatoes
1/2	cup dry white wine
1	tablespoon minced fresh rosemary
	Salt
1/8	teaspoon ground black pepper

1. Squeeze the lemon juice into a large bowl filled with cold water. Drop the spent lemon halves into the water. Prepare the artichokes according to the illustrations on page 7. Drop the artichoke wedges into the bowl of acidulated water until ready to cook.

2. Heat the oil in a large sauté pan or deep skillet over medium-high heat until almost smoking. Add the garlic and cook until

fragrant, about 30 seconds. Drain the artichokes and add them to the pan along with the tomatoes, wine, rosemary, ¼ teaspoon salt, and pepper. Bring to a simmer, cover the pan, turn the heat down to medium, and simmer until the artichokes are tender when pierced with a fork, about 30 minutes. Add more salt, if necessary, to taste. Serve.

EQUIPMENT: Chef's Knives

A good chef's knife is probably the most useful tool any cook owns. Besides chopping vegetables, it can be used for myriad tasks, including cutting up poultry, mincing herbs, and slicing fruit. So what separates a good knife from an inferior one? To understand the answer to this question, it helps to know something about how knives are constructed.

The first pieces of cutlery were made about 4,000 years ago with the discovery that iron ore could be melted and shaped into tools. The creation of steel, which is 80 percent iron and 20 percent other elements, led to the development of carbon-steel knives—the standard for 3,000 years. Although this kind of steel takes and holds an edge easily, it also stains and rusts. Something as simple as cutting an acidic tomato or living in the salt air of the seacoast can corrode carbon steel.

Today, new alloys have given cooks better options. Stainless steel, made with at least 4 percent chromium and/or nickel, will never rust. Used for many cheap knives, stainless steel is also very difficult to sharpen. The compromise between durable but dull stainless steel and sharp but corrodible carbon steel is a material called high-carbon stainless steel. Used by most knife manufacturers, this blend combines durability and sharpness.

Until recently, all knives were hot drop forged—that is, the steel was heated to 2,000 degrees, dropped into a mold, given four or five shots with a hammer, and then tempered (cooled and heated several times to build strength). This process is labor intensive (many steps must be done by hand), which explains why many chef's knives cost almost $100.

A second manufacturing process feeds long sheets of steel through a press that punches out knife after knife, much like a cookie cutter slicing through dough. Called stamped blades, these knives require some hand finishing but are much cheaper to produce because a machine does most of the work.

While experts have long argued that forged knives are better than stamped ones, our testing did not fully support this position. We liked some forged knives and did not like others. Likewise, we liked some stamped knives and did not like others. The weight and shape of the handle (it must be comfortable to hold and substantial but not too heavy), the ability of the blade to take an edge, and the shape of the blade (we like a slightly curved blade, which is better suited to the rocking motion often used to mince herbs or garlic than a straight blade) are all key factors in choosing a knife.

When shopping, pick up the knife and see how it feels in your hand. Is it easy to grip? Does the weight seem properly distributed between the handle and the blade? In our testing, we liked knives made by Henckels and Wüsthof. An inexpensive knife by Forschner, with a stamped blade, also scored well.

THE BEST CHEF'S KNIVES

The Henckels Four Star (right) and Wüsthof-Trident Grand Prix (center) are top choices, but expect to spend about $80 for one of these knives. The Forschner (Victorinox) Fibrox (left) is lighter but still solid and costs just $30.

ASPARAGUS

ASPARAGUS PRESENTS ONE MAIN PREPARATION ISSUE—SHOULD THE spears be peeled, or is it better to discard the tough, fibrous ends entirely? In our tests, we found that peeled asparagus have a silkier texture, but we preferred the contrast between the crisp peel and the tender inner flesh. Peeling also requires a lot of work. We prefer to simply snap off the tough ends and proceed with cooking.

In terms of shopping, we prefer asparagus of medium thickness—about ⅝ inch thick. Very thick asparagus can be tough and woody and really should be peeled, even if you snap off the tough ends. Pencil-thin asparagus, which often command a premium price at the market, are very easy to overcook.

Also, don't be swayed by asparagus in pretty colors. Our tasters detected no flavor differences between purple and green asparagus in a blind taste test. (The purple spears turn green when cooked anyway.) Although our tasters enjoyed the sweet, buttery flavor of white asparagus, we preferred the slightly sharp flavor of plain old green spears. The price difference (white asparagus often costs twice as much as green asparagus) also weighs heavily in favor of traditional green spears.

Asparagus can be cooked in numerous ways. We first investigated moist-heat cooking methods—namely, boiling and steaming. They yielded similar results. Although some sources suggest boiling asparagus, we found that steaming is equally appealing (and easy) and leaves the tips just a bit crisper. Simply arrange the trimmed spears in a steamer basket above boiling water and cook until the asparagus is tender but not mushy, a process

that will take four to five minutes. Steamed asparagus is pretty bland. At the very least, we found that it should be drizzled with good olive oil and sprinkled with salt and pepper. More flavorful dressings are another good option.

A second option for asparagus is stir-frying. Many recipes for stir-fried asparagus begin by steaming or blanching the spears. The asparagus is then quickly stir-fried with the sauce ingredients. There are two problems with this scenario. First, two cooking methods means two dirty pots. Second, the flavor of the asparagus is diluted during the first cooking step, and then the asparagus doesn't spend enough time with the sauce ingredients to absorb much of their character.

We wanted to solve these problems and knew that skipping the precooking part of the recipe would be necessary. But would this work? The answer is yes, as long as you follow a few rules. First, try to use thinner

TRIMMING TOUGH ENDS FROM ASPARAGUS

In our tests, we found that the tough, woody part of the stem will break off in just the right place if you hold the spear the right way. With one hand, hold the asparagus about halfway down the stalk; with the thumb and index finger of the other hand, hold the spear about an inch up from the bottom. Bend the stalk until it snaps.

asparagus that can cook through strictly by stir-frying. If thicker spears are what you have on hand, cut them in half lengthwise so they will cook more quickly.

The second key to success is heat, and plenty of it. Asparagus, even thin spears, will be crunchy if stir-fried for just a minute or two. We found that medium spears cut into 1½-inch lengths need five minutes over intense heat to soften properly. All this heat ensures that the asparagus browns, which improves its flavor. Also, use a skillet large enough to hold the asparagus in a single layer. We also discovered that adding a fairly liquid sauce (which will reduce quickly to a syrup) helps finish the cooking process.

Another cooking option, and one that most cooks don't consider, is grilling or broiling. The intense dry heat concentrates the flavor of the asparagus, and the exterior caramelization makes the spears especially sweet. The result is asparagus with a heightened and, we think, delicious flavor.

The two primary questions related to broiling concerned the thickness of the stalks and the distance they should be kept from the heat source as they cook. In our tests with thicker asparagus, anywhere from ¾ to 1 inch in diameter, the peels began to char before the interior of the spears became fully tender. When we used thinner spears (no thicker than ⅝ inch), the interior was tender by the time the exterior was browned.

We then focused on how far to keep the spears from the heating element. At 3 inches, the asparagus charred a bit. At 5 inches, the asparagus took a little too long to cook, and they failed to caramelize properly. The middle ground, 4 inches, proved perfect for cooking speed, control, and browning.

As with broiling, we found that thicker spears char before they become tender on the grill. Stick with spears ⅝ inch in diameter (or smaller) and the asparagus will be tender by the time the exterior is lightly charred. Grilled and broiled asparagus should be lightly oiled before cooking—use extra-virgin olive oil for the most flavor. After cooking, grilled and broiled asparagus can be tossed or drizzled with a vinaigrette for even more flavor.

Master Recipe for Steamed Asparagus

SERVES 4

To steam asparagus, you will need a collapsible steamer basket that fits into the pot. Make sure the asparagus is above the water level and keep the pot covered. If you are using asparagus with thicker stalks, add a few minutes to the cooking time. You can flavor steamed asparagus with a drizzle of extra-virgin olive oil and salt and pepper, but the recipes that follow use more flavorful vinaigrettes for better results. If the asparagus is not going to be served right away, plunge it into ice water to stop the cooking process. The cooled and drained asparagus can be covered and refrigerated overnight.

1 ½   pounds asparagus, preferably with
      thin stalks about ½ inch in
      diameter, tough ends snapped off
      (see the illustration on page 11)
      Extra-virgin olive oil
      Salt and ground black pepper

1. Place the steamer basket in a large pot or Dutch oven. Add enough water so that the water barely reaches the bottom of the steamer basket. Turn the heat to high and bring the water to a boil. Add the asparagus, cover, and reduce the heat to medium-high. Steam until the asparagus bends slightly when picked up and the stalks yield slightly when squeezed, 4 to 5 minutes.

2. Using tongs, transfer the asparagus to a platter. Drizzle with olive oil to taste and sprinkle with salt and pepper to taste. Serve immediately.

➤ VARIATIONS

Steamed Asparagus with Ginger-Hoisin Vinaigrette

2 ½   tablespoons rice vinegar
1 ½   tablespoons hoisin sauce
2 ½   teaspoons soy sauce
1 ½   teaspoons minced fresh ginger

1 ½   tablespoons canola or vegetable oil
1 ½   teaspoons toasted sesame oil
1   recipe Steamed Asparagus
      (without the olive oil, salt, or pepper)

1. Whisk the vinegar, hoisin sauce, soy sauce, and ginger together in a medium bowl. Whisk in the oils until thoroughly combined.

2. Arrange the steamed asparagus on a platter and drizzle with the dressing. Serve warm or at room temperature.

Steamed Asparagus with Lime-Ginger Vinaigrette

1   teaspoon grated zest and 2 tablespoons
      juice from 1 lime
1 ½   teaspoons minced fresh ginger
½   teaspoon sugar
1   tablespoon chopped fresh
      cilantro leaves
6   tablespoons canola or vegetable oil
      Salt and ground black pepper
1   recipe Steamed Asparagus
      (without the olive oil, salt, or pepper)

1. Whisk the lime zest and juice, ginger, sugar, and cilantro together in a medium bowl. Whisk in the oil until thoroughly

MINCING GINGER

Ginger is highly fibrous, which makes it tricky to mince. A sharp knife is a must.

1. Slice the peeled knob of ginger into thin rounds, then fan the rounds out and cut them into thin matchstick-like strips.

2. Chop the matchsticks crosswise into a fine mince.

STIR-FRY BASICS

To stir-fry properly, you need plenty of intense heat. The pan must be hot enough to caramelize sugars, deepen flavors, and evaporate unnecessary juices. All this must happen in minutes. The problem for most American cooks is that the Chinese wok and the American stovetop are a lousy match that generates moderate heat at best.

Woks are conical because in China they traditionally rest in cylindrical pits containing the fire. Food is cut into small pieces to shorten the cooking time, thus conserving fuel. Only one vessel is required for many different cooking methods, including sautéing (stir-frying), steaming, boiling, and deep-frying.

Unfortunately, what is practical in China makes no sense in America. A wok was not designed for stovetop cooking, where heat comes only from the bottom. On an American stove, the bottom of the wok gets hot, but the sides are only warm. A horizontal heat source requires a horizontal pan. Therefore, for stir-frying at home, we recommend a large skillet, 12 to 14 inches in diameter, with a nonstick coating (see page 91 for details of our testing of nonstick skillets). If you insist on using a wok for stir-frying, choose a flat-bottomed model. It won't have as much flat surface area as a skillet, but it will work better on an American stove than a conventional round-bottomed wok.

Our favorite oil for stir-frying is peanut oil (see page 37), although vegetable oil or canola oil will work. Make sure that the oil is properly heated before adding any food—the oil should almost be smoking before the vegetables are added to the pan.

Many stir-fry recipes add the aromatics (scallions, garlic, and ginger) too early, causing them to burn. In our testing, we found it best to add the aromatics after cooking the vegetables. When the vegetables are done, we push them to the sides of the pan, add a little oil and the aromatics to the center of the pan (see the illustration on page 15), and cook the aromatics briefly until they are fragrant but not colored, about 45 seconds. To keep the aromatics from burning and becoming harsh tasting, we then stir them into the vegetables. At this point, the sauce is usually added to the pan and cooked just until it thickens and coats the vegetables.

---

combined. Season with salt and pepper to taste.

2. Arrange the steamed asparagus on a platter and drizzle with the dressing. Serve warm or at room temperature.

Steamed Asparagus with Roasted Red Pepper Vinaigrette

The roasted red peppers are packed in a vinegary brine that lends a bright flavor to the vinaigrette. See page 44 for more information about buying jarred peppers.

1/4	cup jarred roasted red peppers, chopped coarse
1	tablespoon red wine vinegar
2	medium cloves garlic, minced or pressed through a garlic press
6	tablespoons extra-virgin olive oil
1	tablespoon minced fresh parsley leaves
	Salt and ground black pepper
1	recipe Steamed Asparagus (without the olive oil, salt, or pepper)

1. Combine the peppers, vinegar, garlic, and oil in the workbowl of a food processor. Pulse until thoroughly combined, about 10 seconds. Scrape the dressing into a small bowl. Stir in the parsley and season with salt and pepper to taste.

2. Arrange the steamed asparagus on a platter and drizzle with the dressing. Serve warm or at room temperature.

Master Recipe for Stir-Fried Asparagus

SERVES 4

Really thick spears should be halved lengthwise and then cut into 1½-inch pieces to ensure that the center cooks through. The flavors of chicken broth and garlic are pretty basic; the variations are more intriguing.

½	cup low-sodium chicken broth
½	teaspoon salt
¼	teaspoon ground black pepper
2½	tablespoons peanut oil
1½	pounds asparagus, tough ends snapped off (see the illustration on page 11) and cut on the bias into 1½-inch pieces
3	medium cloves garlic, minced or pressed through a garlic press

1. Mix the broth, salt, and pepper together in a small bowl and set aside.

2. Heat 2 tablespoons of the oil in a large heavy-bottomed nonstick skillet over high heat until almost smoking. Add the asparagus and cook, stirring frequently, until well browned, about 5 minutes.

3. Clear a space in the center of the pan, add the garlic, and drizzle with the remaining ½ tablespoon oil. Cook until fragrant, about 30 seconds, and then mix together with the asparagus. Add the broth mixture and toss to coat the asparagus. Cook until the sauce is syrupy, about 30 seconds. Serve immediately.

➤ VARIATIONS

Stir-Fried Asparagus and Red Pepper with Garlicky Oyster Sauce

To turn this into an entrée that serves three or four, add 1 cup diced firm tofu, drained well, to the red bell pepper in step 2 and serve with steamed rice or Chinese egg noodles. For more information about oyster sauce, see page 15.

2	tablespoons oyster sauce
1	tablespoon soy sauce
1	teaspoon toasted sesame oil
2	tablespoons dry sherry
2½	tablespoons peanut oil
1	medium red bell pepper, stemmed, seeded, and cut into 1 by ¼-inch strips
1½	pounds asparagus, tough ends snapped off (see the illustration on page 11) and cut on the bias into 1½-inch pieces
6	medium cloves garlic, minced or pressed through a garlic press
1	teaspoon minced fresh ginger

1. Mix the oyster sauce, soy sauce, sesame oil, and sherry together in a small bowl and set aside.

2. Heat 2 tablespoons of the peanut oil in a large heavy-bottomed nonstick skillet over high heat until almost smoking. Add the red pepper and cook, stirring frequently, until the pieces start to brown, about 2 minutes. Add the asparagus and cook, stirring frequently, until well browned, about 5 minutes.

3. Clear a space in the center of the pan, add the garlic and ginger, and drizzle with the remaining ½ tablespoon oil. Cook until fragrant, about 30 seconds, and then mix together with the vegetables. Add the oyster sauce mixture and toss to coat the vegetables. Cook until the sauce is syrupy, about 30 seconds. Serve immediately.

Stir-Fried Asparagus with Black Bean Sauce

Chinese fermented black beans are available in Asian food shops. They should be moist and soft to the touch. Don't buy beans that are dried out or shriveled. High-quality fermented beans should not be overly salty.

3	tablespoons dry sherry
2	tablespoons low-sodium chicken broth

<table>
<tbody>
<tr><td>1</td><td>tablespoon soy sauce</td></tr>
<tr><td>1</td><td>tablespoon toasted sesame oil</td></tr>
<tr><td>1</td><td>tablespoon chopped fermented black beans</td></tr>
<tr><td>1</td><td>teaspoon sugar</td></tr>
<tr><td>1/4</td><td>teaspoon ground black pepper</td></tr>
<tr><td>2 1/2</td><td>tablespoons peanut oil</td></tr>
<tr><td>1 1/2</td><td>pounds asparagus, tough ends snapped off (see the illustration on page 11) and cut on the bias into 1 1/2-inch pieces</td></tr>
<tr><td>3</td><td>medium cloves garlic, minced or pressed through a garlic press</td></tr>
<tr><td>1 1/2</td><td>teaspoons minced fresh ginger</td></tr>
<tr><td>2</td><td>medium scallions, white and green parts, sliced thin on the bias</td></tr>
</tbody>
</table>

1. Mix the sherry, broth, soy sauce, sesame oil, black beans, sugar, and pepper together in a small bowl and set aside.

2. Heat 2 tablespoons of the peanut oil

KEEPING GARLIC FROM BURNING IN STIR-FRIES

Many recipes add the garlic as well as the ginger and scallions at the beginning of the stir-frying process. This is a recipe for burnt garlic. We prefer to stir-fry the vegetables until they are crisp-tender, clear the center of the pan, and then add the garlic and other aromatics to the clearing. We usually drizzle a little oil over the garlic and other aromatics to help them cook. Once the aromatics are fragrant, they should be stirred back into the vegetables, and the sauce should be added to keep them from burning.

in a large heavy-bottomed nonstick skillet over high heat until almost smoking. Add the asparagus and cook, stirring frequently, until well browned, about 5 minutes.

3. Clear a space in the center of the pan, add the garlic and ginger, and drizzle with

INGREDIENTS: Oyster Sauce

Oyster sauce, which is actually called oyster-flavored sauce, is a rich concentrated mixture of oyster extracts, soy sauce, brine, and assorted seasonings. This brown sauce is thick, salty, and strong. It is used sparingly to enhance the flavor of many dishes, including many without any seafood ingredients.

A trip to our local grocery store and Asian market turned up five different brands of bottled oyster sauce. Lee Kum Kee dominated the shelves with three varieties: Choy Sun, Panda Brands, and Premium. Coin Tree and Sa Cheng rounded out the list. Although oyster-flavored sauce is too strong to be used as a condiment, we thought it important to take note of the raw, unadulterated flavor of each bottle before using it in a recipe. Each brand of the potent sauce received the same standard comments: "salty," "biting," and "fishy." However, when we mixed the bottled oyster sauces with other ingredients—sherry, soy sauce, sesame oil, sugar, and freshly ground black pepper—and then made simple stir-fries, our tasters were able to detect a wider range of flavors.

The most authentic of the group was undoubtedly Lee Kum Kee's Premium Oyster Flavored Sauce. Admittedly intense and somewhat fishy, it was the only sauce with true depth of flavor; its saltiness was balanced by sweet caramel undertones, and the oyster flavor was strong. This sauce is not for the faint of heart; one taster proclaimed, "My American taste buds can't take it." According to Jason Wong, president of AsiaFoods.com, Lee Kum Kee's Premium sauce is the favorite among the Asian-American population and the "only one" used in restaurants. All of this notwithstanding, the other favorite among our tasters was Sa Cheng Oyster Flavored Sauce, preferred because it was mild and "gravy like." The other three bottled sauces we tried didn't seem to add much to our stir-fries.

the remaining ½ tablespoon peanut oil. Cook until fragrant, about 30 seconds, and then mix together with the asparagus. Add the black bean mixture and toss to coat the asparagus. Cook until the sauce is syrupy, about 30 seconds. Sprinkle with the scallions and serve immediately.

Stir-Fried Asparagus with Soy Sauce, Maple Syrup, and Scallions

The unusual combination of maple syrup and soy sauce makes a sauce that has a great balance of sweet and salty flavors.

1 ½	tablespoons soy sauce
1 ½	tablespoons maple syrup
1	tablespoon dry sherry
2 ½	tablespoons peanut oil
1 ½	pounds asparagus, tough ends snapped off (see the illustration on page 11) and cut on the bias into 1 ½ -inch pieces
3	medium cloves garlic, minced or pressed through a garlic press
2	medium scallions, white and green parts, sliced thin on the bias

1. Mix the soy sauce, maple syrup, and sherry together in a small bowl and set aside.

2. Heat 2 tablespoons of the oil in a large heavy-bottomed nonstick skillet over high heat until almost smoking. Add the asparagus and cook, stirring frequently, until well browned, about 5 minutes.

3. Clear a space in the center of the pan, add the garlic, and drizzle with the remaining ½ tablespoon oil. Cook until fragrant, about 30 seconds, and then mix together with the asparagus. Add the soy sauce mixture and toss to coat the asparagus. Cook until the sauce is syrupy, about 30 seconds. Sprinkle with the scallions and serve immediately.

Master Recipe for Broiled Asparagus
SERVES 4 TO 6

Choose asparagus no thicker than ⅝ inch.

2	pounds thin asparagus spears, tough ends snapped off (see the illustration on page 11)
1	tablespoon olive oil
	Salt and ground black pepper

Adjust an oven rack to the uppermost position (about 4 inches from the heating element) and heat the broiler. Toss the asparagus with the oil and salt and pepper to taste and then lay spears in a single layer on a heavy rimmed baking sheet. Broil, shaking the pan halfway through to turn the spears, until the asparagus is tender and lightly browned, 8 to 10 minutes. Cool the asparagus 5 minutes and arrange them on a serving platter.

➤ VARIATIONS

Broiled Asparagus with Reduced Balsamic Vinaigrette and Parmesan

The balsamic glaze can be made ahead; it will keep in the refrigerator, covered, for up to a week.

¾	cup balsamic vinegar
1	recipe Broiled Asparagus
¼	cup extra-virgin olive oil
¼	cup shaved Parmesan cheese (see the illustration on page 25)

Bring the vinegar to a boil in an 8-inch skillet over medium-high heat. Reduce the heat to medium and simmer slowly until the vinegar is syrupy and reduced to ¼ cup, 15 to 20 minutes. Arrange the broiled asparagus on a serving platter. Drizzle the balsamic glaze and oil over the asparagus. Sprinkle with the cheese and serve immediately.

Broiled Asparagus with Soy-Ginger Vinaigrette

Putting the garlic through a press ensures that the pieces are very fine. If you don't own a press, mince the garlic to a paste with a knife (see the illustration on page 127).

2	medium scallions, white and green parts, minced
1	tablespoon minced fresh ginger
2	small cloves garlic, minced or pressed through a garlic press
3	tablespoons toasted sesame oil
3	tablespoons soy sauce
1/4	cup juice from 2 large limes
1	tablespoon honey
1	recipe Broiled Asparagus

Whisk the scallions, ginger, garlic, oil, soy sauce, lime juice, and honey together in a small bowl. Arrange the asparagus on a serving platter. Drizzle the vinaigrette over the asparagus and serve immediately.

Broiled Prosciutto-Wrapped Asparagus with Mascarpone

SERVES 8 AS AN APPETIZER

Mascarpone is a mildly flavored Italian cheese with a consistency similar to that of cream cheese. It can be found in the specialty cheese section of most large grocery stores. The asparagus will have to be broiled in two batches so the prosciutto can brown properly. Keep the uncooked, prosciutto-wrapped asparagus in the refrigerator until it is ready to be broiled.

1/2	cup mascarpone cheese
12	ounces prosciutto, cut into 4 by 1-inch strips
2	pounds thin asparagus spears, tough ends snapped off (see the illustration on page 11) Ground black pepper

1. Adjust an oven rack to the uppermost position (about 4 inches from the heating element) and heat the broiler. Smear a scant teaspoon of mascarpone onto each strip of prosciutto. Tightly wrap each asparagus spear in a strip of prosciutto (starting with the tip of the asparagus), securing the end with a toothpick. Place half of the spears in a single layer on a heavy rimmed baking sheet, leaving about 1/2 inch of space between the spears.

2. Broil, turning the spears with tongs halfway through the cooking time, until the asparagus is tender and the prosciutto is lightly browned, 8 to 10 minutes. Transfer the broiled asparagus to a serving platter. Broil the remaining asparagus on the empty baking sheet. Transfer the second batch of broiled asparagus to the platter, season with pepper to taste, and serve warm.

Master Recipe for Grilled Asparagus

SERVES 4

Thick spears will burn on the surface before they cook through. Use spears no thicker than 5/8 inch.

1 1/2	pounds asparagus, tough ends snapped off (see the illustration on page 11)
1	tablespoon extra-virgin olive oil Salt and ground black pepper

1. Toss the asparagus with the oil in a medium bowl or on a rimmed baking sheet.

2. Grill the asparagus over a medium-hot fire (you should be able to hold your hand 5 inches above the cooking grate for 3 to 4 seconds), turning once, until tender and streaked with light grill marks, 5 to 7 minutes. Transfer the grilled asparagus to a platter. Season to taste with salt and pepper. Serve hot, warm, or at room temperature.

Grilled Asparagus with Grilled Lemon Vinaigrette

Grilling the lemon not only mellows its flavors but also helps to release its juices.

1	lemon, cut in half crosswise
6	tablespoons extra-virgin olive oil
1	medium shallot, minced
1/2	teaspoon minced fresh thyme leaves
	Salt and ground black pepper
1	recipe Grilled Asparagus

1. Place the lemon halves on the grill, cut-side down, and grill until tender and streaked with light grill marks, about 3 minutes. When the lemon is cool enough to handle, squeeze and strain the juice into a medium nonreactive bowl; you should have about 2 tablespoons. Whisk in the oil, shallot, and thyme. Season with salt and pepper to taste.

2. Arrange the grilled asparagus on a platter and drizzle with the dressing. Serve immediately.

Grilled Asparagus with Orange-Sesame Vinaigrette

Tahini is a paste made from ground sesame seeds and is used in Middle Eastern cooking. If tahini is unavailable, increase the sesame seeds to 3 tablespoons and the sesame oil to 1 teaspoon; instead of whisking the ingredients together, pulse them in a food processor for 10 seconds.

1	tablespoon sesame seeds
1	teaspoon tahini
1	teaspoon grated zest and 1 tablespoon juice from 1 orange
1	tablespoon rice vinegar
1	teaspoon soy sauce
1/2	teaspoon minced fresh ginger
1/2	teaspoon toasted sesame oil
6	tablespoons extra-virgin olive oil
	Salt and ground black pepper
1	recipe Grilled Asparagus

1. Toast the sesame seeds in a dry skillet over medium heat until fragrant, about 5 minutes. Combine the seeds, tahini, orange zest and juice, vinegar, soy sauce, ginger, and oils in a medium bowl and whisk thoroughly to combine. Season with salt and pepper to taste.

2. Arrange the grilled asparagus on a serving platter and drizzle with the dressing. Serve immediately.

ASPARAGUS SALADS

LONG, GRACEFUL ASPARAGUS SPEARS can be an excellent addition to a leafy green salad. But the beauty of these salads is often only skin deep. Either bland or overseasoned, mushy or nearly raw, this first-course tease can prove to be an unsatisfying encounter. Tired of this ongoing disappointment, we wanted some recipes for asparagus salad that combined good taste with good looks: the asparagus perfectly cooked and seasoned; other fresh and flavorful ingredients added in a way that let the flavors unify; and the salad overall both attractive and easy to assemble.

We knew that boiling or steaming asparagus would introduce water that would dilute (or at the very least, not enhance) their flavor. Grilling or broiling would concentrate their flavor, but these were unwanted added steps. We soon found that quickly sautéing and caramelizing the asparagus over high heat was the best way to concentrate flavor. Best of all, this skillet method was ideal for adding other ingredients right to the pan, where the flavors could meld.

The vinaigrette was all about balance. Adding the bold flavors of shallots, garlic, jalapeños, fresh herbs, or even tart cornichons and salty capers to the oil and vinegar made for a zesty dressing that contrasted nicely with the mellow asparagus. To offset the leanness of the lettuce and the vegetables and to counter the sharpness of the dressing, we added a small amount of nuts, beans, cheese, or hard-cooked eggs, making the salads more substantial as well as flavorful.

Asparagus and Mesclun Salad with Capers, Cornichons, and Hard-Cooked Eggs

SERVES 4 TO 6
AS A FIRST COURSE

See page 20 for information on hard-cooking eggs.

5	tablespoons extra-virgin olive oil
I	pound asparagus, tough ends snapped off (see the illustration on page II) and cut on the bias into I-inch pieces
	Salt and ground black pepper
2	tablespoons white wine vinegar
I	small shallot, minced (about 2 tablespoons)
2	tablespoons minced cornichons
I	teaspoon minced capers
2	teaspoons chopped fresh tarragon leaves
6	ounces mesclun
3	large hard-cooked eggs, chopped medium

1. Heat 1 tablespoon of the oil in a 12-inch nonstick skillet over high heat until almost smoking. Add the asparagus, ¼ teaspoon salt, and ¼ teaspoon pepper and cook until browned and tender-crisp, about 4 minutes, stirring once every minute. Transfer the asparagus to a large plate and cool for 5 minutes.

2. Meanwhile, whisk the remaining 4 tablespoons oil, vinegar, shallot, cornichons,

capers, tarragon, and ¼ teaspoon pepper together in a medium bowl until combined. In a large bowl, toss the mesclun with 2 tablespoons dressing and divide among individual salad plates. Toss the asparagus with the remaining dressing and place a portion over the mesclun. Divide the chopped eggs among the salads and serve immediately.

Asparagus, Red Pepper, and Spinach Salad with Goat Cheese

SERVES 4 TO 6
AS A FIRST COURSE

6	tablespoons extra-virgin olive oil
I	small red bell pepper, stemmed, seeded, and cut into I by ¼-inch strips
I	pound asparagus, tough ends snapped off (see the illustration on page II) and cut on the bias into I-inch pieces
	Salt and ground black pepper
I	medium shallot, sliced thin (about ¼ cup)
I	tablespoon plus I teaspoon sherry vinegar
I	medium clove garlic, minced or pressed through a garlic press (about I teaspoon)
I	(6-ounce) bag baby spinach
4	ounces goat cheese, cut into small chunks

1. Heat 2 tablespoons of the oil in a 12-inch nonstick skillet over high heat until almost smoking. Add the red pepper and cook until lightly browned, about 2 minutes, stirring only once after 1 minute. Add the asparagus, ¼ teaspoon salt, and ⅛ teaspoon pepper and cook until the asparagus is browned and almost tender, about 2 minutes,

HARD-COOKED EGGS

We have always considered hard-cooking an egg to be a crapshoot. There's no way to watch the proteins cook under the brittle shell of an uncracked egg, and you certainly can't poke it with an instant-read thermometer, as you would with so many other foods. Often the eggs are overcooked, with rubbery whites and chalky yolks. Of course, undercooked eggs without fully set yolks are even more problematic, especially when you're trying to dice or crumble them for use in a recipe.

There are two general methods for boiling eggs: starting them in cold water and then bringing them to a simmer and lowering them into already simmering water. The first method is not terribly precise. When do you start the clock—when the eggs go into the water or when the water starts to boil? Also, what temperature is right for simmering? Everyone knows what boiling water looks like (and the temperature is always 212 degrees at sea level), but simmering water can be 180, 190, or even 200 degrees. We never developed a reliable timing mechanism with this technique.

Lowering eggs into simmering water is not easy either, because the eggs are likely to crack. Some sources suggest poking a thumb tack through the large end of the egg where the air hole typically sits, but we had inconsistent results with this "trick." Again, the issue of defining "simmering water" proved problematic.

Not satisfied with either method, we tried a third method—starting the eggs in cold water, bringing the water to a boil, and then turning off the heat. The pan is covered, and the eggs are set aside to cook by residual heat for 10 minutes. There's no need to define "simmer" with this method. As long as you can recognize when water is at a boil and can time 10 minutes, you are guaranteed hard-cooked eggs with bright, creamy yolks and tender whites.

Foolproof Hard-Cooked Eggs

MAKES 6

You can double or triple this recipe as long as you use a pot large enough to hold the eggs in a single layer, covered by an inch of water. You can also cook fewer eggs if you like.

6 large eggs

1. Place the eggs in a medium saucepan, cover with 1 inch of water, and bring to a boil over high heat. Remove the pan from the heat, cover, and let sit for 10 minutes. Meanwhile, fill a medium bowl with 1 quart of water and 1 tray of ice cubes (or the equivalent).

2. Transfer the eggs to the ice bath with a slotted spoon and let sit 5 minutes. Peel the eggs according to the illustrations at right.

PEELING HARD-COOKED EGGS

1. Tap the egg all over against the counter surface and then roll it gently back and forth a few times on the counter to crack the shell all over.

2. Begin peeling from the air pocket (the wider end of the egg). The shell should come off in spiral strips attached to a thin membrane.

stirring only once after 1 minute. Stir in the shallot and cook until it is softened and the asparagus is tender-crisp, about 1 minute, stirring occasionally. Transfer the vegetables to a large plate and cool for 5 minutes.

2. Meanwhile, whisk the remaining 4 tablespoons oil, vinegar, garlic, ¼ teaspoon salt, and ⅛ teaspoon pepper in a medium bowl until combined. In a large bowl, toss the spinach with 2 tablespoons dressing and divide among individual salad plates. Toss the asparagus mixture with the remaining dressing and place a portion over the spinach. Divide the goat cheese among the salads and serve immediately.

Asparagus, Watercress, and Carrot Salad with Thai Flavors

SERVES 4 TO 6 AS A FIRST COURSE

The asparagus in this salad tastes best chilled. To chill, place the plate of just-cooked asparagus in the freezer. Toast the peanuts in a dry skillet over medium heat until lightly browned and fragrant, about 6 minutes.

2	tablespoons juice from 1 lime
2	tablespoons fish sauce
2	teaspoons sugar
1	small clove garlic, minced or pressed through a garlic press (about ³/₄ teaspoon)
1	small jalapeño chile, stemmed, seeded, and minced (about 1 tablespoon)
2	medium carrots, peeled and cut into thin matchsticks (about 1½ cups)
1	tablespoon peanut or vegetable oil
1	pound asparagus, tough ends snapped off (see the illustration on page 11) and cut on the bias into 1-inch pieces

1	large bunch watercress (about 6 ounces), washed, dried, and stemmed (about 6 cups loosely packed)
¼	cup chopped fresh mint leaves
⅓	cup chopped unsalted dry-roasted peanuts

1. Whisk the lime juice, fish sauce, 2 tablespoons water, the sugar, garlic, and chile together in a medium bowl until the sugar dissolves. Reserve 1 tablespoon of the dressing in a large bowl; toss the carrots with the remaining dressing and set aside.

2. Heat the oil in a 12-inch nonstick skillet over high heat until almost smoking. Add the asparagus and cook until browned and tender-crisp, about 4 minutes, stirring once every minute. Transfer the asparagus to a large plate and place in the freezer for 5 minutes.

3. Toss the watercress with the reserved 1 tablespoon dressing and divide among individual salad plates. Toss the asparagus and mint with the carrot mixture and place a portion over the watercress. Sprinkle the salads with the peanuts and serve immediately.

Asparagus and Arugula Salad with Cannellini Beans and Balsamic Vinegar

SERVES 4 TO 6 AS A FIRST COURSE

5	tablespoons extra-virgin olive oil
½	medium red onion, sliced thin
1	pound asparagus, tough ends snapped off (see the illustration on page 11) and cut on the bias into 1-inch pieces Salt and ground black pepper
1	(15-ounce) can cannellini beans, drained and rinsed
2	tablespoons plus 2 teaspoons balsamic vinegar

INGREDIENTS: Balsamic Vinegar

There are balsamic vinegars you can buy for $2.50 and ones that nudge the $300 mark. The more expensive vinegars bear the title *tradizionale* or *extra-vecchio tradizionale aceto balsamico* (traditional or extra-old traditional). According to Italian law, these traditional vinegars must come from the northern Italian provinces of Modena and Reggio Emilia and be created and aged in the time-honored fashion.

For hundreds of years, tradizionale balsamico vinegar has been made from Trebbiano grapes grown in the Modena and Reggio Emilia regions of northern Italy. The grapes are crushed and slowly cooked into must over an open flame. The must begins mellowing in a large wooden barrel, where it ferments and turns to vinegar. The vinegar is then passed through a series of barrels made from a variety of woods. To be considered worthy of the tradizionale balsamico title, the vinegar must be moved from barrel to barrel for a minimum of 12 years. An extra-vecchio vinegar must be aged for at least 25 years.

Because of its complex flavor and high production cost, tradizionale balsamico is used by those in the know as a condiment rather than an ingredient. The longer the vinegar ages, the thicker and more intense it becomes, maturing from a thin liquid into a spoon-coating, syrupy one—perfect for topping strawberries or cantaloupe. This is the aristocrat of balsamic vinegars.

The more common varieties, those with a price tag under $30, are categorized as commercial or industrial balsamic vinegars. These vinegars are the kind with which most Americans are familiar and are often used to complete a vinaigrette or flavor a sauce. The flavor profile of commercial balsamic vinegars ranges widely from mild, woody, and herbaceous to artificial and sour, depending on the producer and the style in which the vinegar was made. Commercial balsamic vinegar may or may not be aged and may or may not contain artificial caramel color or flavor.

We wondered how bad—or good—inexpensive commercial balsamic vinegars would be when compared in a blind tasting. To level the playing field—and ease the burden on our budget—we limited the tasting to balsamic vinegars that cost $15 and under. We included samples of the many production styles, including some aged in the traditional fashion, some with added caramel color and flavor, and some made from a blend of aged red wine vinegar and grape must.

We found that a higher price tag did not correlate with a better vinegar. In addition, age seemed to play a less important role than we had expected. Across the board, tasters found balsamic vinegars containing caramel or artificial color or flavor "sour" and "uninteresting." The top brands from our tasting contain no artificial colors or flavors whatsoever. Our findings led us to believe that must is paramount to making a full-flavored balsamic vinegar. As the must ages, it becomes thick and sweet, contributing a character almost like sherry or port. Producers who substitute artificial color and flavor for must end up with a shallow product.

So how can consumers figure out what type of balsamic vinegar to buy? The easy answer is to check the label. If it discloses that artificial ingredients or sweeteners have been added, don't buy it.

THE BEST INEXPENSIVE BALSAMIC VINEGARS

Among the dozen vinegars tested, we preferred 365 Every Day Value (left), Masserie Di Sant'Eramo (center), and Fiorucci Riserva (right).

1   large bunch arugula (about 14 ounces),
     washed, dried, and stemmed
     (about 6 cups lightly packed)

1. Heat 2 tablespoons of the oil in a 12-inch nonstick skillet over high heat until almost smoking. Stir in the onion and cook until it begins to brown, about 1 minute. Add the asparagus, ¼ teaspoon salt, and ¼ teaspoon pepper and cook until the asparagus is browned and tender-crisp, about 4 minutes, stirring once every minute. Off the heat, stir in the beans. Transfer the vegetables and beans to a large plate and cool for 5 minutes.

2. Meanwhile, whisk the remaining 3 tablespoons oil, vinegar, ¼ teaspoon salt, and ⅛ teaspoon pepper together in a medium bowl until combined. In a large bowl, toss the arugula with 2 tablespoons dressing and divide among individual salad plates. Toss the asparagus mixture with the remaining dressing, place a portion over the arugula, and serve immediately.

ASPARAGUS SAUCES FOR PASTA

ASPARAGUS IS A NATURAL STARTING point when trying to make a vegetarian pasta sauce. First, we focused on how to cook the asparagus. We ruled out boiling and steaming because the residual water diluted the flavor. Grilling added bold and smoky characteristics, and broiling also concentrated flavors, but we wanted a simpler method, one that would also allow for the easy introduction of other flavors. The answer, it turned out, was a quick sauté.

We cut the asparagus into 1-inch pieces and sautéed it with other ingredients over high heat. The asparagus caramelized just a bit, and the heat also brought out the flavors of the other ingredients, such as onions,

walnuts, garlic, and shallots. To finish off each dish, we tried a variety of additions, including balsamic vinegar, basil leaves, lemon juice, blue cheese, and arugula. The key, we discovered, is not to overpower the asparagus with too much of one bold ingredient. What's wanted instead is a good balance of salty, sweet, and sour ingredients that allow the asparagus flavor to come through.

Farfalle with Asparagus, Toasted Almonds, and Browned Butter

SERVES 4 TO 6 AS A MAIN DISH

1   tablespoon plus ¹/₂ teaspoon salt
1   pound farfalle
2   tablespoons vegetable oil
1   pound asparagus, tough ends
      snapped off (see the illustration on
      page 11), spears halved lengthwise
      if larger than ¹/₂ inch in diameter
      and cut into 1-inch lengths
3   large cloves garlic, sliced thin
      (about 2 tablespoons)
2   medium shallots, sliced into thin
      rings (about ³/₄ cup)
¹/₂   teaspoon ground black pepper
6   tablespoons unsalted butter,
      cut into 6 pieces
1   cup sliced almonds
¹/₄   cup sherry vinegar
1   teaspoon chopped fresh thyme leaves
1   cup grated Parmesan cheese

1. Bring 4 quarts of water to a boil, covered, in a stockpot. Add 1 tablespoon of the salt and the pasta, stir to separate, and cook until al dente. Drain and return the pasta to the stockpot.

2. While the pasta is cooking, heat the oil in a 12-inch nonstick skillet over high heat

until almost smoking. Add the asparagus and cook, without stirring, until it is beginning to brown, about 1 minute. Add the garlic, shallots, remaining ½ teaspoon salt, and pepper and cook, stirring frequently, until the asparagus is tender-crisp, about 4 minutes. Transfer the asparagus mixture to a large plate and set aside.

3. Return the skillet to high heat and add the butter. When the foaming subsides, add the almonds and cook, stirring constantly, until the almonds are toasted and browned and the butter is nutty and fragrant, 1 to 2 minutes. Off the heat, add the vinegar and thyme. Return the asparagus to the skillet and toss to coat. Add the asparagus mixture and ½ cup of the cheese to the pasta in the stockpot and toss to combine. Serve immediately, passing the remaining ½ cup cheese separately.

Campanelle with Asparagus, Basil, and Balsamic Glaze

SERVES 4 TO 6 AS A MAIN DISH

Campanelle is a frilly trumpet-shaped pasta that pairs nicely with this sauce. If you cannot find it, fusilli works well, too.

1	tablespoon plus ½ teaspoon salt
1	pound campanelle
¾	cup balsamic vinegar
5	tablespoons extra-virgin olive oil
1	pound asparagus, tough ends snapped off (see the illustration on page 11), spears halved lengthwise if larger than ½ inch in diameter and cut into 1-inch lengths
1	medium-large red onion, halved and sliced thin (about 1½ cups)
½	teaspoon ground black pepper
¼	teaspoon hot red pepper flakes
1	cup chopped fresh basil leaves
1	tablespoon juice from 1 lemon
1	cup shaved Pecorino Romano cheese (see the illustration on page 25)

1. Bring 4 quarts of water to a boil, covered, in a stockpot. Add 1 tablespoon of the salt and the pasta, stir to separate, and cook until al dente. Drain and return the pasta to the stockpot.

2. Immediately after putting the pasta in the boiling water, bring the vinegar to a boil in an 8-inch skillet over medium-high heat; reduce the heat to medium and simmer slowly until syrupy and reduced to ¼ cup, 15 to 20 minutes.

3. While the pasta is cooking and the vinegar is reducing, heat 2 tablespoons of the oil in a 12-inch nonstick skillet over high heat until almost smoking. Add the asparagus, onion, black pepper, pepper flakes, and the remaining ½ teaspoon salt and stir to combine. Cook, without stirring, until the asparagus begins to brown, about 1 minute, and then

MAKING CHEESE SHAVINGS

Thin shavings of Parmesan (and other hard cheeses) can be used to garnish vegetable dishes as well as salad or pasta. Simply run a sharp vegetable peeler along the length of a piece of cheese to remove paper-thin curls.

stir and continue to cook, stirring occasionally, until the asparagus is tender-crisp, about 4 minutes longer. Add the asparagus mixture, basil, lemon juice, ½ cup of the cheese, and the remaining 3 tablespoons oil to the pasta in the stockpot and toss to combine. Serve immediately, drizzling 1 to 2 teaspoons balsamic glaze over individual servings and passing the remaining ½ cup cheese separately.

Cavatappi with Asparagus, Arugula, Walnuts, and Blue Cheese

SERVES 4 TO 6 AS A MAIN DISH

Cavatappi is a short, tubular, corkscrew-shaped pasta. Penne is a fine substitute. If you prefer the mild flavor of spinach to the peppery flavor of arugula, substitute an equal amount of baby spinach leaves. The grated apple, added just before serving, balances the other flavors in this dish.

1	tablespoon plus ½ teaspoon salt
1	pound cavatappi
5	tablespoons extra-virgin olive oil
1	pound asparagus, tough ends snapped off (see the illustration on page 11), spears halved lengthwise if larger than ½ inch in diameter and cut into 1-inch lengths
½	teaspoon ground black pepper
1	cup walnuts, chopped
4	cups lightly packed arugula leaves from 1 large bunch, washed and dried thoroughly
6	ounces strong blue cheese, preferably Roquefort, crumbled
2	tablespoons cider vinegar
1	Granny Smith apple, peeled, for grating over pasta

1. Bring 4 quarts of water to a boil, covered, in a stockpot. Add 1 tablespoon of the salt and the pasta, stir to separate, and cook until al dente. Drain and return the pasta to the stockpot.

2. While the pasta is cooking, heat 2 tablespoons of the oil in a 12-inch nonstick skillet over high heat until almost smoking. Add the asparagus, pepper, and the remaining ½ teaspoon salt and cook, without stirring, until the asparagus is beginning to brown, about 1 minute. Add the walnuts and continue to cook, stirring frequently, until the asparagus is tender-crisp and nuts are toasted, about 4 minutes longer. Toss in the arugula until wilted. Add the asparagus mixture, blue cheese, vinegar, and the remaining 3 tablespoons oil to the pasta in the stockpot and toss to combine. Serve immediately, grating the apple over individual servings.

AVOCADO

ALTHOUGH AVOCADO (LIKE THE TOMATO) IS TECHNICALLY A FRUIT, WE often think of it as a vegetable. It falls clearly in the savory rather than sweet category. However, avocado is not cooked. We use it raw in dips and salads.

There are numerous varieties, but only two regularly show up in American markets—small, rough-skinned Hass (also spelled Haas), grown primarily in California and Mexico, and the larger, smooth-skinned Fuerte, grown mostly in Florida. We decided to sample each variety plain and in guacamole. Tasters were unanimous in their preference for the meatier Hass, compared with which the Fuerte tasted "too fruity," "sweet," and "watery."

Regardless of their origin, many supermarket avocados are sold rock hard and unripe. Because these fruits ripen off the tree, that's fine; in two to five days, your avocados are ready to eat. We tested all the supposed tricks to accelerate ripening, from burying the avocados in flour or rice to enclosing them in a brown paper bag, with and without another piece of fruit. We also tried putting them in different areas in the kitchen: light spots and dark, cool spots and warm. In the end, we found that most of these efforts made little difference. The fastest ripening took roughly 48 hours and occurred in a warm, dark spot, but the advantage was minor. From now on, we won't think twice when tossing hard avocados into the fruit bowl on the counter. It's as good an option as any, and easier, too.

Determining ripeness was also straightforward. The skins of Hass avocados turn from green to dark, purply black when ripe, and the fruit yields slightly to a gentle squeeze when held in the palm of your hand. We also discovered a neat trick that involves looking under the tiny stem.

JUDGING THE RIPENESS OF AN AVOCADO

A soft avocado is sometimes bruised rather than truly ripe. To make sure that the avocado is ripe, remove the small stem with your fingers. If you can see green underneath it, the avocado is ripe. However, if the stem does not come off easily or if you see brown underneath, the avocado is not ripe.

GUACAMOLE

THE GUACAMOLE WE ARE SERVED IN restaurants, and even in the homes of friends, often sacrifices the singular, extraordinary character of the avocado—the culinary equivalent of velvet—by adding too many other flavorings. Even worse, the texture of the dip is usually reduced to an utterly smooth, listless puree.

We wanted our guacamole to be different. First, it should highlight the dense, buttery texture and loamy, nutty flavor of the avocado. Any additions should provide bright counterpoints to the avocado without overwhelming it. Just as importantly, the consistency of the dip should be chunky rather than perfectly smooth.

Good guacamole starts with good (i.e., ripe) avocados. Assuming you have ripe avocados, how should you handle and mix them with the other ingredients? Most guacamole recipes direct you to mash all the avocados, and some recipes go so far as to puree them in a blender or food processor. After making dozens of batches, we came to believe that neither pureeing nor simple mashing was the way to go. Properly ripened avocados break down very easily when stirred, and we were aiming for a chunky texture. To get it, we mashed only one of the three avocados in our recipe lightly with a fork and mixed it with most of the other ingredients, and then we diced the remaining two avocados into substantial ½-inch cubes and mixed them into the base using a very light hand. The mixing action breaks down the cubes somewhat, making a chunky, cohesive dip.

Other problems we encountered in most recipes were an overabundance of onion and a dearth of acidic seasoning. After extensive testing with various amounts of onion, we found that 2 tablespoons of finely minced or grated onion gave guacamole a nice spike without

DICING AN AVOCADO

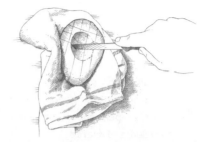

1. Use a dish towel to hold the avocado steady. Make ¹/₂-inch crosshatch incisions in the flesh of each avocado half with a dinner knife, cutting down to but not through the skin.

2. Separate the diced flesh from the skin using a spoon inserted between the skin and the flesh and gently scooping out the avocado cubes.

an overwhelming onion flavor. We also tried various amounts of fresh lemon and lime juice. The acid was absolutely necessary, not only for flavor but also to help preserve the mixture's green color. Tasters preferred 2 tablespoons of lime juice in our three-avocado guacamole.

Master Recipe for Chunky Guacamole

MAKES 2 ¹/₂ TO 3 CUPS

To minimize the risk of discoloration, prepare the minced ingredients first so they are ready to mix with the avocados as soon as they are cut. Ripe avocados are essential here (see page 26 for information on testing avocados for ripeness). If you like, garnish the guacamole with diced tomatoes and chopped cilantro just before serving.

3	medium, ripe avocados (preferably pebbly-skinned Hass)
2	tablespoons minced onion
1	medium clove garlic, minced or pressed through a garlic press
1	small jalapeño chile, stemmed, seeded, and minced
¼	cup minced fresh cilantro leaves Salt
½	teaspoon ground cumin (optional)
2	tablespoons juice from 1 lime

1. Halve 1 avocado, remove the pit, and scoop the flesh into a medium bowl. Mash the flesh lightly with the onion, garlic, chile, cilantro, ¼ teaspoon salt, and cumin (if using) with the tines of a fork until just combined.

2. Halve, pit, and cube the remaining 2 avocados, following illustrations 1 and 2 on page 27. Add the cubes to the bowl with the mashed avocado mixture.

3. Sprinkle the lime juice over the diced avocado and mix the entire contents of the bowl lightly with a fork until combined but still chunky. Adjust the seasonings with salt, if necessary, and serve. (Guacamole can be refrigerated for up to 1 day. Return the guacamole to room temperature before serving; remove the plastic wrap at the last moment.)

➤ VARIATION

Guacamole with Bacon, Scallions, and Tomato

Follow the master recipe, substituting 3 large scallions, sliced thin (about ⅓ cup), for the onion and adding 6 slices cooked, drained, and crumbled bacon with 1 teaspoon rendered fat and ½ medium tomato, seeded and diced small.

CREAMY AVOCADO DIP

GUACAMOLE ISN'T THE ONLY DIP YOU can make with avocados. Because of their rich flavor and soft texture, avocados work well in creamy dairy-based dips. After playing around with several classic recipes, we found that a combination of mayonnaise and sour

PITTING AN AVOCADO

Digging out the pit with a spoon can mar the soft flesh and is generally a messy proposition. This method avoids that problem.

1. Start by slicing around the pit and through both ends with a chef's knife.

2. With your hands, twist the avocado to separate the two halves. Strike the blade of the chef's knife sharply into the pit. Lift the knife, twisting the blade to loosen and remove the pit.

3. Don't pull the pit off the knife with your hands. Instead, use a large wooden spoon to pry the pit safely off the knife.

cream is the ideal medium for carrying fresh and vibrant flavors. This combination also has the perfect consistency for dipping and scooping. As for the ratio of mayonnaise to sour cream, we found equal portions to be ideal. The mayonnaise adds body and richness, while the sour cream brings a bright freshness to the dip. We found that "light" mayonnaise and sour cream fare pretty well in this dip, in part because the avocado has so much fat.

As for the other ingredients, tasters liked Mexican flavors—lime juice, cilantro, scallions, and chiles. We tested various fresh chiles, but in the end, we preferred the smoky flavor of canned chipotle chiles.

We found it best to prepare this dip an hour in advance so the flavors could blend. The dip should be refrigerated during this time so it will be cool (and creamy) when you want to serve it.

Smoky, Spicy Avocado Dip with Cilantro

MAKES ABOUT 2 1/4 CUPS

Chipotle chiles in adobo sauce are dried, smoked jalapeños packed in a tomato-vinegar sauce. See the illustrations at right for more information about storing the extra chiles once the can has been opened.

3/4	cup sour cream (regular or light)
3/4	cup mayonnaise (regular or light)
1	medium, ripe avocado, halved, pitted, and flesh scooped from skin
1	tablespoon juice from 1 lime
1/2	cup packed fresh cilantro leaves
1 1/2	chipotle chiles in adobo sauce, plus 1 teaspoon adobo sauce
2	medium scallions, sliced thin
	Salt and ground black pepper

Process the sour cream, mayonnaise, avocado, lime juice, cilantro, and chiles and adobo sauce in the workbowl of a food processor until smooth and creamy and the cilantro is chopped fine, scraping down the sides of the bowl once or twice. Transfer the mixture to a medium bowl and stir in the scallions. Season with salt and pepper to taste. Cover with plastic wrap and chill until the flavors meld, at least 1 hour and up to 1 day.

FREEZING CHIPOTLE CHILES IN ADOBO SAUCE

Chipotles (dried, smoked jalapeño chiles) are among our favorite chiles because they are so flavorful. Chipotles are often packed in adobo sauce (a vinegary tomato sauce flavored with garlic) and canned. Because a little chipotle goes a long way, it can be difficult to use up an entire can once it has been opened. Rather than letting the remaining chiles go bad in the refrigerator, try this trick we also use with tomato paste.

1. Spoon out the chipotles, each with a couple teaspoons of adobo sauce, onto different areas of a baking sheet lined with parchment or waxed paper. Place the baking sheet in the freezer.

2. Once frozen, the chipotles should be transferred to a zipper-lock plastic bag and stored in the freezer. You can remove them, one at a time, as needed. They will keep indefinitely.

BEETS

THE BEETS MOST OF US REMEMBER FROM CHILDHOOD ARE THE CANNED version or the pickled kind (the ones nestled among pink pickled eggs in giant jars). They were tart and mushy. Freshly cooked beets are altogether different, with sweet, earthy flavors and firm, juicy texture.

In order to find the best way of cooking beets, we tried three methods: boiling, steaming, and roasting. Boiled beets were diluted in flavor. Looking at the pink water, we knew that some of that flavor had escaped into the cooking water. Steaming was a slightly better method, but the flavors weren't as concentrated as we would have liked. Roasting was the next option. We tried wrapping the beets in foil

as well as leaving them unwrapped. The unwrapped beets dried out and became leathery, but the wrapped beets were juicy and tender with the concentrated sweetness we were looking for. There was another significant advantage with the wrapped beets: The roasting pan remained stain free.

Beets can be peeled after cooking (the skins can be rubbed off with paper towels), which further reduces the mess. We found that an oven temperature of 400 degrees delivered good results. Medium beets were done in 45 minutes to one hour. Smaller beets take less time. We don't recommend roasting very large beets, because they can be woody.

⤙⤚

Master Recipe for Roasted Beets
SERVES 4

To keep your hands from turning a shocking shade of pink, use a paper towel when skinning the beets.

Cradle the roasted beet in the paper towel, pinch the skin between your thumb and forefinger, and peel it off. If the beets do stain your hands or cutting board, see the illustration on page 31 for tips on removing these stains. Serve roasted beets as is or flavor them with a vinaigrette or flavored butter.

4   medium beets (about
       I pound without greens)
2   tablespoons extra-virgin olive oil
       Salt and ground black pepper

1. Adjust an oven rack to the middle position and heat the oven to 400 degrees. Trim all but about 1 inch of the stems from the beets. Wash the beets well and remove any dangling roots. Wrap the beets individually in aluminum foil and place the wrapped beets in a shallow roasting pan or a rimmed baking sheet. Roast until a skewer inserted into a beet comes out easily, 45 minutes to 1 hour.

2. Remove the beets from the oven and

carefully open the foil packet (make sure to keep your hands and face away from the steam). When the beets are cool enough to handle, carefully peel off the skins. Slice the beets ¼ inch thick. Toss the beets, oil, and salt and pepper to taste together in a medium bowl. Serve warm or at room temperature.

➤ VARIATIONS

Roasted Beets with Dill–Walnut Vinaigrette

Dill and beets are a combination frequently found in Russian cuisine. Because dill quickly loses its fresh flavor when heated, it's best suited for cold preparations such as vinaigrettes and dips.

½	cup chopped walnuts
1	tablespoon red wine vinegar
2	teaspoons juice from 1 lemon
1	medium shallot, minced
1 ½	tablespoons minced fresh dill

REMOVING BEET STAINS

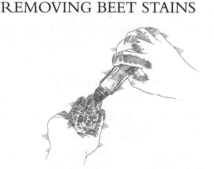

When cut, beets can stain everything they touch, including hands and cutting boards. To help remove these stains, sprinkle the stained area with salt, rinse, and then scrub with soap. The salt crystals help lift the beet juices away.

6	tablespoons extra-virgin olive oil
	Salt and ground black pepper
1	recipe Roasted Beets (without olive oil, salt, and pepper)

1. Place the walnuts in a skillet and toast over medium heat, stirring frequently, until they become fragrant, about 4 minutes.

2. Whisk the vinegar, lemon juice, shallot, dill, and oil together in a small bowl until thoroughly combined. Add salt and pepper to taste. Toss the dressing, sliced beets, and walnuts together in a medium bowl. Serve immediately.

Roasted Beets with Ginger Butter and Chives

To cut the ginger into matchsticks, first slice it into ⅛-inch-thick pieces. Stack the sliced pieces on top of each other and cut them into thin sticks.

4	tablespoons unsalted butter
1	(1-inch) piece fresh ginger, peeled and cut into matchsticks
1	tablespoon minced fresh chives
1	recipe Roasted Beets (without olive oil, salt, and pepper)
	Salt and ground black pepper

Melt the butter in a small skillet over medium heat. When the foaming subsides, add the ginger and cook until the ginger is fragrant and crisp, 3 to 4 minutes. Add the chives. Toss the butter mixture, sliced beets, and salt and pepper to taste together in a medium bowl. Serve immediately.

BOK CHOY

ALTHOUGH A MEMBER OF THE CABBAGE FAMILY, BOK CHOY RESEMBLES leafy greens, especially chard. Its crisp, ivory stalks and crinkly, dark green leaves are easy to recognize. Unlike so many leafy greens, bok choy doesn't shrink down to nothing when cooked. The stalks are crisp and fleshy—like celery but not stringy. In fact, when cooked fully, they become creamy, with an almost meat-like texture and underlying sweetness. In contrast, the leaves become tender and soft, having an earthy, robust flavor similar to chard or even spinach.

But for all bok choy's virtues, there are some issues to look at when cooking this vegetable, especially for American cooks who are not familiar with its

characteristics. If not prepared properly, bok choy can turn mushy and pallid. Our goal was to devise a cooking method that would produce perfectly cooked (and seasoned) bok choy, both the leaves and the stems. (We decided to focus on regular bok choy but also wanted to develop a recipe for baby bok choy—see page 33 for details on bok choy varieties.)

We combed through several dozen cookbooks looking for bok choy recipes. A few non-Chinese sources suggested cooking the stalks and greens together. We were skeptical since all the Chinese sources we consulted called for slicing the stalks and leaves separately so that the stalks could be cooked longer. We went ahead and tried stir-frying roughly chopped bok choy (stalks and greens together) and were disappointed. If the cooking time was brief, the greens were fine but the stalks were way too crunchy, almost like raw celery. Increasing the stir-fry time softened the stalks, but

the leaves turned limp and unappealing.

We needed to separate the white stalks and green leaves before cooking. We started by trimming and discarding the bottom inch of the bunch, which is often tough and blemished. This also separated the stalks so each one could be washed and patted dry individually. With a chef's knife, it's then easy to cut the leafy green portion away from the white stalks (see the illustrations on page 34). For eating purposes, we found it best to slice both the stalks and the leaves thinly.

With the bok choy prepped, it was time to start testing cooking methods. Most methods we uncovered in our research made some effort to deal with the fact that the stalks require a longer cooking time than the greens. We quickly dismissed blanching or steaming the stalks. Steaming was better than blanching (which washed away too much flavor), but both methods made the bok choy watery.

We had better luck stir-frying bok choy in a large nonstick skillet—the test kitchen's preferred vessel for stir-frying because of its wide, flat surface area, especially as compared with a wok. Throwing the sliced stalks into the pan first gave them the necessary head start. After five minutes of stir-frying, the stalks were crisp-tender and beginning to brown. We could then add the leaves and sauce and continue stir-frying for another minute or so until the leaves wilted.

Some sources suggested covering the pan (or wok) once the leaves were added. Although this seemed to cook them a tad faster, it made the stir-fry a bit soupy, since the sauce couldn't evaporate and thicken. We decided it was better to just leave the cover off for the entire cooking time.

INGREDIENTS: Buying Bok Choy

BOK CHOY   **BABY BOK CHOY**   **SHANGHAI**   **BABY SHANGHAI**   **BOK CHOY SUM**

Although most supermarkets carry only one kind of bok choy—the green-leaved, white-stalked variety—in Asian markets, you might see three or four different vegetables labeled "bok choy."

BABY BOK CHOY In addition to varietal differences, bok choy also comes in various sizes, from diminutive baby bok choy that weigh just 4 ounces to mammoth heads that weigh more than 2 pounds. Any variety of bok choy (with either white or green stems) picked at an early age can be called baby bok choy. Most heads weigh just three or four ounces and fit in your hand. Because of their small size, the stalks are fairly tender, so there's no need to cook them separately. Baby bok choy are best halved and seared. (See the recipe on page 37.)

SHANGHAI BOK CHOY has jade-colored stalks that are slightly wider than the ivory stalks on regular bok choy and that are shaped like Chinese soupspoons. Shanghai bok choy can be handled like regular bok choy.

BOK CHOY SUM has small yellow flowers sprouting from the center of its dark green leaves. As with broccoli rabe, the flowers are edible. To keep the flowers bright, slice and cook them with the leaves and stir-fry rather than braise them.

What you are likely to see in the supermarket are medium or large heads of regular bok choy. In general, heads between 1 1/2 and 1 3/4 pounds are your best bet—one head yields four side-dish servings but the stalks are still thin enough to cook up tender. In testing, we've found that stalks on larger heads (weighing 2 pounds or more) can be spongy and woody in the center. In terms of appearance, the leaves should be bright green and crisp. Wilted or yellowing leaves are signs of age. The stalks should be bright white. If the stalks are covered with tiny brown spots, the bok choy is past its prime.

Once you get bok choy home, store it like other leafy greens—in a loosely sealed plastic bag in the refrigerator for up to two or three days. Don't wash bok choy until you are ready to cook it. In tests, we found that prewashing sped up the rotting process.

This stir-fry method has plenty of advantages. It's simple, and the seasonings can be changed endlessly. However, the stalks were still crisp-tender (increasing the stir-frying time didn't seem to help much) and not as creamy as some of the bok choy dishes we've eaten in Chinese restaurants. We liked stir-fried bok choy but wondered if there was another option.

Several recipes we consulted suggested braising bok choy, as you might do with kale or another tough green, in a covered pan with some liquid. We stir-fried the stalks to give them color (and flavor from the browning), added the greens and some broth, and let the bok choy simmer away. After 10 minutes, the stalks were soft but not mushy. Their texture was creamy and delicious. The leaves were completely tender. Best of all, the flavor of the bok choy seemed more robust and earthier.

Both stir-frying and braising have their advantages. Stir-frying results in a fairly dry dish, making bok choy a good partner on most dinner plates. Braising is not much more work than stir-frying. Braised bok choy is very moist and soft, making it an ideal partner

to lean meat, fish, or chicken. The bok choy functions as both vegetable and sauce.

Master Recipe for Stir-Fried Bok Choy with Ginger and Soy

SERVES 4

Stir-frying preserves some of the texture of the bok choy, especially the stalks.

2	tablespoons soy sauce
1	teaspoon sugar
2	tablespoons peanut oil
1	medium head bok choy (1 $^1/_2$ to 1 $^3/_4$ pounds), prepared according to the illustrations below (about 5 cups each sliced stalks and sliced greens)
1	tablespoon minced fresh ginger

1. Combine the soy sauce and sugar in a small bowl.

2. Heat the oil in a large nonstick skillet over high heat until almost smoking. Add the bok choy stalks and cook, stirring occasionally, until lightly browned, 5 to 7 minutes. Add the ginger and cook, stirring

PREPARING BOK CHOY

1. Trim the bottom inch from the head of bok choy. Wash and pat dry the leaves and stalks. With a chef's knife, cut the leafy green portion away from either side of the white stalk.

2. Cut each white stalk in half lengthwise and then crosswise into thin strips.

3. Stack the leafy greens and then slice them crosswise into thin strips. Keep the sliced stalks and leaves separate.

frequently, until fragrant, about 30 seconds. Add the bok choy greens and the soy sauce mixture. Cook, stirring frequently, until the greens are wilted and tender, about 1 minute. Serve immediately.

➤ VARIATIONS

Stir-Fried Bok Choy with Oyster Sauce

This variation is ideal with seafood. If serving meat or chicken, replace the oyster sauce in this recipe with an equal amount of hoisin sauce. See page 15 for more information about oyster sauce. Follow the master recipe, replacing the soy sauce with 2 tablespoons oyster sauce and 1 tablespoon rice vinegar. Add 2 minced garlic cloves along with the ginger.

Stir-Fried Bok Choy in Sweet and Spicy Peanut Sauce

The sweet and salty flavors of the honey-roasted peanuts complement the bok choy nicely. See the illustration on page 280 for tips on grating ginger.

1	tablespoon soy sauce
1	tablespoon hoisin sauce
1	tablespoon smooth peanut butter
1/2	teaspoon sugar
2 1/2	tablespoons peanut oil
1	medium head bok choy (1 1/2 to 1 3/4 pounds), prepared according to the illustrations on page 34 (about 5 cups each sliced stalks and sliced greens)
1	teaspoon hot red pepper flakes
1/2	teaspoon grated fresh ginger
1/3	cup honey-roasted peanuts, chopped coarse

1. Combine the soy sauce, hoisin sauce, peanut butter, and sugar in a small bowl.

2. Heat 2 tablespoons of the oil in a large nonstick skillet over high heat until almost smoking. Add the bok choy stalks and cook, stirring occasionally, until lightly browned, 5 to 7 minutes. Clear a space in the center of the pan and add the pepper flakes, ginger, and the remaining 1/2 tablespoon oil. Cook, stirring frequently, until fragrant, about 30 seconds. Add the bok choy greens and soy sauce mixture. Cook, stirring frequently, until the greens are wilted and tender, about 1 minute. Sprinkle with the peanuts and serve immediately.

Master Recipe for Braised Bok Choy with Garlic

SERVES 4

This dish is fairly saucy, making it an excellent accompaniment to seared pork chops, sautéed chicken breasts, or a firm fish like cod.

2	tablespoons peanut oil
1	medium head bok choy (1 1/2 to 1 3/4 pounds), prepared according to the illustrations on page 34 (about 5 cups each sliced stalks and sliced greens)
4	medium cloves garlic, minced or pressed through a garlic press
3/4	cup low-sodium chicken broth Salt and ground black pepper
1	teaspoon rice vinegar

1. Heat the oil in a large nonstick skillet over high heat until almost smoking. Add the bok choy stalks and cook, stirring frequently, until lightly browned, 5 to 7 minutes. Add the garlic and cook, stirring frequently, until fragrant, about 30 seconds.

2. Add the bok choy greens, broth, and salt and pepper to taste. Cover, reduce the heat to medium-low, and cook, stirring twice, until the bok choy is very tender, 8 to 10 minutes

3. Remove the cover, raise the heat, and

cook until the excess liquid evaporates, 2 to 3 minutes. (The bok choy should be moist but not soupy.) Stir in the vinegar and adjust the seasonings, adding salt and pepper to taste. Serve immediately.

➤ VARIATIONS

Braised Bok Choy with Shiitake Mushrooms

The dried mushrooms add a meaty quality to this dish. See the illustrations at right for tips on rehydrating dried mushrooms.

Soak 6 dried shiitake mushrooms in 1 cup hot water until softened, about 15 minutes. Drain and slice the mushrooms, discarding the stems. Strain the soaking liquid through a sieve lined with a paper towel and reserve. Follow the master recipe, replacing the garlic with 1 tablespoon minced fresh ginger and replacing the broth with the mushroom liquid and sliced mushrooms.

Braised Bok Choy with Bacon and Shallots

Bok choy works well with American flavors, such as bacon and cider vinegar. For additional crunch, add toasted, chopped pecans to this dish along with the bacon.

3	ounces (about 3 strips) bacon, cut into $1/2$-inch pieces
1	medium head bok choy (1 $1/2$ to 1 $3/4$ pounds), prepared according to the illustrations on page 34 (about 5 cups each sliced stalks and sliced greens)
2	small shallots, minced (about $1/4$ cup)
$3/4$	cup low-sodium chicken broth
1	teaspoon cider vinegar
	Salt and ground black pepper

1. Cook the bacon in a large nonstick skillet over medium-high heat until crisp, about 5 minutes. Using a slotted spoon, transfer the bacon to a plate lined with paper towels and set aside.

2. Add the bok choy stalks and shallots to the rendered bacon fat in the skillet (you should have about 2 to 3 tablespoons) and cook, stirring frequently, until browned, 5 to 7 minutes. Add the bok choy greens and broth. Cover, reduce the heat to medium-low, and cook until the bok choy is tender, 8 to 10 minutes.

SOAKING DRIED MUSHROOMS

Dried mushrooms must be reconstituted before being added to recipes. Soak the mushrooms in hot tap water in a small bowl until softened, 10 to 20 minutes, depending on the variety of mushroom. Here's how to make sure any sand or dirt released by the mushrooms doesn't end up in your food.

1. Most of the sand and dirt will fall to the bottom of the bowl, so use a fork to lift the rehydrated mushrooms from the liquid without stirring up the sand.

2. Never discard the flavorful soaking liquid, which can be added to soups, sauces, rice dishes, or pasta sauces. To remove the grit, pour the liquid through a small sieve lined with a single sheet of paper towel and placed over a measuring cup.

3. Remove the cover, raise the heat, and cook until the excess liquid evaporates, 2 to 3 minutes. (The bok choy should be moist but not soupy.) Stir in the vinegar and salt and pepper to taste. Sprinkle the bok choy with the reserved bacon and serve immediately.

Master Recipe for Sesame-Glazed Baby Bok Choy

SERVES 4

This recipe is best with baby bok choy weighing no more than 4 ounces. If your market sells slightly larger baby bok choy, remove a layer or two of large outer stalks so that the vegetable will cook through properly. Toast the sesame seeds in a small skillet over medium heat until fragrant and lightly browned, about 4 minutes.

2   tablespoons soy sauce
2   tablespoons low-sodium chicken broth
1   tablespoon rice vinegar
2   teaspoons toasted sesame oil
1   teaspoon sugar
3   tablespoons peanut oil
4   baby bok choy (about 4 ounces each), each head halved lengthwise
3   medium cloves garlic, minced or pressed through a garlic press
1   tablespoon minced fresh ginger
2   medium scallions, sliced thin
1   tablespoon sesame seeds, toasted

1. Combine the soy sauce, broth, vinegar, sesame oil, and sugar in a small bowl.

2. Heat 2 tablespoons of the peanut oil in a large nonstick skillet over high heat until almost smoking. Place the bok choy, cut-side down, in the skillet in a single layer. Cook without moving until lightly browned, about 2 minutes. Turn the bok choy and cook until lightly browned on the second side, about 1 minute. Transfer the bok choy to a platter.

3. Add the garlic, ginger, and scallions to the empty pan and drizzle with the remaining 1 tablespoon peanut oil. Cook, stirring constantly, until fragrant, about 20 seconds. Add the soy sauce mixture and simmer until thickened, about 20 seconds.

4. Return the bok choy to the pan and cook, turning once, until glazed with the sauce, about 1 minute. Sprinkle with the sesame seeds and serve immediately.

INGREDIENTS: Sesame Oil

Toasted sesame oil, also known as dark or Asian sesame oil, is an aromatic brown oil used as a seasoning in sauces. Because of its low smoke point, it is not used for cooking. Do not substitute regular sesame oil, which is pressed from untoasted seeds and meant for salad dressings and cooking.

Japanese brands of sesame oil are commonly sold in American supermarkets and are generally quite good. Sesame oil tends to go rancid quickly, so store it in a cool cabinet or refrigerate an opened bottle if you will not use it up within a couple of months.

INGREDIENTS: Peanut Oil

You may think all peanut oils are the same. Think again. Highly refined oils, such as Planters, are basically tasteless. They are indistinguishable from safflower, corn, or vegetable oils. In contrast, unrefined peanut oils (also labeled roasted or cold-pressed peanut oil) have a rich nut fragrance straight from the bottle. When heated, these oils smell like freshly roasted peanuts.

In the test kitchen, we find that unrefined or roasted peanut oil is a real plus in simple stir-fries. Like good olive oil, good peanut oil makes many dishes taste better. Three brands that we particularly like are Loriva, Hollywood, and Spectrum.

BROCCOLI

BROCCOLI REQUIRES A MOIST-HEAT COOKING METHOD TO KEEP THE florets tender and to cook through the stalks. We tested boiling, blanching then sautéing, and steaming. Boiled broccoli is soggy tasting and mushy, even when cooked for just two minutes. The florets absorb too much water. We found the same thing happened when we blanched the broccoli for a minute and then finished cooking it in a hot skillet.

Delicate florets are best cooked above the water in a steamer basket. We found that the stalk may be cooked along with the florets as long as it has been peeled and cut into small chunks. Broccoli will be fully cooked after about five minutes of steaming. At this point, it may be tossed with a flavorful dressing. A warning: If you cook broccoli just two or three minutes too long, chemical changes cause this vegetable to lose color and texture.

We tried stir-frying broccoli without pre-cooking and found that the florets started to fall apart long before the stems were tender. While blanching and then stir-frying helped the broccoli to cook more evenly, the florets were soggy. We found that partially cooking the broccoli in the steamer basket and then adding it to a stir-fry pan works best. This technique is best when you want to sauce broccoli rather than dress it with vinaigrette.

Another option (more Italian than Chinese) is to sauté the broccoli for several minutes in hot oil, add some liquid ingredients (chicken broth is ideal), cover, and then let the steam from the liquid finish cooking the broccoli. The advantage of the sauté-then-steam method is that all the cooking takes place in a single pot. In contrast, traditional stir-frying requires two pots—one to steam the broccoli and one to stir-fry it.

Master Recipe for Steamed Broccoli

SERVES 4

Cutting the florets and peeled stems into equal-size pieces ensures that they will all cook at the same rate. The sweet flavor of the steamed broccoli pairs well with bold, bright flavors. Serve it with best-quality olive oil, your favorite vinaigrette, or one of the vinaigrette recipes that follow. For maximum absorption, toss steamed broccoli with the oil or dressing when hot.

1 1/2   pounds broccoli (about 1 medium bunch), prepared according to the illustrations on page 39 (about 8 cups)

2   tablespoons extra-virgin olive oil
Salt and ground black pepper

Fit a wide saucepan with a steamer basket. Add water, keeping the water level below the basket. Bring the water to a boil over high heat. Add the broccoli to the basket. Cover and steam until the broccoli is just tender, 4½ to 5 minutes. Transfer the broccoli to a serving bowl and toss with the oil and salt and pepper to taste. Serve hot or at room temperature.

➤ VARIATIONS

Steamed Broccoli with Sesame Vinaigrette

Sesame seeds can be found in any supermarket but are usually much less expensive at Asian grocery stores.

PREPARING BROCCOLI

1. Place the head of broccoli upside down on a cutting board and trim off the florets very close to their heads with a large knife. Cut the florets into 1-inch pieces.

2. The stalks may also be trimmed and cooked. Stand each stalk up on the cutting board and square it off with a large knife. This will remove the outer ⅛ inch from the stalk, which is quite tough. Now cut the stalk in half lengthwise and into 1-inch pieces.

¼	cup sesame seeds
1	tablespoon soy sauce
1½	tablespoons rice vinegar
1	tablespoon sugar
1	teaspoon toasted sesame oil
6	tablespoons vegetable or canola oil
1	recipe Steamed Broccoli (without olive oil, salt, and pepper)

1. Place the sesame seeds in a dry skillet over medium heat. Cook, shaking the pan occasionally, until the seeds are toasted and fragrant, about 10 minutes.

2. Process the sesame seeds, soy sauce, vinegar, sugar, and oils in the workbowl of a food processor until the sesame seeds are ground and the vinaigrette is well blended, about 15 seconds.

3. Toss the dressing with the steamed broccoli in a serving bowl. Serve hot or at room temperature.

Steamed Broccoli with Balsamic–Basil Vinaigrette

Use a quality balsamic vinegar that's been aged to reduce harshness. See page 22 for more information about balsamic vinegar.

2	tablespoons balsamic vinegar
6	tablespoons extra-virgin olive oil
1	tablespoon minced fresh basil leaves
1	medium clove garlic, minced or pressed through a garlic press
1	small shallot, minced
	Salt and ground black pepper
1	recipe Steamed Broccoli (without olive oil, salt, and pepper)

Mix the vinegar, oil, basil, garlic, shallot, and salt and pepper to taste together in a medium bowl until well blended. Toss the dressing with the steamed broccoli in a serving bowl. Serve hot or at room temperature.

Steamed Broccoli with Lime-Cumin Dressing

This recipe takes its cue from Caribbean cooking. The dressing is quite potent, so a little goes a long way.

1	teaspoon grated zest and 1 tablespoon juice from 1 lime
1/2	teaspoon ground cumin
1/2	teaspoon salt
	Hot pepper sauce, such as Tabasco
3	tablespoons extra-virgin olive oil
1/4	cup minced red onion
1	recipe Steamed Broccoli (without olive oil, salt, and pepper)

Mix the lime zest and juice, cumin, salt, pepper sauce to taste, and oil together in a medium bowl until well blended. Stir in the onion. Toss the dressing with the steamed broccoli in a serving bowl. Serve hot or at room temperature.

SCIENCE: Why Broccoli Turns Olive Green

We've found that broccoli has an internal clock that starts ticking once the broccoli has steamed for seven minutes. At this point, chemical changes begin to occur, which cause an initial undesirable loss of color and texture. This loss intensifies as cooking continues. By nine minutes, the broccoli has become discolored and mushy, and it begins to take on a sulfurous flavor.

This deterioration is due to two distinct actions: heat and acid. As broccoli is heated during cooking, chlorophyll begins to break down, resulting in a change of color and texture. In addition, all vegetables contain acids that leach out during cooking and create an acidic environment, further contributing to the breakdown of the chlorophyll. None of this is an issue as long as the steaming time does not exceed seven minutes. We find that broccoli actually has the best texture, color, and flavor after steaming for just five minutes, which also provides a decent cushion before this chemical reaction begins.

Steamed Broccoli with Spanish Green Herb Sauce

Make sure to scrape down the sides of the workbowl to incorporate all the ingredients into the sauce.

1/2	cup packed fresh parsley leaves
1/2	cup packed fresh cilantro leaves
2	medium cloves garlic, peeled
3	tablespoons extra-virgin olive oil
1	tablespoon juice from 1 lemon
1/2	teaspoon salt
1	recipe Steamed Broccoli (without olive oil, salt, and pepper)

Process the parsley, cilantro, garlic, oil, lemon juice, and salt in the workbowl of a food processor until smooth. Toss the herb sauce with the steamed broccoli in a serving bowl. Serve hot or at room temperature.

Master Recipe for Stir-Fried Broccoli

SERVES 4

Instead of steaming broccoli until tender and tossing it with a dressing, you may partially steam and then stir-fry it with seasonings.

1/2	cup low-sodium chicken broth
1/2	teaspoon salt
	Ground black pepper
1 1/2	tablespoons plus 1 teaspoon peanut oil
1	recipe Steamed Broccoli (page 38), cooked just 2 1/2 minutes and removed from the steamer
3	medium cloves garlic, minced or pressed through a garlic press

1. Mix the broth, salt, and pepper to taste together in a small bowl.

2. Heat 1½ tablespoons of the oil in a large nonstick skillet over high heat until almost smoking. Add the partially steamed

broccoli and cook, stirring every 30 seconds, until fully cooked and heated through, about 2½ minutes.

3. Clear the center of the pan, add the garlic, and drizzle with the remaining 1 teaspoon oil. Mash the garlic with the back of a spatula. Cook 10 seconds and then mix the garlic with the broccoli. Add the broth mixture and cook until the sauce is syrupy, about 30 seconds. Serve immediately.

➤ VARIATIONS

Stir-Fried Broccoli and Red Bell Pepper with Thai Peanut Sauce

SERVES 4 AS A MAIN COURSE
WITH RICE

This stir-fry is interesting enough (and hearty enough) to serve as a main course with rice. Aromatic jasmine rice is ideal, although regular long-grain rice is fine.

³/₄	cup coconut milk
¹/₄	cup water
3	tablespoons smooth peanut butter
3	tablespoons fish sauce
1	teaspoon grated zest plus 1 tablespoon juice from 1 lime
1	tablespoon light brown sugar
¹/₈	teaspoon hot red pepper flakes
1 ¹/₂	tablespoons plus 1 teaspoon peanut oil
1	medium red bell pepper, stemmed, seeded, and cut into ¹/₂-inch strips
1	recipe Steamed Broccoli (page 38), cooked just 2 ¹/₂ minutes and removed from the steamer
1	teaspoon minced fresh ginger

1. Whisk the coconut milk, water, peanut butter, fish sauce, lime zest and juice, brown sugar, and pepper flakes together in a small bowl.

2. Heat 1½ tablespoons of the oil in a large nonstick skillet over high heat until almost smoking. Add the bell pepper and

partially steamed broccoli and cook, stirring every 30 seconds, until fully cooked and heated through, about 2½ minutes.

3. Clear the center of the pan, add the ginger, and drizzle with the remaining 1 teaspoon oil. Mash the ginger with the back of a spatula. Cook 10 seconds and then mix the ginger with the broccoli. Add the peanut sauce and cook until the sauce thickens, about 1 minute. Serve immediately.

Stir-Fried Broccoli with Hot-and-Sour Sauce

Adjust the heat in this dish as desired by increasing or decreasing the amount of chile.

3	tablespoons cider vinegar
1	tablespoon low-sodium chicken broth
1	tablespoon soy sauce
2	teaspoons sugar
1 ¹/₂	tablespoons plus 1 teaspoon peanut oil
1	recipe Steamed Broccoli (page 38), cooked just 2 ¹/₂ minutes and removed from the steamer
1	tablespoon minced fresh ginger
1	tablespoon minced jalapeño chile

1. Mix the vinegar, broth, soy sauce, and sugar together in a small bowl.

2. Heat 1½ tablespoons of the oil in a large nonstick skillet over high heat until almost smoking. Add the partially steamed broccoli and cook, stirring every 30 seconds, until fully cooked and heated through, about 2½ minutes.

3. Clear the center of the pan, add the ginger and chile, and drizzle with the remaining 1 teaspoon oil. Mash the ginger and chile with the back of a spatula. Cook 10 seconds and then mix the ginger and chile with the broccoli. Add the vinegar mixture and cook until the sauce is syrupy, about 30 seconds. Serve immediately.

Stir-Fried Broccoli with Spicy Black Bean Sauce

Black bean sauce is a salty mixture made from small fermented black soybeans and garlic. It can be found in the Asian food section of most large grocery stores.

1/2	cup low-sodium chicken broth
2	tablespoons black bean sauce
1	tablespoon dry sherry
1	teaspoon toasted sesame oil
1	tablespoon sesame seeds
1 1/2	tablespoons peanut oil
1	recipe Steamed Broccoli (page 38), cooked just 2 1/2 minutes and removed from the steamer
1	teaspoon hot red pepper flakes

1. Mix the broth, black bean sauce, sherry, and sesame oil together in a small bowl.

2. Place the sesame seeds in a large non-stick skillet and toast over medium heat, shaking the pan occasionally, until lightly browned, about 5 minutes. Transfer the seeds to another small bowl.

3. Add the peanut oil to the empty skillet and raise the heat to high. When the oil is almost smoking, add the partially steamed broccoli and pepper flakes and cook, stirring every 30 seconds, until fully cooked and heated through, about 2½ minutes. Add the black bean mixture and cook until the sauce is syrupy, about 1 minute. Sprinkle with the toasted sesame seeds and serve immediately.

Master Recipe for Sautéed Broccoli

SERVES 4 TO 6

Adding broth to the sautéing broccoli and steaming it lightly eliminates the need to blanch the broccoli beforehand. This cooking method is well suited to Italian flavors.

2	tablespoons olive oil
1 1/2	pounds broccoli (about 1 medium bunch), prepared according to the illustrations on page 39 (about 8 cups)
1/2	cup low-sodium chicken broth
	Salt and ground black pepper

Heat the oil in a large nonstick skillet over medium-high heat until almost smoking. Add the broccoli and cook, stirring frequently, until the broccoli turns bright green, 2 to 3 minutes. Increase the heat to high and add the broth. Cover and cook until the broccoli begins to become tender, about 2 minutes. Uncover and cook, stirring frequently, until the liquid has evaporated and the broccoli is tender, 3 to 4 minutes longer. Season with salt and pepper to taste and serve immediately.

➤ VARIATION

Sautéed Broccoli with Garlic, Pine Nuts, and Parmesan

The rich flavors in this recipe work well with pizzas and chicken dishes.

2 1/2	tablespoons olive oil
1/4	cup pine nuts
1 1/2	pounds broccoli (about 1 medium bunch), prepared according to the illustrations on page 39 (about 8 cups)
4	medium cloves garlic, sliced thin
1/4	cup low-sodium chicken broth
1/4	cup dry white wine
1/4	cup grated Parmesan cheese
2	tablespoons thinly sliced fresh basil leaves
	Salt and ground black pepper

1. Heat 2 tablespoons of the oil in a large nonstick skillet over medium-high heat until almost smoking. Add the pine nuts and cook, stirring often, until golden, about 2 minutes.

2. Add the broccoli and cook, stirring frequently, until the broccoli turns bright green, 2 to 3 minutes. Clear a space in the center of the pan and add the garlic and the remaining ½ tablespoon oil. Cook until the garlic is fragrant, about 1 minute. Increase the heat to high and add the broth and wine. Stir, cover, and cook until the broccoli begins to become tender, about 2 minutes. Uncover and cook, stirring frequently, until the liquid has evaporated and the broccoli is tender, 3 to 4 minutes longer. Sprinkle with the cheese and basil and season with salt and pepper to taste. Serve immediately.

BROCCOLI SAUCES FOR PASTA

THE ITALIANS WERE THE FIRST TO recognize that broccoli and pasta make a handsome pairing. The crisp texture and hearty vegetal flavor of broccoli marry well with the mild wheaty tones and tender texture of pasta. The problem is figuring out how to properly cook the broccoli. Generally, we are subjected to broccoli's extremes: mushy, overcooked, and dull or undercooked, unyielding, and bland. We set out to find broccoli's happy medium—crisp, sweet, and tender.

First, we tried boiling the broccoli in the pasta water. Picking the vegetable pieces from the water was a bit awkward and beat up the broccoli quite a bit, so we rejected that option. Next, we steamed the broccoli in a steaming basket and then sautéed it with extra-virgin olive oil and lots of garlic. The results were good, but working with the two pans was a bother. We wondered if we could simply sauté the florets and stalks in a frying pan with oil, but we found that the relatively dry heat took awhile to penetrate and cook the vegetable. We were able to speed things up by adding water to the pan. When the cold water hit the hot pan, it turned into steam, and the moisture quickly turned the broccoli bright green and tender. The combination of both dry and moist heat did the trick.

As far as flavorings go, broccoli has an affinity for garlic and anchovies but also works well with heartier combinations such as sausage and peppers or olives and feta.

Farfalle with Broccoli, Olives, and Feta

SERVES 4 TO 6 AS A MAIN DISH

The florets as well as the stalks are used in this recipe and those that follow. For information on trimming the stalks, see the illustration on page 39.

	Salt
1	pound farfalle
4	tablespoons extra-virgin olive oil
9	medium cloves garlic, minced or pressed through a garlic press (3 tablespoons)
1	tablespoon grated zest plus 2 tablespoons juice from 1 lemon
½	teaspoon ground black pepper
2	pounds broccoli (about 1 large bunch), florets cut into 1-inch pieces, stalks peeled, halved lengthwise, and cut into ¼-inch pieces (about 10 cups)
½	cup pitted and quartered Kalamata olives
½	cup chopped fresh parsley leaves
4	ounces feta cheese, crumbled (about ¾ cup)

1. Bring 4 quarts of water to a boil, covered, in a stockpot. Add 1 tablespoon salt and the pasta, stir to separate, and cook until al dente. Drain and return the pasta to the stockpot.

2. While the pasta is cooking, combine

2 tablespoons of the oil, garlic, lemon zest, ½ teaspoon salt, and pepper in a 12-inch nonstick skillet. Cook, stirring constantly, over medium–high heat until fragrant, about 2 minutes. Increase the heat to high and add the broccoli and ½ cup water; cover and cook until the broccoli begins to turn bright green, 1 to 2 minutes. Uncover and cook, stirring frequently, until the water has evaporated and the broccoli is tender, 3 to 5 minutes longer. Stir in the olives and parsley.

3. Add the broccoli mixture, the remaining 2 tablespoons oil, and lemon juice to the pasta in the stockpot and toss to combine. Serve immediately, sprinkling the cheese over individual servings.

Orecchiette with Broccoli, Sausage, and Roasted Peppers

SERVES 4 TO 6 AS A MAIN DISH

Orecchiette is small, ear-shaped pasta. Small shells also work well with this chunky sauce.

	Salt
1	**pound orecchiette**
4	**ounces sweet Italian sausage, casing removed**
9	**medium cloves garlic, minced or pressed through a garlic press (3 tablespoons)**
1	**cup jarred roasted red peppers cut into ½-inch squares**
½	**teaspoon ground black pepper**

INGREDIENTS: Jarred Roasted Red Peppers

Jarred peppers are convenient, but are all brands created equal? To find out, we collected six brands from local supermarkets. The contenders were Divina Roasted Sweet Peppers, Greek Gourmet Roasted Sweet Red Peppers, Lapas Sweet Roasted Peppers, Gaea Flame Roasted Red Peppers, and Peloponnese Roasted Florina Whole Sweet Peppers. Three of these brands identified the type of pepper used (Divina, Gaea, and Peloponnese all use Florina peppers), and we wondered if a company's willingness to identify the variety of pepper it was selling would be an indicator of the quality of the pepper. In other words, would tasters prefer the clearly named Florina peppers over the generics (whose main ingredient was identified only as "peppers")? To more easily identify their preferences, tasters tried the peppers straight from the jar.

We found that tasters did not necessarily prefer the peppers labeled Florina. What counted was the flavor and texture of the pepper itself as well as the flavor of the brine. The top two brands, Divina (roasted Florina pimento red peppers) and Greek Gourmet (fire-roasted peppers), were preferred for their "soft and tender texture" (the Divinas) and "refreshing," "piquant," "smoky" flavor (the Greek Gourmets). The other brands were marked down for their lack of "roasty flavor" and for the overpowering flavor of their brines. These peppers tasted as if they'd been "buried under brine and acid," or they had a "pepperoncini-like sourness" or a "sweet and acidic aftertaste."

The conclusion? Tasters preferred peppers with a full smoky, roasted flavor, a spicy but not too sweet brine, and a tender-to-the-tooth texture.

THE BEST JARRED ROASTED RED PEPPERS

Divina peppers (left) were the top choice of tasters. Greek Gourmet peppers (right) were a close second.

2 pounds broccoli (about 1 large bunch), florets cut into 1-inch pieces, stalks peeled, halved lengthwise, and cut into $1/_4$-inch pieces (about 10 cups)

1 tablespoon extra-virgin olive oil

1 cup grated Pecorino Romano cheese

1. Bring 4 quarts of water to a boil, covered, in a stockpot. Add 1 tablespoon salt and the pasta, stir to separate, and cook until al dente. Drain and return the pasta to the stockpot.

2. While the pasta is cooking, cook the sausage in a 12-inch nonstick skillet over medium-high heat, breaking it into small pieces with a spoon, until browned, about 5 minutes. Stir in the garlic, roasted peppers, $1/2$ teaspoon salt, and the pepper. Cook, stirring constantly, until fragrant, about 2 minutes. Increase the heat to high and add the broccoli and $1/2$ cup water; cover and cook until the broccoli begins to turn bright green, 1 to 2 minutes. Uncover and cook, stirring frequently, until the water has evaporated and the broccoli is tender, 3 to 5 minutes longer.

3. Add the broccoli mixture, oil, and cheese to the pasta in the stockpot and toss to combine. Serve immediately.

MINCING ANCHOVIES

Anchovies often stick to the side of a chef's knife, making it hard to cut them into small bits. Here are two better ways to mince them.

A. Use a dinner fork to mash delicate anchovy fillets into a paste. Mash the fillets on a small plate to catch any oil the anchovies give off.

B. A garlic press will turn anchovies into a fine puree. This method is especially handy when you have already dirtied the press with garlic.

Spaghetti with Broccoli, Garlic, and Anchovies

SERVES 4 TO 6 AS A MAIN DISH

In these recipes, begin cooking the broccoli immediately after putting the pasta into boiling water. When cut into small pieces, the broccoli takes only a few minutes to cook through. See left for tips on mincing anchovy fillets.

Salt

1 pound spaghetti

4 tablespoons extra-virgin olive oil

5 anchovy fillets, minced to a paste (2 teaspoons)

9 medium cloves garlic, minced or pressed through a garlic press (3 tablespoons)

$1/_2$ teaspoon hot red pepper flakes

2 pounds broccoli (about 1 large bunch), florets cut into 1-inch pieces, stalks peeled, halved lengthwise, and cut into $1/_4$-inch pieces (about 10 cups)

3 tablespoons chopped fresh parsley leaves

1 cup grated Parmesan cheese

1. Bring 4 quarts of water to a boil, covered, in a stockpot. Add 1 tablespoon salt and the pasta, stir to separate, and cook until al dente.

Drain and return the pasta to the stockpot.

2. While the pasta is cooking, combine 2 tablespoons of the oil, anchovies, garlic, pepper flakes, and ½ teaspoon salt in a 12-inch nonstick skillet. Cook, stirring constantly, over medium-high heat until fragrant, about 3 minutes. Increase the heat to high and add the broccoli and ½ cup water; cover and cook until the broccoli begins to turn bright green, 1 to 2 minutes. Uncover and cook, stirring frequently, until the water has evaporated and the broccoli is tender, 3 to 5 minutes longer.

3. Add the broccoli mixture, the remaining 2 tablespoons oil, parsley, and cheese to the pasta in the stockpot and toss to combine. Serve immediately.

EQUIPMENT: Cheese Graters

In the old days, you grated cheese on the fine teeth of a box grater. Now, cheese graters come in several distinct designs. Unfortunately, many of them don't work all that well. With some designs, you need Herculean strength to move the cheese over the teeth with sufficient pressure for grating. With others, you eventually discover that a large portion of the grated cheese has remained jammed in the grater instead of going where it belongs: on your food. Whether you are dusting a plate of pasta or grating a full cup of cheese to use in a recipe, a good grater should be easy to use and efficient.

We rounded up 15 models and set about determining which was the best grater. We found five basic configurations. Four-sided box graters have different-size holes on each side to allow for both fine grating and coarse shredding. Flat graters consist of a flat sheet of metal that is punched through with fine teeth and attached to some type of handle. With rotary graters, you put a small chunk of cheese in a hopper and use a handle to press it down against a crank-operated grating wheel. Porcelain dish graters have raised teeth in the center and a well around the outside edge to collect the grated cheese. We also found a model that uses an electric motor to push and rotate small chunks of cheese against a grating disk.

After grating more than 10 pounds of Parmesan cheese, we concluded that success was due to a combination of sharp grating teeth, a comfortable handle or grip, and good leverage for pressing the cheese onto the grater. Our favorite model was a flat grater based on a small, maneuverable woodworking tool called a rasp. Shaped like a ruler but with lots and lots of tiny, sharp raised teeth, the Microplane grater (as it is called) can grate large quantities of cheese smoothly and almost effortlessly. The black plastic handle, which we found more comfortable than any of the others, also earned high praise. Other flat graters also scored well.

What about traditional box graters? They can deliver good results and can do more than just grate hard cheese. However, if grating hard cheese is the task at hand, a box grater is not our first choice.

We also had good results with rotary graters made from metal, but we did not like flimsy versions made from plastic. A metal arm is rigid enough to do some of the work of pushing the cheese down onto the grating drum. The arms on the plastic models we tested flexed too much against the cheese, thus requiring extra pressure to force the cheese down. Hand strain set in quickly. A rotary grater can also chop nuts finely and grate chocolate.

The two porcelain dish graters we tested were duds; the teeth were quite ineffective. And the electric grater was a loser of monumental proportions. True, the grating effort required was next to nothing, but so were the results.

THE BEST GRATER

This Microplane grater has very sharp teeth and a solid handle, which together make grating cheese a breeze. This grater also makes quick work of ginger and citrus zest.

BROCCOLI RABE

A PERFECT PLATE OF BROCCOLI RABE SHOULD BE INTENSELY FLAVORED
but not intensely bitter. You want to taste the other ingredients and flavors in the
dish. So we set our sights on developing a dependable method of cooking this
vegetable that would deliver less bitterness and a rounder, more balanced flavor.

We found that steaming produced little change in the broccoli rabe—it was still
very intense. When blanched in a small amount of salted boiling water (1 quart of
water for about 1 pound of broccoli rabe), the rabe was better, but the bitterness was
still overwhelming. We finally increased the boiling salted water to 3 quarts, and,
sure enough, the broccoli rabe was delicious; complex, mustardy, and peppery as well

as slightly bitter. Depending on personal
taste, you can reduce the amount of blanching water for stronger flavor or, to really tone
down the bitterness, increase it.

After considerable testing, we found that
the lower 2 inches or so of the stems were
woody and tough, while the upper portions
of the stems were tender enough to include
in the recipes. When we used only the upper
portions, there was no need to go through
the laborious task of peeling the stems.
Cutting the stems into pieces about 1 inch
long made them easier to eat and allowed
them to cook in the same amount of time as
the florets and the leaves.

Once the broccoli rabe has been blanched,
it should be shocked in cool water to stop the
cooking process and then dried well. It can
be dressed with a vinaigrette or quickly sautéed with flavorful ingredients.

Master Recipe for Blanched Broccoli Rabe
SERVES 4

*Using a salad spinner makes easy work of drying
the cooled, blanched broccoli rabe. See page 49 for
tips on buying a salad spinner.*

I   bunch broccoli rabe (about 14 ounces),
     bottom 2 inches of stems trimmed
     and discarded, remainder cut
     into 1-inch pieces (see the
     illustrations on page 48)
2   teaspoons salt

1. Bring 3 quarts of water to a boil in a large
saucepan. Stir in the broccoli rabe and salt and
cook until wilted and tender, 2 to 3 minutes.
Drain the broccoli rabe and set aside.

2. Cool the empty saucepan by rinsing
it under cold running water. Fill the cooled
saucepan with cold water and submerge the

broccoli rabe to stop the cooking process. Drain again; squeeze well to dry and proceed with one of the following variations.

➤ VARIATIONS

Broccoli Rabe with Balsamic Vinaigrette

This sweet vinaigrette complements the bitter, mustardy flavors of the broccoli rabe.

2	tablespoons balsamic vinegar
1	tablespoon maple syrup
1	medium shallot, minced
1/4	teaspoon dry mustard
6	tablespoons extra-virgin olive oil
	Salt and ground black pepper
1	recipe Blanched Broccoli Rabe

Whisk the vinegar, maple syrup, shallot, mustard, and oil together in a medium bowl until well blended. Season with salt and pepper to taste. Add the broccoli rabe and toss to combine. Serve at room temperature.

Broccoli Rabe with Red Bell Pepper, Olives, and Feta

Sweet red bell peppers and briny olives are great complements to the peppery broccoli rabe.

3	tablespoons extra-virgin olive oil
1	medium red bell pepper, stemmed, seeded, and diced
1	recipe Blanched Broccoli Rabe
10	Kalamata olives, pitted and chopped coarse
1	teaspoon minced fresh oregano leaves
	Salt and ground black pepper
1/4	cup crumbled feta cheese

Heat the oil in a large skillet over medium-high heat until almost smoking. Add the bell pepper and cook until barely tender, about 3 minutes. Add the broccoli rabe, olives, and oregano and cook, stirring to coat with oil, until the broccoli rabe is heated through, about 1 minute. Season with salt and pepper to taste, sprinkle with the cheese, and serve immediately.

Broccoli Rabe with Asian Flavors

Although we generally think of broccoli rabe in terms of Italian cooking, its strong mustardy flavor works well with Asian flavorings, too. See the illustration on page 280 for tips on grating ginger.

1	tablespoon soy sauce
1 1/2	teaspoons rice vinegar
1	teaspoon toasted sesame oil
1	teaspoon sugar
2	tablespoons peanut oil

PREPARING BROCCOLI RABE

1. The thick stalk ends on broccoli rabe should be trimmed and discarded. Use a sharp knife to cut off the thickest part (usually the bottom 2 inches) of each stalk.

2. Cut the remaining stalks and florets into bite-size pieces, about 1 inch long.

3   medium cloves garlic, minced or
    pressed through a garlic press
1/2 teaspoon grated fresh ginger
1/4 teaspoon hot red pepper flakes
1   recipe Blanched Broccoli Rabe
    Salt

1. Mix the soy sauce, vinegar, sesame oil, and sugar together in a small bowl.

2. Heat the peanut oil, garlic, ginger, and pepper flakes in a large skillet over medium heat until the garlic starts to sizzle. Increase the heat to medium-high and add the broccoli rabe and the soy sauce mixture. Cook, stirring to coat the broccoli rabe with the other ingredients, until heated through, about 1 minute. Season with salt to taste and serve immediately.

EQUIPMENT: Salad Spinners

The basic design of all salad spinners is similar. A perforated basket is fitted into a larger outer bowl, and gears connected to the mechanism in the lid spin the basket rapidly, creating centrifugal force that pulls the greens to the sides of the basket and the water on the leaves through the perforations into the outer bowl. Beyond this, however, there are three important ways in which various models can differ.

First is the lid, some of which are solid and some of which have a hole so water can be run directly into the basket while you spin. Second is the outer bowl, some of which, like the lids, are solid, while others are perforated so water can flow through. The third major difference is the mechanism that makes the basket spin—pull cord, turning crank, lever crank, or pump knob.

To be fair, all of the eight spinners we tested did a reasonably good job of drying wet lettuce leaves and parsley. Since the differences among them in terms of drying performance are not terribly dramatic, what you really want is a spinner that is well designed, easy to use, and sturdy.

We didn't like the spinners with flow-through lids. The greens we cleaned by running water into the basket tended to bruise from the rushing water and never got clean enough. We also didn't like models with bowls that had holes in the bottom so the water could flow right out. We like to use the outer bowl of the spinner to soak the leaves clean.

As for the turning mechanism, the real standout in terms of design and ease of use was the spinner made by Oxo ($26). You can use the Oxo with just one hand because of its clever no-skid base and the pump knob by which it operates. Pushing the pump down both makes the basket spin and pushes the whole unit down onto the counter. Among the other models tested, the pull cord on the Zyliss ($21) was the easiest to grip.

THE BEST SALAD SPINNERS

With its nonskid base and push-button brake, the Oxo Good Grips spinner (left) requires just one hand to operate. The Zyliss Salad Spinner (right) is especially sturdy and dried greens exceptionally well in our tests.

BRUSSELS SPROUTS

THE TASTE OF BRUSSELS SPROUTS IS OFTEN MALIGNED SIMPLY BECAUSE THE sprouts are not prepared properly. True, they can be bitter and limp if overcooked, but they can also be crisp, tender, and nutty-flavored when handled appropriately.

To find the best and simplest way to prepare Brussels sprouts, we investigated boiling, steaming, microwaving, and braising. The result we were looking for was a tender, not-too-bitter, attractively green-colored Brussels sprout that could be prepared with little fuss.

We began our testing with boiling and steaming, the two most popular methods of cooking vegetables. Since bringing water to a boil can take up to 20 minutes, the added cooking time of eight to 10 minutes—to reach just the right tenderness—meant that boiled Brussels sprouts could take up to 30 minutes to prepare. That would be acceptable had the result been spectacular. We found, however, that boiling produced only a waterlogged, olive-green, bitter sprout.

Steaming was next. Certainly, steaming is a great way to cook vegetables—fewer nutrients are washed away in the water, the vegetables keep their vibrant colors, and since less boiled water is used, the cooking time is dramatically reduced. We were convinced that this would be the ideal cooking method for these "little cabbages." However, after several trials, we found that steamed Brussels sprouts still had quite a bitter taste rather than the nutty flavor we sought, even when we were very careful not to overcook them.

If steaming wasn't the answer, what would produce the tender, tasty sprouts we desired? We considered the microwave, an appliance that, even microwave foes would agree, can beautifully prepare many varieties of vegetables. To find out, we added ¼ cup of water to 1 pound of Brussels sprouts and cooked them, covered, on high power for five to six minutes. They were perfect: green, tender, sweet, and nutty.

A problem arose, however, when we considered that the quantity of Brussels sprouts cooked in the microwave at any one time determined how long they would take to cook. Unlike conventional cooking methods, even a modest adjustment in microwave cooking time could result in completely overcooked vegetables. For those accustomed to microwave cooking and familiar with such timing adjustments, this method would be the easiest and best for preparing sprouts. But what about those who don't know the intricacies of microwave cooking and don't feel comfortable winging it? An overcooked Brussels sprout from the microwave is actually chewy. We felt we needed to continue our investigation.

Braising, which refers to cooking food with a small amount of liquid in a tightly covered pan, was the next and last cooking method we tried. As we thought about it, we realized that microwaved Brussels sprouts actually are braised—rapidly. Perhaps cooking them on the stovetop would produce equally satisfying results. We braised 1 pound of sprouts on top of the stove, using only half a cup of water, cooking them until they were just tender enough to be pierced easily by the tip of a knife, about eight to 10 minutes. This method met all the criteria we had established for the perfectly cooked Brussels sprout by producing a tender, nutty-flavored, bright-green vegetable.

Since braising in water was so successful, we decided to try braising in other liquids as well. First, we tried cooking the sprouts in unsalted butter but found that it was difficult to regulate the heat with the lid on and still keep the butter from burning. They came out tasting fine but took longer to cook and required too much attention. Adding broth to the butter helped reduce the attention needed and produced a very green vegetable, but the taste was merely acceptable. Braising in chicken stock produced a sprout that didn't taste much different from the ones braised in water.

Overall, the tastiest Brussels sprouts we cooked came from braising them in heavy cream, a classic French technique for cooking vegetables. We streamlined the preparation by simply placing the cleaned sprouts in a covered pan with the cream. Lightly seasoned with salt, pepper, and nutmeg, the finished sprouts absorbed most of the cream, creating a slightly sweet, nutty flavor that was in no way bitter. Because the results were so tasty, we almost hesitate to offer any additional ideas for preparing Brussels sprouts. Alas, cooking this healthy vegetable

SCIENCE: Does X Mark the Spot?

What about that age-old idea of cutting a small X in the stem end of each Brussels sprout before cooking? The idea behind this technique is to produce faster, more even cooking throughout by allowing the water or steam to penetrate the thicker stem end. If you have ever practiced this technique, you know that it is time consuming to cut that little X, especially since the sprouts are small and round and tend to roll away from the knife. We thought it would be worthwhile to see if this extra step was really necessary.

We carved an X into the bottoms of half of each batch of Brussels sprouts we tested—whether boiled, steamed, microwaved, or braised. While monitoring cooking times, we tested one sprout with an X and one without. Interestingly, we found that the sprouts with an X cut in the stem end did, indeed, seem to be more evenly cooked when tested early in the cooking, before the sprout was completely tender. However, by the time the sprout top was cooked through, it was impossible to tell the difference in the tenderness or cooking evenness between the marked and unmarked sprouts.

Further tests showed that the same result held true for other vegetables commonly carved with an X for even cooking: broccoli stems and pearl onions. Pearl onions cooked at exactly the same rate whether they had been marked or not. Carved broccoli stalks tested slightly faster up to the three-minute point, after which they showed no difference at all.

In other words, the notorious X appears to be a tenet of kitchen wisdom based on myth. Cutting an X into the stem end of a Brussels sprout, broccoli stalk, or pearl onion has no effect on producing evenly cooked, tender vegetables.

in cream on a regular basis simply goes against the healthy lifestyle conscience. Save this method for the holidays, when you can throw caution to the wind. For every day, you can still produce wonderful sprouts by braising them in water. The braised sprouts should be drained and then seasoned, either simply with just butter or olive oil and salt and pepper or in slightly more complex sauces (several recipes follow).

The best Brussels sprouts are available in late fall through early winter, peaking in late November. They are often associated with the holidays because of their short season. When buying Brussels sprouts, choose those with small, tight heads, no more than 1½ inches in diameter, for the best flavor. Larger sprouts can often be trimmed of loose leaves along the stem and still be quite good. However, because these larger sprouts are more robust, they cook best when cut in half.

Look for firm, compact, bright-green Brussels sprouts. Yellow or brown-tipped leaves usually indicate that they are older. Once purchased, keep the sprouts in a vented container in the refrigerator for no longer than four to five days.

Master Recipe for Braised Brussels Sprouts

SERVES 4

Serve these tender Brussels sprouts seasoned simply with ground black pepper and either butter or extra-virgin olive oil. Or use braised Brussels sprouts in one of the following variations.

1	pound small Brussels sprouts, stem end trimmed with a knife and discolored leaves removed by hand
½	teaspoon salt

Bring the sprouts, ½ cup water, and salt to a boil in a 2-quart saucepan over medium-high heat. Cover and simmer (shaking the pan once or twice to redistribute the sprouts) until a knife tip inserted into the center of a sprout meets no resistance, 8 to 10 minutes. Drain well and season (with ground black pepper and either olive oil or butter) or use in one of the following recipes.

➤ VARIATIONS
Brussels Sprouts with Cider and Bacon

Stay away from maple-flavored bacon; it will give an unpleasant flavor to this dish. To keep the bacon crisp, add the cooked bacon to the Brussels sprouts immediately before serving.

3	ounces (about 3 slices) bacon, cut into ½-inch pieces
2	medium cloves garlic, minced or pressed through a garlic press
½	teaspoon minced fresh thyme leaves
¾	cup cider or apple juice
⅛	teaspoon ground black pepper
1	recipe Braised Brussels Sprouts

1. Cook the bacon in a large skillet over medium-high heat until crisp, about 5 minutes. Use a slotted spoon to transfer the bacon to a plate lined with paper towels; set aside.

2. Add the garlic and thyme to the rendered bacon fat in the skillet (there should be 2 to 3 tablespoons of fat) and cook until fragrant, about 1 minute. Add the cider and pepper and cook until the liquid is reduced by half, about 4 minutes. Add the sprouts and cook until heated through, about 1 minute longer. Sprinkle with the reserved bacon and serve immediately.

Glazed Brussels Sprouts with Chestnuts

If chestnuts are unavailable, substitute ½ cup toasted, chopped hazelnuts.

- 3 tablespoons unsalted butter
- 1 tablespoon sugar
- 1 (16-ounce) can peeled chestnuts in water, drained (about 1 ½ cups)
- 1 recipe Braised Brussels Sprouts
  Salt and ground black pepper

1. Heat 2 tablespoons of the butter and the sugar in a medium skillet over medium-high heat until the butter melts and the sugar dissolves. Stir in the chestnuts. Reduce the heat to low and cook, stirring occasionally, until the chestnuts are glazed, about 3 minutes.

2. Add the remaining 1 tablespoon butter and the sprouts and cook, stirring occasionally, to heat through, about 5 minutes. Season with salt and pepper to taste. Serve immediately.

Curried Brussels Sprouts with Currants

If currants are unavailable, substitute an equal amount of coarsely chopped golden raisins.

- 2 tablespoons unsalted butter
- 1 small shallot, minced (about 2 tablespoons)
- 1 ½ teaspoons curry powder
- ¾ cup low-sodium chicken broth
- 3 tablespoons currants
- 1 recipe Braised Brussels Sprouts
  Salt

Melt the butter in a large skillet over medium heat. When the foaming subsides, add the shallot and curry powder and cook, stirring often, until the shallot softens, 4 to 5 minutes. Turn the heat to medium-high, add the broth and currants, and simmer until the liquid is reduced by half, about 4 minutes. Add the sprouts and cook until heated through, about 1 minute longer. Season with salt to taste and serve immediately.

Brussels Sprouts Braised in Cream

SERVES 4

This rich dish is perfect for holidays. Don't drain the sprouts after braising—the cream reduces to form a thick sauce.

- 1 pound small Brussels sprouts, stem end trimmed with a knife and discolored leaves removed by hand
- 1 cup heavy cream
- ½ teaspoon salt
  Pinch grated nutmeg
  Ground black pepper

Bring the sprouts, cream, and salt to a boil in a 2-quart saucepan over medium-high heat. Cover and simmer (shaking the pan once or twice to redistribute the sprouts) until a knife tip inserted into the center of a sprout meets no resistance, 10 to 12 minutes. Season with nutmeg and pepper to taste and serve immediately.

CABBAGE

COOKED PROPERLY, CABBAGE IS PLIANT AND MILDLY SWEET. IT HAS AN image problem because it turns mushy and smells bad when it is overcooked. We set out to find the best way to cook this surprisingly fickle vegetable, reasoning that quick cooking would minimize the unpleasant side effects.

Focusing on green cabbage, we chose to shred it for the quickest cooking and also to provide the greatest surface area for flavoring. We began with the fastest possible method, blanching. Plunging cabbage into boiling water for exactly one minute produced the desired crisp-tender texture and pleasant, mild flavor, but this technique also left the cabbage waterlogged.

To reduce the water involved, we considered microwaving. We sprinkled shredded cabbage with water and cooked it on high in a covered dish. After one minute, the cabbage was already limp, and by two minutes, it was quite rubbery.

Steaming turned out to be a better solution to the problem of water uptake, but cooking times varied too much: four to six minutes with an electric steamer appliance; two to four minutes on the stovetop in a basket insert; less time for tender specimens, more time for fibrous heads. With steaming, there is a thin line between delicious cabbage and the wan, flavorless, mealy kind.

We were not optimistic about the remaining options. We had heard that cabbage sautés terribly, and we went on to find truth in the rumor. Sautéed cabbage scorched before it could soften and tasted very burned and crunchy. In addition, cooking fat remained resolutely on the surface and contributed nothing to flavor other than an oily taste.

But we were perplexed by the many cabbage recipes that refer to sautéing. Perhaps these cookbook authors, we reasoned, actually had a quick braise-sauté in mind. While braising usually refers to cooking slowly in a covered pan using a small quantity of fat or water-based liquid, we would describe a braise-sauté as a quicker process that employs the fat and the water-based liquid in combination. We hoped this gentle method would preserve texture while encouraging the development of more complex flavor.

We tried braising in cream, a strategy consistent with the notion of braise-sautéing because cream is basically an emulsion of butterfat and milk. Seven minutes later, we had found our ideal. For the first time, we could taste a subtle mix of flavors, complemented by a slight residual crunch. The cream also provided the perfect vehicle for both sweet and savory flavor variations.

The only problem is the inherent decadence of cream in an everyday cooking method.

But the quick braise-sauté also worked with every combination of four water-based liquids (white wine, chicken broth, apple juice, and tomato juice) and three common fats (butter, bacon fat, and vegetable oil). In each case, the cabbage cooked in liquid alone tasted characterless; adding fat lent significant extra depth to the cabbage flavor and also improved its texture.

The quantity of fat required is less than a teaspoon per serving. You can obviously use more, but there is a lower limit, as we learned when we tried using dairy products that were lower in fat than cream. Light cream worked almost as well as heavy cream, but it started to scorch toward the end of cooking. Half-and-half and milk showed a greater affinity for the bottom of the pan than for the cabbage, and the cabbage cooked with them was porous with an insipid taste. Buttermilk and sour cream were wildly unsuccessful.

Contrary to the common advice to buy a tight, heavy head of cabbage, we had better success with smaller, looser heads that were covered with thin outer leaves.

SHREDDING CABBAGE

1. Cut the cabbage into quarters and cut away the hard piece of core attached to each quarter.

2. Separate the cored cabbage into stacks of leaves that flatten when pressed lightly.

3a. Use a chef's knife to cut each stack diagonally (this ensures long pieces) into thin shreds.

3b. Or roll the stacked leaves crosswise to fit them into the feed tube of a food processor fitted with the shredding disk.

Master Recipe for Braised Cabbage with Parsley and Thyme

SERVES 4

This dish is delicate and simple. For additional richness, increase the amount of butter.

1	tablespoon unsalted butter
1/4	cup low-sodium chicken broth
1	pound green cabbage (1/2 medium head), shredded (see the illustrations on page 55)
1/4	teaspoon minced fresh thyme
1	tablespoon minced fresh parsley leaves
	Salt and ground black pepper

Melt the butter in a large skillet over medium-high heat. Add the broth and then the cabbage and thyme. Bring to a simmer, cover, and cook, stirring occasionally, until the cabbage is wilted but still bright green, 7 to 9 minutes. Sprinkle with the parsley and season with salt and pepper to taste. Serve immediately.

➤ VARIATION
Cabbage and Apples Braised in Cider

Because Granny Smith apples maintain their shape during cooking, they are the best choice for this recipe.

2	tablespoons unsalted butter
1	Granny Smith apple, peeled, cored, and cut into 1/2-inch dice (about 1 cup)
1/2	cup cider
1	teaspoon minced fresh thyme leaves
1	teaspoon caraway seeds
1	pound green cabbage (1/2 medium head), shredded (see the illustrations on page 55)
	Salt and ground black pepper

Melt the butter in a large skillet over medium-high heat. When the foaming subsides, add the apple and cook until just beginning to brown, about 5 minutes. Add the cider, thyme, and caraway seeds and simmer until slightly reduced, about 3 minutes. Add the cabbage, stir to combine, cover, and simmer until the cabbage is wilted but still bright green, 7 to 9 minutes. Season with salt and pepper to taste. Serve immediately.

Cabbage Braised in Beer with Sausages

SERVES 4 AS A MAIN COURSE

Use your favorite German sausage in this recipe; chicken or turkey sausage also works as well. Keep the sausages in their casings and allow for one sausage per serving.

2	tablespoons unsalted butter
1	pound sausages, left in their casings
1	tablespoon grainy mustard
1/2	cup beer
1	pound green cabbage (1/2 medium head), shredded (see the illustrations on page 55)
	Salt and ground black pepper

Melt the butter in a large skillet over medium-high heat. When the foaming subsides, add the sausages and cook until browned on all sides, about 5 minutes. Add the mustard and beer and simmer until slightly reduced, about 3 minutes. Add the cabbage, stir to combine, cover, and simmer until the cabbage is wilted but still bright green, 7 to 9 minutes. Season with salt and pepper to taste. Serve immediately.

CABBAGE SALADS

CABBAGE MAKES A GREAT SALAD. NOT just as coleslaw or a picnic side dish but a crunchy, flavorful, dress-up kind of salad. Cabbage's natural spicy-sweetness and crunchy texture work well with many strong and unconventional flavor combinations. Dressings with spicy chiles, sweeteners, tangy acids, and strong herbal or spice flavors highlight the natural flavors in cabbage without overpowering them. Also, unlike lettuce salads, cabbage salads can be made well in advance, and leftovers don't have to go to waste—they make a great addition to a sandwich or lunch box.

One problem with cabbage salads is their tendency to become watery and bland when dressed and allowed to sit. This occurs because the cells of the cabbage are full of water that leaches out into the salad, diluting its consistency and flavor. Salting the cabbage and setting it over a colander allows a good bit of this liquid to be drawn out. Salads made with this salted and drained cabbage do not become overly watery, and the flavors of the dressing remain undiluted (see the photos below). Because salting does soften cabbage a bit, these salads won't have the intense crispness of most coleslaws, but their pickle-crisp texture is ideal for forking and eating.

Red and green cabbage work equally well, either singly or in combination, in these salads.

Sweet and Sour Cabbage Salad with Apple and Fennel

MAKES ABOUT 5 CUPS, SERVING 4

See the illustration on page 120 for tips on coring fennel.

1	pound green or red cabbage ($\frac{1}{2}$ medium head), shredded (see the illustrations on page 55)
	Salt
$\frac{1}{2}$	small red onion, chopped fine
1	tablespoon honey
2	tablespoons rice vinegar
2	tablespoons extra-virgin olive oil
1	teaspoon Dijon mustard
2	teaspoons minced fresh tarragon leaves
1	large Granny Smith apple, peeled, cored, and cut into $\frac{1}{4}$-inch dice
1	medium head fennel, cored and sliced thin (about 2$\frac{1}{2}$ cups)
	Ground black pepper

THE EFFECTS OF SALTING

Unsalted cabbage is too crunchy and leaches moisture, which makes the salad watery (left). Salted cabbage has already shed its moisture and makes a salad that is tender but not watery (right).

1. Toss the cabbage and 1 teaspoon salt in a colander or large mesh strainer set over a medium bowl. Let stand until the cabbage wilts, at least 1 hour or up to 4 hours. Rinse the cabbage under cold running water (or in a large bowl of ice water if serving immediately). Press, but do not squeeze, to drain; pat dry with paper towels. (The cabbage can be stored in a zipper-lock plastic bag and refrigerated overnight.)

2. Stir together the onion, honey, vinegar, oil, mustard, and tarragon in a medium bowl. Immediately toss the cabbage, apple, and fennel in the dressing. Season to taste with salt and pepper. Cover and refrigerate until ready to serve. (The salad is best the day it is made but will keep for several days.)

Confetti Cabbage Salad with Spicy Peanut Dressing

MAKES ABOUT 5 CUPS,
SERVING 6 TO 8

Grate the carrot on the large holes of a box grater or on the shredding disk of a food processor.

1	pound green or red cabbage (¹/₂ medium head), shredded (see the illustrations on page 55)
1	large carrot, peeled and grated
	Salt
2	tablespoons smooth peanut butter
2	tablespoons peanut oil
2	tablespoons rice vinegar
1	tablespoon soy sauce
1	teaspoon honey
2	medium cloves garlic, chopped
1	(1 ¹/₂-inch) piece fresh ginger, peeled
¹/₂	jalapeño chile, stemmed and seeded
4	medium radishes, halved lengthwise and sliced thin
4	medium scallions, sliced thin

1. Toss the cabbage, carrot, and 1 teaspoon salt in a colander or large mesh strainer set over a medium bowl. Let stand until the cabbage and carrot wilt, at least 1 hour or up to 4 hours. Rinse the cabbage and carrot under cold running water (or in a large bowl of ice water if serving immediately). Press, but do not squeeze, to drain; pat dry with paper towels. (The cabbage and carrot can be stored in a zipper-lock plastic bag and refrigerated overnight.)

2. Place the peanut butter, oil, vinegar, soy sauce, honey, garlic, ginger, and chile in the workbowl of a food processor. Process until a smooth dressing is formed. Toss the cabbage and carrot, radishes, scallions, and dressing together in a medium bowl. Season to taste with salt. Cover and refrigerate until ready to serve. (The salad is best the day it is made but will keep refrigerated for several days.)

Cabbage and Red Pepper Salad with Lime-Cumin Vinaigrette

MAKES ABOUT 5 CUPS,
SERVING 6 TO 8

1	pound green or red cabbage (¹/₂ medium head), shredded (see the illustrations on page 55)
	Salt
1	teaspoon grated zest and 2 tablespoons juice from 1 lime
2	tablespoons extra-virgin olive oil
1	tablespoon rice vinegar or sherry vinegar
1	tablespoon honey
1	teaspoon ground cumin
	Pinch cayenne pepper
1	red bell pepper, stemmed, seeded, and cut into thin strips

1. Toss the cabbage and 1 teaspoon salt in a colander or large mesh strainer set over a medium bowl. Let stand until the cabbage wilts, at least 1 hour or up to 4 hours. Rinse the cabbage under cold running water (or in a large bowl of ice water if serving immediately). Press, but do not squeeze, to drain; pat dry with paper towels. (The cabbage can be stored in a zipper-lock plastic bag and refrigerated overnight.)

2. Stir together the lime zest and juice, oil, vinegar, honey, cumin, and cayenne in a medium bowl. Toss the cabbage and red pepper in the dressing. Season to taste with salt. Cover and refrigerate until ready to serve. (The salad is best the day it is made but will keep for several days.)

Coleslaw with Bacon and Buttermilk Dressing

MAKES A SCANT 5 CUPS,
SERVING 4 TO 6

Salting and draining the onion with the cabbage helps mellow the harsh raw onion flavors. The bacon will become soft with time, so this salad is best served the day it is made.

I	pound green or red cabbage (about 1/2 medium head), shredded (see the illustrations on page 55)
I	large carrot, peeled and grated
1/2	medium onion, sliced thin
	Salt
6	ounces bacon (about 6 slices), cut into 1/4-inch pieces
1/2	cup buttermilk
2	tablespoons vegetable oil
2	tablespoons cider vinegar
I	tablespoon caraway seeds
1/4	teaspoon dry mustard
2	teaspoons sugar
	Ground black pepper

1. Toss the cabbage, carrot, onion, and 1 teaspoon salt in a colander or large mesh strainer set over a medium bowl. Let stand until the vegetables wilt, at least 1 hour or up to 4 hours. Rinse the vegetables under cold running water (or in a large bowl of ice water if serving immediately). Press, but do not squeeze, to drain; pat dry with paper towels. (The vegetables can be stored in a zipper-lock plastic bag and refrigerated overnight.)

2. Fry the bacon in a medium skillet over medium heat until crisp and brown, about 6 minutes. Transfer the bacon with a slotted spoon to a plate lined with paper towels; discard the fat.

3. Stir together the buttermilk, oil, vinegar, caraway seeds, mustard, and sugar in a medium bowl. Toss the cabbage, carrot, onion, and bacon in the dressing. Season to taste with salt and pepper. Serve.

CARROTS

GLAZING IS PROBABLY THE MOST POPULAR WAY TO PREPARE CARROTS. However, glazed carrots are often saccharine and ill suited as a side dish on a dinner plate. These defamed vegetables, adrift in a sea of syrup, often lie limp and soggy from overcooking or retain a raw, fibrous resistance from undercooking. Most recipes for glazed carrots are hopelessly dated, residing in books from the Betty Crocker era or in more contemporary tomes by authors who feel obliged to include them. These recipes never deliver what we hope for in glazed carrots: fully tender, well-seasoned carrots with a glossy, clingy, yet modest glaze.

We began with how to prepare the carrots for cooking. Matchsticks were out from the get-go—we were looking for simplicity, not to improve our knife skills. A bag of "baby" carrots unceremoniously emptied into a pan for cooking revealed pieces of wildly different girth, with some more than twice as big around as others. Surely, these would cook unevenly, so we halved the large pieces lengthwise. Gone was the convenience of this product. Once cooked, these baby carrots were shy on both carrot flavor and good looks. We peeled regular bagged carrots and cut them on the bias into handsome oblong shapes. Once cooked, these comely carrots earned much praise for their good flavor. Slender bunch carrots (sold with their tops on and at a higher price), also cut on the bias, were no more flavorful, and their diminutive size lacked presence. Regular bagged carrots were the clear choice.

Most recipes suggest that the carrots need to be steamed, parboiled, or blanched prior to glazing, resulting in a battery of dirtied utensils. Instead, we put the carrots with a bit of liquid into a skillet (nonstick, for the sake of easy cleanup), along with some salt and sugar for flavor, covered the skillet, and simmered. Mission accomplished: The carrots were cooked through without much ado. Chicken broth as a cooking liquid lent the carrots savory backbone and a full, round flavor, whereas water left them hollow and wine turned them sour and astringent. We tried swapping the sugar for more compelling sweeteners but found brown sugar too muddy flavored, maple syrup too assertive, and honey too floral (but good for a variation, we noted). We stood by clean, pure, easy-to-measure granulated sugar.

We moved on to finessing the glaze. After the carrots simmered for a few minutes, when just on the verge of tender (they would see more heat during glazing, so we simmered them shy of done), we lifted the lid from the skillet, stepped up the heat, and let the liquid reduce down to 2 tablespoons. (If the liquid is not reduced, it is thin and watery.) Finally, we added butter (cut into small pieces for quick melting) and a bit more sugar to encourage glaze formation and to favorably increase sweetness. All of this resulted in a light, clingy glaze that, with a few more minutes of high-heat cooking, took on a pale amber hue and a light caramel flavor. A sprinkle of fresh lemon juice gave the dish sparkle, and a twist or two of freshly ground black pepper provided depth. We were surprised, as were our tasters, that glazed carrots could be this good and this easy.

Master Recipe for Glazed Carrots

SERVES 4

Glazed carrots are a good accompaniment to roasts of any kind—beef, pork, lamb, or poultry. A nonstick skillet is easier to clean, but this recipe can be prepared in any 12-inch skillet with a cover.

I	pound carrots (about 6 medium), peeled and sliced $1/4$ inch thick on the bias (see the illustration on page 62)
$1/2$	teaspoon salt
3	tablespoons sugar
$1/2$	cup low-sodium chicken broth
I	tablespoon unsalted butter, cut into 4 pieces
2	teaspoons juice from I lemon
	Ground black pepper

1. Bring the carrots, salt, 1 tablespoon of the sugar, and broth to a boil in a 12-inch nonstick skillet, covered, over medium-high heat. Reduce the heat to medium and simmer, stirring occasionally, until the carrots are almost tender when poked with the tip of a paring knife, about 5 minutes. Uncover,

increase the heat to high, and simmer rapidly, stirring occasionally, until the liquid is reduced to about 2 tablespoons, 1 to 2 minutes.

2. Add the butter and the remaining 2 tablespoons sugar to the skillet. Toss the carrots to coat and cook, stirring frequently, until the carrots are completely tender and the glaze is light gold, about 3 minutes. Off the heat, add the lemon juice and toss to coat. Transfer the carrots to a serving dish, scraping the glaze from the pan into the dish. Season to taste with pepper and serve immediately.

➤ VARIATIONS

Glazed Carrots with Bacon and Pecans

Granulated sugar works best in the master recipe, but in this variation, light brown sugar is the best choice. Its rich caramel flavor goes well with the bacon and pecans.

3	ounces (about 3 slices) bacon, cut into $1/2$-inch pieces
$1/3$	cup chopped pecans
I	pound carrots (about 6 medium), peeled and sliced $1/4$ inch thick on the bias (see the illustration on page 62)
$1/2$	teaspoon salt
3	tablespoons light brown sugar
$1/2$	cup low-sodium chicken broth
$1/2$	teaspoon minced fresh thyme leaves
I	tablespoon unsalted butter, cut into 4 pieces
2	teaspoons juice from I lemon
	Ground black pepper

1. Cook the bacon in a 12-inch nonstick skillet over medium-high heat until crisp. Transfer the cooked bacon to a plate lined with paper towels to drain.

2. Remove all but 1 tablespoon bacon

drippings from the pan. Add the pecans and cook until fragrant and slightly browned, about 3 minutes. Transfer the pecans to the plate with the bacon.

3. Add the carrots, salt, 1 tablespoon of the brown sugar, broth, and thyme to the skillet. Bring to a boil, covered, over medium-high heat. Reduce the heat to medium and simmer, stirring occasionally, until the carrots are almost tender when poked with the tip of a paring knife, about 5 minutes. Uncover, increase the heat to high, and simmer rapidly, stirring occasionally, until the liquid is reduced to about 2 tablespoons, 1 to 2 minutes.

4. Add the butter and the remaining 2 tablespoons brown sugar to the skillet. Toss the carrots to coat and cook, stirring frequently, until the carrots are completely tender, about 3 minutes. Off the heat, add the lemon juice and toss to coat. Transfer the carrots to a serving dish, scraping the glaze from the pan into the dish. Season to taste with pepper and serve immediately.

SLICING CARROTS ON THE BIAS

Cut the carrots on the bias into rounds about ¼ inch thick and 2 inches long.

Glazed Curried Carrots with Currants and Almonds

¼	cup sliced almonds
1 ½	teaspoons curry powder
1	pound carrots (about 6 medium), peeled and sliced ¼ inch thick on the bias (see the illustration at left)
½	teaspoon salt
3	tablespoons sugar
½	cup low-sodium chicken broth
1	tablespoon unsalted butter, cut into 4 pieces
¼	cup currants
2	teaspoons juice from 1 lemon
	Ground black pepper

1. Toast the almonds in a 12-inch nonstick skillet over medium heat until fragrant and lightly browned, about 5 minutes. Transfer the nuts to a small bowl and set them aside.

2. Off heat, sprinkle the curry powder into the empty skillet and stir until fragrant, about 2 seconds. Add the carrots, salt, 1 tablespoon sugar, and chicken broth, cover the skillet, and bring the mixture to a boil over medium-high heat. Reduce the heat to medium and simmer, stirring occasionally, until the carrots are almost tender when poked with the tip of a paring knife, about 5 minutes. Uncover, increase the heat to high, and simmer rapidly, stirring occasionally, until the liquid is reduced to about 2 tablespoons, 1 to 2 minutes.

3. Add the butter, currants, and the remaining 2 tablespoons sugar to the skillet. Toss the carrots to coat and cook, stirring frequently, until the carrots are completely tender and the glaze is light gold, about 3 minutes. Off heat, add the lemon juice and toasted almonds and toss to coat. Transfer the carrots to a serving dish, scraping the glaze from the pan into the dish. Season to taste with pepper and serve immediately.

ROASTED CARROTS

ROASTED CARROTS' SUBLIME NATURE LIES in their rustic charm. Simple, sweet, and pure, their perfectly caramelized outer layer gently gives way to a smooth, tender interior—unless they are undercooked and have a crisp, bitter center or, on the opposite end of the spectrum, are subjected to such intense heat that they become wan, limp, and utterly unpalatable. Our ideal roasted carrot recipe, we decided, would let us throw a couple of ingredients together, toss the carrots into the oven, and let them roast until they were done—a simple and painless side dish.

We started with the basic question of what type of carrot to use. We tested bunch carrots (those with greens still attached), bagged carrots, and bagged baby carrots. The bagged whole carrots were too fibrous and bitter. Baby and bunch carrots were the best—sweet and tender. While the flavor and presentation of bunch carrots edged out the bagged babies (bunch carrots were breathtaking when roasted whole with just a nub of green stem left attached), the baby carrots needed no peeling, trimming, or chopping. They were effortless and easy, just what we had in mind.

Still, without a little help from a fatty cohort, we knew that the glossy, bronzed carrots we envisioned would not be possible. So we tossed batches of carrots with vegetable oil, olive oil, extra-virgin olive oil, butter, and clarified butter and roasted them. We were surprised to discover that our favorite was plain olive oil; it neither masked the carrots' sweetness, as did extra-virgin olive and vegetable oils, nor changed their texture, as did the butter.

We next examined possible roasting methods, times, and temperatures. We tried covering the broiler pan with foil to help keep the carrots moist and hasten the roasting, but when we pulled these carrots out from their sealed bed, they had become reminiscent of cafeteria carrots: slightly bitter, pale, and soggy. Carrots covered for only part of the roasting time fared little better. The best batch was the most straightforward: roasted at 475 degrees, uncovered, for 20 minutes, until the carrots were brown and caramel colored.

We proceeded to roast carrots in different sorts of pans to see which would give us the best color and the easiest cleanup. After pitting broiler pan bottoms against cookie sheets and roasting pans against Pyrex glass dishes and nonstick aluminum pans, we found the broiler-pan bottom to be the best for browning the carrots without burning them.

During this testing, we came to wonder just what a baby carrot was. Bagged baby carrots are made by taking long, thin carrots (usually carrot varieties grown for their high sugar and beta-carotene content, which makes them sweet and bright in color) and forcing them through a carrot-trimming machine that peels the carrots and cuts them down to their ubiquitous baby size.

Real baby carrots are varieties of carrots that are miniature in size when mature; contrary to popular belief, they are not carrots of the standard length that are picked early. Unfortunately, real baby carrots are available only through specialty produce purveyors that sell to restaurants and other professional kitchens. If you are lucky enough to spy true, greens-still-attached, tapered baby carrots in your grocery store or farmers' market, buy them in the cooler months and roast according to our recipe. Baby carrots harvested in the warmer spring and summer months tend to be less sweet and have more of a metallic, turpentine-like flavor.

Master Recipe for Roasted Carrots

SERVES 8

Inspect your bag of baby carrots carefully for pockets of water. Carrots taken from the top of the super-market's carrot pile are often waterlogged. This not only makes the carrots mealy but also dashes any hopes of caramelization in the oven.

2	pounds baby carrots (two 16-ounce bags)
2	tablespoons olive oil
½	teaspoon salt

Adjust an oven rack to the middle position and heat the oven to 475 degrees. Toss the carrots, oil, and salt in the broiler-pan bottom. Spread the carrots into a single layer and roast for 12 minutes. Shake the pan to toss the carrots. Continue roasting, shaking the pan twice more, until the carrots are browned and tender, about 8 minutes longer. Serve immediately.

➤ VARIATIONS

Roasted Baby Carrots with Rosemary, Thyme, and Shallots

Follow the master recipe, tossing 1 table-spoon minced fresh rosemary, 2 teaspoons minced fresh thyme leaves, and 2 sliced shal-lots with the carrots, oil, and salt.

Roasted Baby Carrots with Sage and Walnuts

Toast the walnuts in a small skillet over medium heat until fragrant, about 4 minutes, then cool and chop.

Follow the master recipe, tossing 1 table-spoon minced fresh sage leaves with the carrots, oil, and salt. Just before serving, sprinkle the roasted carrots with ⅓ cup toasted, chopped walnuts.

Roasted Maple Carrots with Browned Butter

Follow the master recipe, decreasing the oil to 1½ teaspoons. After the carrots have roasted for 10 minutes, heat 1 tablespoon butter in a small saucepan over medium heat, swirling the pan occasionally, until deep gold, about 1 minute. Off the heat, stir in 1 tablespoon maple syrup. Drizzle the maple-butter mixture over the carrots after 12 minutes of roasting. Shake the pan to coat and continue roasting as directed.

Roasted Carrots with Ginger-Orange Glaze

Follow the master recipe. After the carrots have roasted for 10 minutes, bring 1 heaping tablespoon orange marmalade, 1 tablespoon water, and ½ teaspoon grated fresh ginger to a simmer in a small saucepan over medium-high heat. Drizzle the marmalade mixture over the carrots after 12 minutes of roasting. Shake the pan to coat and continue roasting as directed.

CAULIFLOWER

MANY OF US IN THE TEST KITCHEN GREW UP EATING SOGGY, OVERCOOKED cauliflower flooded with congealing neon-yellow cheese. Some of us ate the cheesy sauce, but no one remembers liking (or eating) the cauliflower. With time (and experience), we have learned that cauliflower doesn't have to be prepared this way. When properly cooked and imaginatively flavored, cauliflower can be nutty, slightly sweet, and absolutely delicious.

We started our testing by trying to develop a quick stovetop method for cooking this sometimes overcooked vegetable. During our first round at the stove, we made two important observations. First, we noticed that cauliflower

is very porous. This can work to cauliflower's advantage or disadvantage, depending on what the cauliflower absorbs during cooking. We identified two basic cooking methods that went hand-in-hand with this observation. In the first method, the cauliflower is fully cooked (boiled, steamed, or microwaved) and then flavored. In this scenario, keeping the water out is key. In the second method, the cauliflower is flavored as it cooks, which means that you want to get liquid in. Our new goal was to test the variables for both methods and devise two master recipes with plenty of creative variations.

We first worked on perfecting the "cook first, flavor later" technique. In this method, the cauliflower is fully cooked by boiling, steaming, or microwaving and then tossed with a light vinaigrette or sautéed briefly in butter or oil with simple flavorings.

We began by comparing boiling, steaming, and microwaving. The boiled cauliflower

tasted watery; regardless of how long we boiled it, from underdone to overcooked, the first flavor to reach our taste buds was the cooking water. The microwaved cauliflower (cooked on full power for six minutes and left to stand for three minutes) had a sweet, nutty flavor, but some of the florets were perfectly cooked while others were seriously undercooked. Steaming the cauliflower for seven to eight minutes, on the other hand, produced evenly cooked florets with a clean, bright, sweet flavor.

To verify our strong impression that steamed cauliflower was less watery than the boiled version, we compared the raw and cooked weights of cauliflower cooked by each method. With steaming, there was no weight increase. With boiling, the cauliflower gained approximately 10 percent of its original weight.

Next, we moved to the "flavor while cooking" approach. The basic technique was braising, which involves cooking with a small amount of liquid in a covered container. We hoped that the cooking liquid—our foe in the previous method—would now become our friend. But we were curious as to how this was best done. Should the cauliflower simply be braised with no previous cooking? Or should it be sautéed first and then finished by braising? Or what about partially cooking via the steaming method and then braising?

After testing these three methods, we immediately realized the benefits of sautéing the cauliflower first, adding some flavorings and liquids, and then braising the vegetable until tender. Braising the dense vegetable with no precooking simply took too long. Not only did we have to stand over the stove to make sure that the cauliflower did not overcook, but this method also created some of the same problems of liquid absorption that we had found when boiling. When we partially cooked the cauliflower by steaming it and then braising it, the taste was lackluster and flat. Sautéing it for seven minutes on medium-high heat and then braising it, however, intensified the cauliflower's naturally mild flavors. The cauliflower absorbed the flavors from the braising liquid, and the browned cauliflower tasted wonderfully smoky and earthy.

Cooking cauliflower too long can release unpleasant sulfur-containing compounds in the vegetable that break down when exposed to heat. To avoid this problem, we found it best to cut the cauliflower into 1-inch pieces that cook quite quickly. With the brown-and-braise method, we also liked how the cut surface of the florets lay flat in the sauté pan. Those cut surfaces browned beautifully, and the sweetness of those florets was pronounced.

We also discovered that just because the tip of a knife slipped in and out of the stem of the cauliflower easily, it did not necessarily mean the cauliflower was done. The best way to test for doneness is quite simply to sample a piece.

Master Recipe for Steamed Cauliflower
SERVES 4

The best complements to the fresh, delicate flavor of steamed cauliflower are mild herbs, nuts, or citrus. Steamed cauliflower can also be served as is, with just a drizzle of extra-virgin olive oil and a sprinkle of salt.

I   medium head cauliflower, prepared according to the illustrations below (about 6 cups)

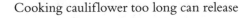

PREPARING CAULIFLOWER

1. Start by pulling off the outer leaves and trimming off the stem near the base of the head.

2. Turn the cauliflower upside down so the stem is facing up. Cut around the core to remove it.

3. Separate the florets from the inner stem using the tip of a chef's knife.

4. Cut the florets in half, or in quarters if necessary, so that individual pieces are about I inch square.

CRUMBLING HARD-COOKED EGGS

For very fine pieces of hard-cooked egg, press the egg through a mesh sieve.

Fit a large saucepan with a steamer basket. Fill the pan with enough water to reach just below the bottom of the basket. Bring the water to a boil over high heat and add the florets to the basket. Reduce the heat to medium, cover, and steam until the cauliflower is tender but firm, about 7 minutes. Remove the cauliflower from the basket and serve or finish with one of the variations.

➤ VARIATIONS

Steamed Cauliflower with Brown Butter, Walnuts, and Crispy Sage

4	tablespoons unsalted butter
1/4	cup walnuts, chopped coarse
1	tablespoon thinly sliced fresh sage leaves
1	recipe Steamed Cauliflower
	Salt and ground black pepper

Heat the butter in a small heavy-bottomed saucepan over medium heat and cook, swirling frequently, until the butter begins to brown, 3 to 4 minutes. Add the walnuts and cook, stirring constantly, until the walnuts become fragrant, about 1 minute longer. Add the sage and cook until the sage becomes crispy, about 30 seconds. Toss the cauliflower gently with the brown butter mixture in a serving bowl. Season with salt and pepper to taste. Serve immediately.

Steamed Cauliflower with Cheddar Mustard Cream Sauce

Because this sauce does not include flour (therefore eliminating the need for the sauce to boil), it is lighter in texture and quicker to make than most other cheese sauces. The combination of cheddar cheese and mustard goes well with the cauliflower.

1	cup heavy cream
4	ounces cheddar cheese, shredded (about 1 cup)
1	tablespoon grainy mustard
	Pinch cayenne pepper
	Salt and ground black pepper
1	recipe Steamed Cauliflower

Place the cream in a small saucepan and bring to a bare simmer over medium heat. When the cream is steaming and just starting to bubble around the edges of the pan, turn off the heat and add the cheese, mustard, and cayenne. Whisk together until smooth. Season to taste with salt and pepper. Toss the cauliflower gently with the cheese sauce in a serving bowl. Adjust the seasonings and serve immediately.

Steamed Cauliflower with Bread Crumbs, Capers, and Chopped Egg

See page 20 for information about hard-cooking an egg. See page 69 for more information about buying capers.

2	tablespoons unsalted butter
3	tablespoons dry bread crumbs
1	recipe Steamed Cauliflower
1 1/2	tablespoons juice from 1 lemon

2   tablespoons minced fresh parsley leaves
2   tablespoons capers
1   large hard-cooked egg, pressed
    through a sieve to crumble very fine
    (see the illustration on page 67)
    Salt and ground black pepper

Heat the butter in a large skillet over medium heat until foaming, about 1½ minutes. Add the bread crumbs and cook, stirring occasionally, until lightly browned, about 5 minutes. Add the cauliflower and cook to heat through, about 1 minute. Add the lemon juice, parsley, capers, and egg and toss lightly to distribute. Season with salt and pepper to taste and serve immediately.

Master Recipe for Braised Cauliflower with Garlic and Tomatoes

SERVES 4

We found that you can braise cauliflower in almost any liquid—broth, canned tomatoes, wine, or coconut milk.

2 ¹/₂   tablespoons olive oil
1   medium head cauliflower, prepared
    according to the illustrations on
    page 66 (about 6 cups)
3   medium cloves garlic, minced or
    pressed through a garlic press
¹/₄   teaspoon hot red pepper flakes
1   (14.5-ounce) can diced tomatoes
2   tablespoons minced fresh basil leaves
    Salt

1. Heat 2 tablespoons of the oil in a large skillet over medium-high heat until almost smoking. Add the cauliflower and cook, stirring occasionally, until the florets begin to brown, 6 to 7 minutes. Clear a space in

the center of the pan and add the garlic, pepper flakes, and the remaining ½ tablespoon oil. Mash and stir the garlic mixture in the center of the pan until the mixture becomes fragrant, about 1 minute. Stir to combine the garlic mixture and cauliflower and cook 1 minute longer.

2. Add the tomatoes, cover, and cook until the cauliflower is tender but still offers some resistance to the tooth when sampled, 4 to 5 minutes. Add the basil and season with salt to taste. Serve immediately.

Braised Cauliflower with Anchovies, Garlic, and White Wine

SERVES 4

Adjust the amount of hot red pepper flakes to increase the heat of this dish. See the illustrations on page 45 for tips on mincing the anchovies.

2 ¹/₂   tablespoons olive oil
1   medium head cauliflower,
    prepared according to the illustrations
    on page 66 (about 6 cups)
2   medium anchovy fillets, minced
3   medium cloves garlic, minced or
    pressed through a garlic press
¹/₂   teaspoon hot red pepper flakes
¹/₃   cup dry white wine
¹/₃   cup low-sodium chicken broth
2   tablespoons minced fresh parsley leaves
    Salt

1. Heat 2 tablespoons of the oil in a large skillet over medium-high heat until almost smoking. Add the cauliflower and cook, stirring occasionally, until the florets begin to brown, 6 to 7 minutes. Clear a space in the center of the pan and add the anchovies, garlic, pepper flakes, and the remaining ½ tablespoon oil. Mash and stir the garlic

mixture in the center of the pan until the mixture becomes fragrant, about 1 minute. Stir to combine the garlic mixture and cauliflower and cook 1 minute longer.

2. Add the wine and broth, cover, and cook until the cauliflower is tender but still offers some resistance to the tooth when sampled, 4 to 5 minutes. Add the parsley and season with salt to taste. Serve immediately.

Braised Cauliflower with Green Curry and Cilantro
SERVES 4

Fish sauce and jarred green curry paste can be found in the Asian food section of most large grocery stores. If fish sauce is not available, rice vinegar can be used.

INGREDIENTS: Capers

Many people associate capers with anchovies and assume that they come from the sea. Others assume that they must be related to peas or beans because of their shape. Capers are actually pickles made from the unopened flower buds of the caper shrub, which grows in the Mediterranean region. These briny morsels are used in countless Italian, Spanish, and Greek recipes.

Capers can be preserved in two ways. More often, the flower buds are soaked in salt water and then packed in brine or a mixture of brine and vinegar. This is how capers are sold in most supermarkets. The other option is to cure them with salt. This kind of caper costs more and is available only in specialty markets.

In addition to differences in preservation technique, capers vary in size. The smallest capers—no larger than small peas—are called nonpareils. There are several more grades, the largest being the size of small olives and called gruesas. If you drink martinis, you may also have seen caperberries. These oval berries form if the flower buds are allowed to open and set fruit. Caperberries are pickled in brine, just like capers.

To make sense of these variables, we purchased six brands of capers and held a small tasting. We tasted small and large capers packed in brine and vinegar as well as

one brand of salted capers. For cooking, tasters agreed that small capers are best because they can be used as is; larger capers are too potent to eat whole and should be chopped. Besides adding an extra step, chopped capers disintegrate when added to sauces.

The taste differences from brand to brand were subtle, although most tasters felt that the brand packed in wine vinegar was the least harsh and therefore the most flavorful. (Labels on the other bottles just said "vinegar.")

Capers packed in salt were unbearably salty straight from the bottle. Rinsing didn't do much to lessen their sting. Soaking in cool water for at least 20 minutes (preferably an hour) washed out enough of the salt to reveal the flavor of the capers. Without the salt (and because there's no vinegar), we picked up hints of herbs (especially oregano) and mustard that we never tasted in the brined capers. These salted capers were delicious, but once we used them in a chicken piccata recipe, their subtle traits faded behind the flavors of the other ingredients.

Many sources suggest rinsing brined capers, too. We think you can skip this step. Drain the capers well and taste one. If they seem very salty or vinegary, you can rinse them. In most cases, this step won't be necessary.

CAPERBERRIES   GRUESAS   NONPAREILS   SALT-CURED CAPERS

2/3 cup coconut milk

1 tablespoon fish sauce or rice vinegar

1 tablespoon light brown sugar

2 teaspoons Thai green curry paste

2 tablespoons peanut oil

1 medium head cauliflower, prepared according to the illustrations on page 66 (about 6 cups)

2 tablespoons minced fresh cilantro leaves

Salt

1. Mix the coconut milk, fish sauce, brown sugar, and curry paste together in a small bowl until smooth; set aside.

2. Heat the oil in a large skillet over medium-high heat until almost smoking. Add the cauliflower and cook, stirring occasionally, until the florets begin to brown, 6 to 7 minutes.

3. Add the coconut milk mixture, stir, and cover. Cook until the cauliflower is tender but still offers some resistance to the tooth when sampled, 4 to 5 minutes. Add the cilantro and season with salt to taste. Serve immediately.

Stir-Fried Cauliflower with Thai Red Curry Sauce

SERVES 4 AS A MAIN COURSE

Stir-frying with a liquidy sauce is a variation on our braising technique. The cauliflower should be cut a bit smaller (¾-inch pieces rather than 1 inch as seen in the illustrations on page 66), and you will need plenty of sauce to give off steam that will help soften the cauliflower. Serve with rice. See the illustration on page 181 for information about stringing snow peas.

1 cup coconut milk

3 tablespoons fish sauce

1 teaspoon grated zest plus 1 tablespoon juice from 1 lime

1 tablespoon light brown sugar

2 teaspoons Thai red curry paste

1/8 teaspoon hot red pepper flakes

1 tablespoon plus 1 teaspoon peanut oil

1 large head cauliflower, trimmed and cut into ¾-inch florets (about 8 cups)

2 medium cloves garlic, minced or pressed through a garlic press

1 teaspoon minced fresh ginger

6 ounces snow peas, strings removed (about 2 cups)

2 tablespoons minced fresh basil or cilantro leaves

1. Mix the coconut milk, fish sauce, lime zest and juice, brown sugar, curry paste, and pepper flakes together in a small bowl until smooth; set aside.

2. Heat 1 tablespoon of the oil in a 12-inch nonstick skillet over high heat until almost smoking. Add the cauliflower and cook, stirring every 10 to 15 seconds, until just barely tender, about 3 minutes. Push the cauliflower to the sides of the skillet, clearing the center of the pan. Add the remaining 1 teaspoon oil, garlic, and ginger to the clearing and mash with the back of a spoon.

INGREDIENTS: Fish Sauce

Just as Chinese and Japanese cooking relies on soy sauce, Southeast Asian cooking depends on salty fish sauce. Fish sauce is a clear, brownish liquid that is pressed from salted and fermented fish, usually anchovies. It has a strong fishy flavor that can be off-putting straight from the bottle. However, the fish flavor fades when cooked, and this sauce adds unusual (and irreplaceable) depth to countless dishes. If shopping in Asian foods stores, look for products labeled *nuoc mam* (Vietnamese) or *nam pla* (Thai). In recent years, fish sauce has become a staple in many American supermarkets.

Cook until fragrant, about 30 seconds, and then stir the mixture into the cauliflower.

3. Reduce the heat to medium-high and stir in the sauce mixture. Simmer, stirring occasionally, until the cauliflower is almost tender, about 2 minutes. Add the snow peas and continue to simmer until the cauliflower is fully tender, about 3 minutes longer. Sprinkle with the basil and serve immediately.

CAULIFLOWER GRATIN

SAUCED WITH CREAM AND CHEESE AND topped with crisp, buttery bread crumbs, cauliflower gratin is a rich and luxurious dish few can resist. There are a few issues, however, that stand in the way of a perfect gratin. First, the cauliflower needs to be cooked just right. When overcooked, it falls apart and has a mealy texture; when underdone, its raw taste and crunch are out of place. The sauce, too, has to be just right, not too rich

and not too thin in both body and flavor.

Starting with the cauliflower, we knew it would have to be partially cooked before being mixed with the sauce and baked in the oven. Most recipes parcook the cauliflower in boiling water for a short time in a process known as blanching. While we found this method to work well, we noticed how important it was to time the cauliflower carefully. Cauliflower's blanching time is directly related to the size of the florets, and tasters preferred florets cut slightly smaller than an inch, making them easy to spear and eat with a fork. We found ¾-inch florets blanched perfectly in 2½ to 3 minutes, at which time the outside is tender while the inside is only softened, retaining some of its toothsome crunch. To keep the florets from cooking further, we ran them under cold water after they were drained. Other tricks we learned along the way include salting the blanching water heavily, which helps to season the cauliflower, and drying the blanched cooked cauliflower by spreading it out on a rimmed baking sheet lined with paper towels.

With perfectly cut and cooked cauliflower, we turned our attention to the sauce. The classic gratin sauce is a béchamel in which cream or milk is thickened with a butter-flour mixture called a roux. After testing béchamel made with heavy cream, half-and-half, and milk, we preferred the rich, lush sauces made with cream. The sauces made with half-and-half and milk lacked appropriate body and heft. Still, although we liked the mouthfeel of the béchamel with cream, we were wary of making it too thick. By using only 1 tablespoon of flour and 2 tablespoons of butter, we were able to make a delicate roux that thickened the cream just slightly. The sauce is classically seasoned with a little nutmeg, to which we added garlic, shallot, fresh thyme, and a pinch of cayenne for a full, round flavor.

Mixing the blanched cauliflower and sauce together, we added a little cheese and topped it all with bread crumbs. We found stronger-flavored cheeses with good melting properties, such as Gruyère, Parmesan, and cheddar, to work best. As for bread crumbs, we found it best to throw a few slices of bread into the food processor with some softened butter instead of using packaged crumbs. These fresh crumbs turned out light and buttery compared with the weighty, overly seasoned packaged crumbs. With the perfectly blanched cauliflower, slightly thickened cream sauce, and fresh bread crumbs, the gratin required only 10 minutes in a 450-degree oven to heat through and brown.

Master Recipe for Cauliflower Gratin

SERVES 6

Gruyère or cheddar can be used in place of the Parmesan. See the illustrations on page 66 for information about cutting the cauliflower into florets but note that this recipe calls for slightly smaller pieces.

TOPPING

4	slices sandwich bread with crusts, each slice torn into quarters
2	tablespoons unsalted butter, softened
1/4	teaspoon salt
1/8	teaspoon ground black pepper

FILLING

Salt

1	large head cauliflower, trimmed and cut into 3/4-inch florets (about 8 cups)
2	tablespoons unsalted butter
1	medium shallot, minced
1	medium clove garlic, minced or pressed through a garlic press
1	tablespoon all-purpose flour
1 1/2	cups heavy cream
	Pinch ground nutmeg
	Pinch cayenne pepper
	Ground black pepper
1	teaspoon minced fresh thyme leaves
1/2	cup plus 2 tablespoons grated Parmesan cheese

1. For the topping: Pulse the bread, butter, salt, and pepper in the workbowl of a food processor fitted with a steel blade until the mixture resembles coarse crumbs, about ten 1-second pulses; set aside.

2. For the filling: Adjust an oven rack to the middle position and heat the oven to 450 degrees. Bring 4 quarts of water to a boil in a large pot and add 1 tablespoon salt. Add the cauliflower and cook until tender on the outside but slightly crunchy inside, 2½ to 3 minutes. Drain the cauliflower in a colander and rinse with cold water to cool. Place the blanched cauliflower on a rimmed baking sheet lined with paper towels.

3. Melt the butter in a large sauté pan over medium heat until the foaming has subsided, about 1 minute. Add the shallot and sauté until softened, 1 to 2 minutes. Add the garlic and cook until fragrant, about 30 seconds. Stir in the flour until well combined, about 1 minute. Whisk in the cream and bring to a boil. Stir in the nutmeg, cayenne, ¼ teaspoon salt, ⅛ teaspoon pepper, thyme, and ½ cup of the cheese until well combined, about 1 minute. Remove the pan from the heat.

4. Arrange the cauliflower in a 3-quart gratin dish. Pour the cream mixture over the cauliflower and mix gently to coat the cauliflower evenly. Sprinkle with the remaining 2 tablespoons cheese. Sprinkle the bread crumb topping evenly over the cheese. Bake until the top is golden brown and the sauce is bubbling around the edges, about 10 minutes. Serve immediately.

➤ VARIATIONS

Cauliflower Gratin with Ham and Cheddar

Cut 6 ounces ham steak into ½-inch cubes (you should have 1 cup). Follow the master recipe, adding the ham steak along with the shallot and substituting cheddar for the Parmesan.

Cauliflower Gratin with Leeks and Gruyère

Halve 3 small leeks lengthwise, using the white and light green parts only, and rinse well; slice crosswise into ¼-inch pieces (you should have about 1 cup). Follow the master recipe, adding the leeks along with the shallot and substituting Gruyère for the Parmesan.

EQUIPMENT: Gratin Dishes

We found that a wide, shallow dish is the key to good cauliflower gratin. Along with a hot oven, the shallow dish ensures that the cauliflower mixture heats up quickly, thus preventing the cauliflower from overcooking and becoming mushy. A gratin dish (*gratin* means "crust" and usually refers to a cheese or bread crumb topping that browns in a hot oven) maximizes the surface area while giving the heat easy access to the crumbs on top.

A tour of any kitchen store, however, doesn't limit the possibilities for dishes that fit this bill. We found eight possible options, priced from $7 to $160, including several specifically labeled "gratin dishes" as well as those sold as "casserole dishes" or "oval dishes." We tested these eight dishes to see what differences, if any, we could find.

First and foremost, you must match the surface area of the dish with the recipe. We found that a dish that is too small causes the crumbs to pack on top of one another, creating a layer beneath the surface that never browns. On the other hand, a dish that is too large causes the crumbs to scatter too far apart so that no cohesive layer can form. A dish that is perfect for one recipe might not work in another, so pay attention to sizes in recipes.

Besides surface area, we also found the depth of the dish to be important. The 4-inch-high sides of the Corning Ware 4-quart oval roaster ($21.99) cast a shadow over the contents that prevented the edges from browning. Most dishes have shallower sides (we found 2 inches to be ideal) that promote better browning.

Another factor is material. Le Creuset's 14-inch oval dish is made of enameled cast iron, which heats up very slowly. The gratins and casseroles made in this dish were still cool by the time the crust was toasted. We found that lighter, faster-heating materials, such as glass, porcelain, and stainless steel, are better choices for a gratin dish. Save cast iron for stews and braises.

Which dish should you buy? We produced hot, nicely browned gratins in several dishes—the Pyrex 2-quart casserole dish ($7), the Emile Henry 13-inch oval dish ($35), the Apilco #14 oval au gratin dish ($68), and the All-Clad Stainless oval au gratin dish ($160). All these dishes have shallow sides, between 1¾ and 2 inches high. More money might buy better looks, but it doesn't buy better performance.

THE BEST GRATIN DISH

In terms of cooking performance, there's little difference between an everyday glass casserole dish and a more expensive porcelain or stainless steel model. We found that a Pyrex casserole dish performs well and costs a fraction of the other options.

CELERY

IN TODAY'S WORLD OF FASHIONABLE VEGETABLES, CELERY IS ABOUT AS hip as bingo night. But as celery fans, we wanted to find a way to transform the crunch of this underrated vegetable into a tasty, tender, cooked side dish. We decided to focus on braising, a method with lots of variations.

When buying celery, we had three choices: loose heads topped with bushy leaves, plastic-bagged celery heads with clipped leaves, and packages labeled "celery hearts" containing two or three dwarfed and cropped heads. We preferred the loose celery—these heads tended to be fuller and fresher, without brownish edges and yellowing leaves. Also, the stalks were glossier and had fewer external

ridges, indicating a less fibrous stalk. The outer stalks' color is a sign of taste and freshness. We found that bleached-out stalks tended to be more pithy, and dark green ones edged on the acrid. The bagged celery hearts had paltry, bitter outer stems and shabby brown edges. Celery stored in the refrigerator lasted for about a week. After that, the flavor faded, and the celery became rather flabby.

Braising—cooking something partially immersed in a liquid while covered—is an easy cooking technique with the added benefit of producing a wonderfully flavored broth. We started cooking the celery in water; not surprisingly, it was pretty lackluster. The braising liquid was perfumed by the celery, but the stalks' well-deserved reputation as diet food needed something to enrich them. Next, we braised the celery in chicken broth, a usual medium for this vegetable, but found that we lost the distinctive celery taste in the broth. Braising the celery in cream

was unappealingly rich. We returned the celery to the water but with bits of butter. We found that a moderate amount of butter added a pleasing finish. We tried braising with olive oil but found that the flavor didn't suit the celery as well as that of butter.

Unfortunately, as the celery cooked, its flavor faded. We tried adding celery leaves, which boosted the taste, but the whole leaves were stringy. Chopping the leaves helped, but the real solution became one of sprinkling celery seed into the liquid, which added the right aromatic punch to both broth and stalks. For another dimension, we tried adding a bit of vermouth or white wine to the braising liquid. The vermouth was the better partner with the celery, contributing a needed touch of herbal sweetness and acidity.

As we tested various braising liquids, we also tested cutting the celery stalks in different ways: curved thin slices, whole and split heads, cut stalks, and peeled and unpeeled. Peeling really improved both the texture and the color of the dish. The unpeeled celery, especially the large outer stems, was like a mouth full of string, even after extended cooking. Peeling also stripped away the surface green color, which tended to go drab when cooked, and the resulting hue of the cooked celery was a pretty sea-washed bottle green.

Although attracted to the idea of cooking whole heads of celery, we found them awkward to peel as well as difficult to fit into a pan. And because of celery stalks' unique bowed shape, the curved thin pieces didn't lie flat when cooking. This in turn increased the amount of water we needed, an undesirable aspect given the fact that the celery itself released liquid during cooking. By splitting the stalks lengthwise, however, and then slicing them into 2-inch-long pieces, we got ample pieces that cooked evenly and were adaptable to numerous variations.

We found that the best cooking procedure was to bring the liquid, flavorings, and celery to a boil in a medium sauté pan, cover the pan, and then simmer the celery for 15 to 20 minutes, until tender but not mushy. Braising in the oven took twice as long to get tender,

REMOVING STRINGS FROM CELERY

Run a vegetable peeler along the outside edge of each stalk to remove the stringy fibers.

and the celery acquired a drab green color.

Depending on how you want to serve the celery, several choices exist for finishing the dish. If you want a very loose broth, the celery can be served at this point or transformed into a gratin. For glazed celery, a favorite in the test kitchen, remove the lid and simmer the broth for five to seven minutes, until the pieces are coated with a light sauce. Glazed celery's pure flavor is a wonderful complement to sautéed fish. If you continue to boil the liquid until it evaporates, the celery can be browned in the residual butter, giving it a nutty edge.

Master Recipe for Braised Celery with Vermouth–Butter Glaze

SERVES 4

See the illustration at left for tips on removing the stringy fibers from each celery stalk.

- 1/2   cup dry vermouth
- 3   tablespoons unsalted butter, cut into small pieces
- 1/4   teaspoon salt
- 1/4   teaspoon celery seeds
- 1/8   teaspoon ground black pepper
- 1   head celery (1 1/2 pounds), leaves trimmed and reserved; stalks separated, rinsed, and outer fibers removed with a vegetable peeler; each stalk halved lengthwise and cut on the bias into 2-inch lengths
- 2   tablespoons minced celery leaves
- 2   tablespoons minced fresh parsley leaves (optional)

Bring 1 cup of water, the vermouth, butter, salt, celery seeds, pepper, and celery to a boil in a medium sauté pan. (The liquid should come about three quarters of the way up the celery pieces.) Reduce the heat, cover, and simmer, stirring several times, until the celery is tender but not mushy, 15 to 20 minutes. Uncover and stir in the celery leaves. Continue to simmer until the broth reduces to a light glaze, 5 to 7 minutes. Sprinkle with the parsley (if using), adjust the seasonings with salt and pepper to taste, and serve.

➤ VARIATIONS

Glazed Celery with Parmesan

Follow the master recipe, adjusting an oven rack to the upper-middle position and heating the broiler. Transfer the cooked celery to an ovenproof dish, sprinkle with ¼ cup grated Parmesan cheese, and broil until the cheese browns, 1 to 3 minutes, depending on the broiler.

Celery-Roquefort Gratin

This celery is braised just until tender and then transferred to a gratin dish and baked. The braising liquid is thickened with a paste of cheese and flour and turns into a sauce in the oven.

½	cup dry vermouth
3	tablespoons unsalted butter, cut into small pieces
¼	teaspoon salt
¼	teaspoon celery seeds
⅛	teaspoon ground black pepper
1	head celery (1 ½ pounds), leaves trimmed and reserved; stalks separated, rinsed, and outer fibers removed with a vegetable peeler; each stalk halved lengthwise and cut on the bias into 2-inch lengths
4	teaspoons unbleached all-purpose flour
3	ounces Roquefort cheese, crumbled (about ⅔ cup)
2	tablespoons minced celery leaves
2	tablespoons minced fresh parsley leaves (optional)
¼	cup chopped walnuts

1. Adjust an oven rack to the middle position and heat the oven to 400 degrees.

2. Bring 1 cup of water, the vermouth, butter, salt, celery seeds, pepper, and celery to a boil in a medium sauté pan. (The liquid should come about three quarters of the way up the celery pieces.) Reduce the heat, cover, and simmer, stirring several times, until the celery is just tender, about 15 minutes. Use a slotted spoon to transfer the celery pieces to a 4-cup gratin dish.

3. With a spoon, beat the flour and cheese in a small bowl until they form a smooth paste. Whisk the cheese mixture into the braising liquid left in the pan. Bring to a simmer and continue to whisk until the liquid thickens, about 1 minute. Stir in the celery leaves and parsley (if using). Pour the cheese sauce over the celery in the gratin dish, shaking the dish to distribute the sauce evenly. Sprinkle the walnuts over the gratin dish.

4. Bake until the sauce is bubbly and the nuts are lightly browned, 25 to 30 minutes. Remove the gratin dish from the oven, cool 5 minutes, and serve.

CHOPPING CELERY QUICKLY

Although you will need longer pieces for braising, many salads, soups, and stews call for chopped celery. Rather than breaking off one or more ribs and ending up with too much, chop the entire bunch across the top. With this method, it's easier to get just the amount you need and, the whole bunch gets shorter as you use it, so it's easier to store.

CELERY ROOT

IN THE TEST KITCHEN, OUR FAVORITE USE FOR CELERY ROOT IS RÉMOULADE, a classic French bistro side dish of raw grated or finely julienned celery root dressed in a mustardy, creamy emulsion. Unlike cooked purees or gratins, celery root salads maintain the vegetable's pristine white appearance, its crunchy coleslaw-like texture, and (most important) its refreshing, herbal flavor, which tastes like a combination of mint, anise, mild radish, and celery.

We began to research and experiment and soon found that fresh celery root salads are straightforward and easy to make. The hardest part of the process was figuring out how to prepare the root vegetable itself: the best and quickest way to peel the bumpy, uneven outer layer and the proper method for cutting or grating it so that it retained some resistance and crunch in the final salad.

To begin, we wanted to find a fast and efficient way to rid the celery root of its dirty, unattractive outer layer and rootlets. After fumbling around with vegetable peelers, different types of knives, and various peeling methods, we settled on the following procedure. First we lopped off about ½ inch on both the root end (the side where there is a mass of rootlets) and the stalk end (the opposite side). Then we sat the vegetable root on either flat end and used a paring knife to cut the outer layer of flesh from top to bottom, rotating it as we cut off its entire circumference.

Now that we had a quick, safe, and easy peeling method, we were ready to explore cutting and grating techniques. We prepared and compared a basic recipe for celery root rémoulade using five different cutting or grating techniques: one cut into fine matchsticks by hand; one using the coarse side of a box grater; one using the fine side; a batch prepared using a rotary grater (or Mouli); and one batch using the grating attachment

PREPARING CELERY ROOT

Cut off about ½ inch from both the root end (where there is a mass of rootlets) and the stalk end (the opposite side). The celery root can now rest flat on a cutting board. To peel, simply cut from top to bottom, rotating the celery root as you remove wide strips of skin.

in the food processor. The salads prepared with the coarse side of the box grater and with the food processor proved to be the best. The celery root developed contrasting textures, softening on the outside while maintaining a good crunch. Unlike the batches made with the rotary grater or the fine side of the box grater, the celery root did not leach out its water. We also liked the ease and speed of using the food processor. It produced nicely grated celery root in a matter of seconds, while cutting the root by hand took considerable time and effort.

Finding the right dressing was the next step. We wanted to develop a dressing that would highlight, not mask, the celery root's fresh, clean, straightforward flavor. We tried several different dressings, including a simple vinaigrette as well as several that were finished with dairy—one with sour cream, one with heavy cream, and one in which crème fraîche was the dominant ingredient. Tasters agreed that the vinaigrette finished with sour cream complemented the celery root the best, contributing a fuller, rounder, and creamier flavor while maintaining the salad's fresh, piquant taste.

The final touches to the master recipe

EQUIPMENT: Cutting Boards

Even though most cooks rarely think about cutting boards, it's nearly impossible to prepare vegetables without one. What separates good cutting boards from bad ones? Is it material? Size, thickness, or weight? Whether the board warps or retains odors with use? And what about the issue of bacteria retention?

To sort all of this out, we gathered boards made from wood, polyethylene (plastic), acrylic, glass, and Corian (the hard countertop material) and used them daily in our test kitchen for eight weeks. We found the two most important factors to be size and material.

In terms of size, large boards provide ample space for both cutting and pushing aside cut foods and waste. The disadvantage of really large boards is that they may not fit in the dishwasher. We are willing to make that sacrifice for the extra work area. If you are not, buy the largest board that will fit in your dishwasher. No matter the dimensions, a board should be heavy enough for stability but not so heavy (or thick and bulky) to impede its easy movement around the kitchen. We found boards in the range of 3 to 4 pounds to be ideal.

Material is important primarily in terms of the way the board interacts with the knife, but it is also relevant to odor retention and warping. We disliked cutting on hard acrylic, glass, and Corian boards because they don't absorb the shock of the knife strike. Plastic and wood boards are softer and therefore cushion the knife's blow, making for more controlled cutting. The pebbly surface texture of the acrylic and glass boards was another point against them. We found that a rough texture promotes knife slide.

There is one advantage to hard boards—they don't retain odors like plastic and wood can. A dishwasher will remove odors from plastic boards as well as specially treated dishwasher-safe wood boards. (Unless treated by the manufacturer with a waterproof coating, wood boards should never go in the dishwasher.)

If your boards are too large to fit in the dishwasher, use one for onions, garlic, and the like; another for raw poultry and meat; and a third for other foods. To remove most odors and bacteria, wash with hot soapy water after each use and then sanitize with a light bleach solution (1 tablespoon of bleach to 1 gallon of water).

Many plastic and wood boards warp over time. Makers of wood boards advise consumers to season their boards with mineral oil to build up water resistance and, thereby, warp resistance. As none of the cooks we know will go this extra mile, plastic boards probably make the most sense for home cooks. Keep them away from the heating element in the dishwasher to prevent warping.

were a matter of personal taste. We added apples for more crunch and acidity as well as a touch of sweetness, thereby giving the salad a necessary spark. Mustard and lemon juice are classic ingredients for celery root rémoulade. Through testing, we found that celery root salads need not be limited to the classic rémoulade flavors. We developed variations that include nuts, fruit, herbs, and fragrant spices to complement the salad.

Master Recipe for Celery Root Salad with Apple and Parsley

SERVES 4 TO 6 AS A SIDE DISH

Although not always available, fresh tarragon complements the flavor of celery root. If you can find it, stir in 2 teaspoons minced fresh tarragon along with the parsley. Add a teaspoon or so more oil to the dressed salad if it seems a bit dry.

2	tablespoons juice from 1 lemon
1 1/2	tablespoons Dijon mustard
1	teaspoon honey
1/2	teaspoon salt
3	tablespoons vegetable or canola oil
3	tablespoons sour cream
1	medium celery root (13 to 14 ounces), peeled (see the illustration on page 77) and rinsed
1/2	medium tart apple, such as Granny Smith, cored and peeled
2	medium scallions, sliced thin
2	teaspoons minced fresh parsley leaves
	Salt and ground black pepper

1. Whisk the lemon juice, mustard, honey, and salt together in a medium bowl.

Whisk in the oil in a slow, steady stream. Add the sour cream and whisk to combine. Set the dressing aside.

2. If using a food processor, cut the celery root and apple into 1½-inch pieces and grate with the shredding disk. (Alternatively, grate the celery root and apple on the coarse holes of a box grater.) You should have about 3 cups total. Immediately add the grated celery root and apple to the prepared dressing (if you wait, they will discolor) and toss to coat. Stir in the scallions and parsley and adjust the seasonings with salt and pepper to taste. Refrigerate until chilled, at least 30 minutes and up to several hours. Serve.

➤ VARIATIONS

Celery Root Salad with Pear and Hazelnuts

For this salad, toast the hazelnuts in a small dry skillet over medium-high heat until fragrant, about 5 minutes. Rub the toasted nuts in a clean kitchen towel to remove as much skin as possible.

Follow the master recipe, substituting ½ firm pear, grated, for the apple and adding ¼ cup toasted, skinned hazelnuts along with the parsley.

Celery Root Salad with Red Onion, Mint, Orange, and Fennel Seeds

Follow the master recipe, substituting 2 tablespoons finely chopped red onion for the scallions and adding 2 teaspoons minced fresh mint leaves, ½ teaspoon grated orange zest, and 1 teaspoon fennel seeds along with the parsley.

Celery Root Salad with Apple, Caraway, and Horseradish

Follow the master recipe, adding ½ teaspoon caraway seeds and 1½ teaspoons prepared horseradish along with the parsley.

CORN

DESPITE FARMSTAND SIGNS ACROSS THE COUNTRY ANNOUNCING "BUTTER and Sugar" corn for sale, no one really grows old-time butter and sugar corn anymore. Nor does anybody grow most of the other old-fashioned nonhybrid varieties. These bygone varieties of corn have disappeared for a reason. They converted sugar into starch so rapidly once picked that people literally fired up their kettles before going out to gather the corn. Corn has since been crossbred to make for sweeter ears that have a longer hold on their fresh flavor and tender texture.

Basically, there are three hybrid types: normal sugary, sugar enhanced, and supersweet. Each contains dozens of varieties, with fancy names such as Kandy Korn, Double Gem, and Mystique. Normal sugary types, such as Silver Queen, are moderately sweet, with traditional corn flavor. The sugars in this type of corn convert to starch rapidly after being picked. The sugar-enhanced types are more tender and somewhat sweeter, with a slower conversion of sugar to starch. Supersweet corn has heightened sweetness, a crisp texture, and a remarkably slow conversion of sugar to starch after being picked. It is a popular type for growers who supply distant markets and require a product with a longer shelf life. Any corn sold in your supermarket during the off-season is likely a variety of supersweet.

Beyond the above generalizations, it's impossible to tell which kind of corn you have unless you taste it. With that in mind, we developed cooking methods that would work with all three kinds of corn hybrids. Boiling is probably the most all-purpose cooking method. To increase sweetness, we tried adding milk to the water but found it muddied the corn flavor. Salt toughens the corn up a bit and is best added at the table. Sugar can be added to the water to enhance the corn's sweetness, but when we tried this with supersweet corn,

DRAINING BOILED CORN

Hot boiled ears of corn are awkward to drain in a conventional colander. Instead, try draining the bulky ears in a clean dish rack.

it tasted too sweet, almost like dessert.

Grilling is our other preferred method for cooking corn. The ideal grilled corn retains the juiciness of boiled corn without sacrificing the toasty caramelization and smoke-infused graces of the grill. We started our tests with the bare ear of corn cooked directly over a medium-high fire. The outcome seemed too good to be true. The lightly caramelized corn was still juicy but with a toasty hit of grilled flavor and a sweet essence to chase it down. In fact, it *was* too good to be true. The variety of corn we used was fittingly called Fantasy, which is a supersweet variety. When we tried grilling a normal sugary corn variety with the husk off, the outcome was a flavorless, dry, gummy turnoff. The end result was no better with sugar-enhanced corn. The direct heat was just too much for the fleeting flavors and tender texture of the normal sugary and sugar-enhanced corn types.

We went on to test another popular grilling technique: throw the whole ear on the grill, husk and all, as is. We tried this with all three sweet corn types at various heat levels. Half of the ears of corn were soaked beforehand; the other half were not. In sum, the husk-on method makes for a great-tasting ear of corn, and a particularly crisp, juicy one. But if it were not for the sticky charred husks that must be awkwardly peeled away at the table if you are to serve the corn hot, you would think you were eating boiled corn. The presoaked corn in particular just steams in the husk and picks up absolutely no grilled flavor.

Since grilling with the husk off was too aggressive for nonsupersweet varieties and grilling with the husk on was no different from boiled corn, we turned to a compromise approach. We peeled off the outer layers of husk but left the final layer that hugs the ear. This layer is much more

moist and delicate than the outer layers, so much so that you can practically see the kernels through the husk. When cooked over a medium-high fire, this gave the corn a jacket heavy enough to prevent dehydration yet light enough to allow a gentle toasting of the kernels. After about eight minutes (rolling the corn one-quarter turn every two minutes), we could be certain that the corn was cooked just right, because the husk picked up a dark silhouette of the kernels and began to pull back at the corn's tip.

DRY-TOASTING GARLIC

Toasting garlic cloves in a dry skillet tames their harsh flavor and loosens the skins for easy peeling. The garlic does not become soft and creamy like garlic roasted in the oven.

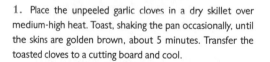

1. Place the unpeeled garlic cloves in a dry skillet over medium-high heat. Toast, shaking the pan occasionally, until the skins are golden brown, about 5 minutes. Transfer the toasted cloves to a cutting board and cool.

2. When cooled, the once-clingy skins peel off readily. The garlic can now be sliced, chopped, or minced as you normally would, but it will have far less bite.

Master Recipe for Boiled Corn

SERVES 8

If you want to serve more corn, bring a second pot of water to a boil at the same time or cook the corn in batches in just one pot. If you know that you have supersweet corn, omit the sugar.

4   teaspoons sugar (optional)
8   ears fresh corn, husks and silk removed
     Salt and ground black pepper
     Plain butter or flavored butter (recipes follow; optional)

Bring 4 quarts of water and the sugar (if using) to a boil in a large pot. Add the corn, return to a boil, and cook until tender, 5 to 7 minutes. Drain the corn. Season the corn with salt and pepper to taste. Serve immediately, with butter (if using).

➤   VARIATIONS

Roasted Garlic and Herb Butter

MAKES ENOUGH FOR 8 EARS OF CORN

Dry-toasting garlic is a good option when you want to mellow the punch of raw garlic but don't have time to roast a whole head of garlic in the oven. See the illustrations on page 81 for more information.

10   medium cloves garlic, skins left on
6   tablespoons unsalted butter, softened
1   tablespoon minced fresh parsley leaves
1   tablespoon minced fresh basil leaves
1/8   teaspoon ground black pepper

1. Toast the garlic cloves in a small skillet over medium-high heat, shaking the pan occasionally, until the garlic becomes fragrant and the skins are golden brown, about 5 minutes. Transfer the toasted garlic cloves to a cutting board. When the cloves are cool enough to handle, skin and press or mince the cloves.

2. Using a fork, beat the butter in a small bowl until light and fluffy. Beat in the garlic, herbs, and pepper until thoroughly combined.

Lime-Cilantro Butter

MAKES ENOUGH FOR 8 EARS OF CORN

6   tablespoons unsalted butter, softened
1 1/2 teaspoons grated zest from 1 lime
1   tablespoon minced fresh cilantro leaves
      Pinch cayenne pepper

Using a fork, beat the butter in a small bowl until light and fluffy. Beat in the lime zest, cilantro, and cayenne until well combined.

Master Recipe for Grilled Corn

SERVES 8

While grilling husk-on corn delivers great pure corn flavor, it lacks the smokiness of the grill; essentially, the corn is steamed in its protective husk. By leaving only the innermost layer, we were rewarded with perfectly tender corn graced with the grill's flavor. Prepared in this way, the corn does not need basting with oil. See the illustration on page 84 for tips on judging when the corn is ready to come off the grill.

8   ears fresh corn, prepared according to the illustrations on page 83
      Salt and ground black pepper
      Butter (optional)

1. Grill the corn over a medium-hot fire (you should be able to hold your hand 5 inches above the cooking grate for 3 to 4 seconds), turning the ears every 1½ to 2 minutes, until the dark outlines of the kernels show through the husk and the husk is charred and beginning to peel away from the tip to expose some kernels, 8 to 10 minutes.

2. Transfer the corn to a platter. Carefully

PREPARING CORN FOR GRILLING

1. Remove all but the innermost layer of the husk. The kernels should be covered by, but visible through, the innermost layer.

2. Use scissors to snip off the tassel, or long silk ends, at the tip of the ear.

remove and discard the charred husks and silk. Season the corn with salt and pepper to taste and butter (if using). Serve immediately.

➤ VARIATIONS

Grilled Corn with Spicy Chili Butter

Sautéing the spices with the butter and garlic brings out their flavor. Because salt does not dissolve readily in butter, it's best to serve the salt on the side.

6	tablespoons unsalted butter
2	medium cloves garlic, minced or pressed through a garlic press
I	teaspoon chili powder
1/2	teaspoon ground cumin
1/2	teaspoon paprika
1/8	teaspoon cayenne pepper
8	ears fresh corn, prepared according to the illustrations above
I	lime, cut into 8 wedges
	Salt

1. Melt the butter in a 10-inch skillet over medium heat. When the foaming subsides, add the garlic, chili powder, cumin, paprika, and cayenne and cook until fragrant, about 1 minute. Turn off the heat and set aside.

2. Grill the corn over a medium-hot fire (you should be able to hold your hand 5 inches above the cooking grate for 3 to 4 seconds), turning the ears every 1½ to 2 minutes, until the dark outlines of the kernels show through the husk and the husk is charred and beginning to peel away from the tip to expose some kernels, 8 to 10 minutes.

3. Transfer the corn to a platter. Carefully remove and discard the charred husks and silk. Using tongs, take each ear of corn and roll it in the butter mixture. Serve immediately, with lime wedges and salt to taste.

Grilled Corn with Soy-Honey Glaze

Corn grilled with soy sauce is a familiar sight at summer fairs and festivals in Japan. Returning the glazed ears of corn to the grill caramelizes the sugar in the sauce and gives the corn a deep, smoky flavor.

- 1/3   cup honey
- 1/3   cup soy sauce
- 8   ears fresh corn, prepared according to the illustrations on page 83

1. Mix the honey and soy sauce together in a 10-inch skillet. Bring to a simmer over medium-high heat. Reduce the heat to medium and simmer until slightly syrupy and reduced to about ½ cup, about 5 minutes. Turn off the heat and set aside.

2. Grill the corn over a medium-hot fire (you should be able to hold your hand 5 inches above the cooking grate for 3 to 4 seconds), turning the ears every 1½ to 2 minutes, until the dark outlines of the kernels show through the husk and the husk is charred and beginning to peel away from the tip to expose some kernels, 8 to 10 minutes.

3. Transfer the corn to a platter. Carefully remove and discard the charred husks and silk. Using tongs, take each ear of corn and roll it in the soy mixture. Return the glazed corn to the grill for an additional 1 to 2 minutes, turning once. Serve immediately.

CORN FRITTERS

CORN FRITTERS ARE BASICALLY CORN kernels (ground, grated, or chopped) enriched with egg and flour and fried until crisp. The ideal fritter is amazingly crisp and golden brown on the outside, creamy and bursting with sweet corn flavor on the inside. As our early tests demonstrated, however, most corn fritters are heavy, dense, greasy cakes with almost no corn flavor.

JUDGING WHEN GRILLED CORN IS DONE

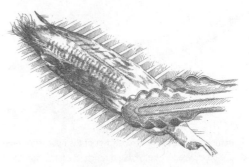

As soon as the husk picks up the dark silhouette of kernels and begins to pull away from the tip of the ear, the corn is ready to come off the grill.

We started our research by collecting as many fritter recipes, corn or otherwise, as possible, detouring around any that began with "Take one can creamed corn . . ." or "Heat up the fry-o-later . . . ." We wanted to use fresh corn and a skillet.

We first looked to see how the corn was treated. The main choices were cut, grated, pureed, and chopped. For our first batch, we simply cut the kernels off the cob and then stirred them into the egg-and-flour batter. The result was a fritter more like a pancake, with a small amount of corn flavor showing up only if one was lucky enough to bite into a kernel. We went to the other extreme and pureed the kernels, but the amount of flour necessary to make the mixture cohesive produced a very bland, pasty fritter. We knew that we were on to something when we tried grating the corn on a box grater. This time, the interior was creamy and flavorful, but the fritters lacked texture. In our next batch, we included whole kernels as well as corn pulp. These fritters were packed with fresh corn flavor and texturally interesting.

Next came the binders. It was obvious that the amount of flour added would make the difference between a delicate fritter and a doorstop. We added just enough flour to keep the fritters from falling apart, but even with this small amount of flour, the corn flavor was dulled significantly. Cornmeal, another binder found in several recipes, was an option, and the corn flavor that it lent was perfect. When used alone, however, the cornmeal compromised the texture of the fritters, making them unpleasantly grainy. We thought that a mixture of the flour and cornmeal would be perfect, and after trying various ratios, we agreed on equal amounts of each.

These fritters had great corn flavor and a tender texture, but they lacked the creamy richness we desired. We first tried adding melted butter, but the fritters were greasy and the butter seemed to dull the fresh corn flavor. Remembering the creamy consistency of the grated corn pulp, we added in turns a small amount of milk, buttermilk, half-and-half, and heavy cream, hoping to closely emulate the creaminess found in the corn itself. Heavy cream proved to be exactly what the batter needed—the higher amount

of fat enriched the fritter yet didn't compromise its sweet corn flavor. At this point, we tried baking soda, which some recipes used to lighten the batter. We didn't care for the puffed, tempura-like appearance and texture of these fritters, so we left it out.

Next, we tested frying the fritters in butter, oil, and a blend of the two. Butter scorched by the time we got around to frying the second half of our batter. Blending the butter with a bit of oil to prevent burning was not worth the trouble. Vegetable oil proved to be the best cooking medium, for both its reluctance to smoke and its neutral taste; it didn't compete with the corn. At this time, we wondered how much oil was really necessary. We found pan-frying in a moderate amount of oil (¼ cup) sufficient to crisp the fritters perfectly.

Finally, we admitted to ourselves that there are times when fresh sweet corn was just not a possibility. We tried our recipe with off-season ears of corn purchased at a local supermarket but found that their moisture content and sweet flavor were greatly diminished. Frozen corn, which is much more flavorful than its canned cousin, was our only option. To obtain a texture similar to the one we got using fresh corn, we pulsed semidefrosted kernels in the food processor. The resulting fritters had great corn flavor and texture—almost as good as those made with fresh corn.

REMOVING KERNELS FROM CORN COBS

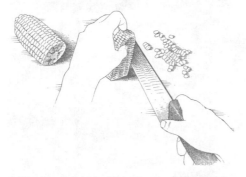

Cutting kernels from long ears of corn can be tricky. Tapered ears can wobble on cutting boards, and kernels can go flying around the kitchen. We avoid these problems by cutting the ear in half crosswise and then standing the ears on their cut surfaces, which are flat and stable.

Master Recipe for Corn Fritters

MAKES TWELVE 2-INCH FRITTERS, SERVING 4 TO 6 AS A FIRST COURSE OR SIDE DISH

See the illustrations on page 87 for tips on cutting the kernels off some ears of corn and grating (milking) the rest of the corn. Serve these fritters with

tartar sauce, hot pepper sauce, or tomato salsa. For breakfast, drizzle with maple syrup.

3–4	medium ears corn, husks and silk removed
1	large egg, beaten lightly
3	tablespoons all-purpose flour
3	tablespoons cornmeal
2	tablespoons heavy cream
1	medium shallot, minced
½	teaspoon salt
	Pinch cayenne pepper
¼	cup vegetable or corn oil, or more as needed

1. Using a chef's knife, cut the kernels from 1 or 2 ears of corn; you should have about 1 cup. Transfer the kernels to a medium bowl. With the back of a knife, scrape any pulp remaining on the cobs and transfer it to the bowl. Grate the kernels from the remaining 1 or 2 ears of corn on the large holes of a box grater, then firmly scrape any pulp remaining on the cobs with the back of a knife; you should have a generous ½ cup kernels and pulp. Transfer the grated kernels and pulp to the bowl with the cut kernels.

2. Mix the egg, flour, cornmeal, cream, shallot, salt, and cayenne into the corn mixture to form a thick batter.

3. Heat the oil in a 12-inch heavy-bottomed skillet over medium-high heat until almost smoking, about 2 minutes. Drop heaping tablespoons of batter into the oil (half the batter, or 6 fritters, should fit into the pan at once). Fry until golden brown, about 1 minute. Using a thin metal spatula, turn the fritters and fry until the second side is golden brown, about 1 minute longer. Transfer the fritters to a plate lined with paper towels. Add more oil to the skillet if necessary and heat until almost smoking. Repeat to fry the remaining batter. Serve immediately.

➤ VARIATIONS

Corn Fritters with Cheddar and Chives

Follow the master recipe, adding ⅓ cup shredded cheddar cheese, 2 tablespoons minced fresh chives, and 1 teaspoon Dijon mustard to the batter.

Out-of-Season Corn Fritters

When fresh corn is out of season, frozen corn makes a fine substitute. Processing the frozen kernels in a food processor approximates the texture achieved by grating fresh corn.

Use the same ingredient list and quantities in the master recipe, substituting 2 cups frozen corn kernels thawed at room temperature for 15 minutes for the fresh corn. Pulse the corn, egg, flour, cornmeal, cream, shallot, salt, and cayenne in the workbowl of a food processor fitted with the steel blade until the mixture forms a thick batter with some whole kernels, about ten 1-second pulses. Continue with the recipe from step 3.

CORN PUDDING

CORN PUDDING IS A COMBINATION of eggs, milk, and cream—basically, a savory corn custard—graced with a generous helping of freshly cut kernels. We set out to develop a recipe for a tender, creamy custard with lots of corn flavor.

We originally thought that this dish would be a no-brainer. Many American cookbooks include recipes for corn pudding, and while some call for cheese and herbs and others add chiles, the recipes invariably boil down to a combination of milk, cream, eggs, and corn. Given the consistency of the recipes, we were quite surprised to find that our first puddings were failures: Each and every one curdled and wept, producing an unwanted pool of watery liquid.

The pudding cooked in a water bath—a large roasting pan filled with hot water—was better than those exposed directly to the oven heat. As with other oven-baked puddings, the water bath tempered the heat and protected the eggs from overcooking. But the water bath alone was not enough to produce a smooth, tender custard. It seemed obvious that the corn in the pudding was the source of the escaping liquid found in every pudding. The question was how to get rid of the moisture in the corn without losing the fresh corn flavor essential to the dish.

After experimenting with various options, we settled on a simple two-step approach. First, we cooked the corn kernels in a little butter, just until the moisture in the pan had almost evaporated. Then we eliminated a bit more of the corn's liquid by simmering the kernels in heavy cream. Because heavy cream, unlike milk or even light cream, can be cooked at a boil without curdling, we reasoned that it would be safe to simmer the corn together with the cream that was already part of the recipe. When we tried this method, we were very happy with the results. When we made the pudding with corn that had been briefly sautéed and then simmered with heavy cream to make a thick mixture, we had a dish with great flavor and without any seeping liquid.

Now we were ready to move on to balancing flavors. The first thing we noticed about our now smooth and creamy custard was the corn—there was too much of it. To reduce the corn-to-custard ratio, we cut back from 4 cups of corn to 3. This helped, but there still seemed to be too many large kernels intruding on the tender custard. Perhaps pureeing some of the corn,

MILKING CORN

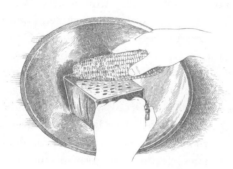

1. Start by grating an ear of corn on the large holes of a box grater.

2. Finish by firmly scraping any remaining pulp off the cob with the back of a butter knife.

we thought, would smooth out the texture without sacrificing any of the intense corn flavor. But pureeing did the job too well; we wanted the pudding to have some chew, and now it didn't have enough. Next, we tried grating some of the corn directly off the cobs on the coarse side of a box grater. This method gave us just what we were looking for in terms of flavor as well as texture.

Now that we had solved the problem of weeping and developed a satisfying texture for the pudding, we thought it was just a bit too rich. We decided to try using whole eggs alone instead of the two whole eggs plus two yolks we had been using. We tried three whole eggs first and liked the pudding better. Next, we tried four whole eggs, and this version was even better. The two extra whites seemed to lighten the dish, while the custard remained smooth and tender—just what we wanted.

Master Recipe for Creamy Corn Pudding

SERVES 6 AS A SIDE DISH

See the illustrations on page 87 for tips on cutting the kernels off some ears of corn and grating (milking) the rest of the corn. Corn pudding must be served hot and cannot be reheated, so plan ahead accordingly.

6	medium ears fresh corn, husks and silk removed
3	tablespoons unsalted butter, plus extra for greasing the baking dish
2/3	cup heavy cream
1 1/2	teaspoons salt
1	teaspoon sugar
1/4	teaspoon cayenne pepper
1 1/3	cups whole milk
4	large eggs, beaten lightly
1	tablespoon cornstarch

1. Cut the kernels from 5 ears of corn and transfer them to a medium bowl. Scrape the cobs with the back of a butter knife to collect the milk in the same bowl (you should have about 2½ cups kernels and milk). Grate the remaining ear of corn on the coarse side of a box grater set in the bowl with the cut kernels (you should have about ½ cup grated kernels). Firmly scrape this cob with the back of a butter knife to collect the pulp and milk in the same bowl.

2. Adjust an oven rack to the lower-middle position, place an empty roasting pan or large baking dish on the rack, and heat the oven to 350 degrees. Generously butter an 8 by 8-inch baking dish. Bring 2 quarts of water to a boil in a kettle or saucepan.

3. Melt the butter in large heavy-bottomed skillet over medium heat. When the foaming subsides, add the contents of the bowl with the corn kernels and pulp. Cook, stirring occasionally, until the corn is bright yellow and the liquid has almost evaporated, about 5 minutes. Add the cream, salt, sugar, and cayenne and cook, stirring occasionally, until thickened and a spoon leaves a trail when the pan bottom is scraped, about 5 minutes. Transfer the corn mixture to a medium bowl. Stir in the milk and then whisk in the eggs and cornstarch. Pour the mixture into the buttered baking dish.

4. Set the dish in the roasting pan or large baking dish already in the oven. Fill the outer pan with boiling water to reach halfway up the inner pan. Bake until the center jiggles slightly when shaken and the pudding has browned lightly in spots, 20 to 25 minutes. Remove the baking dish with the pudding from the water bath. Cool 10 minutes and serve.

→ VARIATION

Corn Pudding with Leeks and Parmesan

Leeks are often filled with sand and must be thoroughly cleaned—see the illustrations on page 148. Use the white and light green parts only; the dark green parts are tough and inedible.

Follow the master recipe, adding 1 medium leek, white and light green parts diced (about 1 cup), along with the corn in step 3. Add ¼ cup grated Parmesan cheese along with the eggs and cornstarch in step 3.

CREAMED CORN

ALTHOUGH CREAMED CORN IS AVAILABLE any time of year out of the can, it doesn't compare with the clean, sweet flavor of late-summer corn gently simmered with fresh cream. But if you don't handle the fresh corn and cream correctly, you wind up with that overcooked, just-out-of-the-can flavor you were trying to avoid.

Many recipes start by boiling the corn on the cob, cutting the kernels off the cob, and mixing them with a cream sauce. This technique, however, loses much of the sweet, delicate corn flavor to the cooking water. We quickly rejected this method in favor of recipes that simmer the corn kernels (which are first cut free from the cobs) directly in the cream. This technique releases their sugary, summery flavor into the sauce, which is where you want it to be.

Simply simmering fresh corn kernels in cream, however, wasn't enough. It produced a thin, lumpy mixture that lacked the thickened, spoonable texture we desired. Scraping the pulp out of the spent cobs helped a bit, but we wanted the sauce a bit thicker. Flour and cornstarch just made the sauce gummy and overwhelmed the flavor of the corn. We then tried grating a few of the ears, which broke

down some of the kernels into smaller pieces. This did the trick. By grating some of the raw kernels off the cob, we were able to release more of the corn's natural thickener.

After making a few batches of this recipe with different types of corn, we realized that the cooking times can differ, depending on the corn's variety and age. While some corn cooked perfectly in only 10 minutes, others needed five minutes longer. We also found that as the corn and cream cook and thicken, the heat needs to be adjusted to keep the mixture at a simmer to prevent the bottom from burning.

As for the other ingredients, we tried using half-and-half instead of heavy cream, but tasters missed the luxurious flavor and heft provided by the latter. A little shallot, garlic, and fresh thyme complemented the delicate flavor of the corn, while a pinch of cayenne added a little kick.

Master Recipe for Creamed Corn

SERVES 6 TO 8

For the best texture and flavor, we like a combination of grated corn, whole kernels (cut away from the cobs with a knife), and corn milk (scraped from all ears with the back of a knife). See the illustrations on page 87 for tips on cutting the kernels off some ears of corn and grating (milking) the rest of the corn.

5	medium ears fresh corn, husks and silk removed
2	tablespoons unsalted butter
1	medium shallot, minced
1	medium clove garlic, minced or pressed through a garlic press
1 ½	cups heavy cream
½	teaspoon minced fresh thyme leaves
	Pinch cayenne pepper
	Salt and ground black pepper

1. Cut the kernels from 3 ears of corn and transfer them to a medium bowl. Firmly scrape the cobs with the back of a butter knife to collect the pulp and milk in the same bowl. Grate the remaining 2 ears of corn on the coarse side of a box grater set in the bowl with the cut kernels. Firmly scrape these cobs with the back of a butter knife to collect the pulp and milk in the same bowl.

2. Melt the butter in a medium saucepan over medium-high heat. When the foaming subsides, add the shallot and cook until softened but not browned, 1 to 2 minutes. Add the garlic and cook until aromatic, about 30 seconds. Stir in the corn kernels and pulp as well as the cream, thyme, cayenne, ¼ teaspoon salt, and ⅛ teaspoon pepper. Bring the mixture to a simmer and cook, adjusting the heat as necessary and stirring occasionally, until the corn is tender and the mixture has thickened, 10 to 15 minutes. Remove the pan from the heat, adjust the seasonings with salt and pepper to taste, and serve immediately.

SCIENCE: Corn Storage

While the general rule of thumb is to buy and eat corn the same day it is harvested (as soon as the corn is harvested, the sugars start converting to starches, and the corn loses sweetness), most of us have been guilty of breaking that rule for one reason or another. We tried a variety of methods for overnight storage using Silver Queen corn, one of the more perishable varieties. We found that the worst thing you can do to corn is to leave it sitting out on the counter. Throwing it into the refrigerator without any wrapping is nearly as bad. Storing in an airtight bag helps, but the hands-down winner entailed wrapping the corn (husk left on) in a wet paper bag and then in a plastic bag (any shopping bag will do). After 24 hours of storage, the corn stored this way was juicy and sweet—not starchy—and fresh tasting.

➤ VARIATION

Creamed Corn with Bacon and Blue Cheese

Use your favorite kind of blue cheese for this variation. Gorgonzola works as well. Because of the saltiness of the bacon and blue cheese, adding salt may not be necessary.

5	medium ears fresh corn, husks and silk removed
4	ounces (about 4 slices) bacon, cut into ½-inch pieces
1	medium shallot, minced
1	medium clove garlic, minced or pressed through a garlic press
1 ½	cups heavy cream
½	teaspoon minced fresh thyme leaves
	Pinch cayenne pepper
2	ounces blue cheese, crumbled (about ½ cup)
	Salt and ground black pepper

1. Cut the kernels from 3 ears of corn and transfer them to a medium bowl. Firmly scrape the cobs with the back of a butter knife to collect the pulp and milk in the same bowl. Grate the remaining 2 ears of corn on the coarse side of a box grater set in the bowl with the cut kernels. Firmly scrape these cobs with the back of a butter knife to collect the pulp and milk in the same bowl.

2. Cook the bacon in a large nonstick skillet over medium-high heat until crisp and brown, about 5 minutes. Transfer the bacon to a plate lined with paper towels to drain; set aside.

3. Remove and discard all but 2 tablespoons rendered bacon fat from the pan. Add the shallot and cook until softened but not browned, 1 to 2 minutes. Add the garlic and cook until aromatic, about 30 seconds. Stir in the corn kernels and pulp as well as

the cream, thyme, and cayenne. Bring the mixture to a simmer and cook, adjusting the heat as necessary and stirring occasionally, until the corn is tender and the mixture has thickened, 10 to 15 minutes. Remove the pan from the heat and stir in the cheese. Adjust the seasonings with salt and pepper to taste and serve immediately.

EQUIPMENT: Inexpensive Nonstick Skillets

Our favorite choice for stir-frying is a large nonstick pan. Although you could spend $100 or more on this pan, most cooks would rather buy a cheaper pan. This makes sense to us, especially when buying nonstick pans, where the increased browning afforded by heavier and more expensive pans is not an issue. To find the best pan for the job, we rounded up eight inexpensive nonstick skillets, all purchased at hardware or discount stores for no more than $50 apiece.

Every pan in our group received a good score in release ability and cleaning tests, the raisons d'être for nonstick. We tested both traits in a purposefully abusive manner by burning oatmeal in the pans over high heat for 45 minutes. That kind of treatment would trash a traditional pan, but the scorched cereal slid out of our nonstick pans with no fuss, and the pans practically wiped clean.

Most manufacturers recommend using plastic, rubber, coated, or wooden utensils to avoid scratching the nonstick coating (and all caution against using any sharp utensil such as a knife, fork, or beater). Makers of only three of our pans, the Farberware, Innova, and Bialetti, actually sanction the use of metal utensils.

In their new, off-the-shelf condition, all of our pans turned in a reasonable-to-good performance cooking the foods best suited to nonstick cooking: eggs and fish. In fact, every pan but the Revere produced evenly cooked omelets and released them with ease. The omelet made in the Farberware pan was especially impressive. The Farberware also did a particularly nice job searing salmon fillets to an even, crusty, medium brown. (Salmon is much higher in fat than skinless chicken breasts and therefore browns more easily, even in a nonstick pan.) Overall, however, our tests indicated that any of these pans could easily handle such light-duty tasks as cooking eggs. Low cost does not mean a big trade-off here.

Sauté speed is also an important measure of a pan's performance. We tested this by sautéing 1 1/2 cups of hand-chopped onions over medium heat for 10 minutes in the hope of ending up with pale gold onions that bore no trace of burning. And you know what? For the most part, we did. The Wearever, T-Fal, Innova, and Revere pans, which were all on the light side in terms of weight, turned out the darkest onions, but they were still well within an acceptable color range. Onions sautéed in the Farberware, Meyer, Calphalon, and Bialetti were a shade lighter, indicating a slightly slower sauté speed. The Farberware onions, however, took top honors based on how evenly all the pieces colored.

Of course, construction quality is a concern with any piece of cookware but especially with inexpensive models. Will the thing hold up, or will you have to replace it in six months? Based on our experience, you may well sacrifice a measure of construction quality with a budget pan. Pans with handles that were welded or riveted on to the pan body, including the Farberware, Innova, Meyer, and Calphalon, all felt solid and permanent. But the heat-resistant plastic (called phenolic) handles on the T-Fal, Revere, Bialetti, and Wearever pans were not riveted in place, and all three of them came loose during testing. That does not bode well for their future.

THE BEST INEXPENSIVE NONSTICK SKILLET

The Farberware Millennium 18/10 Stainless Steel 12-Inch Nonstick Skillet costs around $30, and it delivered superior results in our tests. It was heavier than the other inexpensive pans we tested and had the most solid construction, which contributed greatly to its success.

CUCUMBERS

ALTHOUGH YOU CAN FIND RECIPES THAT CALL FOR COOKING CUCUMBERS, we think cucumbers are at their best in salads. But that doesn't mean that all cucumber salads are good. More often than not, by the time you eat a cucumber salad, the cucumbers have gone soft and watery, losing their appealing texture and diluting the dressing to near tastelessness. This made the primary goal of our testing simple: Maximize the crunch.

The standing recommendation for ridding watery vegetables such as cucumbers, zucchini, and eggplant of unwanted moisture is to salt them. The salt creates a higher concentration of ions (tiny, charged particles) at the surface of the vegetable than exists deep within its cells. To equalize the concentration levels, the water within the cells is drawn out through permeable cell walls. In the case of cucumbers, this leaves them wilted, yet very crunchy. Of course, some culinary questions remain: How much salt should be used? Should the cucumber slices be weighted, or pressed, to squeeze out the liquid? How long should they drain?

To find out if pressing salted cucumbers really squeezes out more liquid, we trimmed and seeded six cucumbers to 8 ounces each,

SALTING CUCUMBERS

1. Peel and halve each cucumber lengthwise. Use a small spoon to remove the seeds and surrounding liquid from each cucumber half.

2. Lay the cucumber halves flat-side down on a work surface and slice them on the bias into 1/4-inch-thick pieces.

3. Toss the cucumbers and salt in a colander set in a bowl. Place a gallon-size plastic bag filled with water on top of the cucumbers to weigh them down and force out the liquid.

sliced them on the bias, and tossed each batch with 1 teaspoon of salt in its own colander set over a bowl. Three of them had zipper-lock freezer bags filled with 1 quart of water placed on top of them; no additional weight was added to the other three. Then we left them all to drain, measuring the liquid each had released after 30 minutes and after one, two, three, and 12 hours. At each time point, the weighted cucumbers had released about 1 tablespoon more liquid than the unweighted cucumbers; 3 tablespoons versus 2 after 30 minutes, 4 versus 3 after one hour, and so on. Interestingly, the weighted cukes gave off no more liquid after 12

hours than they had after three (7 tablespoons at both points). So weighting the cucumbers is worthwhile, but forget about draining the cucumbers overnight; it's not necessary.

At the one-hour mark, we could not detect an appreciable difference in flavor or texture between weighted and unweighted cukes. But we wanted to see how they would perform in salads with different types of dressings. We mixed one batch each of the weighted and unweighted cucumbers with three types of sauces—creamy, oil based, and water based—and allowed each to sit at room temperature for one hour. This is

EQUIPMENT: Vegetable Peelers

You might imagine that all vegetable peelers are pretty much the same. Not so. In our research, we turned up 25 peelers, many with quite novel features. The major differences were the fixture of the blade, either stationary or swiveling; the material of the blade, carbon stainless steel, stainless steel, or ceramic; and the orientation of the blade to the handle, either straight in line with the body or perpendicular to it. The last arrangement, with the blade perpendicular to the handle, is called a harp, or Y, peeler because the frame looks like the body of a harp or the letter Y. This type of peeler, which is popular in Europe, works with a pulling motion rather than the shucking motion of most American peelers.

To test the peelers, we recruited several cooks and asked them to peel carrots, potatoes, lemons, butternut squash, and celery root. In most cases, testers preferred the Oxo Good Grips peeler with a sharp stainless-steel blade that swivels. Peelers with stationary blades are fine for peeling carrots, but they have trouble hugging the curves on potatoes. As for blade material, we found peelers made from stainless steel, carbon steel, and ceramic that were both sharp and dull. We concluded that sharpness is a factor of quality control during the manufacturing process and not blade material.

The Y-shaped peelers tested well, although they

removed more flesh along with the skin on potatoes, lemons, and carrots and therefore did not rate as well as the Oxo Good Grips. The one case where this liability turned into an asset was with butternut squash, where these Y-shaped peelers took off the skin as well as the greenish-tinged flesh right below the skin in one pass. With the Oxo Good Grips, it was necessary to go over the peeled flesh once the skin had been removed. Among Y-shaped peelers, the Kuhn Rikon was preferred by testers. Because both the Oxo Good Grips and Kuhn Rikon peelers can be had for less than $10, we recommend that you purchase both.

THE BEST VEGETABLE PEELERS

The sharp, comfortable Oxo Good Grips Peeler (above) was the best overall peeler we tested. The Kuhn Rikon Peeler (below) takes off very wide, thick strips of peel, making it especially good on winter squash or celery root.

where the true value of better-drained cucumbers became obvious; every single taster preferred the salads made with pressed cucumbers for their superior crunch and less-diluted dressings.

As for the amount of salt, some cooks recommend simply using the quantity with which you would normally season the cucumber, while others say you should use more, up to 2 tablespoons per cucumber, and then rinse off the excess before further use. We tried a few cucumbers, prepared exactly as those described above except with 2 tablespoons of salt. The cucumbers with 2 tablespoons did give up about 1 more tablespoon of liquid within the first hour than those drained with 1 teaspoon had, but they also required rinsing and blotting dry with paper towels. And despite this extra hassle, they still tasted much too salty in the salads. We advise forgoing the extra salt.

Cucumber Salad with Greek Dressing

SERVES 4 AS A SIDE DISH

This juicy salad makes an excellent accompaniment to grilled fish or chicken.

3	medium cucumbers (about 1 1/2 pounds), peeled, halved, seeded, and sliced 1/4 inch thick (see illustrations 1 and 2 on page 92)
1	tablespoon salt
2	tablespoons red wine vinegar
2	teaspoons minced fresh oregano leaves
1	tablespoon minced fresh mint leaves
1	medium clove garlic, minced or pressed through a garlic press
6	tablespoons extra-virgin olive oil
2	ounces feta cheese, crumbled (about 1/2 cup)

1. Toss the sliced cucumbers with the salt in a strainer or colander set over a bowl. Weight the cucumbers (see illustration 3 on page 92) and drain for at least 1 hour and up to 3 hours. Transfer the cucumbers to a medium bowl and set aside.

2. Whisk the vinegar, oregano, mint, garlic, and oil together in a medium bowl. Add the cucumbers and toss to coat. Sprinkle with the cheese and serve immediately.

Cucumber Salad with Spicy Soy Dressing

SERVES 4 AS A SIDE DISH

Red chili paste can be found in the Asian food section of most large grocery stores. If it is unavailable, 1/2 teaspoon hot red pepper flakes can be used instead.

3	medium cucumbers (about 1 1/2 pounds), peeled, halved, seeded, and sliced 1/4 inch thick (see illustrations 1 and 2 on page 92)
1	tablespoon salt
1	tablespoon soy sauce
3	tablespoons rice vinegar
1	teaspoon chili paste
1	medium clove garlic, minced or pressed through a garlic press
1	tablespoon sugar
3	tablespoons toasted sesame oil
1	tablespoon sesame seeds, toasted

1. Toss the sliced cucumbers with the salt in a strainer or colander set over a bowl. Weight the cucumbers (see illustration 3 on page 92) and drain for at least 1 hour and up to 3 hours. Transfer the cucumbers to a medium bowl and set aside.

2. Whisk the soy sauce, vinegar, chili paste, garlic, sugar, oil, and sesame seeds together in a medium bowl. Add the cucumbers and toss to coat. Serve chilled or at room temperature.

INGREDIENTS: Supermarket Extra-Virgin Olive Oils

When you purchase an artisanal oil in a high-end shop, certain informational perks are expected (and paid for). These typically include written explanations of the character and nuances of the particular oil as well as the assistance of knowledgeable staff. But in a supermarket, it's just you and a price tag (usually $8 to $10 per liter). How do you know which supermarket extra-virgin oil best suits your needs? To provide some guidance, we decided to hold a blind tasting of the nine best-selling extra-virgin oils typically available in American supermarkets.

The label extra-virgin denotes the highest quality of olive oil, with the most delicate and prized flavor. (The three other grades are virgin, pure, and olive pomace. Pure oil, often labeled simply olive oil, is the most commonly available.) To be tagged as extra virgin, an oil must meet three basic criteria. First, it must contain less than 1 percent oleic free fatty acids per 100 grams of oil. Second, the oil must not have been treated with any solvents or heat. (Heat is used to reduce strong acidity in some nonvirgin olive oils to make them palatable. This is where the term cold pressed comes into play, meaning that the olives are pressed into a paste using mechanical wheels or hammers and are then kneaded to separate the oil from the fruit.) Third, it must pass taste and aroma standards as defined by groups such as the International Olive Oil Council (IOOC), a Madrid-based intergovernmental olive oil regulatory committee that sets the bar for its member countries.

Tasting extra-virgin olive oil is much like tasting wine. The flavors of these oils range from citrusy to herbal, musty to floral, with every possibility in between. And what one taster finds particularly attractive—a slight briny flavor, for example—another might find unappealing. Also like wine, the flavor of a particular brand of olive oil can change from year to year, depending on the quality of the harvest and the olives' place of origin.

We chose to taste extra-virgin olive oil in its most pure and unadulterated state: raw. Tasters were given the option of sampling the oil from a spoon or on neutral-flavored French bread and were asked to eat a slice of green apple—for its acidity—to cleanse the palate between oils. The olive oils were evaluated for color, clarity, viscosity, bouquet, depth of flavor, and lingering of flavor.

Whereas, in a typical tasting, we are able to identify a clear winner and loser, in this case we could not. In fact, the panel seemed to quickly divide itself into those who liked a gutsy olive oil with bold flavor and those who preferred a milder, more mellow approach. Nonetheless, in both camps, one oil clearly had more of a following than any other—the all-Italian-olive Davinci brand. Praised for its rounded and buttery flavor, it was the only olive oil we tasted that seemed to garner across-the-board approval with olive oil experts and in-house staff alike. Among tasters who preferred full-bodied, bold oils, Colavita and Filippo Berio also earned high marks. Tasters in the mild and delicate camp gave high scores to Pompeian and Whole Foods oils.

THE BEST ALL-PURPOSE OIL
Davinci Extra-Virgin Olive Oil was the favorite in our tasting of leading supermarket brands. It was described as "very ripe," "buttery," and "complex."

THE BEST MILD OIL
Pompeian Extra-Virgin Olive Oil was the favorite among tasters who preferred a milder, more delicate oil. It was described as "clean," "round," and "sunny."

THE BEST FULL-BODIED OIL
Colavita Extra-Virgin Olive Oil was the favorite among tasters who preferred a bolder, more full-bodied oil. It was described as "heavy," "complex," and "briny."

EDAMAME

EDAMAME (EH-DAH-MAH-MEH) ARE SOYBEANS THAT ARE COOKED AND SERVED while still in the pod. They have a sweet, slightly nutty flavor similar to fava beans. In Japanese cuisine, they are served as a snack, often accompanied by cold beer.

Although you may find fresh edamame at farmers' markets, you are most likely to find them frozen at your local supermarket. Occasionally, you will find frozen shelled edamame. We tested this option but found the flavor lackluster and the texture mushy. Stick with frozen edamame still in their green pods.

The main preparation issue here was the cooking method. Various sources suggest either steaming or boiling. Steaming worked well but produced bland beans. The better option was to boil the edamame briefly (three to four minutes is ideal, but carefully test one or two pods before draining) in salted water. For an extra hit of saltiness, sprinkle the drained edamame with coarse salt (kosher is ideal) and serve.

To eat the edamame, use your fingers to pop the soybeans from the pod directly into your mouth (the pods themselves are extremely fibrous and inedible). Make sure to have an empty bowl available for the discarded pods.

Edamame

SERVES 4 AS A SIDE DISH

Frozen edamame are available in most large grocery stores. Use kosher salt for this recipe; the large grains are ideal for sprinkling over the cooked edamame.

1   pound frozen edamame
2   tablespoons kosher salt, plus more to taste

1. Fill a large bowl with cold water and set aside.

2. Bring 2 quarts of water to a boil in a medium saucepan over high heat. Add the edamame and the salt. Bring the water back up to a boil and simmer until the edamame are tender, 3 to 4 minutes. (To test for doneness, use a slotted spoon to fish out one or two pods, carefully pop them open, and taste a bean or two.) Drain the edamame in a colander and transfer them to the bowl of cold water to halt the cooking process. Keep the edamame in the water for just a few seconds if you want to serve them warm, longer if you want to serve the edamame at room temperature. Drain again and spread the edamame onto a sheet tray lined with paper towels to dry. If desired, sprinkle with additional kosher salt to taste. Serve warm, at room temperature, or chilled.

EGGPLANT

EGGPLANT CAN BE PREPARED IN SEVERAL WAYS, INCLUDING SAUTÉING, broiling, grilling, and stir-frying. The biggest challenge that confronts the cook when preparing eggplant is excess moisture. While the grill will evaporate this liquid and allow the eggplant to brown nicely, this won't happen under the broiler or in a hot pan. The eggplant will steam in its own juices. The result can be an insipid flavor and mushy texture.

Salting is the classic technique for drawing moisture out of the eggplant before cooking. We experimented with both regular table salt and kosher salt and preferred kosher salt because the crystals are large enough to wipe away after the salt has done its job. Finer table salt crystals dissolved into the eggplant flesh and had to be flushed out with water. Although traditional recipes call for letting the salted eggplant drain in a colander, we had better results when we placed the salted eggplant on a baking sheet lined with paper towels. In a colander, the eggplant juices tended to fall from one piece to another. On the paper-lined baking sheet, the juices were wicked away as soon as they were drawn out of the eggplant.

The eggplant must then be thoroughly dried, especially if it has been diced for sautéing. We prefer to dice eggplant that will be sautéed to increase the surface area that can brown and absorb flavorings.

Eggplant destined for the broiler should be sliced very thin (about ¼ inch thick) so that the salt can work quickly. The salt will take more time to penetrate thicker slices and will, in the end, be less effective. However, when grilling, you want thicker slices that won't fall apart on the cooking grate. We found ¾-inch rounds perfect for grilling. And because the liquid can fall onto the coals, there's no need to salt eggplant destined for the grill.

Stir-frying is basically the same as sautéing except that the finished dish is saucier. In this case, liquid from the eggplant is not such a problem. The eggplant is browned and then sauced quite generously, so its texture will correctly be soft rather than crisp or firm. In addition, stir-fry sauces often contain soy sauce and are quite salty. For all these reasons, we found it best to skip salting eggplant when using it in a stir-fry. However, stir-frying will work best with small, firm eggplant (sometimes labeled Asian eggplant in markets). Rather than dicing the eggplant (as we do for sautéing), we had the best results when we cut small eggplant in half lengthwise and then crosswise into ½-inch-thick half-moons.

Master Recipe for Sautéed Eggplant

SERVES 4

Very small eggplants (weighing less than 6 ounces each) may be cooked without salting. However, we found that larger eggplants generally have a lot of moisture, which is best removed before cooking.

1	large eggplant (about 1 1/2 pounds), ends trimmed, cut into 3/4-inch cubes
1	tablespoon kosher salt
2	tablespoons extra-virgin olive oil Ground black pepper
1	medium clove garlic, minced or pressed through a garlic press
2	tablespoons minced fresh parsley or finely shredded fresh basil leaves

1. Place the eggplant cubes on a rimmed baking sheet lined with paper towels and sprinkle the cubes with the salt, tossing to coat them evenly. Let the eggplant stand for at least 30 minutes. Using additional paper towels, pat excess moisture from the eggplant.

2. Heat the oil in a 12-inch heavy-bottomed skillet over medium-high heat until almost smoking. Add the eggplant cubes and cook until they begin to brown, about 4 minutes. Reduce the heat to medium-low and cook, stirring occasionally, until the eggplant is fully tender and lightly browned, about 10 minutes. Stir in pepper to taste and add the garlic. Cook to blend the flavors, about 2 minutes. Off the heat, stir in the parsley. Serve immediately.

↪ VARIATIONS

Sautéed Eggplant with Cumin and Garlic

Sautéing the spices in the oil makes their flavors bloom.

1	large eggplant (about 1 1/2 pounds), ends trimmed, cut into 3/4-inch cubes
1	tablespoon kosher salt
2	tablespoons vegetable oil
1	teaspoon ground cumin
1/2	teaspoon chili powder
2	medium cloves garlic, minced or pressed through a garlic press
1	teaspoon sugar
1	tablespoon minced fresh parsley leaves

1. Place the eggplant cubes on a rimmed baking sheet lined with paper towels and sprinkle the cubes with the salt, tossing to coat them evenly. Let the eggplant stand for at least 30 minutes. Using additional paper towels, pat excess moisture from the eggplant.

THE EFFECTS OF SALTING EGGPLANT

BEFORE SALTING

AFTER SALTING

Salting and pressing eggplant collapses the cell walls, eliminating air pockets that would otherwise soak up fat during cooking.

2. Heat the oil in a 12-inch heavy-bottomed skillet over medium-high heat until almost smoking. Add the cumin and chili powder and cook until fragrant, about 20 seconds. Add the eggplant cubes and cook until they begin to brown, about 4 minutes. Reduce the heat to medium-low and cook, stirring occasionally, until the eggplant is fully tender and lightly browned, about 10 minutes. Stir in the garlic and sugar. Cook to blend the flavors, about 2 minutes. Off the heat, stir in the parsley. Serve immediately.

Sautéed Eggplant with Pancetta and Rosemary

Pancetta is unsmoked Italian bacon (see page 123). It can be found in the deli section of most large grocery stores. If pancetta is unavailable, bacon can be substituted.

1   large eggplant (about 1 1/2 pounds), ends trimmed, cut into 3/4-inch cubes
1   tablespoon kosher salt
3   ounces pancetta, diced fine
1   small onion, halved and sliced thin
1/2 teaspoon minced fresh rosemary
    Ground black pepper

1. Place the eggplant cubes on a rimmed baking sheet lined with paper towels and sprinkle the cubes with the salt, tossing to coat them evenly. Let the eggplant stand for at least 30 minutes. Using additional paper towels, pat excess moisture from the eggplant.

2. Cook the pancetta in a 12-inch heavy-bottomed skillet over medium-high heat until crisp, about 5 minutes. Use a slotted spoon to transfer the pancetta to a plate. Add the onion and rosemary to the rendered fat in the pan and cook, stirring frequently, until golden, about 4 minutes. Add the eggplant cubes and cook until they begin to brown, about 4 minutes. Reduce the heat to medium-low and cook, stirring occasionally, until the eggplant is fully tender and lightly browned, about 10 minutes. Stir in the pancetta and pepper to taste. Serve immediately.

INGREDIENTS: Miso

Most miso pastes are made from a combination of fermented soybeans and white rice. Some miso may contain just soybeans, while others may replace the white rice with brown rice or barley. White miso (*shiromiso*) is the type commonly used to make miso soup. This and other types of miso and their flavor characteristics are described below. Any type of miso can be used in the sesame-miso glaze on page 100, although each will yield slightly different results.

WHITE MISO (*Shiromiso*): White miso is the type Westerners are most likely to be familiar with. It is brownish yellow in color—not pure white, as its name may lead you to believe—and its flavor is mellow, with a light sweetness, a light saltiness, and a delicacy that can range from fruity to nutty, depending on the brand. White miso is the favorite in the test kitchen.

BROWN or **RED MISO** (*Akamiso*): Brown or red miso has a darker color and a saltier, more assertive flavor that lacks the delicate sweet quality of white miso. It has a meaty, roasted quality.

BROWN RICE MISO (*Genmaimiso*): Like brown or red miso, brown rice miso is darker in color than white miso, and it lacks the subtleties of white miso. Brown rice miso has a strong saltiness, a soy sauce–like flavor, a hefty smokiness, and a few faint but detectable sour notes.

BARLEY MISO (*Mugimiso*): Barley miso resembles white miso in appearance, but its flavor is distinctly malty. Our tasters also identified sweet, nutty, and tea-like flavor characteristics.

Master Recipe for Broiled Eggplant

SERVES 4

Make sure to slice the eggplant thin so that the slices will cook through by the time the exterior is browned.

1   large eggplant (about 1 1/2 pounds), ends trimmed, sliced crosswise into 1/4-inch-thick rounds
1   tablespoon kosher salt
3   tablespoons extra-virgin olive oil
2   tablespoons minced fresh parsley or finely shredded basil leaves
     Ground black pepper

1. Place the eggplant slices on a rimmed baking sheet lined with paper towels and sprinkle both sides of the eggplant with the salt. Let the eggplant stand for at least 30 minutes. Using additional paper towels, pat any excess moisture from the eggplant.

2. Adjust an oven rack to the highest position (about 4 inches from the heating element) and heat the broiler. Arrange the eggplant slices on a foil-lined baking sheet. Brush both sides with the oil. Broil the eggplant slices until the tops are mahogany brown, 3 to 4 minutes. Turn the slices over and broil until the other side browns, another 3 to 4 minutes.

3. Remove the eggplant from the broiler and sprinkle with the parsley. Season with pepper to taste and serve immediately.

➤ VARIATIONS

Broiled Eggplant with Sesame-Miso Glaze

Mirin is a sweet Japanese cooking wine. It is available in the Asian food section of most large grocery stores. If it is unavailable, sherry may be substituted. See page 99 for information about buying miso.

1   large eggplant (about 1 1/2 pounds), ends trimmed, sliced crosswise into 1/4-inch-thick rounds
1   tablespoon kosher salt
1   tablespoon miso
3   tablespoons mirin
1   tablespoon tahini
3   tablespoons vegetable or canola oil
1   tablespoon sesame seeds
1   medium scallion, sliced thin

1. Place the eggplant slices on a rimmed baking sheet lined with paper towels and sprinkle both sides of the eggplant with the salt. Let the eggplant stand for at least 30 minutes. Using additional paper towels, pat any excess moisture from the eggplant.

2. Whisk the miso, mirin, and tahini together in a small bowl.

3. Adjust an oven rack to the highest position (about 4 inches from the heating element) and heat the broiler. Arrange the eggplant slices on a foil-lined baking sheet. Brush both sides with the oil. Broil the eggplant slices until the tops are mahogany brown, 3 to 4 minutes. Turn the slices over and broil until the other side browns, another 3 to 4 minutes.

4. Brush the miso glaze on each of the eggplant slices and then sprinkle them with sesame seeds. Return the eggplant to the broiler and broil until the miso and seeds are browned, about 2 minutes. Transfer the eggplant to a platter, sprinkle with the scallion, and serve immediately.

Broiled Eggplant with Herbed Goat Cheese

The fresh basil and mint complement the salty goat cheese nicely. Do not substitute dried herbs in this recipe. The eggplant is cut a bit thicker in this variation so that the slices can support the goat cheese topping.

1   large eggplant (about 1 1/2 pounds),
    ends trimmed, sliced crosswise into
    1/2-inch-thick rounds (you should
    have about 10 slices)
1   tablespoon kosher salt
6   ounces goat cheese
2   tablespoons finely shredded
    fresh basil leaves
2   tablespoons minced fresh mint leaves
1   small clove garlic, minced or pressed
    through a garlic press
    Ground black pepper
3   tablespoons extra-virgin olive oil,
    plus more for drizzling

1. Place the eggplant slices on a rimmed baking sheet lined with paper towels and sprinkle both sides of the eggplant with the salt. Let the eggplant stand for at least 30 minutes. Using additional paper towels, pat any excess moisture from the eggplant.

2. With a fork or rubber spatula, mix the goat cheese, basil, mint, garlic, and pepper to taste together in a medium bowl.

3. Adjust an oven rack to the highest position (about 4 inches from the heating element) and heat the broiler. Arrange the eggplant slices on a foil-lined baking sheet. Brush both sides with the oil. Broil the eggplant slices until the tops are mahogany brown, 4 to 6 minutes. Turn the slices over and broil until the other side browns, another 4 to 6 minutes.

4. Remove the eggplant from the broiler and spread each slice with some of the goat cheese mixture. Return the eggplant slices to the broiler and broil until the goat cheese melts and browns slightly. Remove the eggplant from the broiler, drizzle with olive oil to taste, and serve immediately.

Master Recipe for Grilled Eggplant
SERVES 4

There's no need to salt eggplant destined for the grill. The intense grill heat will vaporize excess moisture.

3   tablespoons extra-virgin olive oil
2   medium cloves garlic, minced or
    pressed through a garlic press
2   teaspoons minced fresh thyme or
    oregano leaves
    Salt and ground black pepper
1   large eggplant (about 1 1/2 pounds),
    ends trimmed, cut crosswise into
    3/4-inch-thick rounds

1. Combine the oil, garlic, herb, and salt and pepper to taste in a small bowl. Place the eggplant on a platter and brush both sides with the oil mixture.

2. Grill the eggplant over a medium–hot fire (you should be able to hold your hand 5 inches above the cooking grate for 3 to 4 seconds), turning once, until both sides are

marked with dark stripes, 8 to 10 minutes. Serve hot, warm, or at room temperature.

Grilled Eggplant with Basil Oil

Make sure to cook the garlic until it is barely starting to sizzle. The oil will then be just hot enough to slightly wilt the basil when processed together.

1/4	cup extra-virgin olive oil
1	medium clove garlic, minced or pressed through a garlic press
1/2	cup packed fresh basil leaves
	Salt and ground black pepper
1	recipe Grilled Eggplant

1. Place the oil and garlic in a skillet and turn the heat to medium. Cook until the garlic just starts to sizzle and becomes fragrant, about 2 minutes.

2. Place the basil in the workbowl of a food processor. Very carefully pour the hot oil over the basil. Process until the mixture is fragrant and almost smooth, about 30 seconds. Season with salt and pepper to taste.

3. Transfer the grilled eggplant to a platter and drizzle with the basil oil. Serve immediately.

Grilled Eggplant with Cherry Tomato and Cilantro Vinaigrette

Grape tomatoes can also be used in this recipe. Choose the ripest tomatoes for the best, most flavorful vinaigrette.

1/2	pint cherry tomatoes, each tomato quartered (about 1 cup)
1/4	teaspoon salt
	Pinch cayenne pepper
1	medium shallot, minced
2	tablespoons minced fresh cilantro leaves
2	tablespoons juice from 1 lime
6	tablespoons extra-virgin olive oil
1	recipe Grilled Eggplant

1. Mix the tomatoes, salt, cayenne, shallot, cilantro, lime juice, and oil together in a medium bowl. Let stand at room temperature until juicy and seasoned, about 20 minutes.

2. Transfer the grilled eggplant to a platter. Pour the vinaigrette over the grilled eggplant and serve immediately.

Master Recipe for Stir-Fried Eggplant
SERVES 4

Choose small eggplants (preferably those weighing about 8 ounces each) for this recipe.

1/4	cup low-sodium chicken broth
2	tablespoons soy sauce
1 1/2	teaspoons toasted sesame oil
1	tablespoon plus 1 teaspoon peanut oil
2	small eggplants (about 8 ounces each), ends trimmed, sliced in half lengthwise, and cut crosswise into 1/2-inch-thick half-moons
1	medium clove garlic, minced or pressed through a garlic press
1	teaspoon minced or grated fresh ginger
2	medium scallions, sliced thin

1. Whisk the broth, soy sauce, and sesame oil together in a small bowl and set the mixture aside.

2. Heat 1 tablespoon of the peanut oil in a 12-inch heavy-bottomed nonstick skillet over high heat until almost smoking. Add the eggplant and cook, stirring frequently, until browned, about 3 minutes. Clear a space in the center of the pan and add the garlic, ginger, and the remaining 1 teaspoon oil. Cook until fragrant, about 10 seconds.

Stir the garlic mixture into the eggplant and add the broth mixture. Cover, reduce the heat to medium, and cook until the sauce thickens and the eggplant has softened, about 3 minutes. Garnish with the scallions and serve immediately.

➤ VARIATION

Stir-Fried Eggplant with Ground Pork and Peanut Sauce

Although this dish is intended as a side dish for four, with rice it could feed two or three as a main course.

2/3	cup low-sodium chicken broth
1	tablespoon hoisin sauce
1	tablespoon soy sauce
2	tablespoons smooth peanut butter
1	tablespoon plus 2 teaspoons peanut oil
6	ounces ground pork
2	small eggplants (about 8 ounces each), ends trimmed, sliced in half lengthwise, and cut crosswise into 1/2-inch-thick half-moons
1	medium clove garlic, minced or pressed through a garlic press
1	teaspoon minced or grated fresh ginger
1/4	teaspoon hot red pepper flakes
2	medium scallions, sliced thin

1. Whisk the broth, hoisin sauce, soy sauce, and peanut butter together in a medium bowl. (The peanut butter will not totally dissolve until it is added to the skillet.) Set aside.

2. Heat 1 teaspoon of the oil in a 12-inch heavy-bottomed nonstick skillet over high heat until almost smoking. Add the pork and cook, stirring to break up the meat, until thoroughly cooked, about 3 minutes. Transfer the pork to a plate and set it aside.

3. Add 1 tablespoon of the oil to the empty pan, swirl to coat the pan, and add the eggplant. Cook, stirring frequently, until browned, about 3 minutes. Clear a space in the center of the pan and add the garlic, ginger, pepper flakes, and the remaining 1 teaspoon oil. Cook until fragrant, about 10 seconds. Stir in the cooked pork and the broth mixture. Cover, reduce the heat to medium, and cook until the sauce thickens and the eggplant has softened, about 4 minutes. Garnish with the scallions and serve immediately.

BABA GHANOUSH

THE DRIVING FORCE BEHIND BABA ghanoush is grill-roasted eggplant, sultry and rich. Its beguiling creaminess and haunting flavor come from sesame tahini paste, cut to the quick with a bit of garlic, brightened with lemon juice, and flounced up with parsley. In Middle Eastern countries, baba ghanoush is served as part of a *mezze* platter—not unlike an antipasto in Italy—which might feature salads, various dips, small pastries, meats, olives, other condiments, and, of course, bread.

There is no doubt that the eggplant is a majestic fruit—shiny, sexy, and brilliantly hued. But its contents can be difficult to deal with. Baba ghanoush often turns up as a plate of gray matter intersected by pita triangles. Its taste can be bitter and watery, green and raw, metallic with garlic, or occluded by tahini paste.

The traditional method for cooking eggplant for baba ghanoush is to scorch it over a hot, smoky grill. There the purple fruit grows bruised and then black, until its insides fairly slosh within their charred carapace. The hot, soft interior is scooped out with a spoon and the outer ruins discarded. Having eaten our share of baba ghanoush that had not experienced the thrill of the grill, we were amazed at what an improvement live coals made. The smokiness of the fire induced other ingredients to relate to one another in a more interesting way.

Another thing we realized is that baba made with eggplant not cooked to the sloshy

soft stage simply isn't as good. Undercooked eggplant, while misleadingly soft to the touch (eggplant has, after all, a yielding quality), will taste spongy-green and remain unmoved by additional seasonings.

Another question was whether a decent

EQUIPMENT: Herb Choppers

Is there an easier way to achieve finely minced piles of parsley, basil, and mint than rocking a chef's knife back and forth a hundred times? We tested several kinds of herb choppers and mincers to find out.

The first gadgets tested were herb mills: a stainless-steel mill by KüchenProfi and a plastic mill by Zyliss. Each has a hopper in which you put the herbs and a series of small blades that chop them when you turn a hand crank. For all of the herb choppers tested, we used basil, parsley, rosemary, and garlic. The seemingly solid KüchenProfi gagged on each one, and they had to be pinched and pried out of the hopper. The Zyliss didn't choke, but it could not mince either. Shreds of leafy herb and shards of garlic would be more like it.

Next in line were herb rollers, which depend on a row of wheel-like blades that are pushed back and forth over the item to be minced by means of a handle (as in the Oxo we tested) or some sort of protective casing (as in the International Cutlery). Rollers are comfortable, easy to use, and fast—so fast that they crushed and bruised the parsley and basil leaves into a slimy green mush in about 30 seconds. The rosemary and garlic didn't fare much better, being reduced to odd-shaped bits and pieces, and the garlic tended to stick to the blades.

The most newfangled entry in our lineup was the Rev'n Chef by Chef'n, a round plastic case with a rip cord inside that, when pulled and released, turned a blade that tore up everything we gave it into large, rough, unevenly sized pieces. And more pulls of the rip cord didn't help much. A beat-up clove of garlic looked much the same after 75 pulls as it did after 25.

The only worthwhile alternative to a chef's knife was the mezzaluna, a cutting tool named for its half-moon shape that has been in use for hundreds of years. We

tried three styles: one with a single handle and a single blade meant to be used in a wooden bowl, one with a single blade and two handles, and one with two blades and two handles. The first of these minced well but was a bit awkward to use as well as labor intensive. The latter pair, each with a handle on either end, let you get a rocking motion going that cut through herbs—especially tough, woody rosemary—cleanly and quickly. The double-bladed mezzaluna was faster (usually 30 to 60 seconds faster than the single blade when producing $\frac{1}{4}$ cup of minced herbs), but it was tough on the basil, bruising it badly. None of the mezzalunas could mince garlic as perfectly as a garlic press.

What do we recommend? If your knife skills aren't quite what you'd like them to be, try a single-bladed, two-handled mezzaluna. It's not only effective but fun. And purchase one with a 7-inch blade rather than a 6-inch blade. The 7-inch really rocks.

THE BEST HERB CHOPPER

When it comes to mincing and chopping herbs, a single-bladed, two-handled mezzaluna is the only real alternative to a chef's knife. Although the mezzaluna is not superior to a chef's knife, it is its equal, and the mezzaluna works far better than the other herb choppers on the market. If you are going to buy a mezzaluna, we recommend a model with a 7-inch blade.

baba ghanoush could be made without a grill. Taking instruction from the hot fire we had used, we roasted a few large eggplants in a 500-degree oven. It took about 45 minutes to collapse the fruit and transform the insides to pulp. Though the babas made with grill-roasted eggplant were substantially superior to those made with oven-roasted fruit, the latter were perfectly acceptable.

Eggplant suffers from persistent rumors that it is bitter. Most baba ghanoush recipes call for discarding the seedbed. But the insides of the eggplants we were roasting were veritably paved with seeds. We thought it impractical and wasteful to lose half the fruit to mere rumor, so we performed side-by-side tests comparing versions of the dip with and without seeds. We found no tangible grounds for seed dismissal. The dip was not bitter. The seeds stayed.

Other sources suggest one variety of eggplant over another, so we made baba ghanoush with standard large globe eggplants, with compact Italian eggplants, and with long, lithe Japanese eggplants. All were surprisingly good. The globe eggplants made a baba that was slightly more moist. The Italian eggplants were drier and contained fewer seeds. The Japanese eggplants were also quite dry. Their very slenderness allowed the smoke to permeate the flesh completely, and the resulting dip was meaty and delicious. (Given a choice, we would definitely select Italian or Japanese eggplant.)

Once the eggplants are roasted and scooped, you are about five minutes away from removing your apron. The eggplant can be mashed with a fork, but we prefer the food processor, which makes it a cinch to add the other ingredients and to pulse the eggplant, leaving the texture slightly coarse.

As for the proportions of said ingredients, tests indicated that less was always more.

Minced garlic gathers strength on-site and can become aggressive when added in abundance. Many recipes we saw also called for tahini in amounts that overwhelmed the eggplant. Likewise with lemon juice: Liberal amounts dash the smoky richness of the eggplant with astringent tartness.

If you're serving a crowd, the recipe can easily be doubled or tripled. Time does nothing to improve the flavor of baba ghanoush. An hour-long stay in the refrigerator for a light chilling is all that's needed.

Master Recipe for Baba Ghanoush

MAKES ABOUT 2 CUPS

When buying eggplants, select those with shiny, taut, and unbruised skins and an even shape (eggplants with a bulbous shape won't cook evenly). We prefer to serve baba ghanoush only lightly chilled. If yours is cold, let it stand at room temperature for about 20 minutes before serving. Baba ghanoush does not keep well, so plan to make it the day you want to serve it. Pita bread, black olives, tomato wedges, and cucumber slices are nice accompaniments.

2   pounds eggplant (about 2 large globe eggplants, 5 medium Italian eggplants, or 8 small Japanese eggplants), each eggplant poked uniformly over the entire surface with a fork to prevent it from bursting

1   tablespoon juice from 1 lemon

1   small clove garlic, minced or pressed through a garlic press

2   tablespoons tahini paste

1   tablespoon extra-virgin olive oil, plus extra for serving
    Salt and ground black pepper

2   teaspoons chopped fresh parsley leaves

1. Grill the eggplants over a hot fire (you should be able to hold your hand 5 inches above the grill grate for only 2 seconds) until the skins darken and wrinkle on all sides and the eggplants are uniformly soft when pressed with tongs, about 25 minutes for large globe eggplants, 20 minutes for Italian eggplants, and 15 minutes for Japanese eggplants, turning the eggplants every 5 minutes. Transfer the eggplants to a rimmed baking sheet and cool 5 minutes.

2. Set a small colander over a bowl or in the sink. Trim the top and bottom off each eggplant. Slit the eggplants lengthwise. Use a spoon to scoop the hot pulp from the skins and place the pulp in the colander (you should have about 2 cups packed pulp); discard the skins. Let the pulp drain 3 minutes.

3. Transfer the pulp to the workbowl of a food processor. Add the lemon juice, garlic, tahini, oil, ¼ teaspoon salt, and ¼ teaspoon pepper and process until the mixture has a coarse, choppy texture, about eight 1-second pulses. Adjust the seasoning with salt and pepper to taste. Transfer to a serving bowl, cover with plastic wrap flush with the surface of the dip, and refrigerate until lightly chilled, 45 to 60 minutes. To serve, use a spoon to make a trough in the center of the dip and spoon the olive oil into it. Sprinkle with the parsley and serve.

➤ VARIATIONS

Baba Ghanoush, Oven Method

Adjust an oven rack to the middle position and heat the oven to 500 degrees. Line a rimmed baking sheet with foil, set the eggplants on the baking sheet, and roast, turning every 15 minutes, until the eggplants are uniformly soft when pressed with tongs, about 60 minutes for large globe eggplants, 50 minutes for Italian eggplants, and 40 minutes for Japanese eggplants. Cool the eggplants on the baking sheet 5 minutes and then proceed with the master recipe from step 2.

Baba Ghanoush with Sautéed Onion

Sautéed onion gives the baba ghanoush a sweet, rich flavor.

Heat 1 tablespoon extra-virgin olive oil in a small skillet over low heat until almost smoking. Add 1 small onion, chopped fine, and cook, stirring occasionally, until the edges are golden brown, about 10 minutes. Follow the master recipe, stirring the onion into the dip after processing.

Israeli-Style Baba Ghanoush

Replacing the sesame paste with mayonnaise makes this baba ghanoush pleasantly light and brings out the smoky flavor of charcoal-grilled eggplant.

Follow the master recipe, substituting an equal amount of mayonnaise for the tahini.

RATATOUILLE

THINK, FOR A MOMENT, OF RATATOUILLE as French soul food. A well-made ratatouille embodies the essence of flavors from the South of France, including firm eggplant, zucchini, caramelized onions, heady garlic, and garden-fresh herbs. Bringing the mixture together are the ripest of tomatoes, cooked just enough to lend their sweet juices to the mix.

Now think of the last time you had ratatouille for brunch at a second-rate local eatery. The ingredients were indistinguishable in taste, color, and texture. That's because each of the vegetables has its own set of cooking problems. If each is not handled properly, the resulting dish is a mess. Eggplant soaks up oil and leaches liquid into the pan. Zucchini's problem is lack of flavor. Cooked too little, it is pretty to look at but tastes like nothing; cooked enough to become flavorful, it turns into army green mush. Ripe and juicy tomatoes break down to a runny sauce in minutes, especially when mixed with other vegetables.

The name ratatouille is derived from the French *touiller,* meaning "to stir." When it comes to interpretation of the method, there are two schools of thought. Included in the testing were the classic French preparation, in which vegetables are sautéed in olive oil in batches and combined at the last minute with minimal stirring, and a typical American ratatouille, in which everything is tossed into the pot at once and stewed until tender. In American-style ratatouille, it was difficult to distinguish eggplant from zucchini, and the whole amalgamation tasted like watery tomatoes. The batch-cooked ratatouille fared much better, although it was oily from the more than 1 cup of olive oil needed to keep the vegetables from sticking to the pan. On the plus side, the vegetables remained relatively intact, and the stew carried the flavors particular to each component. So we set out to deal with each

ANY EGGPLANT WILL DO

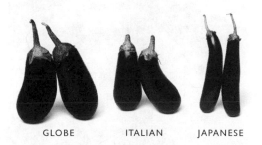

GLOBE   ITALIAN   JAPANESE

Some ratatouille recipes call for Japanese or Italian eggplant, each of which is thought to be superior to globe eggplant in flavor and texture. In a head-to-head comparison of the three in our recipe, we found that neither the Japanese nor the Italian eggplant had anything on the common globe eggplant.

vegetable individually, hoping to maximize texture and flavor while minimizing the amount of oil.

We quickly discovered that sautéing eggplant has its problems. Eggplant is mostly water, which turns to steam and bursts through the cell walls, causing them to collapse in the process. The result is a soggy, soupy mess. Eggplant is also extremely absorbent, thanks to millions of air pockets built into its cell walls, and will soak up as much oil as you give it. To avoid these problems, cooks typically salt eggplant and allow it to drain before cooking. Using this method, however, the eggplant in our test kitchen still soaked up 1 cup of oil when sautéed. The next time around, we pressed the eggplant chunks firmly with paper towels after salting to extract most of the moisture and to rid the pieces of their oil-absorbing air pockets. This time, the eggplant was dense and firm, and it soaked up ¾ cup of oil, still a large amount. We had to find a method for cooking the eggplant and zucchini that highlighted their natural flavors, provided good texture, and did not require an obscene amount of olive oil.

Because high heat draws out liquid and intensifies flavor, our next stop was the broiler. Still using the salting/pressing preparation for the eggplant, we tossed the chunks with a little oil and slipped them under the broiler. The results were less than satisfying. The extreme heat from the broiler caused the eggplant to burn before the pieces were sufficiently dehydrated. Then we turned to a high-heat oven set at 500 degrees, thinking that it would present no direct threat from the broiler element. Eureka! The eggplant was firm and toothsome, with no sign of sponginess, and the flavor was rich and intense. Next, we tried the zucchini (which was simply cut into chunks and lightly oiled) and found that it also benefited from the oven-roasting method. It was tender and flavorful. Left undisturbed in the oven, the zucchini retained its shape, and the chunky pieces gave the stew a fresh appearance.

No small advantage of using the oven to roast the eggplant and zucchini was the now-minuscule amount of oil that was required. Batch-cooking the stew entirely on the stovetop had necessitated at least ¾ cup of oil, mostly for the eggplant. Now, a total of only 2 tablespoons was needed to coat both the zucchini and the eggplant, and they could be spread and roasted on sheet pans at the same time.

Any hopes of making this an entirely in-oven operation came to a screeching halt when we tested roasting the onions, garlic, and tomatoes. If the onions were to roast evenly, they would have to be sliced rather than chopped, and tasters found the long strands texturally unappealing. Chopping and then sautéing them until caramel colored and soft gave them a delicate flavor that blended well with the sweet tomatoes. Garlic also performed better in the sauté pan. But rather than subject it to the same slow caramelization as the onions, we found that a quick blast of heat best allowed the flavor to bloom. There was no mistaking its presence in the ratatouille. Finally, the roasted plump tomatoes turned to mush well before any increase in flavor occurred. We found that it was much better to add the tomatoes near the end of cooking, giving them just enough time to start breaking down and supply a bit of moisture to hold the stew together.

Although the test kitchen usually prefers canned tomatoes to most produce aisle specimens, this is one recipe in which the real thing is mandatory, for authenticity as well as for texture and flavor. In fact, buying the right tomato and preparing it correctly can make or break a ratatouille. First, we tried the compact Roma tomato, but its lack of liquid gave the stew the appearance of thick chutney. Round tomatoes, especially the rugged beefsteak variety, worked exceptionally well. Their robust flavor, substantial size, and abundance of fleshy meat added just the right amount of texture and freshness to the mélange.

We found it necessary to first peel the tomatoes, a process that goes quickly by dropping them into boiling water for a few seconds, followed by shocking them in ice water. But no matter what kind of tomato we used, we found that it was better to leave the seedbed in place. The seeds carry quite a bit of liquid, so removing them resulted in a dry ratatouille.

At last, we tested the herbs. Fresh herbs are an important part of Provençal cookery, and this dish is no exception. Basil is by far the herb called for most often in ratatouille, due in no small part to its growing schedule,

which is simultaneous with that of the other ingredients. In the end, we chose to combine chopped fresh basil with bright green parsley and woody-flavored thyme. We also found that the full-flavored vegetables demanded a bounty of herbs—a whopping 5 tablespoons in total. Adding the herbs just before serving ensures that they will remain bright in color and flavor and complement the intensely flavored vegetables perfectly.

Ratatouille
SERVES 4 TO 6

For the best-flavored ratatouille, we recommend very ripe beefsteak tomatoes. See page 295 for tips on peeling the tomatoes.

2	large eggplants (2 to 2 $\frac{1}{2}$ pounds), ends trimmed and cut into 1-inch cubes
	Salt
2	large zucchini (about 1 $\frac{1}{2}$ pounds), scrubbed and cut into 1-inch cubes
4	tablespoons extra-virgin olive oil
1	large onion, chopped large
2	medium cloves garlic, minced or pressed through a garlic press
3	medium ripe tomatoes (about 1 pound), cored, peeled, and cut into 2-inch cubes
2	tablespoons chopped fresh parsley leaves
2	tablespoons chopped fresh basil leaves
1	tablespoon minced fresh thyme leaves
	Ground black pepper

1. Place the eggplant in a large colander set over a large bowl. Sprinkle the eggplant with 2 teaspoons salt and toss to distribute the salt evenly. Let the eggplant stand at least 1 hour or up to 3 hours. Rinse the eggplant well under running water to remove the salt and spread it in an even layer on a triple thickness of paper towels. Cover with another triple thickness of paper towels. Press firmly on the eggplant with your hands until the eggplant is dry and feels firm and compressed (see the photograph on page 98).

2. Adjust one oven rack to the upper-middle position and the second rack to the lower-middle position and heat the oven to 500 degrees. Line two rimmed baking sheets with aluminum foil.

3. Toss the eggplant, zucchini, and 2 tablespoons of the oil together in a large bowl. Divide the vegetables evenly between the prepared baking sheets, spreading them in a single layer on each sheet. Sprinkle with salt to taste and roast, stirring every 10 minutes, until well browned and tender, 30 to 40 minutes, rotating the baking sheets from top to bottom halfway through the roasting time. Set the roasted eggplant and zucchini aside.

4. Heat the remaining 2 tablespoons oil in a heavy-bottomed Dutch oven over medium heat until almost smoking. Add the onion, reduce the heat to medium-low, and cook, stirring frequently, until softened and golden brown, 15 to 20 minutes. Stir in the garlic and cook until fragrant, about 30 seconds. Add the tomatoes and cook until they release their juices and begin to break down, about 5 minutes. Add the roasted eggplant and zucchini, stirring gently but thoroughly to combine. Cook until just heated through, about 5 minutes. Stir in the parsley, basil, and thyme and adjust the seasonings with salt and pepper to taste. Serve hot or warm. (The ratatouille can be refrigerated in an airtight container for up to 3 days.)

ENDIVE

RAW BELGIAN ENDIVE, WITH ITS SHARP AND PLEASANTLY BITTER FLAVOR, may be an acquired taste. The right cooking method, however, transforms endive into a vegetable side dish of uncommonly complex flavor—at once mellow, sweet, and rich, yet still faintly bitter. According to generations of French and Belgian cooks, braising is the cooking method of choice. Just try to find a classic French cookbook without a braised endive recipe, along with the suggestion that it accompany a simple roast chicken, veal, or pork supper.

Most recipes for braised endive follow the same protocol: Brown the endive in fat and then finish cooking it, covered, in a small amount of liquid over low heat.

The challenge is to develop the deep flavor, richness, and gentle sweetness necessary to balance the endive's natural bite.

Available year-round, Belgian endive heads should have tightly packed leaves and a torpedo-like shape. The white leaves, essentially devoid of color because they are grown in the dark, are tinged slightly with yellow at the tip. It is said that if the yellow tinge is particularly deep, the endive will taste more bitter than usual. Our observations confirmed that notion when we tasted the endive raw, but we noted no effect on the flavor once the endive had been braised.

The first question was whether the endive really had to be browned before being braised. None of our tasters was impressed with the sharp, shallow flavor of endive that had not been browned, so we kept that step. We tested both butter and olive oil, and the former won hands down—the milk solids in the butter turn an appealing nut-brown

as they cook, and, overall, the butter adds a deeper, richer flavor. We took this notion one step further and lightly caramelized the endive using the butter and a pinch of sugar. The butter and sugar provided rich, sweet undertones that complemented the endive's bitterness nicely, without overpowering it. We added extra dimension to the flavor with some minced fresh herbs (tasters preferred thyme and parsley) and a small amount of fresh lemon juice for brightness.

The braising liquid also had a considerable impact on the flavor of the dish. Water, a common choice, had few supporters among our tasters. Cream was too rich and cider too seasonal for a year-round recipe. White wine made the dish too acidic, and while chicken broth tasted deep and round, it obscured the flavor of the endive. The ideal balance resided in a mixture of equal parts white wine and chicken broth, which produced deep yet brightly flavored endive that retained a hint of its own bitterness, something we wanted to preserve. We made the most of the braising liquid by reducing it to make a light sauce after the endive finished cooking, thereby concentrating its sweetness and richness.

Our last question concerned the cooking process. Classic technique dictates that endive be covered with a piece of buttered parchment and then cooked in a warm oven for a long period. In our tests, however, we achieved excellent flavor and texture simply by leaving the endive in a single layer in the same skillet used to brown it and braising on the stovetop with the pan's lid in place of the parchment. This method was not only straightforward but quick—the endive became completely tender within 15 minutes. Stovetop cooking also left plenty of room in the oven for a roast to complete the meal.

Although braising is the most traditional method for cooking endive, we've found that grilling is another option. The texture softens (but less so than when braised), and the vegetable easily holds its shape. Like braising, grilling softens the bitter flavor of endive.

We tried grilling endive whole, but it charred on the outside before the interior cooked through. We had far better results when we sliced each head in half lengthwise (just as we had done before braising). With a piece of the core still attached, the layers of leaves stay together on the grill. Since the core is exposed, it softens quickly and is crisp-tender by the time the exterior is streaked with dark grill marks.

Master Recipe for Braised Belgian Endive

SERVES 4

To avoid discoloration, do not cut the endive far in advance of cooking. Delicate endive can fall apart easily if not handled gently. Move the halved endive in the pan by grasping the curved sides gingerly with tongs and supporting the cut sides with a spatula while lifting and turning. You will need a skillet with a tight-fitting lid for this recipe.

3   tablespoons unsalted butter
½   teaspoon sugar
      Salt

PREPARING ENDIVE

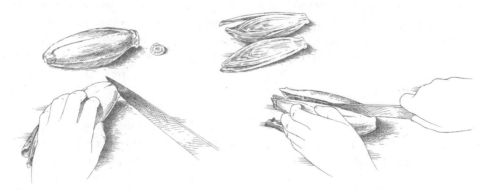

1. With a knife, shave off the discolored end of the endive. Cut the thinnest slice possible—you want the layers of leaves to remain intact as the endive cooks.

2. Cut the endive in half lengthwise through the core end.

4   medium Belgian endive (about
     4 ounces each), wilted or bruised
     outer leaves discarded, root ends
     trimmed, and each endive halved
     lengthwise (see the illustrations
     on page 111)
¼   cup dry white wine
¼   cup low-sodium chicken broth
½   teaspoon minced fresh thyme leaves
1   teaspoon juice from 1 lemon
1   tablespoon minced fresh parsley leaves
     Ground black pepper

1. Heat 2 tablespoons of the butter in a 12-inch heavy-bottomed skillet over medium-high heat. When the foaming subsides, sprinkle the sugar and ¼ teaspoon salt evenly over the skillet and set the endive, cut-sides down, in the pan in a single layer. Cook, shaking the skillet occasionally to prevent sticking and adjusting the burner if browning too quickly, until golden brown, about 5 minutes. Turn the endive over and cook until the curved sides are golden brown, about 3 minutes longer. Carefully turn the endive cut-sides down again. Add the wine, broth, and thyme. Reduce the heat to low, cover the skillet tightly, and simmer, checking occasionally and adding 2 tablespoons water if the pan appears dry, until the leaves open up slightly and the endive are tender throughout when pierced with the tip of a paring knife, 13 to 15 minutes. Transfer the endive to a warmed serving platter; set aside.

2. Increase the heat to medium-high to bring the liquid in the skillet to a boil and simmer until reduced to a syrupy consistency, 1 to 2 minutes. Off the heat, whisk in the remaining 1 tablespoon butter, lemon juice, and parsley. Adjust the seasoning with salt and pepper to taste, spoon the sauce over the endive, and serve immediately.

➤ VARIATIONS

Braised Belgian Endive with Gruyère and Canadian Bacon

Gruyère is a hard Swiss cheese with a mellow, nutty flavor. Because this version is finished under a broiler, you will need an ovenproof skillet (no plastic or wooden parts).

2   tablespoons unsalted butter
2   ounces Canadian bacon (about
     5 slices), cut into thin strips
½   teaspoon sugar
     Salt
4   medium Belgian endive (about
     4 ounces each), wilted or bruised
     outer leaves discarded, root ends
     trimmed, and each endive halved
     lengthwise (see the illustrations
     on page 111)
¼   cup low-sodium chicken broth
¼   cup heavy cream
½   teaspoon minced fresh thyme leaves
3   ounces Gruyère cheese, grated
     (about 1 cup)
     Ground black pepper

1. Heat the butter in a 12-inch heavy-bottomed ovenproof skillet over medium-high heat. When the foaming subsides, add the Canadian bacon and cook until lightly browned, about 4 minutes. Remove the bacon to a plate; set aside.

2. Adjust an oven rack to the upper-middle position (so that the rack is about 6 inches from the heating element) and heat the broiler.

3. Sprinkle the sugar and ¼ teaspoon salt evenly over the fat in the empty skillet and set the endive, cut-sides down, in the pan in a single layer. Cook, shaking the skillet occasionally to prevent sticking and adjusting the burner if browning too quickly, until golden brown, about 5 minutes. Turn the

EQUIPMENT: Pepper Mills

Most pepper mills work by similar means. Peppercorns are loaded into a central chamber through which runs a metal shaft. Near the bottom of the mill, the shaft is connected to a grinding mechanism that consists of a rotating, grooved "male" head that fits into a stationary, grooved "female" ring. Near the top of the male piece, the large grooves crack the peppercorns and then feed the smaller pieces downward to be ground between the finer grooves, or teeth, of the male and female components.

To a reasonable point, the finer the grind, the more evenly the pepper will be distributed throughout a dish. Likewise, the coarser the grind, the better for dishes like steak au poivre. Thus, the quality of a pepper mill's fine and coarse grinds (are all the bits fine or coarse, or does the mill yield a mix of fine and coarse bits at the same time?) is more important than options for an endless range of grinds beyond fine, medium, and coarse.

The industry experts we queried explained that the specifics of the grinding mechanism are key to grind quality. A related consideration, according Tom David, president of Tom David, Inc., maker of the Unicorn Magnum Plus mill, is how well the male and female grinding pieces are machined (how well the process used to cut the grooves works). Sharper teeth combined with a very tight tolerance between the pieces yield a finer grind. Unfortunately, none of these details are evident on inspecting a pepper mill in a kitchen store.

In addition to having an excellent grind quality, Unicorn Magnum Plus managed an awesome output. In one minute of grinding, the Magnum produced an amazing average of 7.3 grams, or about 3½ teaspoons, of fine-ground pepper. By comparison, honors for the next-highest average output went to the Oxo Grind It, at 5.1 grams, while about half the pack came in around the 2 grams-or-less mark (which, at roughly 1 teaspoon in volume, is perfectly acceptable).

The ease of adjusting the grind was another factor we considered. Changing the grind from fine to coarse involves changing the tolerances of, or distances between, the male and female grinding components. The more space between them, the larger the pepper particles and the coarser the grind. Traditionally, a knob at the top of the mill, called the finial, is used to adjust the grind. This was our least favorite design for two reasons. First, the finial must be screwed down very tight for a fine grind, which not only requires significant finger strength but also makes the head (or the crank) of the mill more difficult to turn. Second, the finial usually has to be removed entirely to fill the mill, which means you have to readjust the grind with each filling. We preferred mills like the Unicorn Magnum Plus, which use a screw or dial at the base of the grinding mechanism.

Grind quality and speed are only half the battle—especially if most of your peppercorns land on the floor when you try to fill the mill. So we appreciated mills with wide, unobstructed filler doors that could accommodate the lip of a wide funnel or, better yet, the lip of a bag or jar so that we could dispense with the funnel altogether. The East Hampton Industries (FHI) Peppermate took high honors in this category, with a lid that snaps off to create a gaping 3-inch opening. Along the same lines, the more peppercorns a mill can hold, the less often it has to be filled. The Zyliss held a full cup, and the Unicorn Magnum Plus trailed behind by just 1 tablespoon.

THE BEST PEPPER MILLS

The Unicorn Magnum Plus (far left) has a huge capacity and awesome speed. The East Hampton Industries Peppermate (second from left) has a detachable cup that captures ground pepper and makes measuring easy. The Oxo Good Grips Grind It (second from right) is lightning fast, but it can be tricky to adjust the grind on the mill. The Zyliss Large Mill (far right) has a huge capacity and an excellent range of grinds, but it is slower than the other top models.

endive over and cook until the curved sides are golden brown, about 3 minutes longer. Carefully turn the endive cut-sides down again. Add the broth, cream, and thyme. Reduce the heat to low, cover the skillet tightly, and simmer until the leaves open up slightly and the endive are tender throughout when pierced with the tip of a paring knife, 13 to 15 minutes.

4. Sprinkle the reserved Canadian bacon and the cheese over the endive and season with salt and pepper to taste. Place the pan in the oven and broil until the cheese is melted and lightly browned, 2 to 3 minutes. Serve immediately.

Braised Belgian Endive with Parmesan Bread Crumbs

For the bread crumbs, use a hearty, high-quality white bread (we like Pepperidge Farm Hearty White).

    5   slices high-quality white bread,
        crusts removed and torn into
        rough 1 1/2-inch pieces
    2   tablespoons unsalted butter
        Pinch cayenne pepper
    1/4 cup grated Parmesan cheese
        Salt
    1   recipe Braised Belgian Endive

1. Place the bread in the workbowl of a food processor and process until the crumbs are even and fine textured, 20 to 30 seconds.

2. Heat the butter in a 12-inch heavy-bottomed skillet over medium-high heat. When the foaming subsides, add the bread crumbs and cayenne and cook, tossing to coat with the butter, until the bread crumbs just begin to color, about 10 minutes. Transfer the bread crumbs to a medium bowl. Add the cheese and toss to combine. Season with salt to taste and set the crumbs aside.

3. Wipe out the skillet and prepare the endive as directed. Just before serving, sprinkle the bread crumbs over the braised endive and sauce.

Cider-Braised Belgian Endive with Apples

Because the apples absorb some of the braising liquid, more cider is added to the pan before the sauce is reduced.

    3   tablespoons unsalted butter
    1/2 teaspoon sugar
        Salt
    4   medium Belgian endive (about
        4 ounces each), wilted or bruised
        outer leaves discarded, root ends
        trimmed, and each endive halved
        lengthwise (see the illustrations
        on page 111)
    1   medium Granny Smith apple, peeled,
        cored, and cut into 1/4-inch wedges
    1/2 cup plus 2 tablespoons cider
    1/2 teaspoon minced fresh thyme leaves
    1   tablespoon minced fresh parsley leaves
        Ground black pepper

1. Heat 2 tablespoons of the butter in a 12-inch heavy-bottomed skillet over medium-high heat. When the foaming subsides, sprinkle the sugar and 1/4 teaspoon salt evenly over the skillet and set the endive, cut-sides down, in the pan in a single layer. Add the apple slices to the pan as well. Cook, shaking the skillet occasionally to prevent sticking and adjusting the burner if browning too quickly, until golden brown, about 5 minutes. Turn the endive over and cook until the curved sides are golden brown, about 3 minutes longer. Carefully turn the endive cut-sides down again. Add 1/2 cup of the cider and the thyme. Reduce the heat to low, cover the skillet tightly, and simmer, checking occasionally and adding 2 tablespoons water if the pan

appears dry, until the leaves open up slightly and the endive are tender throughout when pierced with the tip of a paring knife, 13 to 15 minutes. Transfer the endive and apples to a warmed serving platter; set aside.

2. Add the remaining 2 tablespoons cider to the empty pan, increase the heat to medium-high to bring the liquid in the skillet to a boil, and simmer until it has reduced to a syrupy consistency, 1 to 2 minutes. Off the heat, whisk in the remaining 1 tablespoon butter and the parsley. Adjust the seasoning with salt and pepper to taste, spoon the sauce over the endive and apples, and serve immediately.

Master Recipe for Grilled Belgian Endive

SERVES 6 TO 8

Delicate endive can fall apart easily if not handled gently. Move the halved endive on the grill by grasping the curved sides gently with tongs and supporting the cut sides with a spatula while lifting and turning.

8   medium heads endive (about 4 ounces
     each), wilted or bruised outer leaves
     discarded, root ends trimmed, and
     each endive halved lengthwise (see the
     illustrations on page 111)
3   tablespoons extra-virgin olive oil
     Salt and ground black pepper

1. Toss the endive halves and oil in a large bowl until the endive is well coated with oil. Season with salt and pepper to taste.

2. Grill the endive over a medium-hot fire (you should be able to hold your hand 5 inches above the cooking grate for 3 to 4 seconds), turning once, until dark grill marks appear and the center of each is crisp-tender, 5 to 7 minutes. Serve hot or at room temperature.

➤ VARIATION

Grilled Belgian Endive with Lemon-Garlic Butter

The lemon zest, garlic, and thyme need to be cooked only until they are fragrant. If the zest is overcooked, it will become bitter.

6   tablespoons unsalted butter
1   medium clove garlic, minced or
     pressed through a garlic press
1   teaspoon grated zest from 1 lemon
1/2 teaspoon minced fresh thyme leaves
1   recipe Grilled Endive
     Salt and ground black pepper

Place the butter in a small skillet or saucepan over medium heat. When the butter has melted, add the garlic, lemon zest, and thyme and cook until fragrant, about 2 minutes. Drizzle over the grilled endive and season the endive with salt and pepper to taste. Serve immediately.

ESCAROLE

ESCAROLE IS A LEAFY GREEN THAT LOOKS MUCH LIKE GREEN LEAF LETTUCE. Its gently bitter flavor makes it an excellent choice for the salad bowl. However, unlike lettuce, escarole stands up well to cooking. Although most Americans are unfamiliar with escarole prepared in this fashion, Italians often cook this leafy green.

To find the best cooking method, we tried blanching, steaming, and braising. Both blanching and steaming made the escarole soggy and bland. Braising turned out to be the best method. Not only was braising the fastest method (no need to wait for water to boil), but it also allowed the addition of other ingredients, such as olive oil, garlic, and herbs, which complemented the bitter flavors of the escarole.

To get the escarole ready for cooking, we simply washed it and then shook the leaves dry. The moisture clinging to the leaves will turn to steam once the escarole is added to a hot pan. A cover will trap this steam and wilt the escarole quickly. There's no need to add any other braising liquid to the pan. We found that the tough white stems (the portion at the bottom of each leaf) did not soften at the same rate as the green leaves, so we decided to remove them before cooking the escarole.

Of course, escarole can also be used in salads. Its bitter flavor works especially well with sweet oranges and briny olives.

Braised Escarole with Garlic and Thyme
SERVES 4 AS A SIDE DISH

After washing the escarole, there is no need to dry the leaves too thoroughly. Any water remaining on the leaves will help braise the escarole in the pan. Be sure to remove the tough white stems of the escarole.

2   tablespoons extra-virgin olive oil
2   medium cloves garlic, sliced
1/8 teaspoon hot red pepper flakes
1   teaspoon minced fresh thyme leaves
1   large head escarole (about 1 1/2 pounds), washed, shaken dry, tough white stems discarded, and leaves torn into 2-inch pieces
     Salt

Place the oil, garlic, and pepper flakes in a Dutch oven and turn the heat to medium. Cook until the garlic turns golden, taking care not to let the garlic burn and adjusting the heat as necessary, about 5 minutes. Add the thyme and escarole, stir to coat the leaves with oil, and cover. Cook, stirring occasionally, until the escarole is wilted, about 5 minutes. Season with salt to taste. Serve immediately.

Escarole and Orange Salad with Green Olive Vinaigrette

SERVES 4 TO 6 AS A FIRST COURSE

When arranging the orange segments on the greens, leave behind any juice that is released; it will dilute the dressing. Grate the zest from one of the oranges before segmenting it and then use the orange zest in the dressing. Toast the almonds in a dry skillet over medium heat until golden, about 7 minutes.

2 tablespoons sherry vinegar
$\frac{1}{2}$ cup pitted and chopped green olives
1 large shallot, minced (about $\frac{1}{4}$ cup)
1 medium clove garlic, minced or pressed through a garlic press
1 teaspoon grated zest from 1 orange
$\frac{1}{3}$ cup extra-virgin olive oil
Salt and ground black pepper
1 large head escarole (about 1 $\frac{1}{2}$ pounds), washed, dried, tough white stems discarded, and leaves torn into bite-size pieces
2 large oranges, segmented (see the illustrations below)
$\frac{1}{2}$ cup slivered almonds, toasted

1. Whisk the vinegar, olives, shallot, garlic, and orange zest together in a large bowl. Whisk in the oil and season with salt and pepper to taste. Add the escarole and toss to coat evenly.

2. Divide the greens among individual plates. Arrange a portion of the orange segments over each salad and sprinkle with the almonds. Serve immediately.

SEGMENTING AN ORANGE

When presentation matters, you should remove the segments from an orange without any white pith or membranes. Use the same technique with tangerines and grapefruit.

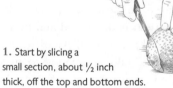

1. Start by slicing a small section, about $\frac{1}{2}$ inch thick, off the top and bottom ends.

2. With the fruit resting flat, use a paring knife to slice off the rind and the white pith. Slide the knife from top to bottom, closely following the outline of the fruit to minimize waste.

3. Working over a bowl to catch the juice, slip the blade between a membrane and a section and slice to the center, separating one side of the section.

4. Turn the blade so that it is facing out. Slide the blade from the center out along the other membrane to free the section. Continue until all the sections are removed.

FENNEL

ALTHOUGH FENNEL IS ALMOST ALWAYS AVAILABLE IN SUPERMARKETS these days, most Americans have little idea what to do with this anise-flavored vegetable. Maybe it's the funny Italian name, *finocchio*, or its odd appearance. A white, squat bulb narrows into several light green stems, which are topped with feathery, dark green fronds.

Raw fennel is crisp and has a fairly strong anise flavor. Cooking softens the fennel and causes this licorice flavor to fade. No matter how it is cooked, fennel will be slightly sweet. Although each portion—the bulb, stems, and fronds—has different culinary uses, for most recipes only the white bulb is used. The stems

can be reserved for making stock, while the fronds can be minced and used as a garnish for dishes made with the bulb.

At the outset, our goals were twofold: We wanted to figure out how to prepare fennel for cooking, and we wanted to find which cooking methods would deliver the best results. We soon realized that these two questions are intertwined. The tricks with cooking fennel are to cook it evenly and to use methods that accentuate its subtle anise sweetness. To do that, you must combine the proper cooking method with the proper way of cutting the vegetable.

The first step in slicing fennel is to remove the long green stems and fronds. A heavy chef's knife can be used to cut through the bottom of the stems where they meet the white bulb. Most fennel bulbs, especially larger ones, have an outer layer of dried or blemished flesh. Of course, when at the market, you should try to pick firm bulbs with a

bright white color and as little blemishing as possible. But even on the freshest fennel, the outer layer should be removed, much as you might peel away the outer layer on a large onion. We find it best to start out by trimming a thin slice from the bottom of the bulb. Invariably, this flesh is discolored and needs to be removed. This cut usually loosens the outer layer on the bulb sufficiently so that it can be peeled away with your fingers. If the outer layer will not yield to your fingers, make a shallow vertical cut through this layer and then slide your fingers into the cut to pry off this first layer of the bulb.

Now that the tough portions of the bulb have been removed, there are several options for slicing. Fan-shaped wedges are good for grilling (these large pieces won't fall through the grates) or for braising. To form these wedges, simply cut the bulb vertically so that each slice includes a portion of the base, which will serve to hold the various layers together.

Most cooking methods other than grilling or braising rely on smaller pieces. In this case, we find it useful to cut the bulb in half through the base. Each half contains a small portion of the core at its base. Use a small, sharp knife to remove this pyramid-shaped piece. This small refinement helps promote even cooking, because the core can remain tough long after the rest of the bulb has softened.

The next step is to lay each fennel half on a work surface with the flat-side down and then cut each half crosswise. These slices can then be cut lengthwise to yield long strips that are about ½ inch thick. We find this size perfect for sautéing and roasting. Larger slices take too long to soften with either method, and the exterior can burn before the interior is fully cooked. In contrast, this is not such a problem when braising, because the liquid prevents too much browning. That's why fennel for braising can be left in larger pieces.

Now that we had figured out how to slice this odd-looking bulb, it was time to start cooking fennel. Fennel generally responds best to dry-heat methods. Sautéing, grilling, and roasting cause the natural sugars in the fennel to caramelize, thereby enhancing its flavor. The exception to the "dry heat is best" rule is braising. This method involves wet heat, with the fennel absorbing flavors from the cooking liquid (usually stock or wine) and, therefore, delivering very good results.

The common thread in all our testing was to achieve uniform tenderness throughout the fennel pieces. It's easy enough to cook fennel until mushy, but we prefer that it offer some resistance. However, fennel that is soft on the exterior and crunchy on the inside is not to our taste either. Fairly slow cooking turned out to be the key. Sautéing over medium heat for a considerable period (about 15 minutes), braising for 30 minutes,

and roasting for 35 minutes all worked beautifully. Attempts to hurry fennel along by using faster methods such as boiling and microwaving did not succeed; the fennel became mushy with both methods, and boiling also washed out much of its flavor. Steaming not only was time consuming and turned the fennel a bit mushy, but it also did little to elicit or enhance its sweet flavor because steaming did not brown the fennel.

Unlike most vegetables, raw fennel has a long history of use in salads or antipasti. Italians often put out strips of fennel along with a bowl of fine olive oil and salt as a quick antipasto. The fennel is simply dipped in the oil, sprinkled with salt, and enjoyed with cocktails. Raw fennel can also be cut into thin strips or diced and used in salads. Add a handful of diced fennel to a leafy salad or use thin strips of fennel in a citrus salad.

Master Recipe for Sautéed Fennel with Garlic and Parsley

SERVES 4

Sautéing causes the anise flavor of fennel to fade but concentrates the natural sugars in the vegetable. This side dish complements poultry and seafood particularly well.

- 2 medium fennel bulbs (about 2 pounds)
- 3 tablespoons extra-virgin olive oil
- 4 medium cloves garlic, minced or pressed through a garlic press
  Salt and ground black pepper
- 2 tablespoons minced fresh parsley leaves

1. Remove the stems, fronds, and any blemished portions from the fennel bulbs (see illustrations 1 and 2 on page 120). Mince and reserve 1 tablespoon fronds and discard the stems. Halve the bulbs through the base.

Use a paring knife to remove the pyramid-shaped piece of core attached to each half (see illustration 4 below). With the cut-side down and the knife parallel to the work surface, slice each fennel half crosswise. Then, with the knife perpendicular to the work surface, cut each fennel half lengthwise into long, thin strips (see illustration 5 below).

2. Heat the oil in a large skillet over medium heat until almost smoking. Add the garlic and sauté until lightly colored, about 1 minute. Add the fennel strips and cook, stirring often, until the fennel has softened considerably but still offers some resistance, about 15 minutes. Season generously with salt and pepper to taste. Stir in the minced fronds and parsley and serve immediately.

➤ VARIATION

Sautéed Fennel with Tarragon and Walnuts

The anise flavors lost during sautéing can be brought back with the addition of fresh tarragon and fennel seeds.

2	medium fennel bulbs (about 2 pounds)
3	tablespoons extra-virgin olive oil
4	medium cloves garlic, minced or pressed through a garlic press
I	teaspoon fennel seeds
	Salt and ground black pepper
2	tablespoons minced fresh tarragon leaves
3	tablespoons coarsely chopped walnuts

PREPARING FENNEL

1. Cut off the stems and feathery fronds. (The fronds can be minced and used for a garnish.)

2. Trim a very thin slice from the base and remove any tough or blemished outer layers from the bulb.

3. For braising or grilling, slice the bulb vertically through the base into 1/2-inch-thick slices that resemble fans.

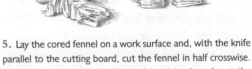

4. For sautéing, roasting, or salads, cut the bulb in half through the base. Use a small, sharp knife to remove the pyramid-shaped core.

5. Lay the cored fennel on a work surface and, with the knife parallel to the cutting board, cut the fennel in half crosswise. With the knife perpendicular to the cutting board, cut the fennel pieces lengthwise into 1/2-inch-thick strips.

1. Remove the stems, fronds, and any blemished portions from the fennel bulbs (see illustrations 1 and 2 on page 120). Mince and reserve 1 tablespoon fronds and discard the stems. Halve the bulbs through the base. Use a paring knife to remove the pyramid-shaped piece of core attached to each half (see illustration 4 on page 120). With the cut-side down and the knife parallel to the work surface, slice each fennel half crosswise. Then, with the knife perpendicular to the work surface, cut each fennel half lengthwise into long, thin strips (see illustration 5 on page 120).

2. Heat the oil in a large skillet over medium heat until almost smoking. Add the garlic and fennel seeds and cook until lightly colored and fragrant, about 1 minute. Add the fennel strips and cook, stirring often, until the fennel has softened considerably but still offers some resistance, about 15 minutes. Season generously with salt and pepper to taste. Stir in the minced fronds and tarragon. Transfer the fennel to a serving bowl and garnish with the walnuts. Serve immediately.

Master Recipe for Braised Fennel with White Wine and Parmesan

SERVES 4

In this recipe, the fennel cooks slowly in butter and white wine until tender and then receives a dusting of cheese just before serving. This rich side dish works well with either beef or veal.

3 tablespoons unsalted butter
3 small fennel bulbs (about 2 1/4 pounds), stems and fronds discarded, blemished portions of bulbs trimmed, and bulbs cut vertically into 1/2-inch-thick slices (see illustrations 1 through 3 on page 120)
Salt and ground black pepper

1/3 cup dry white wine
1/4 cup grated Parmesan cheese

1. Melt the butter over medium heat in a sauté pan large enough to hold the fennel in almost a single layer. When the foaming subsides, add the fennel and sprinkle with salt and pepper to taste. Add the wine, cover, and simmer for 15 minutes. Turn the slices and continue to simmer, covered, until the fennel is quite tender, has absorbed most of the pan liquid, and starts to turn golden, about 10 minutes longer. Turn the fennel again and continue cooking, covered, until the fennel starts to color on the other side, about 4 minutes longer.

2. Sprinkle the fennel with the cheese. Transfer the fennel to a platter and serve immediately.

VARIATIONS
Braised Fennel with Olives, Sun-Dried Tomatoes, and Pecorino Romano

Like Parmesan, Pecorino Romano is a hard, white cheese, traditionally made from sheep's milk and designed for grating. It has a pungent, peppery flavor and pairs well with dishes with assertive ingredients such as olives and sun-dried tomatoes.

3 tablespoons extra-virgin olive oil
3 small fennel bulbs (about 2 1/4 pounds), stems and fronds discarded, blemished portions of bulbs trimmed, and bulbs cut vertically into 1/2-inch-thick slices (see illustrations 1 through 3 on page 120)
Salt and ground black pepper
1/3 cup low-sodium chicken broth
4 medium oil-packed sun-dried tomatoes, chopped
10 black olives, pitted and sliced
1/4 cup grated Pecorino Romano cheese

1. Heat the oil over medium heat in a sauté pan large enough to hold the fennel in almost a single layer. When the oil begins to shimmer, add the fennel and sprinkle with salt and pepper to taste. Add the broth, tomatoes, and olives, cover, and simmer over medium heat for 15 minutes. Turn the slices and continue to simmer, covered, until the fennel is quite tender, has absorbed most of the pan liquid, and starts to turn golden, about 10 minutes longer. Turn the fennel again and continue cooking, covered, until the fennel starts to color on the other side, about 4 minutes longer.

2. Sprinkle the fennel with the cheese. Transfer the fennel to a platter and serve immediately.

Braised Fennel with Pancetta and Onion

Pancetta can be found in the specialty deli section of most large grocery stores. See page 123 for more information.

- 2 tablespoons extra-virgin olive oil
- 2 ounces pancetta, chopped fine
- I medium onion, chopped fine
- 3 small fennel bulbs (about 2 1/4 pounds), stems and fronds discarded, blemished portions of bulbs trimmed, and bulbs cut vertically into 1/2-inch-thick slices (see illustrations I through 3 on page 120)
  Salt and ground black pepper
- 1/3 cup dry white wine
- 1/4 cup grated Parmesan cheese

1. Heat the oil over medium-high heat in a sauté pan large enough to hold the fennel in almost a single layer. When the oil begins to shimmer, add the pancetta and onion and cook until the pancetta is crisp and the onion begins to turn golden brown, 4 to 5 minutes,

adjusting the heat as necessary to prevent burning. Add the fennel and sprinkle with salt and pepper to taste. Add the wine, cover, reduce the heat to medium, and simmer for 15 minutes. Turn the slices and continue to simmer, covered, until the fennel is quite tender, has absorbed most of the pan liquid, and starts to turn golden, about 10 minutes longer. Turn the fennel again and continue cooking, covered, until the fennel starts to color on the other side, about 4 minutes longer.

2. Sprinkle the fennel with the cheese. Transfer the fennel to a platter and serve immediately.

Master Recipe for Grilled Fennel

SERVES 4

Fennel grills beautifully. Its anise flavor is complemented by the caramelization of natural sugars on the surface of the vegetable. The biggest challenge when grilling fennel is slicing the bulb so that the pieces pick up as much flavor as possible without falling through the grill grate. Make sure to slice the bulb through the core end into fan-shaped pieces. With a piece of the core still attached, the various layers will remain intact as a single piece. With two flat sides, fan-shaped pieces also have plenty of surface area, so they pick up a lot of grill flavor.

- 2 medium fennel bulbs (about 2 pounds), stems and fronds trimmed and discarded, base shaved off, tough or blemished outer layers removed, and cut vertically through the base into 1/4-inch-thick slices (see illustrations I through 3 on page 120)
- 3 tablespoons extra-virgin olive oil
  Salt and ground black pepper

1. Toss the fennel and oil together in a large bowl. Season to taste with salt and pepper.

2. Grill the fennel over a medium-hot fire (you should be able to hold your hand 5 inches above the cooking grate for 3 to 4 seconds), turning once, until tender and streaked with dark grill marks, 7 to 9 minutes. Transfer the grilled fennel to a platter and leave as is or drizzle with any of the following vinaigrettes. Serve hot, warm, or at room temperature.

Grapefruit Vinaigrette

MAKES ABOUT $1/2$ CUP

If your grapefruit is especially tart, you may want to add more honey.

$3/4$	cup juice from 1 pink grapefruit
$1/4$	teaspoon finely minced or grated fresh ginger
1	medium shallot, minced
1	teaspoon honey, or more to taste
6	tablespoons extra-virgin olive oil
	Salt and ground black pepper

1. Bring the grapefruit juice to a simmer in a 10-inch nonstick skillet over medium-high heat. Reduce the heat and simmer the juice gently, adjusting the heat as necessary,

INGREDIENTS: Pancetta

Pancetta and American bacon come from the same part of the pig—the belly—but the curing process is different. American bacon is cured with salt, sugar, and spices (the mix varies from producer to producer) and smoked. Pancetta is not smoked, and the cure does not contain sugar—just salt, pepper, and, usually, cloves. Pancetta is usually cured for two weeks, rolled up tightly like a jelly roll, and packed into a casing.

until the juice has reduced to a syrupy glaze (you should have about 2 tablespoons), about 15 minutes.

2. Whisk the reduced grapefruit juice, ginger, shallot, honey, and oil together in a small bowl. Season with salt and pepper to taste and add more honey if necessary.

Mint and Tarragon Vinaigrette

MAKES ABOUT $1/2$ CUP

The anise flavors of the tarragon and fennel are highlighted by the brightness of the mint.

6	tablespoons extra-virgin olive oil
2	tablespoons white wine vinegar
2	teaspoons minced fresh tarragon leaves
$1 1/2$	teaspoons minced fresh mint leaves
	Salt and ground black pepper

Whisk the oil, vinegar, and herbs together in a small bowl. Season with salt and pepper to taste.

Master Recipe for Roasted Fennel

SERVES 4 TO 6

Roasting is an easy way of caramelizing the sugars in the fennel. We found that cutting the fennel into small pieces and roasting it for a considerably long time ensured that the fennel's natural sweetness was brought out. Tossing the fennel pieces with extra-virgin olive oil prior to roasting produced the most flavorful results. The fennel's subtle anise flavors were muted by butter, and vegetable oil added nothing. The fresh, grassy flavors of the olive oil complemented the fennel nicely. The only things needed to complete this simple dish were salt, pepper, and a sprinkling of fresh parsley. If you like, sprinkle the roasted fennel with freshly grated Parmesan, Pecorino Romano, or crumbled feta just before serving.

3   small fennel bulbs (about 2 1/4 pounds)
2   tablespoons extra-virgin olive oil
     Salt and ground black pepper
2   tablespoons minced fresh parsley leaves

1. Adjust the oven rack to the lower-middle position and heat the oven to 425 degrees.

2. Remove and discard the stems, fronds, and any blemished portions from the fennel bulbs (see illustrations 1 and 2 on page 120). Halve the bulbs through the base. Use a paring knife to remove the pyramid-shaped piece of core attached to each half (see illustration 4 on page 120). With the cut-side down and the knife parallel to the work surface, slice each fennel half in half crosswise. Then, with the knife perpendicular to the work surface, cut each fennel half lengthwise into long, thin strips (see illustration 5 on page 120).

3. Toss the fennel and oil together in a large roasting pan. Season with salt and pepper to taste. Roast, turning the fennel once after 20 minutes, until the fennel is tender, 35 to 40 minutes. Garnish with the parsley and serve immediately.

⋟ VARIATION
Roasted Fennel and Onion with Apple Cider Glaze

For reducing the cider, we recommend a nonstick skillet for two reasons. The first is ease of cleanup. The second reason is that the surface is nonreactive and therefore will not react with the acid in the cider.

3   small fennel bulbs (about 2 1/4 pounds)
1   small onion, cut into 1/2-inch wedges
1   teaspoon minced fresh thyme leaves
2   tablespoons extra-virgin olive oil
     Salt and ground black pepper
1   cup cider

1. Adjust the oven rack to the lower-middle position and heat the oven to 425 degrees.

2. Remove and discard the stems, fronds, and any blemished portions from the fennel bulbs (see illustrations 1 and 2 on page 120). Halve the bulbs through the base. Use a paring knife to remove the pyramid-shaped piece of core attached to each half (see illustration 4 on page 120). With the cut-side down and the knife parallel to the work surface, slice each fennel half in half crosswise. Then, with the knife perpendicular to the work surface, cut each fennel half lengthwise into long, thin strips (see illustration 5 on page 120).

3. Toss the fennel, onion, thyme, and oil together in a large roasting pan. Season with salt and pepper to taste. Roast, turning the vegetables once after 20 minutes, until the fennel is tender, 35 to 40 minutes.

4. Meanwhile, place the cider in a small nonstick skillet over medium-high heat and bring to a simmer. Reduce the heat to medium-low and simmer gently until the cider has reduced to about 1/4 cup, 15 to 20 minutes.

5. Transfer the roasted vegetables to a platter and drizzle with the cider glaze. Serve immediately.

⋟
Fennel and Olive Salad with Creamy Herb Vinaigrette

SERVES 4

This salad is best served as a first course.

2   small fennel bulbs (about 1 1/2 pounds)
1   tablespoon sour cream
1   teaspoon grated zest and 1 tablespoon juice from 1 lemon
2   tablespoons extra-virgin olive oil
1   tablespoon minced fresh parsley leaves
     Salt and ground black pepper
2   cups frisée leaves, arugula, or mesclun, rinsed and dried
1/4 cup Niçoise olives

1. Remove the stems, fronds, and any blemished portions from the fennel bulbs (see illustrations 1 and 2 on page 120). Mince and reserve 1 tablespoon fronds and discard the stems. Halve the bulbs through the base. Use a paring knife to remove the pyramid-shaped piece of core attached to each half (see illustration 4 on page 120). With the cut-side down and the knife parallel to the work surface, slice each fennel half in half crosswise. Then, with the knife perpendicular to the work surface, cut each fennel half lengthwise into long, thin strips (see illustration 5 on page 120).

2. Whisk the sour cream, lemon zest and juice, oil, parsley, minced fennel fronds, and salt and pepper to taste together in a medium bowl. Add the fennel and toss to coat.

3. Arrange the salad greens on individual plates. Mound the fennel on top of the greens and garnish with the olives. Serve immediately.

Fennel and Tangerine Slaw
SERVES 4

Serve this refreshing slaw as a side dish with grilled fish, chicken, or pork. Make sure to reserve the juice from the tangerines as you segment them.

2   medium fennel bulbs (about 2 pounds)
2   tangerines or small oranges, peeled
    and segmented (see the illustrations
    on page 117), segments halved
    crosswise and seeded
1/4 cup chopped fresh parsley leaves
2   tablespoons juice from 1 lemon
2   tablespoons grainy mustard
1   medium clove garlic, minced or
    pressed through a garlic press
1/2 cup extra-virgin olive oil
    Salt and ground black pepper

1. Remove and discard the stems, fronds, and any blemished portions from the fennel bulbs (see illustrations 1 and 2 on page 120). Halve the bulbs through the base. Use a paring knife to remove the pyramid-shaped piece of core attached to each half (see illustration 4 on page 120). With the cut-side down and the knife parallel to the work surface, slice each fennel half crosswise into 1/2-inch-thick slices. Then, with the knife perpendicular to the work surface, cut each fennel half lengthwise into long, thin strips (see illustration 5 on page 120). Coarsely chop the fennel strips.

2. Toss the fennel, tangerines, and parsley together in a large bowl. Whisk the lemon juice, mustard, garlic, and oil together in a small bowl. Toss the dressing with the fennel mixture and season with salt and pepper to taste. Serve. (The slaw can be refrigerated in an airtight container for 2 days.)

GARLIC

GARLIC FALLS INTO TWO PRIMARY CATEGORIES: HARDNECK AND SOFTNECK. The garlic that most of us cook with is softneck, so-called because its neck is soft and braidable. Softneck garlic contains a circle of plump cloves shrouding a second circle of smaller cloves, all enveloped by many papery layers. Because softneck garlic is heat tolerant and produces and stores well, it has become the favored commercial garlic. Supermarket garlics are almost invariably softneck.

Hardneck, which is the original cultivated garlic variety, is distinguished by its stiff center staff, around which large uniform cloves hang. Hardneck garlic has a relatively sparse parchment wrapper that makes it easier to peel (and damage) than softneck. It is considered superior in flavor—more complex and intense than softneck. Its thinly wrapped cloves lose moisture quickly, however, and do not winter over, as do the cloves of the robust softneck.

We tasted eight garlic varieties, softneck and hardneck, raw and cooked, and found a wide range of flavors. We enjoyed several softneck and hardneck varieties. However, our two favorite varieties were Porcelain Zemo and Rocambole Carpathian, both of which are hardnecks.

Minced, chopped, or sliced garlic is used in countless recipes. However, whole heads of garlic can be cooked on their own and served as is (on bread) or used to flavor mashed potatoes, stews, sauces, or dressings. Roasting is a simple way to mellow garlic's harsh flavors.

Most recipes call for wrapping a whole head of garlic in foil and then roasting it in the oven until very soft. A few sources suggest poaching the garlic first (in chicken stock, wine, or milk) and then roasting it, but we quickly dismissed this notion because poaching tended to weaken the garlic flavor.

Some recipes coat the head of garlic with oil before it is wrapped in foil, and others

TWO TYPES OF GARLIC

HARDNECK
GARLIC

SOFTNECK
GARLIC

Hardneck garlic has a stiff center staff around which the large, uniformly sized cloves hang. Softneck garlic, the kind found most commonly in supermarkets, has cloves of varying sizes (larger on the outside, smaller near the center) and no central staff.

omit this step. We roasted two heads of garlic, each in a separate foil pack, one with oil and one without. The garlic roasted without the oil was pale and steamy. Using a small amount of extra-virgin olive oil helped to caramelize the garlic and gave the cloves a deeper, toasty flavor. Don't go overboard with the oil. Too much oil (one head needs just 1 teaspoon of oil) makes the garlic greasy and unappetizing.

Next, we wondered if separating the cloves would result in a shorter cooking time. It did, but the separated cloves dried out and became leathery. Keeping the head intact helped to keep the cloves juicy and

cooked them evenly. The last thing to test was the oven temperature. We tried temperatures from 300 to 500 degrees and found that 425 degrees produced the best results, with garlic that was slightly caramelized on the outside and creamy on the inside.

Roasted Garlic

SERVES 2 TO 4

Serve roasted garlic with toasted Italian or French bread. Squeeze a clove of the roasted garlic onto the bread and drizzle with extra-virgin olive oil, if desired. Roasted garlic can also be used to flavor mashed potatoes, soups, pasta sauces, or spreads (see the variation that follows).

- 1   medium head garlic, outer skin removed but head left intact
- 1   teaspoon extra-virgin olive oil

1. Adjust an oven rack to the lower-middle position and heat the oven to 425 degrees.
2. Slice off the top ½ inch from the head of garlic to expose the cloves. Place the garlic on a piece of aluminum foil measuring at least 10 by 10 inches. Pour the oil over the garlic and then wrap the garlic securely in the foil.

PEELING GARLIC

Unless whole cloves are needed, we crush garlic cloves with the side of a large chef's knife to loosen their skins and make them easier to remove.

MINCING GARLIC TO A PASTE

Here's how to produce very fine, smooth bits of garlic without a garlic press. If possible, use kosher or coarse salt; the larger crystals do a better job of breaking down the garlic than fine table salt.

1. Mince the garlic as you normally would on a cutting board. Sprinkle the minced garlic with salt.

2. Drag the side of the knife over the garlic-salt mixture to form a fine puree. Continue to mince and drag the knife as necessary until the puree is smooth.

EQUIPMENT: Garlic Presses

Most cooks dislike the chore of mincing garlic, and many turn to garlic presses. We know that many professional cooks sneer at this tool, but we have a different opinion. In hundreds of hours of use in our test kitchens, we have found that this little tool delivers speed, ease, and a comfortable separation of garlic from fingers.

The garlic press offers other advantages. First is flavor, which changes perceptibly depending on how the cloves are broken down. The finer a clove of garlic is cut, the more flavor is released from its broken cells. Fine mincing or pureeing, therefore, results in a fuller, more pungent garlic flavor. A good garlic press breaks down the cloves more than the average cook would with a knife. Second, a good garlic press ensures a consistently fine texture, which in turn means better distribution of the garlic throughout the dish.

The question for us, then, was not whether garlic presses work but which of the many available presses work best. Armed with 10 popular models, we pressed our way through a mountain of garlic cloves to find out.

Garlic press prices can vary by as much as a shocking 700 percent, from about $3 up to $25. Some are made from metal and others from plastic. Some offer devices to ease cleaning, and most show subtle differences in handle and hopper design.

Most garlic presses share a common design consisting of two handles connected by a hinge. At the end of one handle is a small, perforated hopper; at the end of the other is a plunger that fits snugly inside the hopper. The garlic cloves in the hopper get crushed by the descending plunger when the handles are squeezed together, and the puree is extruded through the perforations in the bottom of the hopper.

Some presses employ a completely different design—a relatively large cylindrical container with a tight-fitting screw-down plunger. These presses are designed for large capacity, but the unusual design failed to impress us. The screw-type plungers required both pressure and significant repetitive motion, which contributed to hand fatigue. This seemed like a lot of work just to press garlic. Matters did not improve when the hoppers were loaded with multiple garlic cloves. Even greater effort was required to twist down the plungers, and the texture of the garlic puree produced was coarse and uneven.

A good garlic press should not only produce a smooth, evenly textured puree but also be easy to use. To us, this meant that different users should be able to operate it without straining their hands. With several notable exceptions, all of our presses performed reasonably well in this regard.

Several of our test cooks wondered if we could make an easy task even easier by putting the garlic cloves through the presses without first removing their skins. Instructions on the packaging of the Zyliss and Bodum presses specified that it was OK to press unpeeled cloves, and our tests bore out this assertion. Though the directions for several other presses did not address this issue specifically, we found that the Oxo and the Endurance also handled unpeeled garlic with ease. We did note, however, that the yield of garlic puree was greater across the board when we pressed peeled cloves. While we were at it, we also tried pressing chunks of peeled fresh ginger. The Zyliss, Kuhn Rikon, and Oxo were the only three to excel in this department, and we found that smaller chunks, about ½ inch, were crushed much more easily than larger, 1-inch pieces.

When all was said and pressed, the traditionally designed, moderately priced Zyliss turned out to be comfortable and consistent, and it produced the finest, most even garlic puree. In addition, it handled unpeeled garlic and small chunks of fresh ginger without incident. While other presses got the job done, the Zyliss just edged out the field in terms of both performance and design.

THE BEST GARLIC PRESS

We found that this Zyliss press can handle two cloves at once, producing very finely pureed garlic in a flash.

Place the wrapped garlic on a baking sheet.

3. Roast the garlic until the cloves are soft and the top is golden, 35 to 45 minutes. (You can open the foil packet to check the progress of the garlic but seal it back up if the garlic is not done.) Remove the sealed foil packet from the oven and let cool for 10 minutes. Unwrap the garlic and cool further. When the cloves are cool enough to handle, separate the cloves from the head, and squeeze the cloves onto bread or into a small bowl (if the garlic is to be used in another recipe).

SCIENCE:
Changing Garlic's Flavor

It may seem odd, but the way that garlic is prepared—whether sliced, chopped, or minced—influences the flavor it contributes to a dish. Raw garlic cloves contain a sulfur-based compound called *alliin* and an enzyme called *alliinase*. These two elements are not in contact in raw garlic, which is why a head of garlic has almost no aroma. When the garlic is cut, the enzyme comes into contact with the alliin and converts it to *allicin*, a new and very pungent compound that gives garlic its typical aroma. This compound also gives garlic its bite.

When you slice garlic, only a small amount of the enzyme and the sulfur compound come into contact with each other, so just a small amount of allicin is produced. The result is a mild garlic flavor. When you chop garlic, a bit more allicin is produced and so the garlic flavor is a bit stronger. When you mince garlic, even more allicin is produced because there's more contact between the sulfur compound and the enzyme. More allicin means more aroma and flavor. For the strongest garlic flavor, put the cloves through a press or mince them into a smooth paste.

Because heat breaks down the enzyme alliinase, roasting or toasting garlic cloves before adding them to a dish will pretty much eliminate the development of any harsh garlic flavor.

➤ VARIATION
Roasted Garlic and Sun-Dried Tomato Cream Cheese

MAKES ABOUT 1 CUP

Garlic lovers will like this spread on their bagels or sandwiches.

1	recipe Roasted Garlic
8	ounces cream cheese, softened
2	medium oil-packed sun-dried tomatoes, drained and chopped (about 2 tablespoons)
1	tablespoon minced fresh basil leaves
	Salt and ground black pepper

When the roasted cloves are cool enough to handle, separate the cloves from the head and squeeze the cloves into a medium bowl. Using a fork, mash the garlic into a smooth paste. Add the cream cheese, tomatoes, and basil and mix together thoroughly. Season with salt and pepper to taste. (The spread can be refrigerated in an airtight container for several days.)

CLEANING A GARLIC PRESS

Garlic presses make quick work of garlic but are notoriously hard to clean. Recycle an old toothbrush with a worn brush for this job. The bristles will clear bits of garlic from the press and are easy to rinse clean.

GREEN BEANS

THERE ARE TWO BASIC TREATMENTS FOR GREEN BEANS. IN THE FIRST, THE beans are cooked until crisp-tender, drained, drizzled with oil, seasoned, and served. In the second, they are braised in a covered pan, usually with tomatoes, stock, or cream, until they are extremely tender (some would say overcooked).

For the first method, green beans are boiled or steamed and then sautéed or simply dressed with flavorful ingredients. Sounds simple (and it is), but we still had questions. Is boiling better than steaming? Should beans be cut (either into pieces or lengthwise) before cooking? Should salt be added to the water? How long should beans cook? Should they be refreshed in cold water?

After a number of experiments with boiling and steaming, we came to prefer boiling for several reasons. Steaming takes twice as long as boiling, and when steaming a pound or more of beans, we found it necessary to turn them during cooking because those at the bottom were cooking faster than those at the top of the pile. Finally, boiling cooks each bean more evenly; steamed beans are often tender on the outside but raw tasting in the middle.

Just as important, boiling permits the addition of salt during cooking. The beans need additional salting after they are drained, but adding salt during cooking results in more even seasoning because the salt has time to be absorbed into the beans.

As for preparation, we prefer to tip the tops and tails with our fingers but leave the beans whole otherwise. Cutting the beans into shorter lengths exposes the tender flesh to too much heat. Because the skin cooks more slowly than this exposed flesh, the inside of the beans tends to become mushy. We also are not enthusiastic about "frenching" (see page 132 for details).

Another batch of tests centered around refreshing the beans in cold water. We found that this "tip" advocated by many cookbook authors makes the beans soggy tasting. If you want to use the beans later and need to stop the cooking process, we would suggest spreading the beans out over a baking sheet, an idea we picked up from Alice Waters' *Chez Panisse Vegetables* (HarperCollins, 1996). The beans cool off fairly quickly and do not soften further.

Boiling times vary greatly in the sources we consulted. One respected Italian cookbook author recommends cooking green beans for 20 to 25 minutes. Another suggests 1½ minutes. Could they be writing about the same vegetable?

We found that the freshness and the thickness of the beans greatly affect cooking time.

Really fresh, thin beans, not much thicker than a strand of linguine, may be done in as little as two minutes. Most beans in the supermarket, though, have traveled some distance and are considerably thicker. Due to their age and size, they need five to six minutes to become tender. We don't like mushy green beans, but beans that are too crisp or raw tasting are likewise unappealing.

After boiling and prompt draining, beans may be flavored in two ways. They can be "dressed" (drizzled with a flavorful oil or vinaigrette) or quickly sautéed. If dressing the beans, do so when they are hot for maximum absorption. Beans that will be sautéed can be set aside at room temperature for a few hours. Whether dressing or sautéing beans, use very flavorful ingredients—a drizzle of walnut oil and the addition of toasted walnuts and tarragon, for example, or a quick sauté with onions that have been browned in bacon fat.

The second method for preparing green beans (cook and flavor at the same time) is slower than the first method but allows the beans to absorb flavors as they cook. Tomatoes, cream, or stock can be used as a braising liquid. While the principle is quite simple, we did have a few questions. Could the bright green color be preserved by blanching the beans before braising? And what kind of heat was best—long and slow or fast and furious? Also, how long should the beans be braised so they pick up a good amount of flavor from the braising liquid but still keep some of their original color and texture?

After several attempts at blanching beans before braising (for 30 seconds, one minute, and two minutes), we realized this path was going nowhere. Even short blanching reduced braising time dramatically so the beans didn't spend enough time in the braising pan to pick up flavors. More important, blanching before braising failed to keep the color bright; no matter what we tried, the color of the braised beans faded to an olive green.

As for the cooking time, we found that the beans need at least 15 or 20 minutes to pick up enough flavor to make this method worthwhile. More time (like 45 minutes) added little in terms of flavor but did hurt both color and texture.

As we continued to experiment, we began to realize that the choice between these two distinct methods should be made on the basis of the beans that you are cooking. Really fresh beans are best boiled and seasoned, retaining much of their flavor and texture. But older, tougher beans benefit from slow cooking in a covered pan. The beans will lose some color, but they pick up wonderful flavors from the braising medium.

Natural variations in the size and quality of the beans make a real difference, so it's worthwhile to keep a few points in mind while shopping. A green bean is a legume that is harvested when the pod is tender and the seeds are immature. However, there are times when the beans are harvested too late. Very thick pods swollen with not-so-immature seeds should be avoided. They do

TRIMMING ENDS FROM GREEN BEANS

Instead of trimming the end from one green bean at a time, line up the beans on a cutting board and trim all the ends with just one slice.

not possess the gentle sweetness we associate with good green beans and can remain tough and chewy after cooking. Also, spend some time choosing pods that are fairly uniform in size. Thickness determines cooking time, so this is important.

The two cooking methods just outlined can be used with regular green beans. Haricots verts—very thin green beans—should be boiled and then flavored. Two to three minutes in boiling water will make these beans tender. The sweet flavor and delicate texture of these beans make them ill suited to braising.

EQUIPMENT: Bean Slicers

As best we can tell, "frenching" (cutting thick beans in half lengthwise) is supposed to turn thick green beans into delicate haricots verts. Or at least several cookbooks mention "frenching" as a method of making haricots verts at half the price.

To do this, each bean must be sliced lengthwise with a small knife or with a gadget like a bean slicer. A knife is very tedious for this task and self-inflicted wounds are a real possibility. A bean slicer works better, but we must say we don't get the point.

A bean slicer has a sharp stationary blade in the top loop for cutting the top and tail of the bean. However, each bean must be inserted, one at a time, into the loop and forced down against the blade to remove the end. It's faster to squeeze off the top and tail with your fingers or to cut a whole row of beans on a cutting board at one time.

For frenching, each bean must be inserted into the funnel-like hole and then forced through several sharp blades, which yield several (not two) thin strips per green bean. Although this method beats working with a knife, the bean slicer doesn't make a real haricot vert.

The pods on real haricots verts completely encase the flesh and prevent the insides from overcooking. Frenched beans will always cook unevenly because the slower-to-soften skin and the flesh are both exposed.

Master Recipe for Blanched Green Beans
SERVES 4

Add some chopped toasted nuts, diced tomatoes, or sautéed bacon and onions to jazz up the beans.

1	teaspoon salt
1	pound green beans, ends trimmed (see the illustration on page 131)
1	tablespoon extra-virgin olive oil
1	tablespoon minced fresh basil, tarragon, or parsley leaves

Bring 2½ quarts of water to a boil in a large saucepan over high heat. Add the salt and beans and cook until tender, about 5 minutes. Drain the beans well and transfer them to a bowl. Toss with the oil and herb and serve immediately.

➤ VARIATIONS
Green Beans with Quatre Épices

Quatre épices is a classic French blend of four spices. There is no set recipe or combination, but it is usually made from any four of the following: ginger, cloves, black or white pepper, nutmeg, cinnamon, or allspice.

1	teaspoon salt, plus more to taste
1	pound green beans, ends trimmed (see the illustration on page 131)
2	tablespoons unsalted butter
¼	teaspoon ground black pepper
⅛	teaspoon ground cloves
¼	teaspoon ground nutmeg
¼	teaspoon ground ginger
3	tablespoons heavy cream

1. Bring 2½ quarts of water to a boil in a large saucepan over high heat. Add the salt and beans and cook until tender, about 5 minutes. Drain the beans well.

2. Melt the butter in a 12-inch skillet over medium-high heat. When the foaming subsides, add the spices and cook, stirring frequently, until fragrant, about 30 seconds. Add the cream and the beans and cook until heated through, about 1 minute. Season to taste with salt and serve immediately.

Green Beans with Sautéed Shallots and Vermouth

See below for information about buying vermouth.

- 1 teaspoon salt, plus more to taste
- 1 pound green beans, ends trimmed (see the illustration on page 131)
- 4 tablespoons unsalted butter
- 4 large shallots, sliced thin (about 2 cups)
- 2 tablespoons dry vermouth
  Ground black pepper

1. Bring 2 ½ quarts of water to a boil in a large saucepan over high heat. Add the salt and beans and cook until tender, about 5 minutes. Drain the beans well.

2. Meanwhile, heat 2 tablespoons of the butter in a 12-inch skillet over medium heat. When the foaming subsides, add the shallots and cook, stirring often, until golden brown and just crisp around the edges, about 10 minutes. Add the vermouth and bring to a simmer. Whisk in the remaining 2 tablespoons butter, 1 tablespoon at a time. Add the beans and toss to combine. Season with salt and pepper to taste and serve immediately.

INGREDIENTS: Vermouth

Though it's often used in cooking, and even more often in martinis, dry vermouth is a potable that is paid very little attention. Imagine our surprise, then, when we did a little research and turned up nearly a dozen different brands. We pared them down to eight and tasted the vermouths straight (chilled) and in simple pan sauces (containing only shallots, chicken broth, and butter in addition to the vermouth).

First, a quick description of what dry vermouth is: Its base is a white wine, presumably not of particularly high quality, as evidenced by the relatively low prices of most vermouths. The wine is fortified with neutral grape spirits, which hike the alcohol level up a few percentage points to between 16 and 18 percent, and it is "aromatized" or infused with "botanicals," such as herbs, spices, and fruits. In this country, dry vermouth, also called extra-dry vermouth, is imported from France and Italy (Italian vermouths being most common here) or is made domestically in California.

Two vermouths found their way into the top three in both tastings: Gallo Extra Dry and Noilly Prat Original French Dry. Gallo is the fruitier of the two and made the favorite pan sauce, which tasters called balanced, complex, smooth, and round. Noilly Prat is more woodsy and herbaceous and made a pan sauce that tasted fresh and balanced.

THE BEST VERMOUTHS

Gallo Extra Dry Vermouth (left) has floral and fruity flavors, with hints of melons and apples and was tied for first place in our tasting of eight leading brands. Noilly Prat Original French Dry Vermouth (right) was the other top choice. Tasters described it as honeyed, herbaceous, and woodsy, with faint anise notes and a subtle bitterness.

EQUIPMENT: Large Saucepans

When blanching vegetables, we reach for a 3- to 4-quart saucepan. Which begs an obvious question: Does the brand of pan matter? With prices for these large saucepans ranging from $24.99 for a Revere stainless-steel model with thin copper cladding at the base up to $140 for an All-Clad pan with a complete aluminum core and stainless-steel interior and exterior cladding, a lot of money is riding on the answer. To offer guidance, we tested eight models, all between 3 and 4 quarts in size, from well-known cookware manufacturers.

The tests we performed were based on common cooking tasks and designed to highlight specific characteristics of the pans' performance. Sautéing minced onions illustrated the pace at which the pan heats up and sautés. Cooking white rice provided a good indication of the pan's ability to heat evenly as well as how tightly the lid sealed. Making pastry cream let us know how user-friendly the pan was—was it shaped such that a whisk reached into the corners without trouble, was it comfortable to pick up, and could we pour liquid from it neatly? These traits can make a real difference when you use a pan day in and day out.

Of the tests we performed, sautéing onions was the most telling. In our view, onions should soften reliably and evenly (and with minimal attention and stirring) when sautéed over medium heat. In this regard, the All-Clad, Calphalon, KitchenAid, and Sitram pans all delivered. The Chantal and Cuisinart pans sautéed slightly faster, necessitating a little more attention from the cook, but still well within acceptable bounds. Only the Revere and Farberware Millennium sautéed so fast that we considered them problematic.

Incidentally, the Revere and Farberware pans that sautéed onions too fast for us were the lightest pans of the bunch, weighing only 1 pound, 10 ounces and 2 pounds, 6 ounces, respectively. This indicates that they were made from thinner metal, which is one reason they heat quickly. On the flip side of the weight issue, however, we found that too heavy a pan, such as the 4-pound Calphalon, could be uncomfortable to lift when full. We felt that around $3\frac{1}{2}$ pounds was the ideal weight; pans near this weight, including the All-Clad, KitchenAid, Chantal, Sitram, and Cuisinart, balanced good heft with easy maneuverability.

While none of the pans failed the rice test outright, there were performance differences. In the Sitram, Revere, and Farberware pans, the rice stuck and dried out at the bottom, if only a little bit. Although this did not greatly affect the texture, the flavor, or the cleanup, we'd still choose a pan for which this was not an issue.

Every pan in the group turned out perfect pastry cream. During this test, we did observe one design element that made it easy to pour liquid from the pan neatly, without dribbles and spills. A rolled lip that flares slightly at the top of the pan helped control the pour. Only two pans in the group did not have a rolled lip: the All-Clad and the Calphalon.

So which pan do you want to buy? That depends largely on two things: your budget and your attention as a cook. Based on our tests, we'd advise against really inexpensive pans (those that cost less than $50). For between $50 and $100, you can get a competent pan such as the Chantal, Sitram, or Cuisinart. The only caveat is that you may have to watch them carefully; they offer less room for error than our favorite pans, made by All-Clad, Calphalon, and KitchenAid.

THE BEST SAUCEPANS

The All-Clad (left), Calphalon (center), and KitchenAid (right) saucepans are our favorites, but they are not flawless. The Calphalon ($110) is heavy, both it and the All-Clad pan ($140) lack rolled lips, and the KitchenAid pan ($119) has a relatively short curved handle. However, these three pans provide moderate, steady heat, even when you are distracted.

Green Beans with Garlic

The green beans served in Chinese restaurants are actually Chinese long beans. They have a flavor similar to green beans and can grow up to 3 feet in length. Green beans make a perfectly fine substitute and are much more readily available. Because the beans are cooked in the skillet with the seasonings for some time, the blanching time should be reduced.

1	teaspoon salt, plus more to taste
1	pound green beans, ends trimmed (see the illustration on page 131)
3	teaspoons vegetable oil
3	medium cloves garlic, minced or pressed through a garlic press
1	teaspoon minced fresh ginger
1/4	teaspoon hot red pepper flakes
1	tablespoon soy sauce

1. Bring 2 1/2 quarts of water to a boil in a large saucepan over high heat. Add the salt and beans and cook until crisp-tender, 3 to 4 minutes. Drain the beans well.

2. Heat 2 teaspoons of the oil in a 12-inch nonstick skillet over high heat until almost smoking. Add the beans and cook, stirring frequently, until the beans are spotty brown, about 2 minutes. Clear a space in the center of the pan and add the garlic, ginger, and pepper flakes. Drizzle the remaining 1 teaspoon oil over the aromatics. Cook, stirring frequently, until fragrant, about 15 seconds. Add the soy sauce, mix together, and serve immediately.

Green Beans with Buttered Bread Crumbs and Almonds

1	slice high-quality white bread, crust removed and torn into rough 1 1/2-inch pieces
2	tablespoons sliced almonds, crumbled by hand into 1/4-inch pieces
2	medium cloves garlic, minced or pressed through a garlic press
2	teaspoons chopped fresh parsley leaves Salt and ground black pepper
1	pound green beans, ends trimmed (see the illustration on page 131)
4	tablespoons unsalted butter

1. Process the bread in the workbowl of a food processor until even and fine textured, 20 to 30 seconds. (You should have about 1/4 cup fresh bread crumbs.) Transfer the crumbs to a dry 10-inch nonstick skillet, add the almonds, and toast over medium-high heat, stirring constantly, until golden brown, about 5 minutes. Off the heat, stir in the garlic and parsley and season with salt and pepper to taste. Set the crumbs aside but do not wash the skillet.

2. Bring 2 1/2 quarts of water to a boil in a large saucepan over high heat. Add 1 teaspoon salt and the beans and cook until tender, about 5 minutes. Drain the beans well and arrange them on a serving platter.

3. As the beans cook, melt the butter over medium-high heat in the same skillet used to toast the crumbs. When the foam subsides, add the bread crumb mixture and heat, stirring frequently, until fragrant, 1 to 2 minutes. Spoon the buttered bread crumb mixture over the beans and serve immediately.

Master Recipe for Braised Green Beans

SERVES 4

Here's a way to use older, end-of-season green beans.

1	tablespoon extra-virgin olive oil
1	medium shallot, minced
1/2	teaspoon minced fresh thyme leaves
1	pound green beans, ends trimmed (see the illustration on page 131)

¾ cup low-sodium chicken broth
Salt and ground black pepper

Heat the oil in a large sauté pan over medium heat until almost smoking. Add the shallot and cook until golden, about 5 minutes. Add the thyme, beans, and broth. Stir, cover, and reduce the heat to low. Simmer, stirring occasionally, until the beans are tender but still offer some resistance to the bite, 15 to 20 minutes. Season to taste with salt and pepper and serve immediately.

➤ VARIATIONS
Green Beans Braised in Tomatoes

This Italian recipe uses a simple tomato sauce flavored with onions and garlic as the braising medium. Add the parsley (or some basil) at the end of cooking for extra color.

2 tablespoons extra-virgin olive oil
I small onion, diced
2 medium cloves garlic, minced or pressed through a garlic press
I cup diced canned tomatoes
I pound green beans, ends trimmed (see the illustration on page 131)
Salt and ground black pepper
2 tablespoons minced fresh parsley leaves

1. Heat the oil in a large sauté pan over medium heat until almost smoking. Add the onion and cook until softened, about 5 minutes. Add the garlic and cook until fragrant, about 1 minute. Add the tomatoes and simmer until the juices thicken slightly, about 5 minutes.

2. Add the beans, ¼ teaspoon salt, and pepper to taste. Stir, cover, and cook, stirring occasionally, until beans are tender but offer some resistance to the bite, about 20 minutes. Stir in the parsley and adjust the seasonings, adding salt and pepper to taste. Serve immediately.

Green Beans Braised with Shiitake Mushrooms

Dried shiitakes have a fabulous earthy, smoky flavor. They are often used in Japanese cooking to flavor soups. You can find them in the Asian food section of most large grocery stores. See page 36 for tips on rehydrating dried mushrooms.

½ ounce dried shiitakes (about 6 small or 4 medium caps)
I tablespoon soy sauce
I teaspoon sugar
I teaspoon vegetable oil
I teaspoon finely minced or grated fresh ginger
I pound green beans, ends trimmed (see the illustration on page 131)
Salt and ground black pepper

1. Place the shiitakes in a medium bowl. Add 1 cup boiling water, cover the bowl with plastic wrap, and let the shiitakes steep for 5 minutes. Remove the shiitakes from the water (reserving the liquid), let cool, remove and discard the stems, and dice the shiitake caps. Strain the soaking liquid through a sieve lined with a paper towel. Add the soy sauce and sugar to the shiitake liquid. Set aside.

2. Heat the oil in a large sauté pan over medium-high heat until almost smoking. Add the ginger and cook until fragrant, about 30 seconds. Add the beans, shiitakes, and the shiitake broth. Stir, cover, and reduce the heat to low. Simmer, stirring occasionally, until the beans are tender but still offer some resistance to the bite, 15 to 20 minutes. Season to taste with salt and pepper and serve immediately.

GREENS

MANY COOKS THINK THEY CAN TREAT ALL LEAFY GREENS THE SAME WAY, even though some are delicate enough for salads while others seem as tough as shoe leather. After cleaning, stemming, and cooking more than 100 pounds of leafy greens, we found that they fell into two categories, each of which is handled quite differently.

Spinach (which is also good in salads; see page 282), beet greens, and Swiss chard are tender and rich in moisture. They require no additional liquid during cooking. They taste of the earth and minerals but are still rather delicate. Kale and mustard, turnip, and collard greens are tougher and require the addition of some

liquid as they cook. Their flavor is much more assertive, even peppery in some cases, and can be overwhelming.

We tested boiling, steaming, and sautéing tender greens. Boiling produced the most brilliantly colored greens, but they were also very mushy and bland. The water cooked out all their flavor and texture. Steamed greens were less mushy, but clearly these tender greens did not need any liquid. Damp greens that were tossed into hot oil (which could be flavored with aromatics and spices) wilted in just two or three minutes in a covered pan. Once they wilted, we found it best to remove the lid so the liquid in the pan would evaporate. This method has the advantage of flavoring the greens as they cook.

Tougher greens don't have enough moisture to be wilted in a hot pan; they scorch before they wilt. Steaming these greens produces a better texture but does nothing to tame their bitter flavor. Oddly, it turned them

an unattractive jaundice green. It was clear to everyone in the test kitchen that tough greens benefit from cooking in some water, which will wash away some of their harsh notes.

We tested boiling 2 pounds of greens in either an abundant quantity of salted water or what might be called shallow-blanching in several cups of salted water. Greens blanched in larger quantities of salted water had a lot going for them. They were tender, brilliantly colored, and less bitter than those cooked by other methods; also the salt rounded out their flavor. However, blanching greens this way was not ideal. Once boiled, drained, rinsed, and squeezed, the greens had lost much of their individual character and tasted rather pallid. Cooking the greens in lots of water diluted their flavor too much.

So we tried cooking these assertive greens in small quantities of water. We started by cooking leaves from 1 pound of greens in 1 cup of salted water, checking at five and then again at seven minutes. The five-minute leaves had a sharp, raw bite and were starting to acquire that dull look. The seven-minute greens were fully cooked but still tasted bitter. We decided to double the water from 1 to 2 cups. The greens cooked in this quantity of water weren't as grossly bitter as those cooked in only 1 cup of liquid, but they were still a bit too bold. On the verge of settling for conventional blanching, we gave this shallow-cook method one more shot, by once again doubling the water from 2 cups to 1 quart and cooking the greens the full seven minutes. The resulting greens offered the perfect balance we wanted: good color, full flavor without bitterness, and tenderness. They were ready for a quick, final cooking to unite them with other flavorful ingredients.

When you think about it, it stands to reason that a shallow blanch would work best with assertive greens. The more water you use when blanching porous vegetables, the more diluted the flavor of the vegetables becomes. That's one reason why steaming is the preferred way to cook so many vegetables—you want as little of the flavor as possible to escape into the cooking liquid. Assertive greens are different. You want to rid them of some of the bitterness, but not all of it. A shallow blanching erases enough bitterness to make these greens palatable but not so much as to rob them of their character.

Shallow blanching not only preserves the greens' color and flavor but also saves time. We were surprised to learn that a gallon of water takes almost 20 minutes to boil. Two quarts (the amount you need to cook greens for four) can be brought to a boil in half the time.

We found that cut leaves cook faster than whole ones, but the leaves are much easier to cut when cooked. Tediously stacking 2 pounds of leaves in batches, rolling them up like big cigars, and cutting them into ribbons seemed a waste of time when the same leaves boiled down to just 2 cups seven minutes later. We found it simpler to rough-chop them before blanching. Then, after blanching, it was easy to cut the dramatically shrunken greens as fine as we liked. Once the blanched greens have been cut, they can be quickly cooked with seasonings.

PREPARING LEAFY GREENS

SWISS CHARD, KALE, COLLARDS, AND MUSTARD GREENS
To prepare Swiss chard, kale, collards, and mustard greens, hold each leaf at the base of the stem over a bowl filled with water and use a sharp knife to slash the leafy portion from either side of the thick stem.

TURNIP GREENS
1. Turnip greens are most easily stemmed by grasping the leaf between your thumb and index finger at the base of the stem and stripping it off by hand.
2. When using this method, the very tip of the stem will break off along with the leaves. It is tender enough to cook along with the leaves.

Master Recipe for Sautéed Tender Greens

SERVES 4

To stem spinach and beet greens, simply pinch off the leaves where they meet the stems. A thick stalk runs through each Swiss chard leaf, so it must be handled differently; see the illustration on page 138 for information on this technique. A large, deep Dutch oven or soup kettle is best for this recipe. The greens should be moist but not soaking wet when they go into the pot.

3	tablespoons extra-virgin olive oil
2	medium cloves garlic, minced or pressed through a garlic press
2	pounds damp tender greens, such as spinach, beet greens, or Swiss chard; stemmed, washed in several changes of cold water, shaken to remove excess water, and coarsely chopped
	Salt and ground black pepper
	Lemon wedges (optional)

Heat the oil and garlic in a Dutch oven or other deep pot over medium-high heat until the garlic sizzles and turns golden, 1 to 2 minutes. Add the wet greens, cover, and cook, stirring occasionally, until the greens completely wilt, 2 to 3 minutes. Uncover and season with salt and pepper to taste. Raise the heat to high and cook until the liquid evaporates, 2 to 3 minutes. Serve immediately (with lemon wedges, if using).

➤ VARIATIONS

Sautéed Tender Greens with Pine Nuts and Currants

Raisins (either black or yellow) can be used in place of the currants.

3	tablespoons extra-virgin olive oil
1	medium clove garlic, minced or pressed through a garlic press
¼	cup pine nuts, chopped coarse
2	tablespoons currants
2	pounds damp tender greens, such as spinach, beet greens, or Swiss chard; stemmed, washed in several changes of cold water, shaken to remove excess water, and coarsely chopped
	Salt and ground black pepper

Heat the oil, garlic, and pine nuts in a Dutch oven or other deep pot over medium-high heat until the garlic and nuts sizzle and turn golden, 1 to 2 minutes. Add the currants and wet greens, cover, and cook, stirring occasionally, until the greens completely wilt, 2 to 3 minutes. Uncover and season with salt and pepper to taste. Raise the heat to high and cook until the liquid evaporates, 2 to 3 minutes. Serve immediately.

Sautéed Tender Greens with Cumin, Tomatoes, and Cilantro

Indian flavors enliven greens in this simple recipe. See page 294 for information about seeding plum tomatoes.

DRAINING LEAFY GREENS

Many recipes for greens recommend adding the greens to the cooking pot with a little water from their washing still clinging to their leaves. To keep the damp leaves from turning your work surface into a watery mess, let them drain in an empty dish rack next to the sink.

3 tablespoons vegetable or canola oil
1 small onion, minced
2 medium cloves garlic, minced or
   pressed through a garlic press
1 medium jalapeño chile, stemmed,
   seeded, and minced
1 1/2 teaspoons ground cumin
2 large plum tomatoes, cored,
   seeded, and chopped
2 pounds damp tender greens, such as
   spinach, beet greens, or Swiss chard;
   stemmed, washed in several changes
   of cold water, shaken to remove
   excess water, and coarsely chopped
2 tablespoons minced fresh cilantro leaves
   Salt and ground black pepper
   Lime wedges (optional)

Heat the oil and onion in a Dutch oven or other deep pot over medium–high heat until the onion sizzles and softens, about 2 minutes. Add the garlic, chile, and cumin and cook until fragrant, about 1 minute. Add the tomatoes and cook until they release their juices, about 1 minute. Add the wet greens, cover, and cook, stirring occasionally, until the greens completely wilt, 2 to 3 minutes. Uncover, stir in the cilantro, and season with salt and pepper to taste. Raise the heat to high and cook until the liquid evaporates, 2 to 3 minutes. Serve immediately (with lime wedges, if using).

Sautéed Tender Greens with Mustard and Pecans

For best results, use grainy mustard. If it is unavailable, regular Dijon mustard can be substituted.

1/4 cup chopped pecans
1 tablespoon grainy mustard
1 teaspoon light or dark brown sugar
3 tablespoons extra-virgin olive oil
1 medium shallot, minced

2 pounds damp tender greens,
   such as spinach, beet greens, or
   Swiss chard; stemmed, washed in
   several changes of cold water,
   shaken to remove excess water,
   and coarsely chopped
   Salt and ground black pepper

1. Toast the pecans in a dry skillet over medium heat until fragrant, about 4 minutes. Set aside.

2. Mix the mustard, brown sugar, and 2 tablespoons water together in a small bowl. Set aside.

3. Heat the oil and shallot in a Dutch oven or other deep pot over medium-high heat until the shallot sizzles and turns golden, about 2 minutes. Add the wet greens and mustard mixture, cover, and cook, stirring occasionally, until the greens completely wilt, 2 to 3 minutes. Uncover and season with salt and pepper to taste. Raise the heat to high, and cook until the liquid evaporates, 2 to 3 minutes. Garnish with the toasted pecans and serve immediately.

Sautéed Tender Greens with Bacon and Red Onion

This dish also makes a great filling for omelets.

2 ounces (about 2 slices) bacon, cut
   crosswise into 1/2-inch strips
1/2 small red onion, minced
1 medium clove garlic, minced or
   pressed through a garlic press
1/2 teaspoon minced fresh thyme leaves
2 pounds damp tender greens,
   such as spinach, beet greens, or
   Swiss chard; stemmed, washed in
   several changes of cold water,
   shaken to remove excess water,
   and coarsely chopped
   Salt and ground black pepper

1. Cook the bacon in a Dutch oven or other deep pot over medium heat until the bacon is crisp, about 5 minutes. Use a slotted spoon to transfer the bacon to a plate lined with paper towels, leaving the bacon drippings in the pot.

2. Raise the heat to medium-high. Add the onion to the drippings and cook, stirring frequently, until golden brown, about 3 minutes. Stir in the garlic and cook until fragrant, about 1 minute longer. Add the thyme and wet greens, cover, and cook, stirring occasionally, until the greens completely wilt, 2 to 3 minutes. Uncover and season with salt and pepper to taste. Raise the heat to high and cook until the liquid evaporates, 2 to 3 minutes. Garnish with the reserved bacon and serve immediately.

Sautéed Tender Greens with Caramelized Onions and Dried Apricots

Adding sugar to the onions speeds their cooking time and balances the sherry vinegar in this recipe.

I	tablespoon extra-virgin olive oil
I	tablespoon unsalted butter
I	large onion, chopped fine
I	teaspoon sugar
2	medium cloves garlic, minced or pressed through a garlic press
2	medium anchovy fillets, minced
1/4	cup chopped dried apricots
I	tablespoon sherry vinegar
2	pounds damp tender greens, such as spinach, beet greens, or Swiss chard; stemmed, washed in several changes of cold water, shaken to remove excess water, and coarsely chopped
	Salt and ground black pepper

Heat the oil and butter in a Dutch oven or other deep pot over medium heat. When the foaming subsides, add the onion and sugar and cook, stirring often, until the onion is soft and golden, about 10 minutes. Add the garlic and anchovies and cook, mashing the anchovies to a paste with a wooden spoon, until fragrant, about 1 minute. Stir in the apricots, vinegar, and wet greens. Raise the heat to medium-high, cover, and cook, stirring occasionally, until the greens completely wilt, 2 to 3 minutes. Uncover and season with salt and pepper to taste. Raise the heat to high and cook until the liquid evaporates, 2 to 3 minutes. Serve immediately.

Master Recipe for Blanched Assertive Greens

MAKES ABOUT 2 CUPS

Once the greens have been blanched and drained, they can be used in any of the recipes that follow.

I 1/2	teaspoons salt
2	pounds assertive greens, such as kale, collards, mustard, or turnip greens; stemmed, washed in several changes of cold water, and coarsely chopped

Bring 2 quarts of water to a boil in a Dutch oven or other deep pot. Add the salt and greens and stir until wilted. Cover and cook until the greens are just tender, about 7 minutes. Drain in a colander. Rinse the Dutch oven or pot with cold water to cool and then refill with cold water. Pour the greens into the cold water to stop the cooking process. Gather a handful of greens, lift out of the water, and squeeze dry. Repeat with the remaining greens. Roughly cut each bunch of greens and proceed with one of the following recipes.

Assertive Greens with Bacon and Onion

SERVES 4

The strong flavors of bacon and sautéed onions are a good match with the greens.

2   ounces (about 2 slices) bacon, cut crosswise into thin strips
    Vegetable oil
1/2 medium onion, chopped fine

2   medium cloves garlic, minced or pressed through a garlic press
1   recipe Blanched Assertive Greens
1/4 cup low-sodium chicken broth
2   teaspoons cider vinegar
    Salt

1. Fry the bacon in a large sauté pan over medium heat until crisp, about 5 minutes. Use a slotted spoon to transfer the bacon to a plate lined with paper towels, leaving the bacon drippings in the pan.

2. If necessary, add oil to the bacon drippings in the pan to make 2 tablespoons. Add the onion and cook until softened, about 3 minutes. Add the garlic and cook until fragrant, about 30 seconds. Add the greens and stir to coat them with the fat. Add the broth, cover, and cook until the greens are heated through, about 2 minutes. If any excess liquid remains, remove the lid and continue to simmer until the liquid has thickened slightly, about 1 minute longer. Sprinkle the greens with the vinegar and bacon bits and season with salt to taste. Serve immediately.

DRAINING BLANCHED GREENS

Assertive greens should be blanched, drained, and then sautéed with seasonings. After blanching, it's important to squeeze out as much water as possible. Here's an unusual but quick way to accomplish this task.

1. Instead of squeezing the greens by hand, place them in the hopper of a potato ricer.

2. Close the handle and squeeze the water from the greens. Don't squeeze harder than is necessary or you might puree the greens.

Assertive Greens with Kielbasa

SERVES 4

Kielbasa is a smoked Polish sausage usually made from pork or a combination of pork and beef. Its mildness complements the slightly bitter flavor of the greens.

2   tablespoons unsalted butter
4   ounces kielbasa, cut into 1/2 -inch dice
1   recipe Blanched Assertive Greens
1/4 cup low-sodium chicken broth
1/2 teaspoon sugar
    Salt and ground black pepper

Melt the butter in a large sauté pan over medium-high heat. When the foaming

EQUIPMENT: Dutch Ovens

We find that a Dutch oven (also called a lidded casserole) is almost essential to making stews and braises. It's also ideal for wilting large quantities of greens or frying. A Dutch oven is nothing more than a wide, deep pot with a cover. It was originally manufactured with "ears" on the side (small, round tabs used to pick up the pot) and a top that had a lip around the edge. The latter design element was important because a Dutch oven was heated through coals placed both underneath and on top of the pot. The lip kept the coals on the lid from falling off. One could bake biscuits, cobblers, beans, and stews in this pot. It was, in the full sense of the word, an oven. And this "oven" was a key feature of chuck wagons and essential in many Colonial American households, where all cooking occurred in the fireplace. This useful pot supposedly came to be called "Dutch" because at some point the best cast iron came from Holland.

Now that everyone in America has an oven, the Dutch oven is no longer used to bake biscuits or cobblers. However, it is essential for dishes that start on top of the stove and finish in the oven, like many stews. To make some recommendations about buying a modern Dutch oven, we tested 12 models from leading makers of cookware.

We found that a Dutch oven should have a capacity of at least 6 quarts to be useful. Eight quarts is even better. As we cooked in the pots, we came to prefer wider, shallower Dutch ovens because it's easier to see and reach inside them, and they offer more bottom surface area to accommodate larger batches of meat for browning. This reduces the number of batches required to brown a given quantity of meat and, with it, the chances of burning the flavorful pan drippings. Ideally, a Dutch oven should have a diameter twice as wide as its height.

We also preferred pots with a light-colored interior finish, such as stainless steel or enameled cast iron. It is easier to judge the caramelization of the drippings at a glance in these pots. Dark finishes can mask the color of the drippings, which may burn before you realize it. Our favorite pots are the 8-quart All-Clad Stainless Stockpot (despite the name, this pot is a Dutch oven) and the 7-quart Le Creuset Round French Oven, which is made of enameled cast iron. These pots are quite expensive, costing at least $150, even when on sale. A less expensive alternative is the 7-quart Lodge Dutch Oven, which is made from cast iron. This pot is extremely heavy (making it a bit hard to maneuver), it must be seasoned (wiped with oil) regularly, and the dark interior finish is not ideal, but it does brown food quite well and costs just $45.

THE BEST DUTCH OVENS

Our favorite Dutch ovens are the 8-quart All-Clad Stainless Stockpot (top) and the 7-quart Le Creuset Round French Oven (center). A much less expensive alternative is the 7-quart Lodge Dutch Oven (bottom).

subsides, add the kielbasa and cook, stirring occasionally, until browned, about 3 minutes. Add the greens and stir to coat them with the fat. Stir in the broth and sugar, cover, and cook until the greens are heated through, about 2 minutes. If any excess liquid remains, remove the lid and continue to simmer until the liquid has thickened slightly, about 1 minute longer. Season with salt and pepper to taste and serve immediately.

Assertive Greens with Shallots and Cream

SERVES 4

The sweetness of the shallots and the richness of the cream mellow the bitterness of the greens.

2	tablespoons unsalted butter
2	medium shallots, chopped fine
1	recipe Blanched Assertive Greens
1/4	cup heavy cream
1/2	teaspoon sugar
1/2	teaspoon minced fresh thyme leaves
1/8	teaspoon ground nutmeg
	Salt and ground black pepper

Melt the butter in a large sauté pan over medium heat. When the foaming subsides, add the shallots and cook, stirring frequently, until golden brown, 3 to 4 minutes. Add the greens and stir to coat them with the fat. Stir in the cream, sugar, thyme, and nutmeg. Cover and cook until the greens are heated through, about 2 minutes. If any excess liquid remains, remove the lid and continue to simmer until the cream has thickened slightly, about 1 minute longer. Season with salt and pepper to taste and serve immediately.

Assertive Greens with Honey Mustard Sauce

SERVES 4

Serve this dish with German sausages and boiled potatoes for a hearty dinner.

1 1/2	tablespoons Dijon or grainy mustard
1	tablespoon honey
1/4	cup low-sodium chicken broth
2	tablespoons unsalted butter
1	medium clove garlic, minced or pressed through a garlic press
1	recipe Blanched Assertive Greens
	Salt and ground black pepper

1. Mix the mustard, honey, and broth together in a small bowl.

2. Heat the butter in a large sauté pan over medium heat. When the foaming subsides, add the garlic and cook until the garlic is fragrant and starts to sizzle, about 1 minute. Add the greens and stir to coat them with the fat. Stir in the mustard mixture. Cover and cook until the greens are heated through, about 2 minutes. If any excess liquid remains, remove the lid and continue to simmer until the liquid has thickened slightly, about 1 minute longer. Season with salt and pepper to taste and serve immediately.

KOHLRABI

KOHLRABI IS A PALE-GREEN BULB THAT RESEMBLES A TURNIP IN APPEAR-ance and a broccoli stalk in flavor. When the thick stalks and leafy greens are attached (as is the case at many farmers' markets), kohlrabi is quite striking (and hard to miss). This vegetable is commonly used in Eastern European cuisine. Although kohlrabi may not be a staple in most American kitchens, its mellow, slightly sweet flavor should make it a household favorite.

If you buy kohlrabi with the stalks and leaves attached, trim them. The bulb, which is actually a swollen portion of the stalks, is the part of the plant that is usually cooked. Smaller bulbs (the size of an orange) are sweeter and more tender than larger bulbs (the size of a grapefruit), which can be woody or spongy.

Once the stalks and leaves have been trimmed, the thick skin on the bulb must be peeled. A paring knife (rather than a vegetable peeler) is the best tool for this task. After the kohlrabi has been peeled, it can be cut into bite-size chunks and cooked.

Our goal was to find the best cooking method. Although some sources suggest blanching or steaming kohlrabi, we found that these cooking methods made the kohlrabi bland and soggy. It also didn't stand up well to the high heat of stir-frying (by the time the inside was done, the outside was almost burnt).

Roasting the kohlrabi proved to be the best (and simplest) solution. A fairly hot oven (450 degrees) browns the kohlrabi, and ¾-inch pieces cook in just 30 minutes. As the kohlrabi roasts, make sure to shake the pan once or twice to encourage even browning.

Occasionally, we encountered problems with pieces of kohlrabi sticking to the pan. More oil just made the kohlrabi greasy, but lining the baking sheet with foil solved the problem.

Since kohlrabi has such a mild flavor, we found it best to keep the seasonings simple. Extra-virgin olive oil, salt, and pepper are sufficient, although slightly more complex (but not aggressive) combinations are also possible.

Master Recipe for Roasted Kohlrabi

SERVES 4

When peeling the kohlrabi, make sure to remove the outer ⅛ inch of the vegetable, so that the skin and fibrous green parts are removed and only the pale flesh remains.

3 medium kohlrabi bulbs (about
   1 ½ pounds), peeled and cut
   into ¾-inch cubes

2 tablespoons extra-virgin olive oil
Salt and ground black pepper
1 tablespoon minced fresh
parsley leaves

1. Adjust an oven rack to the middle position and heat the oven to 450 degrees.

2. Toss the kohlrabi, oil, and salt and pepper to taste together in a large bowl until combined. Spread the kohlrabi onto a foil-lined rimmed baking sheet in a single layer. Roast, shaking the pan occasionally, until the kohlrabi is browned and tender, about 30 minutes.

3. Transfer the kohlrabi to a bowl, sprinkle with the parsley, and adjust the seasonings, adding salt and pepper to taste. Serve immediately.

➤ VARIATION

Roasted Kohlrabi with Crunchy Seeds

Seeds are usually toasted before being included in a dish. The high heat of the oven eliminates that step in this recipe. See the illustrations below for tips on chopping fennel seeds.

3 medium kohlrabi bulbs (about
1 ½ pounds), peeled and cut
into ¾-inch cubes
2 tablespoons extra-virgin olive oil
2 teaspoons sesame seeds
1 teaspoon poppy seeds
½ teaspoon fennel seeds, coarsely chopped
Salt and ground black pepper

1. Adjust an oven rack to the middle position and heat the oven to 450 degrees.

2. Toss the kohlrabi, oil, seeds, and salt and pepper to taste together in a large bowl until combined. Spread the kohlrabi onto a foil-lined rimmed baking sheet in a single layer. Roast, shaking the pan occasionally, until the kohlrabi is browned and tender, about 30 minutes.

3. Transfer the kohlrabi to a bowl and adjust the seasonings, adding salt and pepper to taste. Serve immediately.

CHOPPING FENNEL SEEDS

Small, hard seeds like fennel (and cumin) are seemingly impossible to chop because they scatter all over the counter when you bear down on them. Here's how to overcome this problem.

1. Place the measured seeds in a small pile on a cutting board. Pour just enough water or oil on the seeds to moisten them.

2. The seeds can now be chopped with a chef's knife and will not fly all over the kitchen.

LEEKS

THE UNIQUE, ONION-LIKE SWEETNESS OF LEEKS MAKES THEM A DELICIOUS vegetable side dish, equally good whether served hot or cold. Leeks come in all sizes, but in most stores they are bundled together without regard for this. To ensure even cooking times, make your own bundles of same size leeks. In our testing, we didn't find any difference between larger and smaller leeks, in either taste or texture. As long as the leeks are firm and have sprightly, unblemished leaves, bulbs 2 inches in diameter should be just as tender as smaller ones only ½ inch thick. Try to buy the leeks with the longest white stems, since you get more usable, tender parts that way. The white parts can vary from 4 inches long up to 8 inches long.

Some supermarkets sell leeks trimmed down to the lighter base part. At first, this seems like a good deal because you aren't paying for the upper leaves, which are discarded anyway. However, after buying and cooking these trimmed-down leeks, we found the actual purpose of this procedure was to trim away aging leaves and make tough, old leeks look fresher to the unwary consumer.

At home, trimming is essential because it is the only way to expose the many layers of the leek and clean it properly. Instead of following the often-recommended technique of slicing off the leaves right where they lighten into the white base of the leek, we found you could move about 2 inches upward into the leaves, to the point at which the light green part turns dark green, without any ill effect.

The next step is to clean the leeks. Since leeks grow underground, during the process of pushing upward they collect dirt between their layers. We've come across leeks that had only a few grains of dirt between the layers, but we've also found leeks with mud jammed in the crevices. See the illustrations on page 148 for tips on washing leeks.

In researching the best way to cook leeks, we found that, apart from a few chefs who braised leeks in the oven, most advocated boiling them. Our first test was to boil leeks in water for 10 to 15 minutes. The resulting leeks were moist, and their color was good. They were a bit misshapen, however, so we tried tying them in bundles the way one recipe suggested. The results didn't justify the trouble. All you really need to do, we found, is arrange the leeks on the plate or platter after cooking, taking care to coax them into shape. This method would have been fine if the leeks tasted better. But all that boiling had washed away too much leek flavor. We also tried boiling the leeks in chicken broth instead of water. This produced better results.

But we were looking for a stronger leek flavor, not one dominated by the broth.

The next cooking process we tried was braising, defined as first browning in fat and then covering tightly and continuing to cook with a small amount of liquid at low heat for a long time. We tried braising the leeks in water, chicken broth, wine, and combinations of all three. Water made the leeks bland; wine alone was too harsh. Chicken broth worked well, as did a combination of equal parts wine and broth. Removing the lid during the last few minutes of cooking reduced the braising liquid, making a flavorful sauce that went well with everything from fish and chicken to pasta and potatoes.

We felt that braising was better than boiling in broth (at least in terms of introducing flavor to the leeks). Since braising makes the leeks especially tender (and prone to falling apart), we decided to cut the leeks into ½-inch lengths before cooking rather than trying to cook them whole. Our braising method was set, but we still wanted to find a way to cook whole leeks. We wanted a cooking method that would intensify the basic leek flavor rather than supplement it with other flavors.

We tried baking the leeks three ways: wrapping them in foil with butter, wrapping them in foil with a bit of water, and brushing them with butter and baking them unwrapped. None of the methods proved satisfactory. In all three cases, the texture suffered. The wrapped leeks were tough and dry, while the naked ones were too tough to chew.

Next, we turned to the sauté pan. This method yielded leeks that were well browned on the outside, which provided an initial flavor boost that we liked; however, when we cut into the leeks, we found that the centers were not cooked and the outer layers were

tough. The leeks also needed to cook in a generous amount of butter to keep them sizzling without burning. We rolled out the grill and threw some leeks on it, brushing them first with butter. No matter how much butter we lavished on them, though, the leeks came out charred on the outside but still uncooked, tough, and stringy inside.

CLEANING LEEKS

Leeks are often quite dirty and gritty, so they require thorough cleaning. Both of the following methods require that you first cut the green portion into quarters lengthwise, leaving the root end intact.

A. Hold the leek under running water and shuffle the cut layers like a deck of cards.

B. Slosh the cut end of the leek up and down in a bowl of water. Repeat as necessary.

Fortunately, the last method that we tried turned out to be the hands-down winner. When we steamed leeks, the results were full flavored, moist, and tender. Steamed leeks not only tasted better than boiled leeks, with a stronger and sweeter onion-like flavor, but also retained more of their nutritional value. As an added bonus, no butter, oil, or complicated cooking techniques were required when leeks were steamed.

Steaming turned out to be not only an excellent method of cooking leeks but also a very useful intermediate step when cooking leeks by other methods. Steaming softens the leeks and leaves them better suited to sautéing, grilling, or baking.

Master Recipe for Steamed Leeks

SERVES 4

Leeks are grown in sandy soil and frequently have lots of grit between the leaves. Rinse them thoroughly before cooking—see the illustrations on page 148. This recipe offers pure leek flavor. The variations are more complex.

  4   small to medium leeks (between ¾ inch and 1 ¼ inches in diameter)
  2   tablespoons extra-virgin olive oil
     Salt and ground black pepper

1. Trim the leeks about 2 inches beyond the point where the leaves start to darken. Trim the root end, keeping the base intact. Slit each leek lengthwise upward through the leaves, leaving the base intact. Rinse the leeks thoroughly to remove all traces of dirt.

2. Fill a large pot with enough water to come to a depth of 1 inch. Cover and bring the water to a boil over high heat. Arrange the leeks in a single layer in a steamer basket.

SCIENCE: Storing Leeks

To find the best way to store leeks at home, we tried: just leaving them on the refrigerator shelf; putting them on the refrigerator shelf in a plastic bag; putting them in the vegetable crisper bin both unwrapped and wrapped in plastic; and refrigerating them, wrapped in paper bags, thinking that this method might allow the leeks to breathe and not "sweat," as sometimes happens when they're wrapped in plastic. We also tried "misting" the leeks to keep them moist.

After a few days, all of the leeks had become somewhat limp and dry, except those wrapped in plastic and kept in the vegetable crisper. Therefore, we recommend you store your leeks completely enclosed in plastic bags in the crisper. However you store them, leeks should be used within five days of purchase.

When the water comes to a boil, carefully place the steamer basket with the leeks into the pot. Cover and steam until the leeks are tender and the tip of a knife inserted into the thickest part of a leek meets no resistance, 10 to 12 minutes. Place the leeks on a serving platter, drizzle the oil over the leeks, and season to taste with salt and pepper. Serve immediately.

VARIATIONS

Steamed Leeks with Herb Butter
Feel free to use your favorite herbs in this recipe. Tarragon, mint, and chervil also complement the mild, sweet flavor of the leeks.

  1   recipe Steamed Leeks (without oil, salt, or pepper)
  3   tablespoons unsalted butter, softened
  ½   teaspoon minced fresh dill
  ½   teaspoon minced fresh chives
  ½   teaspoon minced fresh parsley leaves
  ¼   teaspoon salt
  ⅛   teaspoon ground black pepper

1. Prepare and cook the leeks as directed in the master recipe.

2. While the leeks are steaming, use a fork to mix the butter, herbs, salt, and pepper together in a small bowl.

3. Arrange the steamed leeks on a platter. Evenly distribute bits of the herb butter over the leeks and serve immediately.

Steamed Leeks with Ginger Sauce

Grating ginger is faster and releases more juices than mincing. Our favorite tool for this task is the Microplane grater—see page 46. You can also find porcelain or plastic ginger graters at Asian markets. The fine holes on a box grater will also work. See page 280 for tips on grating ginger.

I	recipe Steamed Leeks (without olive oil, salt, and pepper)
I	teaspoon grated fresh ginger
3	tablespoons soy sauce
I	tablespoon sugar

1. Prepare and cook the leeks as directed in the master recipe.

2. While the leeks are steaming, whisk the ginger, soy sauce, and sugar together in a small bowl.

3. Arrange the steamed leeks on a platter. Drizzle the ginger sauce over the leeks and serve hot or warm.

Baked Leeks with Bacon and Gruyère

This recipe is much richer than the other variations.

I	ounce (about I slice) bacon, cut into small dice
I	large egg
1/4	cup milk
1/4	cup low-sodium chicken broth
	Salt and ground white pepper

I	ounce Gruyère cheese, grated (about 1/3 cup)
I	recipe Steamed Leeks (without oil, salt, or pepper)
I	tablespoon dry bread crumbs
I	tablespoon minced fresh parsley leaves

1. Adjust an oven rack to the center position and heat the oven to 350 degrees.

2. Fry the bacon in a small skillet over medium-high heat until the fat is rendered and the bacon is crisp, 3 to 5 minutes. Transfer the bacon to a small plate lined with a paper towel. Discard the bacon fat.

3. Whisk the egg, milk, broth, and salt and pepper to taste together in a small bowl. Stir in the cheese.

4. Arrange the leeks in a single layer in a baking dish just large enough to hold them. Pour the egg mixture over the leeks and then sprinkle with the bacon and bread crumbs.

5. Bake until the top is browned and the egg mixture has set, about 30 minutes. Sprinkle with the parsley and serve immediately.

Master Recipe for Braised Leeks

SERVES 4

Serve these leeks with grilled fish or chicken or try them mixed into mashed potatoes. This recipe is very plain. The variations that follow, which replace some of the chicken broth with either white wine or cream, are more complex.

4	small to medium leeks (between 3/4 inch and 1 1/4 inches in diameter)
2	tablespoons unsalted butter
1/2	cup low-sodium chicken broth
	Salt and ground black pepper

1. Trim the leeks about 2 inches beyond the point where the leaves start to darken. Trim

the root end and cut the leeks in half lengthwise and then crosswise into ½-inch pieces. Place the leek pieces in a large bowl filled with cold water and rinse thoroughly. Lift the leeks out of the water (the soil will have sunk to the bottom) and into a colander to drain.

2. Melt the butter in a 12-inch skillet over medium-high heat. When the foaming subsides, add the leeks and cook, stirring occasionally, until they start to soften, about 5 minutes. Add the broth, cover, and simmer until the leeks are tender, about 5 minutes. Remove the lid and cook until the braising liquid thickens, about 2 minutes. Season to taste with salt and pepper and serve immediately.

➤ VARIATIONS

Braised Leeks with White Wine and Thyme

The sugar may not be necessary if you are using a sweeter white wine. Taste the finished leeks and add the sugar along with the salt and pepper if needed.

4	small to medium leeks (between ¾ inch and 1 ¼ inches in diameter)
2	tablespoons unsalted butter
¼	cup low-sodium chicken broth
¼	cup white wine
1	teaspoon minced fresh thyme leaves
¼	teaspoon sugar (optional)
	Salt and ground black pepper

1. Trim the leeks about 2 inches beyond the point where the leaves start to darken. Trim the root end and cut the leeks in half lengthwise and then crosswise into ½-inch pieces. Place the leek pieces in a large bowl filled with cold water and rinse thoroughly. Lift the leeks out of the water (the soil will have sunk to the bottom) and into a colander to drain.

2. Melt the butter in a 12-inch skillet over medium-high heat. When the foaming subsides, add the leeks and cook, stirring

occasionally, until they start to soften, about 5 minutes. Add the broth, wine, and thyme. Cover and simmer until the leeks are tender, about 5 minutes longer. Remove the lid and cook until the braising liquid thickens, about 2 minutes. Season with the sugar (if using) and salt and pepper to taste and serve immediately.

Leeks Braised in Cream with Garlic and Lemon

Serve these leeks with buttered egg noodles or creamy polenta.

4	small to medium leeks (between ¾ inch and 1 ¼ inches in diameter)
2	tablespoons unsalted butter
2	medium cloves garlic, minced or pressed through a garlic press
¼	cup heavy cream
¼	cup low-sodium chicken broth
½	teaspoon grated zest from 1 lemon
1	tablespoon minced fresh parsley leaves
	Salt and ground black pepper

1. Trim the leeks about 2 inches beyond the point where the leaves start to darken. Trim the root end and cut the leeks in half lengthwise and then crosswise into ½-inch pieces. Place the leek pieces in a large bowl filled with cold water and rinse thoroughly. Lift the leeks out of the water (the soil will have sunk to the bottom) and into a colander to drain.

2. Melt the butter in a 12-inch skillet over medium-high heat. When the foaming subsides, add the leeks and garlic and cook, stirring occasionally, until the leeks start to soften, about 5 minutes. Add the cream, broth, and zest. Cover and simmer until the leeks are tender, about 5 minutes. Remove the lid and cook until the braising liquid thickens, about 2 minutes. Sprinkle with the parsley, season with salt and pepper to taste, and serve immediately.

Master Recipe for Grilled Leeks

SERVES 4

Once the leeks have been steamed, they can be grilled and seasoned simply with salt, pepper, and olive oil or with your favorite vinaigrette. See the illustrations on page 148 for tips on rinsing the leeks.

4	small to medium leeks (between ³/₄ inch and 1 ¹/₄ inches in diameter)
3	tablespoons extra-virgin olive oil
	Salt and ground black pepper

1. Trim the leeks about 2 inches beyond the point where the leaves start to darken. Trim the root end, keeping the base intact. Slit each leek lengthwise upward through the leaves, leaving the base intact. Rinse the leeks thoroughly to remove all traces of dirt.

2. Fill a large pot with enough water to come to a depth of 1 inch. Cover and bring the water to a boil over high heat. Arrange the leeks in a single layer in a steamer basket; when the water comes to a boil, carefully place the steamer basket with the leeks into the pot. Cover and steam until the leeks are tender and the tip of a knife inserted into the thickest part of a leek meets no resistance, 10 to 12 minutes. Remove the leeks from the steamer and place them on a platter.

3. Brush the leeks with the oil and season with salt and pepper to taste. Grill the leeks over a medium-hot fire (you should be able to hold your hand 5 inches above the cooking grate for 3 to 4 seconds), turning once, until the leeks are streaked with light grill marks, 3 to 4 minutes. Serve hot, warm, or at room temperature.

➤ VARIATION

Grilled Leeks with Orange-Tarragon Vinaigrette

The fresh, licorice flavor of the tarragon works well with the orange and the leeks.

1	recipe Grilled Leeks
4	tablespoons extra-virgin olive oil
1	medium shallot, minced
¹/₂	teaspoon grated zest and 4 teaspoons juice from 1 orange
¹/₈	teaspoon sugar
1	teaspoon minced fresh tarragon leaves
	Salt and ground black pepper

1. Prepare and cook the leeks as directed in the master recipe.

2. While the leeks are cooking, whisk the oil, shallot, orange zest and juice, sugar, and tarragon together in a small bowl. Season with salt and pepper to taste.

3. Arrange the grilled leeks on a serving platter. Drizzle them with the vinaigrette and serve hot, warm, or at room temperature.

MUSHROOMS

WHITE MUSHROOMS HAVE A LOUSY REPUTATION. COOKS WHO OOH AND aah over porcini, portobellos, shiitakes, and other exotic mushrooms often find the white mushroom, also called the button, to be beneath their consideration. But button mushrooms are inexpensive and almost always available (they are the only choice in some markets), which gives them at least some appeal. We figured there must be a way of cooking them that would bring out the deep, rich, earthy flavors for which their tonier cousins are so highly prized.

The most common method of cooking mushrooms is sautéing. The sautéing time seemed crucial, so we cut a handful of mushrooms into uniform ⅜-inch slices and sautéed them in a bit of oil over medium-high heat for times ranging from three minutes to eight minutes, removing one slice from the pan every minute. We preferred those cooked for six minutes, since at this point the mushrooms were moist all the way through—a condition we had learned to recognize as indicating doneness—and slightly browned but not burnt on the exterior. Much of the moisture had been cooked out and evaporated, but some still remained in the pan. These mushrooms also tasted pretty good, with a fairly deep, somewhat complex, nutty flavor from the exterior browning. The texture, however, was not ideal; while tender, the mushrooms were also a bit rubbery.

We tried sautéing the mushrooms until they exuded no more liquid, as suggested in several cookbooks. This took about 12 minutes, though, and by that time the mushrooms had acquired a dark, almost burnt taste and again were slightly rubbery. Not terrible, but not great either.

We finally started to have some success when we cut the mushrooms into larger pieces. Rather than thin slices, we halved smaller mushrooms and quartered larger ones. The mushrooms were less likely to dry out, and their texture was meatier and more substantial. We tested cooking the mushrooms over various heat levels and found that medium-high heat is best at drawing out the excess liquid from the mushrooms and then browning them. As for the cooking medium, a combination of butter and oil had just the right balance of flavor and richness.

Because mushrooms naturally contain a lot of moisture, the mushrooms will release quite a bit of liquid as they cook. Luckily, this juice acts like a braising liquid, poaching the mushrooms in their own flavorful juices and eliminating the need for broth or water. As the liquid evaporates, the mushrooms

153

become golden and slightly crisp; so much better than their pale, tasteless counterparts.

Although we were pleased with our success on the stovetop, we decided to try some methods that mimicked even more closely the cooking of meat—that is, roasting. We reasoned that an initial burst of high heat to brown the mushrooms, followed by a longer cooking period, might give us even better results. So we tried both sautéing and high-heat roasting for the preliminary browning, followed by a longer roasting at a somewhat lower temperature. We also decided to throw in a slightly bizarre method suggested to us by a friend, who swore that it had been suggested to him by a celebrity chef: boiling the mushrooms for one minute before cooking them. This, he claimed, somehow extracted the liquid from the mushrooms and made them brown up quicker and better.

We divided a group of mushrooms of approximately equal size into three batches. The first we blanched in boiling water for one minute; the second we sautéed for four minutes over medium-high heat, reasoning that we should not fully cook them since they would finish in the oven; the third we tossed with a bit of oil and roasted for 10 minutes at 450 degrees, which was just long enough to get them nicely browned on the exterior. We then tossed each batch with a teaspoon of olive oil, put each of them in a separate small bowl, and roasted them all at 400 degrees for 20 minutes.

The differences were substantial. The preboiled mushrooms were an unappetizing tan color and retained a vegetal taste that we did not particularly like. The presautéed mushrooms had less than a teaspoon of liquid in the bowl and were moist throughout and relatively well browned. They also had a pleasant, rather rich flavor.

The preroasted mushrooms, however, were the clear favorite. Slight brown marks on the bottom of the bowl were all that remained of the evaporated liquid, and the mushrooms

---

SCIENCE: To Wash or Not to Wash Mushrooms

Common culinary wisdom dictates that mushrooms should never, ever be washed. Put these spongy fungi under the faucet or in a bowl, the dictum goes, and they will soak up water like a sponge.

Like most cooks, we had always blindly followed this precept. But when we learned that mushrooms were over 80 percent water, we began to question their ability to absorb yet more liquid. As we so often do in situations like this, we consulted the works of food scientist and author Harold McGee. Sure enough, in his book *The Curious Cook* (North Point Press, 1990), we found an experiment he had devised to test this very piece of accepted mushroom lore. We decided to duplicate McGee's work in our test kitchen.

We weighed out 6 ounces of white mushrooms, put them into a bowl, added water to cover, and let them sit. After five minutes, we shook off the surface water and weighed them

again. Our results replicated McGee's—the total weight gain for all the mushrooms together was 1/4 ounce, which translates to about 1 1/2 teaspoons of water.

We suspected that even this gain represented mostly surface moisture rather than absorption, so we repeated the experiment with 6 ounces of broccoli, which no one would claim is an absorbent vegetable. The weight gain after a five-minute soak was almost identical—1/5 ounce—suggesting that most of the moisture was clinging to the surface of both vegetables rather than being absorbed by them.

So, as it turns out, mushrooms can be cleaned in the same way as other vegetables are—rinsed under cold water. However, it's best to rinse them just before cooking and to avoid rinsing altogether if you are using them uncooked, since the surfaces of wet mushrooms turn dark and slimy when they're exposed to air for more than four or five minutes.

not only were moist all the way through but had a deep, rich, pronounced flavor that seemed at once meaty and nutty. This was the real mushroom flavor that we had been trying to coax from this everyday mushroom. After further testing of both higher and lower oven temperatures, we found that we could simply roast the mushrooms at a constant 450 degrees, as long as we turned them once near the end of the cooking time.

Although we liked simply tossing these roasted mushrooms with spice mixes or combinations of herbs and garlic, we started wondering if preroasting would improve that old cocktail party standby, the stuffed mushroom cap. A final taste test showed that, as we'd expected, roasted caps had a fuller, deeper flavor than those we'd stuffed raw and roasted; the filling was also less soggy and more flavorful.

Master Recipe for Sautéed Mushrooms

SERVES 4

Serve these basic mushrooms as a side dish with meat or poultry or use them as a pizza topping or in a salad. Cremini are light brown mushrooms commonly sold in supermarkets. They have a bit more flavor than white button mushrooms, but either variety will work well in these recipes.

I	tablespoon unsalted butter
I	tablespoon extra-virgin olive oil
I	medium shallot, minced
I	pound white or cremini mushrooms (or a combination of both), cleaned and cut into halves if small, quarters if large
½	teaspoon minced fresh thyme leaves
	Salt and ground black pepper

Heat the butter and oil in a large skillet over medium-high heat. When the butter melts and the foam subsides, add the shallot and cook until the shallot is soft, about 2 minutes. Add the mushrooms and thyme and cook, stirring occasionally, until the liquid from the mushrooms has evaporated and the mushrooms are lightly browned, about 12 minutes. Season with salt and pepper to taste and serve immediately.

➤ VARIATIONS

Spicy Sautéed Mushrooms with Anchovy

The anchovies give the mushrooms a rich but not fishy flavor.

I	tablespoon unsalted butter
I	tablespoon extra-virgin olive oil
¼	teaspoon hot red pepper flakes
I	medium clove garlic, minced or pressed through a garlic press
2	medium anchovy fillets
I	pound white or cremini mushrooms (or a combination of both), cleaned and cut into halves if small, quarters if large
	Salt

Heat the butter and oil in a large skillet over medium-high heat. When the butter melts and the foam subsides, add the pepper flakes, garlic, and anchovies and cook, breaking up the anchovy fillets with a wooden spoon, until the mixture is fragrant, about 1 minute. Add the mushrooms and cook, stirring occasionally, until the liquid from the mushrooms has evaporated and the mushrooms are lightly browned, about 12 minutes. Season with salt to taste and serve immediately.

Sautéed Mushrooms with Toasted Garlic and Parsley

I	tablespoon unsalted butter
I	tablespoon extra-virgin olive oil

4   medium cloves garlic, sliced thin
1   pound white button or cremini
       mushrooms (or a combination of
       both), cleaned and cut into halves
       if small, quarters if large
1   tablespoon minced fresh parsley leaves
       Salt and ground black pepper

Heat the butter and oil in a large skillet over medium-high heat. When the butter melts and the foam subsides, add the garlic and cook until golden, about 5 minutes, adjusting the heat as necessary to keep the garlic from burning. Add the mushrooms and parsley and cook, stirring occasionally, until the liquid from the mushrooms has evaporated and the mushrooms are lightly browned, about 12 minutes. Season with salt and pepper to taste and serve immediately.

Quick and Easy Mushroom Burgers

SERVES 4 AS A LIGHT MAIN COURSE

Once you have sautéed (and cooled) the mushrooms, you can make these burgers in a matter of minutes. Feel free to use the master recipe for sautéed mushrooms or any of the variations. Serve these burgers in a bun with lettuce and other fixings.

½   cup unbleached all-purpose flour
1   recipe Sautéed Mushrooms,
       cooled to room temperature
2   slices high-quality white bread,
       crust removed, and roughly torn
1   large egg
1   teaspoon Dijon mustard
1   tablespoon minced fresh parsley leaves
3   tablespoons extra-virgin olive oil

1. Place the flour in a pie plate or wide, shallow plate.

2. Place the mushrooms, bread, egg, mustard, and parsley in the workbowl of a food processor. Pulse until the mushrooms are chopped finely, about fifteen 1-second pulses. Scrape the mixture into a medium bowl and mix together with a rubber spatula to ensure that the mixture is well blended. Shape the mixture into 4 equal-size burgers. Dredge the burgers in the flour, shaking off the excess, and set them aside on a plate.

3. Heat the oil in a 12-inch nonstick skillet over medium-high heat until almost smoking. Add the burgers and cook, turning once, until both sides are golden brown, about 5 minutes per side, adjusting the heat as necessary to prevent burning. Serve immediately.

Master Recipe for Roasted Mushrooms

SERVES 4

This recipe is pretty basic. To add more intriguing flavors, toss the roasted mushrooms with garlic, herbs, vinegar, lemon juice, and/or spices just before serving. See the variations for specific ideas. Cremini are light brown mushrooms commonly sold in supermarkets. They have a bit more flavor than white button mushrooms, but either variety will work well in these recipes.

1   pound white or cremini mushrooms
       (or a combination of both),
       cleaned and cut into halves
       if small, quarters if large
2   tablespoons extra-virgin olive oil
       Salt and ground black pepper

1. Adjust an oven rack to the lowest position and heat the oven to 450 degrees. Line a rimmed baking sheet or a large low-sided roasting pan with aluminum foil.

2. Toss the mushrooms with the oil and salt and pepper to taste in a medium bowl. Arrange the mushrooms in a single layer on the foil-lined pan.

3. Roast until the released juices have nearly evaporated and the mushroom surfaces facing the pan are browned, 12 to 15 minutes. Remove the pan from the oven and turn the mushrooms with a metal spatula or tongs. Return the pan to the oven; continue to roast until the mushroom liquid has completely evaporated and the mushrooms are brown all over, 5 to 10 minutes longer. Serve immediately.

➤ VARIATIONS
Roasted Mushrooms with Greek Flavors

If desired, sprinkle the finished mushrooms with ⅓ cup crumbled feta. See page 44 for information about buying jarred roasted peppers.

4	tablespoons extra-virgin olive oil
I	teaspoon minced fresh oregano leaves
I	tablespoon juice from I lemon
¼	cup jarred roasted red peppers, chopped coarse
I	pound white or cremini mushrooms (or a combination of both), cleaned and cut into halves if small, quarters if large
	Salt and ground black pepper

1. Adjust an oven rack to the lowest position and heat the oven to 450 degrees. Line a rimmed baking sheet or a large low-sided roasting pan with aluminum foil.

2. Mix 2 tablespoons of the oil with the oregano, lemon juice, and peppers in a medium bowl.

3. In a separate medium bowl, toss the mushrooms with the remaining 2 tablespoons oil and salt and pepper to taste. Arrange the mushrooms in a single layer on the foil-lined pan.

4. Roast until the released juices have nearly evaporated and the mushroom surfaces facing the pan are browned, 12 to 15

minutes. Remove the pan from the oven and turn the mushrooms with a metal spatula or tongs. Return the pan to the oven; continue to roast until the mushroom liquid has completely evaporated and the mushrooms are brown all over, 5 to 10 minutes longer.

5. Add the mushrooms to the bowl with the pepper mixture and toss to combine. Adjust the seasonings, adding salt and pepper to taste. Serve immediately.

Roasted Mushrooms with Rosemary and Cracked Black Pepper

Peppercorns are usually crushed using the bottom of a skillet. In this case, since only a small amount is being used, use the bottom of a heavy glass liquid measuring cup to crush the whole peppercorns. The cup not only is smaller and easier to manipulate than a skillet but also has the additional bonus of a see-through bottom, so that you can keep an eye on the peppercorns.

½	teaspoon whole black peppercorns
2	tablespoons extra-virgin olive oil
I	teaspoon minced fresh rosemary
I	pound white or cremini mushrooms (or a combination of both), cleaned and cut into halves if small, quarters if large
	Salt

1. Adjust an oven rack to the lowest position and heat the oven to 450 degrees. Line a rimmed baking sheet or a large low-sided roasting pan with aluminum foil.

2. Place the peppercorns on a cutting board. Using the bottom of a heavy glass liquid measuring cup, crush the peppercorns until they are broken into small pieces. Toss the pepper, oil, rosemary, and mushrooms together in a medium bowl. Arrange the mushrooms in a single layer on the foil-lined pan.

3. Roast until the released juices have nearly evaporated and the mushroom surfaces facing the pan are browned, 12 to 15 minutes. Remove the pan from the oven and turn the mushrooms with a metal spatula or tongs. Return the pan to the oven; continue to roast until the mushroom liquid has completely evaporated and the mushrooms are brown all over, 5 to 10 minutes longer. Season with salt to taste and serve immediately.

Roasted Mushroom Caps

MAKES ENOUGH MUSHROOM
CAPS TO SERVE 4 TO 6

These caps can be stuffed (see the recipe that follows) and served as an appetizer. Roast the stems along with the caps and use them in the filling.

24	large white mushrooms, stems and caps separated and washed
2	tablespoons extra-virgin olive oil
	Salt and ground black pepper

1. Adjust an oven rack to the lowest position and heat the oven to 450 degrees.

2. Toss the mushroom caps and stems, oil, and salt and pepper to taste in a medium bowl. Arrange the caps, gill side down, in a single layer on a large low-sided roasting pan or rimmed baking sheet with the stems placed alongside.

3. Roast until the mushrooms have released some juice and are brown around the edges facing the pan, 12 to 15 minutes. Remove the pan from the oven and turn the caps over with a metal spatula. Continue to roast until the mushroom liquid has completely evaporated and the mushroom caps and stems are brown all over, 5 to 10 minutes longer. Use with the filling at right or any other filling of your choice.

Mushrooms Stuffed with Bacon, Spinach, and Blue Cheese

MAKES 24 STUFFED MUSHROOMS

This is our favorite stuffing for roasted mushroom caps.

1	recipe Roasted Mushroom Caps
6	ounces (about 6 slices) bacon, cut crosswise into 1/4-inch strips
1/2	medium red onion, minced
1	large clove garlic, minced or pressed through a garlic press
6	ounces spinach, stems removed, washed thoroughly and chopped coarse
1/4	cup dry bread crumbs
3	tablespoons ricotta cheese
2	ounces blue cheese, crumbled
	Salt and ground black pepper

1. Follow the recipe for Roasted Mushroom Caps, adjusting an oven rack to the center position and leaving the oven temperature at 450 degrees. With the cooked mushroom caps still on the roasting pan, remove the cooked stems and set them aside.

2. Meanwhile, fry the bacon in a large skillet over medium heat until crisp, 5 to 7 minutes. Transfer the bacon to a plate lined with paper towels.

3. Discard all but 1 tablespoon of the bacon drippings from the skillet. Add the onion and cook until soft, about 6 minutes. Add the garlic and cook until fragrant, about 1 minute. Add the spinach and cook until wilted, about 2 minutes. Transfer the spinach mixture to a large bowl and let cool for 10 minutes.

4. Transfer the spinach mixture to a food processor, along with the bread crumbs, ricotta, half of the blue cheese, and roasted mushroom stems. Process to a chunky puree, scraping down the sides of the processor at

least once to ensure an even texture. Return the spinach mixture to the large bowl and stir in the bacon bits and salt and pepper to taste. Fill each mushroom cap with a heaping teaspoon of filling and top each with a portion of the remaining blue cheese.

5. Roast the stuffed mushrooms until the cheese is melted and the filling is hot throughout, about 8 minutes. Serve warm.

GRILLED PORTOBELLOS

IN SOME CIRCLES, GRILLED PORTOBELLOS have become the new "burger." Although we are happy to use meaty grilled portobellos in sandwiches, they are ideal as a side dish or as a salad ingredient. Unfortunately, many grilled portobellos are flaccid. Ideally, they should be plump, juicy, and slightly charred.

With portobellos ranging from 4 to 6 inches in diameter, the first pitfall we encountered was how to develop an across-the-board grilling method for both smaller and larger mushrooms. This, we knew, would be difficult since we wanted to keep the grilling temperature relatively high. We wanted to be able to grill portobellos side by side with meat, which needs a hot fire.

Grilling directly on the rack over the fire proved problematic because the larger portobellos were charred to a black crisp by the time they had cooked through. Seeking refuge, we elevated the mushrooms on a grill rack, but now they took eons to cook through. We suspected that if we found a way to shield the mushrooms from the fire, we could grill them until entirely cooked through and also infuse them with a pure, smoky flavor without the bitterness associated with the direct-grilling method. We called upon an old campfire friend—aluminum

foil—and loosely wrapped each mushroom in a handcrafted foil packet. We placed the portobellos gill-side up (through our endeavors we had learned that this method traps juices) on the grill. After about 10 minutes, the mushrooms were tender and juicy to the core, without sacrificing any of the grill's smoky attributes.

Pumping up flavor was our next concern, and we began brushing our way through a long list of marinades before finding that a simple combination of chopped garlic, lemon juice, olive oil, and salt worked best. After a one-hour marinade, the mushrooms, when grilled, developed a slightly tangy and complex flavor, with a tinge of garlicky oomph. At the end of cooking, we stripped the portobellos of their foil jackets and seared them briefly, infusing them with the smoky essence of summertime grilling.

Master Recipe for Grilled Portobellos

SERVES 4

We prefer large 5- to 6-inch portobellos for grilling because they are sold loose, not prepackaged, and are typically fresher. However, if you cannot find large ones, use six 4- to 5-inch portobellos, which are usually sold three to a package; decrease their grilling time, wrapped in foil, to about 9 minutes.

½	cup extra-virgin olive oil
3	tablespoons juice from 1 lemon
6	medium cloves garlic, minced fine or pressed through a garlic press (about 2 tablespoons)
¼	teaspoon salt
4	portobello mushrooms, each 5 to 6 inches (or about 6 ounces each), stems removed and discarded, caps wiped clean

1. Combine the oil, lemon juice, garlic, and salt in a large zipper-lock plastic bag. Add the mushrooms, seal the bag, and gently shake to coat the mushrooms with the marinade. Let stand at room temperature for 1 hour. Meanwhile, cut four 12 by 12-inch pieces of foil (or six 9 by 9-inch pieces if using smaller mushrooms).

2. Remove the mushrooms from the marinade. Place a foil square on a work surface and set a mushroom on top, gill-side up. Fold the foil edges over to enclose the mushroom and seal the edges shut. Grill the mushrooms over a medium-hot fire (you should be able to hold your hand 5 inches above the cooking grate for 3 to 4 seconds), with the sealed side of the foil packet facing up, until the mushrooms are juicy and tender, 10 to 12 minutes. Using tongs, unwrap the mushrooms and discard the foil. Return the unwrapped mushrooms to the grill, gill-side up, and cook until grill marked, 30

to 60 seconds. Remove from the grill and serve hot or warm or use in the following recipes.

➤ VARIATIONS
Grilled Portobellos with Tarragon
This variation is great served with a grilled steak or a juicy hamburger.

2	teaspoons rice vinegar
1	medium clove garlic, minced or pressed through a garlic press
1	tablespoon chopped fresh tarragon leaves
¼	teaspoon salt
2	teaspoons vegetable or canola oil
1	recipe Grilled Portobellos, cut into ½-inch cubes
	Ground black pepper

Combine the vinegar, garlic, tarragon, and salt in a medium bowl and then whisk in

---

Taking the Temperature of a Grill Fire

Use the chart below to determine the intensity of the fire. The terms *hot*, *medium-hot*, *medium*, and *medium-low* are used throughout this book. When using a gas grill, ignore dial readings such as medium or medium-low in favor of actual measurements of the temperature, as described here.

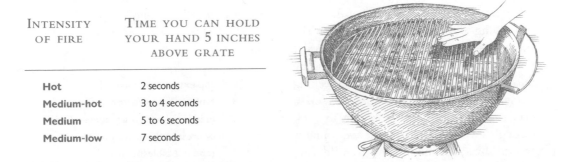

INTENSITY OF FIRE	TIME YOU CAN HOLD YOUR HAND 5 INCHES ABOVE GRATE
Hot	2 seconds
Medium-hot	3 to 4 seconds
Medium	5 to 6 seconds
Medium-low	7 seconds

Once the coals have been spread out in the bottom of the grill, put the cooking grate in place and put the cover on for five minutes to heat up the grate. (On gas grills, preheat with the lid down and all burners on high for 15 minutes.) Scrape the cooking grate clean and then take the temperature of the fire by holding your hand 5 inches above the cooking grate and counting how long you can comfortably leave it in place. If the fire is not hot enough, add more coals and wait 10 minutes for them to light. If the fire is too hot, wait for the coals to cool slightly.

the oil. Add the mushrooms and pepper to taste and toss to coat. Serve immediately or cover with plastic wrap and let stand at room temperature up to 30 minutes.

Grilled Portobello and Spinach Salad with Caramelized Onion Vinaigrette

SERVES 4 AS A FIRST COURSE

For convenience, we like the prewashed baby spinach, sold in 5-ounce packages in most supermarkets. If you choose to use bunched baby spinach instead, make sure to wash and dry the leaves well.

6	tablespoons extra-virgin olive oil
1	small onion, chopped fine (about ¹/₂ cup)
2	tablespoons balsamic vinegar
1	teaspoon minced fresh thyme leaves
	Salt and ground black pepper
1	recipe Grilled Portobellos, halved and cut into ¹/₂-inch-thick slices
5	ounces baby spinach, washed and dried thoroughly (about 6 cups)

1. Heat 2 tablespoons of the oil in a small skillet over medium-high heat until almost smoking. Add the onion and lower the heat to medium. Cook, stirring frequently, until the onions are golden brown, adjusting the heat as necessary to prevent burning, about 10 minutes.

2. Scrape the cooked onions into a large bowl. Whisk in the remaining 4 tablespoons oil, vinegar, and thyme. Season the dressing with salt and pepper to taste.

3. Add the mushrooms and spinach to the bowl and toss to combine. Serve immediately.

EQUIPMENT: Grill Tongs

Each grilling season brings with it a truckload of snazzy new barbecue utensils. We wondered if any were worth a second look.

Testing all manner of tongs, we groped and grabbed kebabs, asparagus, chicken drumsticks, and 3-pound slabs of ribs and found tong performance differed dramatically. Grill tongs by Progressive International, Charcoal, Lamson, Oxo Good Grips, and AMC Rosewood were heavy and difficult to maneuver, and their less delicate pincers couldn't get a grip on asparagus. Other problems included sharp, serrated edges that nicked the food, flimsy arms that bent under the strain of heavy food, and pincers whose spread could not even accommodate the girth of a chicken leg. A new tong on the scene, the Lamson multipurpose, had a spatula in place of one pincer, rendering its grasp almost useless.

The winner was a pair of 16-inch stainless-steel kitchen tongs by Amco. Not only did they grip, turn, and move food around the grill easily, but they also were long enough to keep the cook a safe distance from the hot coals. So forget about all those flashy new grill utensils and simply bring your kitchen tongs outside.

THE BEST GRILL TONGS

A pair of 16-inch stainless-steel kitchen tongs made by Amco outperformed other tongs especially designed for use at the grill. Save money and use the same pair of tongs indoors and outdoors.

OKRA

OKRA HAS A FRESH, SLIGHTLY SWEET FLAVOR, SOMEWHAT LIKE A CROSS between a zucchini and a green bean. However, the most memorable characteristic of okra may be its texture. The interior of the okra pod contains a substance that becomes gelatinous as it is boiled or braised, which is how many Southern cooks prepare this vegetable.

We wanted to find a way to prepare okra so that it would appeal to all Americans, not just Southerners raised on this summer vegetable. Our okra could not be slimy. As we soon found out, prolonged cooking exacerbates the problem. The longer okra simmers or stews, the more objectionable it becomes. In addition, moist heat (such as in boiling or braising) tends to accelerate the softening of this vegetable. We needed to cook okra with dry heat so that it would remain crisp-tender, like other green vegetables.

We had seen several recipes that called for sautéing. Our first test was a revelation. Sautéing whole pods over medium-high heat not only minimizes the slipperiness but also maintains their fresh flavor and crisp texture. Even test cooks who claimed not to like okra were happily munching on whole pods that had been quickly sautéed in olive oil and flavored with garlic.

As we later discovered, shopping is the other key factor involved in preparing crisp rather than slimy okra. Small pods (no longer than 3 inches) will stay crisp when cooked this way, but larger pods tended to become slimy, no matter how we cooked them. The keys to crowd-pleasing okra are simple—buy small pods and sauté them quickly.

Master Recipe for Sautéed Okra
SERVES 4 TO 6

Okra pods that are less than 3 inches in length will be the most tender.

2   tablespoons plus 1 teaspoon extra-virgin olive oil
1   pound small okra (no more than 3 inches long), stems removed
1   medium clove garlic, minced or pressed through a garlic press
    Salt and ground black pepper

Heat 2 tablespoons of the oil in a large skillet over medium-high heat until almost smoking. Add the okra and cook, stirring occasionally, until the okra is bright green, 3 to 4 minutes. Clear a space in the center of the pan, add the garlic and the remaining 1 teaspoon oil, and cook until fragrant, about

15 seconds. Stir the garlic mixture into the okra, season with salt and pepper to taste, and serve immediately.

➤ VARIATION

Sautéed Okra with Quick Tomato Sauce

Tomatoes and okra are a classic combination. This juicy side dish, served with rice or pasta, makes a perfect accompaniment to chicken or fish, such as halibut or catfish.

3	tablespoons extra-virgin olive oil
1	pound small okra (no more than 3 inches long), stems removed
	Salt and ground black pepper
4	medium cloves garlic, minced or pressed through a garlic press
½	teaspoon hot red pepper flakes
1	(14.5-ounce) can diced tomatoes
1	teaspoon sugar
1	tablespoon minced fresh basil leaves

1. Heat 2 tablespoons of the oil in a large skillet over medium-high heat until almost smoking. Add the okra and cook, stirring occasionally, until the okra is bright green, 3 to 4 minutes. Season with salt and pepper to taste and transfer the okra to a bowl.

2. Add the remaining 1 tablespoon oil to the empty pan. Add the garlic and pepper flakes and cook until fragrant, about 15 seconds. Stir in the tomatoes and sugar, bring to a simmer, and cook until slightly reduced, about 2 minutes. Stir in the okra and cook for 1 minute longer. Stir in the basil and adjust the seasonings, adding salt and pepper to taste. Serve immediately.

INGREDIENTS: Canned Tomatoes

Canned whole tomatoes are the closest product to fresh. Whole tomatoes, either plum or round, are steamed to remove their skins and then packed in tomato juice or puree. We prefer tomatoes packed in juice; they generally have a fresher, livelier flavor than tomatoes packed in puree, which has a cooked tomato flavor that imparts a slightly stale, tired taste to the whole can.

To find the best canned whole tomatoes, we tasted 11 brands, both straight from the can and in a simple tomato sauce. Muir Glen (an organic brand available in most supermarkets and natural foods stores) finished at the head of the pack. Progresso was a close second in the tasting and is also recommended.

Diced tomatoes are simply whole tomatoes that have been roughly chopped during processing and then packed with juice. For pasta sauces, we prefer diced tomatoes because they save time and effort. Why chop canned tomatoes (a messy proposition at best) if you don't have to? There are not as many brands of diced tomatoes to choose from, although this seems to be changing as more companies realize that consumers want this product. Among the brands we tested, Muir Glen was our favorite. Unless otherwise indicated, use the entire contents of the can (both the diced tomatoes and the juice) in recipes.

THE BEST CANNED TOMATOES

Muir Glen diced tomatoes have a fresh, lively flavor (they are packed in juice, not puree) and are recipe-ready.

ONIONS

THERE ALWAYS SEEMS TO BE A BAG OF ONIONS HANGING AROUND, EVEN when the vegetable bin in the refrigerator is bare. For this reason, it makes sense to know how to treat onions as a vegetable side dish, not just as a flavoring agent for other dishes. In this chapter, we examine how to caramelize, roast, and grill onions as well as how to cook small pearl onions.

SCIENCE: Onions and Crying

When an onion is cut, the cells that are damaged in the process release sulfuric compounds as well as various enzymes, notably one called sulfoxide lyase. Those compounds, which are separated in the onion's cell structure, activate and mix to form the real culprit behind crying, a volatile new compound called thiopropanal sulfoxide. When thiopropanal sulfoxide evaporates in the air, it irritates the eyes, causing us to cry.

Over the years, we've collected more than 20 ideas from readers, books, and conversations with colleagues all aimed at reducing tears while cutting onions. We decided to put those ideas to the test. The ideas ranged from the commonsense (work underneath an exhaust fan or freeze onions for 30 minutes before slicing) to the comical (wear ski goggles or hold a toothpick in your teeth).

Overall, the methods that worked best were to protect our eyes by covering them with goggles or contact lenses or to introduce a flame near the cut onions. The flame, which can be produced by either a candle or a gas burner, changes the activity of the thiopropanal sulfoxide by completing oxidizing it. Contact lenses and goggles form a physical barrier that the thiopropanal cannot penetrate.

CARAMELIZED ONIONS

SWEET, GLOSSY, WITH COMPLEX FLAVOR, caramelized onions have a pedigree far superior to the mongrel side dish offered at your local steakhouse. Made with only four ingredients (not counting salt, pepper, and water) and featuring the most common of all pantry staples, caramelized onions easily play a wide range of culinary roles, from condiment for burgers to sauce for roast chicken. Caramelized onions can also team up with bacon and sour cream to make a classic dip or be used on their own as a topping for steak.

As simple as caramelized onions are, we soon discovered that poor technique can yield onions that are dried out, burnt, bland, gummy, and/or greasy. Among the half dozen recipes we tried, some produced onions that were much too sweet, while others seemed barely cooked. One recipe produced a sticky mass of onion-flavored goo that tasters had a hard time identifying. What we were looking for were soft yet lightly toothsome onions with a deep, complex character and a lustrous, dark golden hue.

MINCING ONIONS

There are lots of ways to mince an onion. This method is the easiest one we've tested.

1. Start with a peeled, quartered onion. Working with one quarter at a time, place the quarter with one flat side down on a cutting board. Make two or three slices across the quarter and down to, but not through, the root end.

2. Turn the quarter onto its other flat side and repeat the slicing.

3. Using the claw grip, with your fingertips folded inward toward your palm to hold the onion in place, cut across the existing slices to make an even dice.

To start, we tried several different methods of caramelizing onions: in a roasting pan in the oven as well as on top of the stove in a regular skillet, a nonstick skillet, and a Dutch oven. The oven dried out the onions before they had a chance to fully caramelize; on the stovetop, the onions were easier to regulate throughout the cooking process. In terms of the pan used, the high sides of the Dutch oven encouraged condensation, causing the reduction and caramelization process to take about 15 minutes longer with no discernible difference in flavor or texture. The low-sided skillets caramelized the onions more quickly. When it came to choosing between regular and nonstick, we decided on the slippery, nonstick surface. This pan was easier to clean, and the flavorful juices did not cling to the pan but were instead forced to mingle with the onions.

After this first round of tests, we realized that the process of caramelization cannot begin until the onions start to release their juices. This release of moisture is an indication that cell walls are breaking down, turning complex starches within the cells into simple sugars. These sugars then caramelize and, owing to a series of chemical reactions, turn darker and add a variety of complex flavors. The question was how to get this process started as soon as possible.

The recipes consulted employed a variety of techniques. Some added salt and sugar at the beginning of the cooking process; some started cooking the onions under a lid; still others noted the importance of cutting the onion with the "grain" (slicing stem to root), which is said to encourage the release of juices. We tested all three methods and found that while adding salt and sugar at the outset did not encourage faster caramelization, it did give the resulting onions a fuller, more impressive flavor. Using a lid for all or even part of the caramelizing process did speed things up, but the resulting onions had a stale, steamed flavor that tasters didn't like. Slicing with or against the grain made absolutely no difference. After much additional testing, we finally discovered the secret to jump-starting caramelization: Start the onions off over a high flame for five minutes to quickly release their moisture.

The next question was what to do with the flame after the initial five-minute blast. Several cookbooks note the importance of cooking the onions over low heat to allow the sugars to caramelize slowly, while others call for high heat, claiming that caramelization will take only 15 minutes. To test these theories, we took three pans of onions through the initial five-minute blast and then put one over a very low flame, put another over a medium flame, and left the last over the high flame. The results were

as expected: The onions cooked over a low flame took nearly two hours to fully caramelize, those cooked over a medium flame took a total of 45 minutes, and those blasted over high heat took about 20 minutes. The differences in flavor were as dramatic as the cooking times. The slowly cooked onions were extremely sweet, with a stringy, dried-out texture. The quickly cooked onions were invitingly dark and glossy but had a shallow, slightly charred flavor. The moderately cooked onions, on the other hand, were perfect. With varying shades of brown, these onions had a complex, multi-

---

INGREDIENTS: Choosing an Onion for Caramelizing

The type of onion you choose for camelizing has a tremendous effect on flavor. Although the caramelizing times of these various onions are consistent, our tasters' preferences were not. Some liked a sweeter, more mellow flavor, while others liked their onions with more bite. Tasters with a sweet tooth gravitated to the white and Vidalia onions (the latter being the sweeter of the two). Those who preferred a heartier onion flavor with only moderate sweetness were drawn to Spanish onions.

SPANISH ONION Most tasters liked this onion for its "deep and complex" flavor and "meaty" texture. While its "heartiness," tempered only by a "moderate sweetness," ranked highly with some, it was considered a bit "harsh" by others.

YELLOW ONION  Tasters found this onion to strike a "good balance between savory and sweet," with a "mild onion flavor" and "beautiful color." A few found it unpleasantly "gummy," with a "bitter finish." Nobody loved it; nobody hated it.

RED ONION When caramelized, this onion turned very dark. Its flavor ranked neither high nor low. Tasters found it "pleasantly sweet," with a "good onion flavor," despite its "sticky" and "jammy" consistency.

WHITE ONION  This controversial onion was rated both at the top and at the bottom of the tasters' charts. Some liked its simple, "sugary," "mellow" flavor, while others found it "too sweet" and "one dimensional," with "no texture."

VIDALIA ONION It came as no surprise that the Vidalia—a notably sweet variety similar to Maui and Walla Walla—was the sweetest sample. Its texture was less pleasing, however, and deemed both a bit "chalky" and "gummy."

layered flavor and struck the perfect balance of palatable flavor and pleasing texture.

Making four batches, we tested olive oil, vegetable oil, butter, and a combination of vegetable oil and butter. The olive oil was overpowering, with a slightly bitter edge. The vegetable oil allowed for a clean, onion flavor, while the butter tasted extremely round and muted. The combination of vegetable oil and butter was the winner, releasing a clean, well-defined onion flavor lightly tempered with the rich taste of butter.

Finally, we tried adding flavorings such as broth, wine, and vinegar, but tasters preferred the flavor of the onions with the help of only a little light brown sugar (it brought out a heartier flavor than granulated sugar), salt, and black pepper. One tablespoon of water gathered up the drops of caramelized onion juice from around the edges of the pan without diminishing the flavor or texture of the onions.

STORING VIDALIA ONIONS

The sugar content of Vidalia, Walla Walla, and Maui onions, which is what endears them to many cooks, also makes them spoil more quickly if they are stored touching each other. To prolong their freshness, place one onion in the leg of an old but clean pair of pantyhose. Tie a knot in the hose, just above the onion. Repeat this process up the entire leg of the pantyhose. To use an onion, just cut off the lowest one, below the knot.

Master Recipe for Caramelized Onions

MAKES 1 CUP

Caramelized onions are easily added to most any meal. Try them in an omelet, frittata, or strata or with scrambled eggs and home fries. They taste fantastic on grilled cheese sandwiches, BLTs, and burgers or thrown into pasta, potato, or green salads. Add them to stuffings, gratins, casseroles, and savory tarts or sprinkle them over bruschetta, focaccia, or pizza. They spiff up baked and mashed potatoes, rice, risotto, and polenta. Last, try caramelized onions with apples and a good cheese for dessert.

1	tablespoon unsalted butter
1	tablespoon vegetable oil
1/2	teaspoon salt
1	teaspoon light brown sugar
2	pounds onions (see page 166), halved and sliced 1/4 inch thick
1	tablespoon water
	Ground black pepper

Heat the butter and oil in a 12-inch nonstick skillet over high heat. When the foaming subsides, stir in the salt and brown sugar. Add the onions and stir to coat. Cook, stirring occasionally, until the onions begin to soften and release some moisture, about 5 minutes. Reduce the heat to medium and cook, stirring frequently, until the onions are deeply browned and slightly sticky, about 40 minutes longer. (If the onions are sizzling or scorching, reduce the heat. If the onions are not browning after 15 to 20 minutes, raise the heat.) Off the heat, stir in the water and season with pepper to taste. (The onions can be refrigerated in an airtight container for up to 7 days.)

167

Caramelized Onion Sauce with White Wine

MAKES ABOUT 2 CUPS

This sauce is an excellent accompaniment to a simple pork roast or roast chicken.

1	tablespoon unsalted butter
1	tablespoon vegetable oil
½	teaspoon salt, plus more to taste
1	teaspoon light brown sugar
2	pounds onions (see page 166), halved and sliced ¼ inch thick
1	medium clove garlic, minced or pressed through a garlic press
1	small shallot, minced
1	cup low-sodium chicken broth
½	cup dry white wine
3	tablespoons cold unsalted butter, cut into 3 pieces
	Ground black pepper

1. Heat the 1 tablespoon butter and oil in a 12-inch nonstick skillet over high heat. When the foaming subsides, stir in the salt and brown sugar. Add the onions and stir to coat. Cook, stirring occasionally, until the onions begin to soften and release some moisture, about 5 minutes. Reduce the heat to medium and cook, stirring frequently, until the onions are deeply browned and slightly sticky, about 40 minutes longer. (If the onions are sizzling or scorching, reduce the heat. If the onions are not browning after 15 to 20 minutes, raise the heat.) Add the garlic and shallot and cook until fragrant, about 1 minute.

2. Stir in the broth and wine and simmer until the mixture reduces to about 2 cups, 2 to 3 minutes. Off the heat, whisk in the 3 tablespoons butter, 1 tablespoon at a time. Adjust the seasonings, adding salt and pepper to taste. Serve immediately.

Caramelized Onion Jam with Dark Rum

MAKES ABOUT 1 CUP

Spread this jam on a sandwich with cream cheese or serve it on a platter with cheese and crackers.

1	tablespoon unsalted butter
1	tablespoon vegetable oil
½	teaspoon salt, plus more to taste
1	teaspoon plus 1 tablespoon light brown sugar
2	pounds onions (see page 166), halved and sliced ¼ inch thick
2	tablespoons dark rum
1	teaspoon minced fresh thyme leaves
½	teaspoon cider vinegar
	Ground black pepper

1. Heat the butter and oil in a 12-inch nonstick skillet over high heat. When the foaming subsides, stir in the salt and 1 teaspoon of the brown sugar. Add the onions and stir to coat. Cook, stirring occasionally, until the onions begin to soften and release some moisture, about 5 minutes. Reduce the heat to medium and cook, stirring frequently, until the onions are deeply browned and slightly sticky, about 40 minutes longer. (If the onions are sizzling or scorching, reduce the heat. If the onions are not browning after 15 to 20 minutes, raise the heat.)

2. Off the heat, stir in the rum. Wave a lit match over the skillet until the rum ignites. Shake the skillet until the flames subside.

3. Transfer the onions to the workbowl of a food processor along with the thyme and the remaining 1 tablespoon brown sugar and pulse to a jam-like consistency, about five 1-second pulses. Transfer the mixture to a bowl and stir in the vinegar and salt and pepper to taste. (The jam can be refrigerated in an airtight container for up to 7 days.)

Bacon, Scallion, and Caramelized Onion Dip

MAKES ABOUT 1 ½ CUPS

This recipe uses only ½ cup—or a half recipe—of caramelized onions.

3	ounces (about 3 slices) bacon, cut into ¼-inch pieces
½	cup Caramelized Onions
2	medium scallions, minced
½	teaspoon cider vinegar
¾	cup sour cream
	Salt and ground black pepper

1. Fry the bacon in a small skillet over medium heat until crisp, about 5 minutes. With a slotted spoon, transfer the bacon to a plate lined with paper towels.

2. Combine the caramelized onions, scallions, vinegar, sour cream, and bacon in a medium bowl. Season with salt and pepper to taste and serve. (The dip can be refrigerated in an airtight container for up to 3 days.)

ROASTED ONIONS

ROASTING PRODUCES CLEAN, PURE-tasting onions because it requires considerably less fat than other cooking methods. Roasting instructions, however, vary widely with regard to cutting and peeling the onions, oven temperature and timing, and the use of fats and liquids. By testing all the variables, we wanted to come up with roasted onions that met three criteria. First, the interior should be tender and moist throughout all the layers, rather than mushy on the inside and leathery toward the outside. Second, for a pleasing presentation, we wanted to serve them reasonably intact, perhaps halved or whole, like a baked potato. Finally, we wanted caramelization on at least some of the surfaces.

We started by trying to determine whether onions for roasting should be cut and, if so, how. Roasting onions whole, whether peeled or not, worked poorly because they became caramelized only at the small points where they touched the baking pan. We tried rolling them around from time to time during the cooking to increase the contact area

CARAMELIZING ONIONS, STEP BY STEP

Raw onions will nearly fill a 12-inch skillet (left). After 5 minutes over high heat, the onions will soften and release some moisture (center). Reduce the heat to medium and cook until the onions are glossy, soft, and deeply browned, about 40 minutes longer (right).

between onion and pan, but repeatedly opening the oven door to do so was a nuisance. Quartered onions caramelized better because they had more surface area to touch the pan, but the presentation fell short: Even with the root end intact, the quarters disintegrated into their separate sections, many of which turned mushy or dry during cooking.

Then we tried a straightforward method described by Jacques Pépin in his book *Cooking with Claudine* (KQED Books, 1996), in which he halved unpeeled onions crosswise (which helps keep them from falling apart) and roasted them cut-side down in a pan rubbed with a small amount of oil. These were the best of the bunch by far. All the layers were fully tender, neither mushy nor dry, and the caramelization of the cut surface was impressive. With good results and final preparation limited to a quick chop, this method clearly showed promise.

Moving forward with the halved onions, we set out to determine the optimum oven temperature and whether to cover the onions with foil during cooking.

With a dozen 2-pound bags of yellow onions in the kitchen, we tried 15-minute time intervals between 15 and 60 minutes; 25-degree temperature intervals between 350 and 500 degrees; pans both uncovered and covered with foil for the full cooking time and half the cooking time; and different oven rack adjustments, including directly on the oven floor. Among all those variations, the onions cooked for 30 minutes, at 400 degrees, uncovered, with the rack positioned just off the floor, turned out best—and quite beautifully at that. The layers were perfectly and evenly tender, and cut surfaces were caramelized to a dark brown, though the outside rings of the onions were lighter than the inside rings because they had popped up off the pan surface during cooking.

KEEPING ONIONS ORGANIZED

It's always best to use up onions that have been sitting in the pantry before breaking into a fresh supply. Here's how we keep track of older versus younger onions. Using a permanent marker, lightly mark a small X on the skin of each onion now in your storage bin. Leave any new onions you add to the bin unmarked, so that you'll know to reach for the marked onions first. When all of the marked onions have been used, mark the remaining onions.

With the basic questions answered, we went after the other variables. Our research turned up variations that called for peeling the onions, soaking them in water, rubbing them all over with fat, roasting in butter rather than oil, and roasting with various liquids, from water to vermouth to broth to vinegar, in the pan. Though none of these experiments improved the onions, we did discover a minor beneficial change. During cooking, the outer rings of onion rose off the pan, so they caramelized less than the inner rings. The remedy we devised was to cut two small X's at the top of each onion half, near the root and stem, with the tip of a knife. This provided a means for evaporated moisture to escape during cooking, which helped limit the elevation of the outer rings. We never found a way to keep them completely level on the pan, but we did note that a five-minute rest before removing the onions from the pan allowed the outer rings to settle back into position for an improved presentation.

Master Recipe for Roasted Onions

SERVES 6

Roasted onions make a fine side dish, alone or with a glaze made from the onion pan drippings and ⅓ cup balsamic vinegar, boiled until reduced by almost half. Roasted onions can be peeled and cut into salads, mixed with white beans, used as a bruschetta topping sprinkled with minced fresh parsley or oregano leaves and shaved Parmesan, or served with other small bites as part of an antipasto.

1	tablespoon olive oil
6	medium yellow onions
	Salt and ground black pepper

1. Adjust an oven rack to the lowest position and heat the oven to 400 degrees. Line a rimmed baking sheet with aluminum foil and rub the foil with the oil.

2. Halve the onions crosswise (do not peel them) and then cut two small X's in both the root and stem end with a paring knife to help steam escape. Place the onions cut-side down on the baking sheet. Roast the onions until dark brown around the bottom edge and tender when pierced with a thin skewer or knife tip, about 30 minutes. Transfer the pan to a wire rack and let the onions rest for 5 minutes before lifting them off the pan with a metal spatula. Peel if desired, season with salt and pepper to taste, and serve.

➤ VARIATIONS

Roasted Onions with Cumin

There will be enough juice on the cut side of the onion to form a paste when the cumin mixture is added.

1	tablespoon olive oil
1 ½	teaspoons ground cumin
1	tablespoon light or dark brown sugar
⅛	teaspoon cayenne pepper
	Salt
6	medium yellow onions
	Ground black pepper

1. Adjust an oven rack to the lowest position and heat the oven to 400 degrees. Line a rimmed baking sheet with aluminum foil and rub the foil with the oil. Mix the cumin, brown sugar, cayenne, and ½ teaspoon salt together in a small bowl; set the cumin mixture aside.

2. Halve the onions crosswise (do not peel them) and then cut two small X's in both the root and stem end with a paring knife to help steam escape. Sprinkle about ½ teaspoon of the cumin mixture onto the cut end of each onion and rub lightly to form a paste. Place the onions cut-side down on the baking sheet. Roast the onions until dark brown around the bottom edge and tender when pierced with a thin skewer or knife tip, about 30 minutes. Transfer the pan to a wire rack and let the onions rest for 5 minutes before lifting them off the pan with a metal spatula. Peel if desired, season with salt and pepper to taste, and serve.

Roasted Onion and Bacon Dip

MAKES 3 CUPS

With its fresh ingredients, this dip tastes like an uptown version of the old standby made with powdered onion soup mix. Serve with chips or crudités.

1	recipe Roasted Onions, cooled, peeled, and chopped fine
6–8	slices bacon, cooked until crisp, drained on paper towels, and crumbled
2	cups sour cream
2	teaspoons Worcestershire sauce
1	teaspoon Dijon mustard

½ teaspoon celery seed

3 tablespoons minced fresh chives

½ teaspoon salt

Ground black pepper

Mix all the ingredients, including pepper to taste, in a medium bowl. Serve immediately or chill. (The dip can be covered and refrigerated for 1 day.)

GRILLED ONIONS

GRILLING ONIONS SOUNDS LIKE A GREAT idea. Ideally, the onions will caramelize on the grill and become crisp in spots. Slices expose the greatest surface area and make the most sense. However, as the slices cook, the rings separate and can easily fall down onto the coals as you try to flip or move the onions. To keep the slices from falling apart, we found that it is necessary to skewer each onion slice crosswise (from side to side) so that it will rest flat on the grill and can be easily turned. Thick slices are best for skewering—anything less than ½ inch thick will be difficult to work with.

It's easier to work with large onions rather than smaller ones. In our tests, we particu-larly liked red, Vidalia, and Spanish, in part because it's easier to find oversized versions of these varieties. The Vidalias were particu-larly sweet, while the Spanish onions were heartier and not really sweet at all. The red onions were right in between and appealed to tasters who wanted their grilled onions neither too sweet nor too savory.

Master Recipe for Grilled Onions

SERVES 4

These onions are wonderful on burgers or served with just about any grilled meat, game, or poultry. The onions sweeten and caramelize as they cook on the grill.

2 large onions (about 1 ¼ pounds), papery skins removed and cut crosswise into ½-inch-thick rounds

2 tablespoons extra-virgin olive oil

Salt and ground black pepper

1. Place the onion slices on a baking sheet and brush with the oil. Season with salt and pepper to taste on both sides. Thread the onions onto skewers (see the illustrations below).

PREPARING ONIONS FOR GRILLING

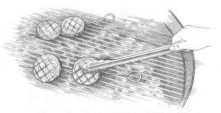

1. Cut thick slices (at least ½ inch) from large red, Vidalia, or Spanish onions and then impale each slice all the way through with a slender bamboo skewer that is about the same thick-ness as a toothpick or with a thin metal skewer. If using longer skewers, thread two slices on each skewer.

2. The skewered onion slices remain intact as they grill so no rings can fall onto the coals. Best of all, the onions are easily flipped with tongs.

2. Grill the onions over a medium-hot fire (you should be able to hold your hand 5 inches above the cooking grate for 3 to 4 seconds), turning once, until streaked with dark grill marks, 10 to 12 minutes. Serve hot or at room temperature.

➤ VARIATION

Grilled Onion Relish
MAKES 2 CUPS
Serve this relish with hamburgers, hot dogs, or any other grilled meat. You can also toss it together with your favorite green salad. Use the same baking sheet to hold the onions before and after grilling.

2	large onions (about 1 ¼ pounds), papery skins removed and cut crosswise into ½-inch-thick rounds
2	tablespoons extra-virgin olive oil
	Salt and ground black pepper
1	large red bell pepper
2	medium Italian or Greek pepperoncini (pickled peppers), chopped fine
¼	cup red wine vinegar
1	teaspoon sugar

1. Place the onion slices on a baking sheet and brush with the oil and season with salt and pepper to taste on both sides. Thread the onions onto skewers (see the illustration on page 172).

2. Grill the onions over a medium-hot fire (you should be able to hold your hand 5 inches above the cooking grate for 3 to 4 seconds), turning once, until streaked with dark grill marks, 10 to 12 minutes. When the onions are done, transfer them to the baking sheet and let cool for 10 minutes. At the same time as you are cooking the onions, grill the bell pepper, turning it every 3 or 4 minutes, until all sides are blistered and charred, about 15 minutes. When the pepper is done, place it in a bowl and cover the bowl with plastic wrap; allow to steam for 15 minutes.

3. Chop the grilled onions into ¼-inch dice and mix together with the pepperoncini, vinegar, and sugar in a medium bowl. Using your fingers, peel the blackened skin from the bell pepper. Remove and discard the core and seeds. Chop the pepper into ¼-inch dice and mix the pepper with the onion mixture. Let stand at least 30 minutes to blend flavors. Serve warm or at room temperature.

PEARL ONIONS
PEARL ONIONS (ALSO KNOWN AS BOILING onions) are tiny onions that measure about 1 inch in diameter. They are usually found mixed in with frozen peas, but many cooks braise pearl onions on their own to bring out the onions' sweet flavors.

Pearl onions must first be blanched in order to loosen the outer layers. We found that two minutes of blanching was sufficient to loosen the skins. Don't let the onions cook longer or they may become soggy. To prevent overcooking, we found it best to transfer the blanched and drained onions to a bowl of ice water. Once the onions are blanched and cooled, the skins can be easily slipped off. After trying various methods, we found it best to shave the thinnest slices possible from the root end and tip. The paper skin will then come right off.

Onions have a high sugar content, and browning them in a combination of butter and olive oil brought out their natural sweetness. As for braising liquids, we tried water, wine, and chicken broth. Water made the onions taste bland, and wine was too harsh. Chicken broth was the right choice here, resulting in onions that were rich and flavorful. Adding brown sugar and rosemary and reducing the liquid to a glaze deepened the flavors even further.

Master Recipe for Glazed Pearl Onions

SERVES 4

When trimming the root ends of the blanched onions, shave off the thinnest slice possible. If too much is taken off, the onion will fall apart. Serve glazed pearl onions with any roast; they are a natural on the holiday table.

I	pound small pearl onions
I	tablespoon extra-virgin olive oil
I	tablespoon unsalted butter
¹/₂	cup low-sodium chicken broth
I ¹/₂	tablespoons light or dark brown sugar
¹/₂	teaspoon minced fresh rosemary
	Salt and ground black pepper

1. Bring 2 quarts of water to a boil in a large saucepan. Add the onions and cook for 2 minutes. Drain and shock the onions in a large bowl filled with ice water. Let the onions cool; drain them again. Using a paring knife, shave off the root ends and cut off the very tips. Peel off the skins with your fingers.

2. Place the oil and butter in a large skillet over medium heat. When the butter has melted and is beginning to sizzle, add the onions and cook, shaking the pan to turn the onions occasionally, until lightly browned, 7 to 9 minutes.

3. Add the broth, brown sugar, and rosemary. Bring to a boil, cover, and reduce the heat to medium-low. Simmer until the onions are tender, about 12 minutes. Remove the lid, raise the heat to medium-high, and simmer until the liquid reduces to a glaze-like consistency, 4 to 5 minutes. Season with salt and pepper to taste and serve immediately.

> VARIATIONS

Frozen Glazed Pearl Onions

Frozen pearl onions are already peeled and can be cooked directly from their frozen state. No defrosting is necessary.

Follow the master recipe, starting at step 2. You may need to increase the browning time in step 2 by a minute or two.

Glazed Pearl Onions with Sweet and Sour Flavors

I	pound small pearl onions
I	tablespoon extra-virgin olive oil
I	tablespoon unsalted butter
¹/₂	cup low-sodium chicken broth
I ¹/₂	tablespoons light or dark brown sugar
I	tablespoon balsamic vinegar
¹/₂	teaspoon minced fresh thyme leaves
	Salt and ground black pepper

1. Bring 2 quarts of water to a boil in a large saucepan. Add the onions and cook for 2 minutes. Drain and shock the onions in a large bowl filled with ice water. Let the onions cool; drain them again. Using a paring knife, shave off the root ends and cut off the very tips. Peel off the skins with your fingers.

2. Place the oil and butter in a large skillet over medium heat. When the butter has melted and is beginning to sizzle, add the onions and cook, stirring occasionally, until lightly browned, 7 to 9 minutes.

3. Add the broth, brown sugar, vinegar, and thyme. Bring to a boil, cover, and reduce the heat to medium-low. Simmer until the onions are tender, 12 to 15 minutes. Remove the lid, raise the heat to medium-high, and simmer until the liquid has reduced slightly, 4 to 5 minutes. Season with salt and pepper to taste and serve immediately.

EQUIPMENT: Colander

A colander is essentially a perforated bowl designed to allow liquid to drain through the holes. Any vegetable that is boiled will end up in a colander before it is served. In our initial survey of models, we were not surprised to find colanders made from a range of materials: plastic, enameled steel, stainless steel, anodized aluminum, and wire mesh (which is like a screen). What did surprise us—and how—was the range of prices: from $4 to $115.

We put the colanders through a battery of tests to obtain an objective assessment of their performance. We drained pounds and pounds of cooked spaghetti, orzo, and frozen baby peas in each one. Early in the testing, we splashed scalding water and hot pasta out of a tiny 3-quart model by pouring it too fast from the cooking pot, so we eliminated that size from the running. The 5- and 7-quart models (10 altogether) performed on par, so we included both in our tests.

Most colanders on the market come with one of two types of bases, either a circular metal ring attached to the bottom, on which the bowl sits pedestal style, or individual feet soldered to the bottom of the bowl. No matter which type it is, the base should be unfailingly stable to prevent spills. Our research and reading on colanders consistently noted the superiority of the ring over the feet, claiming that a colander on feet is less stable because it touches the ground in only three or four spots. That sounded like a reasonable theory to us, until we tested the two models in the group with feet, which did not tip or spill during any of our tests. In our experience, then, though most colanders on the market have ring bases, you needn't shy away from a model with feet if that's what you happen to find.

We also expected that the size, placement, and pattern of the drainage holes would be key for quick, efficient draining. Seven of our 10 colanders had the look we expected, that of a metal or plastic bowl with perforations arranged in straight lines, starbursts, or circles; the remaining three had more unusual designs. True to its name, the Endurance Colander/Strainer was a hybrid with a metal bowl that was so thoroughly perforated it almost looked like wire mesh. Two other colanders, the Harold Imports and the Norpro expandable colander, were made from wire mesh, like a strainer. The three latter colanders had more holes than their more traditional counterparts, and each one performed very well, draining quickly and completely, with no pooling of water and no food—even the wily orzo—slipping through the holes. The traditional colanders with larger holes did allow some orzo to slip through (anywhere from just a few pieces for the Rösle to almost three quarters of a cup for the Silverstone), but only the Silverstone allowed so much orzo through that it merited a downgrade in the ratings.

When all was said and drained, every colander in the group got the job done, be it the $4 Hoan plastic model or the gleaming $115 Rösle stainless-steel model. To make a recommendation, then, we have to be a bit more subjective than usual. So here it is: Based on this testing and our gut feeling, the colander we'd most like to bring home is the Endurance Colander/Strainer. It's reasonably priced at $25, it's solid and comfortable to wield, it drains like a pro and keeps all its contents in check, and many editors here considered it to be an unusually handsome specimen of a colander. When it comes to this basic kitchen utensil, extra money is not well spent.

THE BEST COLANDER

The Endurance Colander/Strainer has a mesh-like perforated bowl that traps even the smallest bits of food.

PARSNIPS

MANY PEOPLE IGNORE PARSNIPS, PROBABLY BECAUSE THESE ROOT VEG-
etables look like dirty, anemic carrots. When our shopper started buying parsnips
for this article, people stopped her in the supermarket checkout line to ask what
they were and how she cooked them. Pounds of parsnips later, we had the answer
for those people. Parsnips shouldn't be thought of as a pale version of a carrot.
They're sweeter, richer, and more assertive and should be used in recipes where
they can shine. For the most part, this means pureeing or roasting them.

To arrive at this culinary understanding, we tried substituting parsnips for
mashed or grated potatoes and carrots in cakes, puddings, and breads. The results
were disappointing (and expensive). We also tried eating parsnips raw in salads and blanched with a dip. The flavor was bland and the texture was unpleasantly chewy. We sautéed them and wished we had used potatoes.

We did find that parsnips responded well to roasting, becoming soft and sweet on the inside and crisp and caramelized on the outside. We found that the parsnips cooked best at 425 degrees—they were lightly browned on the outside and creamy on the inside. At higher oven temperatures, they tended to scorch, and at lower temperatures, they did not brown sufficiently and were lacking in flavor. Coating the parsnips (which should be cut into chunks) with olive oil promoted even better browning and added flavor. Shaking the baking pan halfway through the 30-minute roasting time turned the parsnip pieces and promoted even browning.

As good as our roasted parsnips are, many test cooks in our kitchen ended up preferring parsnips when they were pureed. Although many recipes call for boiling parsnips until tender before pureeing them, we found that the best flavor resulted from steaming them for about 10 minutes and then pureeing. Use small, firm parsnips without dark spots and with a base of no more than 1 to 1¼ inches in diameter. Larger ones have a woody core that takes as long as 20 minutes to cook and offers little flavor. If you get stuck with large ones, cut out this woody core before cooking.

Unless you truly despise peeling, we recommend you peel parsnips before steaming or boiling. After cooking, the skin will rub off, but a fair amount of flesh comes off with it.

You can puree parsnips with any of the tools you use to mash potatoes. However, since they are not as high in starch as potatoes, they can also be pureed in a food processor without turning into a gummy mess. This is definitely the easiest and quickest method.

Master Recipe for Pureed Parsnips

SERVES 4

Since the vegetables are steamed, the flavor of this puree is sweet and intense. The puree can be refrigerated for up to 3 days. Larger parsnips should be quartered lengthwise and then cored. To do this, lay the piece of parsnip flat-side down on a cutting board and trim the woody core that runs along the interior of the piece. Medium parsnips (about an inch in diameter) have tender cores that don't have to be removed.

I ½   pounds parsnips, peeled, cut into
 2 ½-inch lengths, and halved (or
 quartered and cored, if necessary)
I ½   tablespoons unsalted butter, softened
 Salt and ground white pepper

1. Place the parsnips in a steamer basket in a large saucepan filled with 1 inch of water. Bring the water to a boil, cover, and steam over high heat until the parsnips can be easily pierced with a thin-bladed knife, about 10 minutes. Reserve the cooking liquid.

2. Transfer the parsnips to the workbowl of a food processor or to a food mill. Puree, adding reserved cooking liquid (about ¼ cup) to achieve the desired consistency. Return the puree to a skillet and reheat, stirring in the butter. Season to taste with salt and pepper. Serve immediately.

➤ VARIATION

Creamy Parsnip Puree with Shallots
This puree can be served as a side dish with roast pork or roast chicken.

I ½   pounds parsnips, peeled, cut into
 2 ½-inch lengths, and halved (or
 quartered and cored, if necessary)
I   tablespoon unsalted butter

3   medium shallots, chopped
¼   cup low-sodium chicken broth
¼   cup milk, or more to taste
 Salt and ground white pepper

1. Place the parsnips in a steamer basket in a large saucepan filled with 1 inch of water. Bring the water to a boil, cover, and steam over high heat until the parsnips can be easily pierced with a thin-bladed knife, about 10 minutes.

2. While the parsnips are cooking, melt the butter in a large skillet over medium heat. When the foaming subsides, add the shallots and cook until golden, 2 to 3 minutes. Set the mixture aside.

3. Transfer the steamed parsnips to the workbowl of a food processor or to a food mill. Puree the parsnips along with the broth. Add the puree to the skillet with the shallots and warm over medium-low heat. Stir in the milk and season to taste with salt and pepper. Serve immediately.

Master Recipe for Roasted Parsnips

SERVES 4

All the parsnip pieces should be the same size. Larger parsnips (thicker than 1 ½ inches) should be quartered lengthwise and then cored. To do this, lay the piece of parsnip flat-side down on a cutting board and trim the woody core that runs along the interior of the piece. Smaller parsnips (about an inch in diameter) should be halved lengthwise.

2   pounds parsnips, peeled, cut into
 I-inch lengths, and halved (or
 quartered and cored, if necessary)
2   tablespoons extra-virgin olive oil
 Salt and ground black pepper
I   tablespoon minced fresh parsley leaves

1. Adjust an oven rack to the lower-middle position and heat the oven to 425 degrees.

2. Toss the parsnips, oil, and salt and pepper to taste together in a large bowl. Spread the parsnips out in a single layer on a rimmed baking sheet. Roast until the parsnips are golden and tender, about 30 minutes, shaking the pan halfway through the cooking time. Add the parsley and adjust the seasonings, adding salt and pepper to taste. Serve immediately.

➤ VARIATIONS

Roasted Parsnips with Warm Spices

The butter, spices, and honey will be easier to mix together if the butter is hot. The butter shouldn't be hot enough to sizzle, but it should be very warm to the touch.

2	tablespoons unsalted butter, melted
1/8	teaspoon ground allspice
1/8	teaspoon ground nutmeg
1/4	teaspoon ground ginger
1	teaspoon honey
2	pounds parsnips, peeled, cut into 1-inch lengths, and halved (or quartered and cored, if necessary) Salt and ground black pepper
1	tablespoon minced fresh parsley leaves

1. Adjust an oven rack to the lower-middle position and heat the oven to 425 degrees.

2. Whisk the butter, spices, and honey together in a large bowl. Add the parsnips and salt and pepper to taste and toss to combine. Spread the parsnips out in a single layer on a rimmed baking sheet. Roast until the parsnips are golden and tender, about 30 minutes, shaking the pan halfway through the cooking time. Add the parsley and adjust the seasonings, adding salt and pepper to taste. Serve immediately.

Roasted Parsnips with Bacon and Rosemary

The earthy flavors of the parsnips and rosemary are delicious with the smoky bacon. This dish goes well with roast chicken or pork.

3	ounces (about 3 slices) bacon, cut into 1/2-inch pieces
2	pounds parsnips, peeled, cut into 1-inch lengths, and halved (or quartered and cored, if necessary)
1	tablespoon minced fresh rosemary Salt and ground black pepper

1. Adjust an oven rack to the lower-middle position and heat the oven to 425 degrees.

2. Fry the bacon in a large skillet over medium heat until crisp, about 5 minutes. Using a slotted spoon, transfer the bacon to a plate lined with paper towels; set aside.

3. Turn off the heat under the skillet and add the parsnips and rosemary to the bacon fat. Stir to coat the parsnips with the fat and season with salt and pepper to taste. Spread the parsnips out in a single layer on a rimmed baking sheet. Roast until the parsnips are golden and tender, about 30 minutes, shaking the pan halfway through the cooking time. Add the bacon and adjust the seasonings, adding salt and pepper to taste. Serve immediately.

PEAS

THERE ARE THREE VARIETIES OF PEAS SOLD IN MOST MARKETS—SHELL peas, sugar snap peas, and snow peas. We find that shell peas are generally mealy and bland. Frozen peas are usually sweeter and are the better option. Frozen peas are best blanched and then buttered or sauced. Nothing could be simpler.

The flat, light green snow pea has a long history, especially in the Chinese kitchen. The peas are immature, and the pod is tender enough to eat. Sugar snap peas are a relatively recent invention, which date back just 20 years. They are a cross between shell peas and snow peas. The sweet, crisp pod is edible and holds small, juicy peas. Good sugar snaps look like compact fresh garden peas in the

shell. They are firm and lustrous with barely discernible bumps along the pods. Expect to find robust fresh peas from late spring through summer.

Sugar snap and snow peas should be cooked quickly so that they retain some crunch and color. Stir-frying works well with snow peas, which have a fairly sturdy pod. However, sugar snap peas are too delicate for such intense heat. We found the pods become mushy by the time the peas inside are actually heated through.

We found that microwaving did not cook the sugar snap peas evenly. Opening the microwave and stirring helped, but we soon abandoned this method. Steaming yielded tender sugar snap peas, but they tasted flat. We found that sugar snaps greatly benefit from the addition of some salt as they cook, something that can only be done if the peas are blanched.

Although blanching yielded sugar snap peas with excellent taste and texture, we found that the blanched sugar snaps tended to shrivel or pucker a bit as they cooled. We solved this problem by plunging the cooked peas into ice water as soon as they were drained. This also helped set their bright color and prevent further softening from residual heat.

Once blanched and shocked, the sugar snap peas can be held for up to an hour before seasoning. Here you have two options—a quick sauté with butter or oil and other flavorful ingredients (garlic, herbs, nuts) or dressing with a vinaigrette.

Master Recipe for Buttered Peas

SERVES 4

Frozen peas may just be the perfect vegetable. They're not only inexpensive but require no washing, stemming, or chopping and cook in a matter of minutes.

I   (16-ounce) bag frozen peas

I   teaspoon salt, plus more to taste

I   tablespoon unsalted butter

     Ground black pepper

1. Bring 2 quarts of water to a boil in a large saucepan. Add the peas and salt and cook until the peas are bright green, about 2 minutes. Drain the peas and set aside.

2. Melt the butter in a 10-inch skillet over medium-high heat. When the foaming subsides, add the peas and cook, stirring frequently, until the peas are coated with butter and hot, about 2 minutes. Season to taste with salt and pepper and serve immediately.

➤ VARIATION

Frozen Peas and Ham with Béchamel Sauce

We prefer thick-cut ham or ham steaks for this recipe.

I   (16-ounce) bag frozen peas

I   teaspoon salt, plus more to taste

2   tablespoons unsalted butter

6   ounces ham, cut into ¼-inch dice
       (about I cup)

2   teaspoons all-purpose flour

⅔   cup whole milk
       Cayenne pepper

1. Bring 2 quarts of water to a boil in a large saucepan. Add the peas and salt and cook until the peas are bright green, about 2 minutes. Drain the peas and set aside.

2. Melt 1 tablespoon of the butter in a 10-inch skillet over medium-high heat. When the foaming subsides, add the ham and cook, stirring frequently, until the ham is lightly browned, about 3 minutes. Transfer the ham to a plate.

3. Reduce the heat to medium and add the remaining 1 tablespoon butter. Sprinkle the flour into the pan. Using a wooden spoon, stir until the flour is well mixed. Add the milk and continue to stir until no lumps remain. Bring to a simmer and cook until the sauce thickens, about 1 minute. Add the peas and ham, stir, and cook until the peas are hot, about 1 minute. Season to taste with salt and cayenne and serve immediately.

≁

Master Recipe for Stir-Fried Snow Peas

SERVES 4

Snow peas are sturdier than sugar snap peas and hold up well when stir-fried.

¼   cup low-sodium chicken broth

¼   teaspoon salt
       Ground black pepper

I   tablespoon plus I teaspoon peanut oil

I   pound snow peas (about 4 cups),
       tips pulled off and strings removed
       (see the illustration on page 181)

2   medium cloves garlic, minced or
       pressed through a garlic press

1½   teaspoons minced fresh ginger

1. Mix the broth, salt, and pepper to taste in a small bowl.

2. Heat 1 tablespoon of the oil in a 12-inch nonstick skillet over high heat until almost smoking. Add the snow peas and cook, stirring frequently, until bright green, about 2 minutes. Clear the center of the pan, add the garlic and ginger, and drizzle with the remaining 1 teaspoon oil. Mash the garlic and ginger with the back of a spatula. Cook for 10 seconds and then mix with the snow peas. Off the heat, add the broth mixture (it should immediately reduce down to a glaze). Serve immediately.

➤ VARIATION
Stir-Fried Snow Peas with Tofu

Be sure to drain the tofu well and pat it dry with paper towels. If the tofu is too wet, it will splatter when it hits the hot oil.

1	tablespoon hoisin sauce
1	tablespoon Worcestershire sauce
1	tablespoon soy sauce
3	tablespoons dry sherry
1	teaspoon toasted sesame oil
2	tablespoons peanut oil
8	ounces tofu, drained, dried well with paper towels, and cut into 1 by 1 by ¹/₂-inch cubes
1	pound snow peas (about 4 cups), tips pulled off and strings removed (see the illustration below)
2	medium cloves garlic, minced or pressed through a garlic press
¹/₂	teaspoon minced fresh ginger

1. Mix the hoisin sauce, Worcestershire sauce, soy sauce, sherry, and sesame oil together in a small bowl. Set aside.

2. Heat 1 tablespoon of the peanut oil in a 12-inch nonstick skillet over high heat until almost smoking. Add the tofu and cook until golden brown, 1 to 2 minutes. Flip the tofu over and cook until the other side is golden brown, 1 to 2 minutes longer. Transfer the tofu to a plate.

3. Add 2 teaspoons of the peanut oil to the empty skillet and swirl to coat. Add the snow peas and cook, stirring frequently, until bright green, about 2 minutes. Clear the center of the pan, add the garlic and ginger, and drizzle with the remaining 1 teaspoon peanut oil. Mash the garlic and ginger with the back of a spatula. Cook for 10 seconds and then mix with the snow peas. Add the tofu and sauce, stir, and cook for 1 minute longer. Serve immediately.

Master Recipe for Blanched Sugar Snap Peas
SERVES 4

Have a bowl of ice water ready to shock the drained peas and prevent further softening and shriveling. Snow peas can be used in any of the following recipes, although they are probably best stir-fried (see page 180).

1	teaspoon salt, plus more to taste
1	pound sugar snap peas (about 4 cups), stems snapped off and strings removed if needed
1	tablespoon unsalted butter
	Ground black pepper

1. Bring 6 cups of water to a boil in a large saucepan. Add the salt and peas and cook until crisp-tender, 1½ to 2 minutes. Drain the peas, shock them in ice water, and drain again. Dry the peas well on a rimmed baking sheet lined with paper towels.

2. Place the butter in a large skillet and turn the heat to medium-high. When the foaming subsides, add the peas and cook, stirring frequently, until the peas are heated through, 1 to 2 minutes. Season to taste with salt and pepper and serve immediately.

STRINGING SNOW PEAS

Rip off the tip of the snow pea and pull along the flat side of the pod to remove the string at the same time.

➤ VARIATIONS

Sugar Snap Peas with Pine Nuts and Garlic

Nuts burn very easily. Keep a sharp eye on the pine nuts in the pan and adjust the heat as necessary.

- I teaspoon salt, plus more to taste
- I pound sugar snap peas (about 4 cups), stems snapped off and strings removed if needed
- I tablespoon extra-virgin olive oil
- ¼ cup pine nuts, chopped coarse
- I medium clove garlic, minced or pressed through a garlic press Ground black pepper

1. Bring 6 cups of water to a boil in a large saucepan. Add the salt and peas and cook until crisp-tender, 1½ to 2 minutes. Drain the peas, shock them in ice water, and drain again. Dry the peas well on a rimmed baking sheet lined with paper towels.

2. Heat the oil in a large skillet over medium heat until almost smoking. Add the pine nuts and cook, stirring frequently, until they are light golden brown, 1 to 2 minutes. Stir in the garlic and cook until fragrant, 30 seconds. Add the peas and cook, stirring frequently, until the peas are heated through, 1 to 2 minutes. Season to taste with salt and pepper and serve immediately.

Sugar Snap Peas with Sesame Seeds

Sesame oil has a low smoking point and should not be used in high-heat cooking. It is usually used at the end of cooking, or as a condiment. There are two different kinds of sesame oil: toasted and plain. Toasted sesame oil is golden in color and has a distinct, nutty aroma. See page 37 for more information about sesame oil.

- I teaspoon salt, plus more to taste
- I pound sugar snap peas (about 4 cups), stems snapped off and strings removed if needed
- 2 teaspoons vegetable oil
- 2 tablespoons sesame seeds
- I teaspoon toasted sesame oil Ground black pepper

1. Bring 6 cups of water to a boil in a large saucepan. Add the salt and peas and cook until crisp-tender, 1½ to 2 minutes. Drain the peas, shock them in ice water, and drain again. Dry the peas well on a rimmed baking sheet lined with paper towels.

2. Heat the vegetable oil in a large skillet over medium heat until almost smoking. Add the sesame seeds and cook, shaking the pan occasionally, until the seeds are light golden brown and begin to pop, 1 to 2 minutes. Add the sesame oil and peas and cook, stirring frequently, until the peas are heated through, 1 to 2 minutes. Season to taste with salt and pepper and serve immediately.

Sugar Snap Peas with Asian Dressing

To mingle the flavors, you can let the peas and dressing stand for up to 10 minutes at room temperature. After that, the peas start to lose their bright green color.

- 2 teaspoons sesame seeds
- 2 tablespoons orange juice
- 2 tablespoons rice vinegar
- I teaspoon honey
- ½ teaspoon soy sauce
- I medium scallion, sliced thin
- ½ teaspoon grated fresh ginger
- 2 tablespoons peanut oil
- I teaspoon toasted sesame oil
- I teaspoon salt, plus more to taste

Ground black pepper

1 pound sugar snap peas (about 4 cups), stems snapped off and strings removed if needed

1. Toast the sesame seeds over medium heat in a small skillet, shaking the pan often to promote even cooking, until light brown and fragrant, 4 to 5 minutes.

2. Meanwhile, combine the orange juice, vinegar, honey, soy sauce, scallion, and ginger in a small bowl. Whisk in the oils.

Season to taste with salt and pepper. Stir in the sesame seeds. (The dressing can be set aside for several hours.)

3. Bring 6 cups of water to a boil in a large saucepan. Add 1 teaspoon salt and the peas and cook until crisp-tender, 1½ to 2 minutes. Drain the peas, shock them in ice water, and drain again. Dry the peas well on a rimmed baking sheet lined with paper towels.

4. Toss the peas with the dressing, adjust the seasonings with salt and pepper to taste, and serve immediately.

INGREDIENTS: Soy Sauce

Few condiments are as misunderstood as soy sauce, the pungent, fragrant, fermented flavoring that's a mainstay in Asian cooking. Its simple, straightforward composition—equal parts soybeans and a roasted grain, usually wheat, plus water and salt—belies the subtle, sophisticated contribution it makes as an all-purpose seasoning, flavor enhancer, tabletop condiment, and dipping sauce.

The three products consumers are likely to encounter are regular soy sauce, light soy sauce (made with a higher percentage of water and hence lower in sodium), and tamari (made with fermented soybeans, water, and salt—no wheat). Tamari generally has a stronger flavor and thicker consistency than soy sauce. It is traditionally used in Japanese cooking.

In a tasting of leading soy sauces, we found that products aged according to ancient customs were superior to synthetic sauces, such as La Choy's, which are made

in a day and almost always contain hydrolyzed vegetable protein. Our favorite soy sauce, Eden Selected Shoyu Soy Sauce (*shoyu* is the Japanese word for soy sauce), is aged for three years. Tasters also liked products made by San-J and Kikkoman.

THE BEST SOY SAUCE
Eden Selected Shoyu Soy Sauce was described by tasters as "toasty, caramely, and complex." The saltiness was tangible but not overwhelming. Among the 12 brands tested, it was the clear favorite.

PEPPERS

THE ROASTING OF BELL PEPPERS HAS BECOME VERY POPULAR, AND FOR very good reasons. When roasted, sweet red bell peppers assume a whole new layer of complex, smoky flavor. In testing the many different methods of roasting peppers, we sought the most efficient way to achieve tender but not mushy flesh, smoky flavor, and skin that would peel off easily.

After flaming (over a gas burner), broiling, baking, and steaming dozens of peppers, we found that oven broiling is clearly superior. It's neater and faster, and the peppers are delicious.

We found that you must take care not to overroast the peppers. When the skin

of the pepper just puffs up and turns black, you have reached the point at which flavor is maximized and the texture of the pepper flesh is soft but not mushy. After this point, continued exposure to heat will result in darkened flesh that is thinner, flabby textured, and slightly bitter.

Some details from our testing: The first method we tested was using the stovetop gas burner. The one benefit of this method is that whole peppers retain the liquid that would be released during roasting by other methods. The disadvantages, however, are many. The peppers require constant tending and must be turned with tongs after each exposed area of flesh has charred. The clever tong manipulation doesn't end there, as both ends of the pepper need to be charred to promote even peeling. Also, only two peppers can be roasted at a time, unless you want to try to double this number by using two burners at a time. That,

however, requires two pairs of tongs and deft eye-hand coordination and invites both arm scorching and overroasting. Forget about using a long-handled fork instead of tongs. After three or four minutes, we found that the softened pepper will fall off the fork right onto the burner flame.

The second approach we tested was oven-roasting at 550 degrees. Whether the peppers are kept whole or split open and flattened, this method takes longer, usually from 12 to 15 minutes, which in turn creates overcooked, soggy flesh. Lower oven temperatures also yielded overcooked peppers and required even longer cooking times—up to one hour at 325 degrees.

Broiling peppers does present some challenges, although it is certainly better than either the flame-roasting or oven-roasting methods. The broiler element in most ovens is approximately 3 inches away from the upper rack, which means that whole peppers usually touch the element. A lower rack level takes too long and cooks the flesh too much.

After some trial and error, we found that the answer is to cut the peppers. This method yields less juice (some does collect in the bowl as the peppers steam), but that's an easy tradeoff given the many benefits of this method. Primary among these is that the peppers consistently achieved a meaty texture and rich flavor. In addition, peppers that have been cut open and roasted under the broiler are easier to peel than peppers roasted by any other method. The skin blackens and swells up like a balloon and lifts off in whole sections. By comparison, roasting over an open flame results in small patches of skin peeling off, at best.

Peppers should not be rubbed with oil before they are roasted. The skins will char and blister faster without the oil coating. It does help to line the baking pan with foil. Without foil, sticky, dark spots formed on the baking sheet where the juices dripped and evaporated during roasting.

Unless you have asbestos fingers, roasted peppers need time to cool before handling, and steaming during this time does make the charred skin a bit easier to peel off. The ideal steaming time is 15 minutes—any less and the peppers are still too hot to work with comfortably. Any more time (we tested lengths up to one hour) provided no discernible advantage. The best method is to use a heat-resistant bowl (glass, ceramic, or metal) with a piece of plastic wrap secured over the top to trap the steam. The wrap holds in the heat, creating more intense steam.

Seeding the peppers before roasting makes it possible to peel the peppers without having to rinse them to wash away the seeds. If you are still tempted to rinse, notice the rich oils that accumulate on your fingers as you work. It seems silly to rinse away those oils rather than savoring them later with your meal.

The way peppers are treated after they are peeled determines how long they keep. Unadorned and wrapped in plastic wrap, peppers will keep their full, meaty texture only about two days in the refrigerator. Drizzled with a generous amount of olive oil and kept in an airtight container, peppers will keep about one week without losing texture or flavor.

Most cooks are familiar with roasting bell peppers for salads, sauces, or dips. However, peppers may also be sliced and cooked by other means as a vegetable side dish. When choosing peppers, we generally avoid green peppers,

INGREDIENTS: Bell Peppers

We had long wondered whether color makes a difference when it comes to roasting bell peppers. After roasting five kinds of bell peppers, we can now say that the answer is an unequivocal yes.

Red peppers gave the best and most even results. Yellow peppers were generally more delicate, their flesh thinner and more prone to overcooking, which gave it a brownish hue. Since they are also more expensive than red peppers, we roast them only if the yellow color is important to a dish. Orange peppers are equally delicate and need careful watching. With both yellow and orange varieties, wait for the skin to just char and lift up, making sure the edges are slightly blistered. At this point, remove these delicate peppers from the broiler. You have more leeway with red peppers and can let them char a bit more, which makes peeling easier.

Based on our kitchen tests, we can confidently say that purple peppers are a waste of money. They lost their color when roasted (or when cooked in any manner), turning a muddy green. Their flavor was bitter, like green peppers, not sweet like the red, yellow, and orange varieties. Lastly, don't bother roasting green peppers. Green peppers, which are simply unripened red peppers, are not sweet and gain nothing by being roasted.

which are unripe and can be quite bitter. Red, yellow, and orange peppers are all fully ripe and much sweeter. Avoid purple peppers, which turn a drab green color when cooked and cost much more than green peppers.

We tested sautéing and stir-frying first and found that both methods yield lightly seared peppers that are still fairly crisp. The peppers were good, but we missed the silky smoothness of roasted peppers. We tried

cooking the peppers more but found that the exterior charred by the time the pepper was fully cooked.

We decided to see what would happen if we put the cover on the skillet after searing them. As we hoped, the peppers steamed in their own juices and became especially tender. We found that the moisture from the peppers is enough to keep them from scorching in the covered pan. We also realized that we now

ROASTING PEPPERS

1. Slice ¼ inch from the top and bottom of the pepper and then gently remove the stem from the top lobe.

2. Pull the core out of the pepper.

3. Make a slit down one side of the pepper and lay it flat, skin-side down, in one long strip. Slide a sharp knife along the inside of the pepper and remove all ribs and seeds.

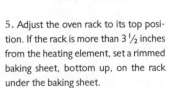

4. Arrange the strips of peppers and the top and bottom lobes, skin-side up, on a foil-lined baking sheet. Flatten the strips with the palm of your hand.

5. Adjust the oven rack to its top position. If the rack is more than 3 ½ inches from the heating element, set a rimmed baking sheet, bottom up, on the rack under the baking sheet.

6. Roast until the skin of the peppers is charred and puffed up like a balloon, but the flesh is still firm. You may steam the peppers at this point or not, as you wish. Start peeling where the skin has charred and bubbled the most. The skin will come off in large strips.

had an opportunity to add another liquid for juicier, seasoned peppers. We found that a little vinegar balances the intense sweetness of the peppers and works especially well.

In addition to sautéing, raw bell peppers can also be grilled. In this case, you need to oil the peppers quite well and to cook them less—just until lightly colored. The skins should wrinkle but not blister. If the skins blister (which can happen rather quickly on the grill), you will be tempted to peel the peppers. If that's the case, you might as well have made roasted peppers. Grilled peppers can be seasoned in numerous ways (again, vinegar is a good option) and make an excellent side dish.

Roasted Red Bell Peppers

MAKES 4 ROASTED PEPPERS,
ENOUGH TO SERVE 8 AS
AN APPETIZER

Cooking times vary, depending on the broiler, so watch the peppers carefully as they roast. You will need to increase the cooking time slightly if your peppers are just out of the refrigerator instead of at room temperature. Yellow and orange peppers roast faster than red ones, so decrease their cooking time by 2 to 4 minutes. Do not roast green or purple peppers—their flavor is bitter and not worth the effort.

4	medium-to-large red bell peppers (6 to 9 ounces each), prepared according to illustrations 1 through 4 on page 186
	Extra-virgin olive oil
	Salt

1. Adjust the oven rack to the top position. The oven rack should be 2½ to 3½ inches from the heating element. If it is not,

set a rimmed baking sheet, turned upside down, on the oven rack to elevate the pan (see illustration 5 on page 186). Turn the broiler on and heat for 5 minutes. Broil the peppers until spotty brown, about 5 minutes. Reverse the pan in the oven and roast until the skin of the peppers is charred and puffed but the flesh is still firm, 3 to 5 minutes longer.

2. Remove the pan from the oven and let the peppers sit until cool enough to handle. (To facilitate peeling, transfer the peppers right out of the oven to a large heat-resistant bowl, cover it with plastic wrap, and let the peppers steam for 15 minutes.) Peel and discard the skin from each piece (see illustration 6 on page 186).

3. To serve, slice the peppers and arrange them on a platter. Drizzle with oil just until lightly moistened and sprinkle with salt to taste.

Sweet and Spicy Roasted Red Pepper Dip

MAKES ABOUT 2 CUPS

Serve this Middle Eastern–style dip with grilled or toasted pita breads that are cut into triangles.

6	tablespoons extra-virgin olive oil
1	small onion, chopped coarse
1	small clove garlic, minced or pressed through a garlic press
1	tablespoon ground cumin
½	medium jalapeño chile, stemmed, seeded, and minced
3	Roasted Red Bell Peppers
¼	cup coarsely chopped fresh parsley leaves
2	tablespoons molasses
2	tablespoons juice from 1 lime
	Salt and ground black pepper

1. Heat the oil in a small skillet over medium-high heat until almost smoking. Add the onion and cook until softened, about 5 minutes. Add the garlic, cumin, and chile and cook until the garlic softens, about 1 minute.

2. Transfer the onion mixture to the workbowl of a food processor. Add the roasted peppers, parsley, molasses, and lime juice and process until smooth. Scrape the mixture into a bowl and season with salt and pepper to taste. (The dip can be covered and refrigerated for several days.)

Roasted Red Pepper Salad with Red Onions and Cucumbers

SERVES 4 TO 6

This salad works well with grilled food.

2   medium cucumbers (about 1 pound),
    peeled, halved, seeded, and sliced
    1/4 inch thick (see illustrations
    1 and 2 on page 92)
2   teaspoons salt, plus more to taste
2   tablespoons balsamic vinegar
    Ground black pepper
4   tablespoons extra-virgin olive oil
1   small red onion, halved and sliced thin
1   recipe Roasted Red Bell Peppers,
    cut into bite-size pieces
2   tablespoons minced fresh mint leaves

1. Toss the sliced cucumbers with 2 teaspoons salt in a strainer or colander set over a bowl. Weight the cucumbers (see illustration 3 on page 92) and drain for at least 1 hour and up to 3 hours. Transfer the cucumbers to a medium bowl and set aside.

2. Meanwhile, whisk the vinegar and salt and pepper to taste together in a medium bowl. Whisk in the oil until smooth. Add the onion and set aside for 30 minutes. Add the cucumbers, roasted peppers, and mint and toss to combine. Adjust the seasonings, adding salt and pepper to taste, and serve immediately.

Fusilli with Roasted Red and Yellow Pepper Sauce

SERVES 4 AS A MAIN COURSE

This recipe looks best with a mixture of red and yellow bell peppers. The peppers can be roasted together, but make sure not to overcook the delicate yellow peppers.

1   recipe Roasted Red Bell Peppers
    (made with 2 red and 2 yellow
    peppers), chopped
6   tablespoons extra-virgin olive oil
1   medium clove garlic, minced or
    pressed through a garlic press
2   tablespoons minced fresh mint leaves
1   tablespoon drained capers
2   teaspoons juice from 1 lemon
    Salt and ground black pepper
1   pound fusilli

1. Combine the roasted peppers, oil, garlic, mint, capers, lemon juice, and salt and pepper to taste in a medium bowl. Cover and set aside for the flavors to blend, at least 30 minutes and up to 2 hours.

2. Bring 4 quarts of water to a boil, covered, in a stockpot. Add 1 tablespoon salt and the pasta, stir to separate, and cook until al dente. Drain the pasta, reserving 1/4 cup of the cooking water. Return the pasta to the stockpot and add the roasted pepper mixture. Toss, adding the reserved water as needed to moisten the pasta. Serve immediately.

Master Recipe for Sautéed Peppers

SERVES 4

A mixture of red, yellow, and orange peppers delivers the sweetest and best results.

2	tablespoons extra-virgin olive oil
4	medium red, yellow, or orange bell peppers (about 1 3/4 pounds), stemmed, seeded, white parts removed, and cut into 1/4-inch-wide strips
1	medium clove garlic, minced or pressed through a garlic press
1	tablespoon chopped fresh oregano, basil, or parsley leaves
	Salt and ground black pepper

Heat the oil in a large skillet or sauté pan over medium-high heat until almost smoking. Add the peppers and cook, stirring occasionally, until the peppers begin to brown, about 5 minutes. Add the garlic and cook for 1 minute. Reduce the heat to low, cover, and cook until the peppers are tender, 4 to 5 minutes. Add the herb and season to taste with salt and pepper. Serve hot, warm, or at room temperature.

➤ VARIATION

Sautéed Peppers with Onions and Andouille

Andouille is a Cajun sausage made from heavily spiced smoked pork. If you prefer a less spicy sausage, use kielbasa instead.

2	tablespoons extra-virgin olive oil
12	ounces andouille sausage, sliced on the bias into 3/4-inch-thick rounds
3	medium red, yellow, or orange bell peppers (about 1 1/4 pounds), stemmed, seeded, white parts removed, and cut into 1/4-inch-wide strips
1	small onion, halved and sliced thin
1	medium clove garlic, minced or pressed through a garlic press
1	tablespoon chopped fresh parsley leaves
	Salt and ground black pepper

1. Heat 1 tablespoon of the oil in a large skillet or sauté pan over medium-high heat until almost smoking. Add the sausage and cook until browned on both sides, about 5 minutes. Transfer the sausage to a plate.

2. Add the remaining 1 tablespoon oil to the pan. Add the peppers and onion and cook, stirring occasionally, until the vegetables begin to brown, about 5 minutes. Add the garlic and cook for 1 minute. Reduce the heat to low, cover, and cook until the peppers are tender, about 4 minutes. Add the sausage and parsley and season to taste with salt and pepper. Serve hot, warm, or at room temperature.

Frittata with Sautéed Peppers and Olives

SERVES 4 AS A MAIN COURSE

Feel free to use feta or Parmesan in place of provolone. Basil, mint, or parsley can be substituted for oregano.

1	tablespoon extra-virgin olive oil
2	large red, yellow, or orange bell peppers (about 1 pound), stemmed, seeded, white parts removed, and cut into 1/4-inch-wide strips
1	medium clove garlic, minced or pressed through a garlic press
1	tablespoon chopped fresh oregano leaves
10	black olives, pitted and chopped coarse
	Salt and ground black pepper
6	large eggs
1/3	cup shredded provolone cheese

1. Adjust the oven rack to the upper-middle position and heat the oven to 350 degrees.

2. Heat the oil in a 10-inch ovenproof skillet over medium-high heat until almost smoking. Add the peppers and cook, stirring occasionally, until the peppers begin to brown, 3 to 4 minutes. Add the garlic and cook for 1 minute. Reduce the heat to low, cover, and cook until the peppers are tender, 4 to 5 minutes. Add the oregano, olives, and salt and pepper to taste.

3. Meanwhile, mix the eggs, cheese, ¼

PREPARING PEPPERS FOR GRILLING

1. Cut each pepper in half lengthwise (through the stem end). Remove the core and seeds.

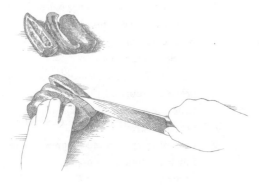

2. Cut the clean halves into thirds lengthwise.

teaspoon salt, and ¼ teaspoon pepper together in a medium bowl.

4. Increase the heat to medium. Pour the egg mixture into the skillet and stir lightly with a fork to evenly distribute the peppers until the eggs begin to set. Once the bottom is firm, use a thin plastic spatula to lift the frittata edge closest to you. Tilt the skillet forward slightly toward you so that the uncooked egg runs underneath. Return the skillet to a level position and swirl gently to evenly distribute the egg. Continue cooking for another 40 seconds and then lift the edge again, repeating the process until the egg on top is no longer runny.

5. Transfer the skillet to the oven and bake until the frittata top is set and dry to the touch, 2 to 4 minutes, removing it as soon as the top is set.

6. Run a spatula around the skillet edge to loosen the frittata. Invert the frittata onto a serving plate and serve warm or at room temperature.

Master Recipe for Grilled Peppers

SERVES 4 TO 6

Sweet bell peppers are especially tasty when grilled. Serve them as a side dish or as part of an antipasto platter with cold cuts, olives, marinated mushrooms, and marinated artichoke hearts.

3   large red, yellow, or orange bell peppers (about 1 ½ pounds), prepared according to the illustrations at left
2   tablespoons extra-virgin olive oil
     Salt and ground black pepper

1. Toss the peppers and oil together in a large heat-resistant bowl. Season to taste with salt and pepper. Transfer the peppers to a grill, reserving the bowl with the residual

oil for the grilled peppers.

2. Grill the peppers over a medium-hot fire (you should be able to hold your hand 5 inches above the cooking grate for 3 to 4 seconds), turning every 2 minutes, until dark grill marks appear, the skins begin to wrinkle, and the peppers are crisp-tender, 8 to 10 minutes total.

3. Place the peppers back in the bowl and toss to coat with the residual oil. Allow the peppers to cool slightly and then cut them into thinner strips. Serve warm or at room temperature.

➤ VARIATION
Grilled Peppers with Mint and Feta
The Greek flavors in this recipe go well with lamb.

3	large red, yellow, or orange bell peppers (about 1 1/2 pounds), prepared according to the illustrations on page 190
2	tablespoons extra-virgin olive oil
	Salt and ground black pepper
1 1/2	tablespoons red wine vinegar
1	tablespoon minced fresh mint leaves
1	tablespoon minced fresh parsley leaves
1/4	cup crumbled feta cheese

1. Toss the peppers and oil together in a large heat-resistant bowl. Season to taste with salt and pepper. Transfer the peppers to a grill, reserving the bowl with the residual oil for the grilled peppers.

2. Grill the peppers over a medium-hot fire (you should be able to hold your hand 5 inches above the cooking grate for 3 to 4 seconds), turning every 2 minutes, until dark grill marks appear, the skins begin to wrinkle, and the peppers are crisp-tender, 8 to 10 minutes total.

3. Place the peppers back in the bowl and toss to coat with the residual oil. Allow the peppers to cool slightly and then cut them into thinner strips. Return the peppers to the bowl. Add the vinegar, mint, and parsley and toss to combine. Transfer the pepper mixture to a serving bowl. Sprinkle with the cheese and serve warm or at room temperature.

STUFFED PEPPERS
MENTION STUFFED PEPPERS TO MOST people and they think of an army-green shell crammed with leftovers from the school cafeteria. Although the classic 1950s sweet pepper filled with aromatic rice and beef and topped with ketchup may sound mediocre, this recipe can be delicious if prepared properly.

To get going, we tried a few classic recipes. Although these trial runs produced nothing as bad as what we remembered from the school cafeteria, they were far from perfect. First off, the peppers themselves varied greatly in their degree of doneness. Some were so thoroughly cooked that they slumped onto their sides, unable to support their stuffed weight. On the other end of the spectrum, barely cooked peppers added an unfriendly crunch and bitter flavor to the mix. To be a success, the stuffed peppers would have to yield a tender bite yet retain enough structure to stand up proudly on the plate.

None of the fillings hit home, either. An all-rice version was uninteresting, while another stuffed with all meat was leaden and greasy. One recipe called for small amounts of so many varied ingredients that it made us think its creator just wanted to clean out her refrigerator. We came away from this first round of tests wanting a simple yet gratifying filling, neither humdrum nor packed with odd ingredients.

To start, we needed a solid pepper venue with minimal crunch. So we steamed, microwaved, roasted, or blanched a round of peppers and lined them up for everyone in the test kitchen to examine. The steamed and microwaved examples were bland in both color and flavor. We tried roasting in an uncovered dish containing a little water, an uncovered dish with no water, and a covered dish. Each procedure produced a bitter, subpar pepper. We knew that if we allowed the peppers to roast a little longer, their sugars would eventually caramelize and the peppers would turn sweet. But at that point, their texture would also disintegrate into that of an Italian sandwich ingredient. Tasters unanimously preferred the vibrant color, sturdiness, and overall sweeter flavor of the blanched peppers; the hot water actually seemed to have washed away some of the peppers' bitterness.

Usually, a freshly blanched vegetable is plunged immediately into an ice-cold water bath in a process known as *shocking*. The point is to halt the cooking process at just the right moment while stabilizing the vegetable's brightened color. We find water baths to be a real pain, especially in a kitchen where counter space is prime property. Although the shocked peppers had a slightly brighter hue than those that had been blanched but not shocked, they took much longer to heat through in the oven. So we abandoned shocking and instead fussed with blanching times, being careful to remove the peppers a little early and then allow the residual heat to finish their cooking. We found that a three-minute dip in boiling water followed by a cooling period on the countertop yielded the perfect balance of structure and chew.

Even with a pepper that's cooked to perfection, everyone knows that in this dish the stuffing is the real star of the show. The options for stuffing ingredients are many, including couscous, polenta, and a number of interesting and unusual grains. But we landed on rice. A universal pantry ingredient, it is a classic in American recipes for stuffed peppers.

Because we wanted these stuffed peppers to work as a quick midweek meal, our goal was to keep the rice-based filling simple and satisfying, with a streamlined ingredient list and preparation method. Tasters did not care much for sausage, heavy seasonings, or a mix of too many ingredients. To our surprise, they were big fans of the classic 1950s version of a pepper stuffed with rice and ground beef. Sautéed onions and garlic rounded out the flavors, while tomatoes added a fresh note and some color. Bound together with a little cheese and topped with ketchup, this retro pepper is a model of "make it from what you have in the pantry" simplicity.

Now we had a pepper, and we had a filling. All we had to do was figure out the best

way to get them together. The first trick is to use the boiling water from the blanched peppers to cook the rice. While the peppers cool and the rice cooks, the onions, garlic, and beef can be sautéed quickly. Then the filling and peppers can be assembled and heated through in the oven. The result? Stuffed peppers that take only 45 minutes from start to finish—and that are also truly worth eating.

Master Recipe for Stuffed Bell Peppers

SERVES 4 AS A LIGHT MAIN DISH
OR SIDE DISH

When shopping for bell peppers to stuff, it's best to choose those with broad bases that will allow the peppers to stand up on their own. It's easier to fill the peppers after they have been placed in the baking dish, because the sides of the dish will hold the peppers steady.

KEEPING STUFFED PEPPERS UPRIGHT

Here are four neat ways to keep stuffed peppers from spilling their contents as they bake.

A. Reserve the tops of the peppers, which you cut off to open the peppers for stuffing, and insert them between the stuffed peppers in the pan for added stability.

B. Instead of cooking the peppers in a baking dish, as specified in most recipes, put them in a tube pan. The snug fit makes the peppers sit right up.

C. Place the peppers in the cups of a muffin tin, whose cups hold the peppers firmly in place.

D. Place each stuffed pepper in an individual ovenproof custard cup. This is a great system when you want to cook only a couple of peppers instead of a whole batch.

Salt

4   medium red, yellow, or orange bell
      peppers (about 6 ounces each),
      ½ inch trimmed off the tops, cores
      and seeds discarded

½   cup long-grain white rice

1½   tablespoons extra-virgin olive oil

1   medium onion, chopped fine

12   ounces ground beef, preferably
      ground chuck

3   medium cloves garlic, minced or
      pressed through a garlic press

1   (14.5-ounce) can diced tomatoes,
      drained, ¼ cup juice reserved

5   ounces Monterey Jack cheese,
      shredded (about 1 ¼ cups)

2   tablespoons chopped fresh
      parsley leaves

      Ground black pepper

¼   cup ketchup

1. Bring 4 quarts of water to a boil in a large stockpot or Dutch oven over high heat. Add 1 tablespoon salt and the bell peppers. Cook until the peppers just begin to soften, about 3 minutes. Using a slotted spoon, remove the peppers from the pot, drain excess water from inside the peppers, and place the peppers cut-side up on paper towels. Return the water in the pot to a boil; add the rice and boil until tender, about 13 minutes. Drain the rice and transfer it to a large bowl; set aside.

2. Adjust an oven rack to the middle position and heat the oven to 350 degrees.

3. Meanwhile, heat the oil in a 12-inch heavy-bottomed skillet over medium-high heat until almost smoking. Add the onion and cook, stirring occasionally, until softened and beginning to brown, about 5 minutes. Add the beef and cook, breaking the beef into small pieces with a spoon, until no longer pink, about 4 minutes. Stir in the garlic and cook until fragrant, about 30 seconds.

Transfer the mixture to the bowl with the rice and stir in the tomatoes, 1 cup of the cheese, parsley, and salt and pepper to taste.

4. Stir together the ketchup and reserved tomato juice in a small bowl.

5. Place the peppers cut-side up in a 9 by 9-inch baking dish. Using a soup spoon, divide the filling evenly among the peppers. Spoon 2 tablespoons of the ketchup mixture over each filled pepper and sprinkle each with 1 tablespoon of the remaining cheese. Bake until the cheese is browned and the filling is heated through, 25 to 30 minutes. Serve immediately.

➤   VARIATIONS

Stuffed Bell Peppers with Chicken, Smoked Mozzarella, and Basil

Ground chicken is a neutral background for the Italian flavors in this variation.

      Salt

4   medium red, yellow, or orange
      bell peppers (about 6 ounces each),
      ½ inch trimmed off the tops, cores
      and seeds discarded

½   cup long-grain white rice

1½   tablespoons extra-virgin olive oil

1   medium onion, chopped fine

12   ounces ground chicken

3   medium cloves garlic, minced or
      pressed through a garlic press

1   (14.5-ounce) can diced tomatoes,
      drained

4   ounces smoked mozzarella cheese,
      shredded (1 cup)

2   tablespoons chopped fresh basil leaves

      Ground black pepper

⅓   cup fresh bread crumbs

1. Follow the master recipe for Stuffed Bell Peppers through step 2.

2. Meanwhile, heat the oil in a 12-inch

heavy-bottomed skillet over medium-high heat until almost smoking. Add the onion and cook, stirring occasionally, until softened and beginning to brown, about 5 minutes. Add the chicken and cook, breaking it into small pieces with a spoon, until the chicken becomes opaque, about 4 minutes. Stir in the garlic and cook until fragrant, about 30 seconds. Transfer the mixture to the bowl with the rice. Stir in the tomatoes, cheese, basil, and salt and pepper to taste.

3. Continue with the master recipe from step 5, substituting the bread crumbs for the ketchup mixture and cheese topping.

Stuffed Bell Peppers with Spiced Lamb, Currants, and Feta Cheese

Middle Eastern flavors—ground lamb, warm spices, currants, and feta cheese—are used in this variation.

	Salt
4	medium red, yellow, or orange bell peppers (about 6 ounces each), $1/2$ inch trimmed off the tops, cores and seeds discarded
$1/2$	cup long-grain white rice
$1 1/2$	tablespoons extra-virgin olive oil
1	medium onion, chopped fine
12	ounces ground lamb
1	tablespoon ground cumin
1	teaspoon ground cardamom
$1/2$	teaspoon ground cinnamon
$1/2$	teaspoon hot red pepper flakes
3	medium cloves garlic, minced or pressed through a garlic press
1	tablespoon minced fresh ginger
$1/4$	cup currants
1	(14.5-ounce) can diced tomatoes, drained
6	ounces feta cheese, crumbled (about 1 cup)
2	tablespoons chopped fresh cilantro leaves
	Ground black pepper
$1/3$	cup roughly chopped salted, toasted cashews

1. Follow the master recipe for Stuffed Bell Peppers through step 2.

2. Meanwhile, heat the oil in a 12-inch heavy-bottomed skillet over medium-high heat until almost smoking. Add the onion and cook, stirring occasionally, until softened and beginning to brown, about 5 minutes. Add the lamb, cumin, cardamom, cinnamon, and pepper flakes. Cook, breaking the lamb into small pieces with a spoon until no longer pink, about 4 minutes. Stir in the garlic, ginger, and currants and cook until fragrant, about 30 seconds. Transfer the mixture to the bowl with the rice. Stir in the tomatoes, cheese, cilantro, and salt and pepper to taste.

3. Continue with the master recipe from step 5, substituting the chopped cashews for the ketchup mixture and cheese topping.

PLANTAINS

PLANTAINS ARE A STAPLE IN LATIN AMERICAN CUISINE. THEY ARE WIDELY available in many supermarkets and are certainly sold in Latino markets. You may also see them in some Asian food stores. Although plantains are technically a fruit rather than a vegetable (they closely resemble bananas in appearance), they are usually served as a side dish instead of dessert. They are starchier and less sweet than bananas. Also, if you look closely, you will notice that plantains are larger than most bananas, and their skins have more pronounced ridges that run from tip to tip. Finally, plantains are sold individually rather than in bunches.

Unlike bananas, plantains are used in all three stages of ripeness: green, yellow,

and black. Green plantains are mainly used to make *tostones* (fried flattened plantain slices). The riper yellow and black plantains are a bit sweeter and can be used in a number of different ways because the flesh remains firm no matter how ripe the fruit becomes. Our preference is for very ripe black-skinned plantains. They are easier to peel than less ripe plantains (just cut the plantains into large chunks, slit the skin with a paring knife, and then pull if off with your fingers), and their flesh is a bit sweeter (although not really sugary like a banana).

Sautéing is the easiest and most classic way to prepare ripe plantains. We tried cooking peeled pieces in butter and in oil, and tasters preferred the rich flavor of the plantains cooked in butter. Golden-brown sautéed plantains have so much flavor that they need nothing more than a little salt and a squirt of lime juice, best added at the table.

Ripe plantains can also be peeled and grilled over a moderate fire. We found that the plantains must be oiled before grilling or they will stick to the cooking grate. By the time the plantains are streaked with grill marks, they will be cooked through, tender, and ready to serve.

Master Recipe for Sautéed Plantains
SERVES 4

The peels of ripe plantains should be quite black. Sautéed plantains are the perfect accompaniment to roast pork. They also work well with rice and beans.

- 2 large ripe plantains (10 to 12 ounces each)
- 2 tablespoons unsalted butter
  Salt
- 1 lime, cut into 4 wedges

1. Trim the ends from the plantains and then cut the plantains crosswise into 4 pieces. With a paring knife, make a slit in the peel of each piece, from one end to the other end, and then peel away the skin with your fingers. Cut the plantains crosswise into 1-inch-thick slices.

2. Heat the butter in a 12-inch nonstick skillet over medium-high heat. When the foaming subsides, add the plantains and cook until golden brown, about 4 minutes. Turn and cook until the other side is golden, about 4 minutes longer. Season with salt to taste and serve immediately with the lime wedges

➤ VARIATION

Sautéed Plantains with Brown Sugar

Serve these lightly sweetened plantains as a side dish in lieu of candied sweet potatoes. They are even sweet enough to serve as dessert, perhaps with a scoop of vanilla ice cream.

2	large ripe plantains (10 to 12 ounces each)
2	tablespoons unsalted butter
1/8	teaspoon salt
2	tablespoons light or dark brown sugar
2	tablespoons heavy cream

EQUIPMENT: Paring Knives

A paring knife is useful for coring tomatoes, slivering garlic, and trimming artichokes. But which paring knife is best? Prices range from a modest $5 plus change to a grand $50, which invites the obvious question for a home cook: Is the most expensive knife really 10 times better than the cheapest model? To find out, we put seven all-purpose paring knives through a series of kitchen tests, including peeling and slicing shallots, peeling and slicing apples and turnips, coring tomatoes, peeling and mincing fresh ginger, and slicing lemons and limes.

The way the knives were made (by forging or stamping) wasn't much of a factor in our ratings of paring knives. By definition, a paring knife is used for light tasks where weight and balance are not terribly important (it doesn't take a huge effort to peel an apple). The way the handle felt in testers' hands was much more important. Most testers preferred medium-size, ergonomically designed plastic handles. Slim wooden handles were harder to grasp.

Testers also preferred paring knives with flexible blades, which make it easier to work in tight spots. Peeling turnips or sectioning oranges is much easier with a flexible than a stiff blade. Stiffer blades are slightly better at mincing and slicing, but these are secondary tasks for paring knives. Among the knives tested, expensive forged knives from Wüsthof and Henckels performed well, as did an inexpensive stamped knife made by Forschner.

THE BEST PARING KNIVES

The Wüsthof-Trident Grand Prix (top) is extremely agile and was the clear favorite of our testers. The Forschner (Victorinox) Fibrox (center) is quite light, and the blade is very flexible. The Henckels Four Star (bottom) has an especially comfortable handle, but the blade is a bit less flexible and somewhat less sharp than the blades on our other top picks. Note that the Forschner knife costs just $6, while you should expect to spend about $20 for the Henckels and about $28 for the Wüsthof.

1. Trim the ends from the plantains and then cut the plantains crosswise into 4 pieces. With a paring knife, make a slit in the peel of each piece, from one end to the other end, and then peel away the skin with your fingers. Cut the plantains crosswise into 1-inch-thick slices.

2. Heat the butter in a 12-inch nonstick skillet over medium-high heat. When the foaming subsides, add the plantains and cook until golden brown, about 4 minutes. Turn and cook until the other side is golden, about 4 minutes longer. Add the salt, brown sugar, and cream, mix well, and simmer for 30 seconds. Serve immediately.

Master Recipe for Grilled Plantains

SERVES 4

Plantains absorb the flavors of the grill well and can be served with almost anything. Try these plantains with grilled chicken, fish, beef, or pork. For this recipe, the plantains are quartered, peeled, and then cut in half lengthwise.

2   large ripe plantains
    (10 to 12 ounces each)
2   tablespoons vegetable oil
    Salt

1. Trim the ends from the plantains and then cut the plantains crosswise into 4 pieces. With a paring knife, make a slit in the peel of each piece, from one end to the other end, and then peel away the skin with your fingers. Cut each piece of plantain in half lengthwise. Gently toss the plantains, oil, and salt to taste in a large bowl until the plantains are evenly coated with oil.

2. Grill the plantains over a medium-hot fire (you should be able to hold your hand 5 inches above the cooking grate for 3 to 4 seconds), turning once, until grill marks appear, 7 to 8 minutes. Serve immediately.

➤ VARIATION
Grilled Plantains with Lime and Mint

These grilled plantains are seasoned simply with a squeeze of lime and a sprinkling of mint.

2   large ripe plantains
    (10 to 12 ounces each)
2   tablespoons vegetable oil
    Salt
2   tablespoons minced fresh
    mint leaves
1   lime, cut into 4 wedges

1. Trim the ends from the plantains and then cut the plantains crosswise into 4 pieces. With a paring knife, make a slit in the peel of each piece, from one end to the other end, and then peel away the skin with your fingers. Cut each piece of plantain in half lengthwise. Gently toss the plantains, oil, and salt to taste in a large bowl until the plantains are evenly coated with oil.

2. Grill the plantains over a medium-hot fire (you should be able to hold your hand 5 inches above the cooking grate for 3 to 4 seconds), turning once, until grill marks appear, 7 to 8 minutes. Place the plantains on a serving platter, sprinkle with the mint, and serve immediately with the lime wedges.

GLAZED CURRIED CARROTS WITH CURRANTS AND ALMONDS **PAGE 62**

SESAME-GLAZED BABY BOK CHOY **PAGE 37**

CAMPANELLE WITH ASPARAGUS, BASIL, AND BALSAMIC GLAZE **PAGE 24**

201

GRILLED CORN WITH SPICY CHILI BUTTER **PAGE 83**

CAULIFLOWER GRATIN **PAGE 72**

203

LATKES **PAGE 244**

BRAISED BELGIAN ENDIVE **PAGE 111**

GRILLED POTATO AND ARUGULA SALAD WITH DIJON MUSTARD VINAIGRETTE **PAGE 263**

GREEK-STYLE POTATOES **PAGE 233**

207

TWICE-BAKED POTATOES WITH SMOKED SALMON AND CHIVES **PAGE 220**

ROASTED RED PEPPER SALAD WITH RED ONIONS AND CUCUMBERS **PAGE 188**

CARAMELIZED ONIONS **PAGE 167**

WILTED SPINACH SALAD WITH WARM BACON DRESSING **PAGE 284**

SPRING VEGETABLE SOUP **PAGE 323**

SAUTÉED CHERRY TOMATOES WITH CAPERS AND ANCHOVY **PAGE 294**

213

SAUTÉED SHREDDED ZUCCHINI WITH SWEET CORN AND CHIVES **PAGE 315**

POTATOES

DOZENS OF POTATO VARIETIES ARE GROWN IN THIS COUNTRY, AND AT ANY time you may see as many as five or six in your supermarket. Some potatoes are sold by varietal name (such as Yukon Gold), but others are sold by generic name (baking, all-purpose, etc.). To make sense of this confusion, we find it helpful to group potatoes into three major categories, based on the ratio of solids (mostly starch) to water. The categories are high-starch/low-moisture potatoes, medium-starch/medium-moisture potatoes, and low-starch/high-moisture potatoes.

The high-starch/low-moisture category includes baking, russet, and white creamer potatoes. (The formal name for the russet is russet Burbank potato, named after its developer, Luther Burbank of Idaho. This type of potato is also known as the Idaho. In all of our recipes, we call them russets.) These potatoes are best for baking and mashing. The medium-starch/medium-moisture category includes all-purpose, Yukon Gold, Yellow Finn, and purple Peruvian potatoes. These potatoes can be mashed or baked but are generally not as fluffy as the high-starch potatoes. The low-starch/high-moisture category includes Red Bliss, red creamer, new, white rose, and fingerling potatoes. These potatoes, which are often called waxy potatoes, are best roasted or boiled and used in salad.

Within each category, you can safely make substitutions, but cross-category substitutions can yield in poor results. For instance, if you try to fry red potatoes rather than the recommended russet potatoes, you will get poor results. Likewise, russets are a poor choice for salads.

In addition to categorizing potatoes by starch content, it is useful to divide them into two groups based on how they have been handled after harvesting. Most potatoes are cured after harvesting to toughen their skins and protect the flesh. They are then held in cold storage, often for months. These potatoes are called storage potatoes. Almost all of the potatoes in the supermarket fall into this category.

Occasionally, potatoes are harvested before they have developed their full complement of starch. New potatoes are always low in starch and high in moisture, even if they are actually a high-starch variety. Although all new potatoes are small, not all small potatoes are new. You can pick out a true new potato by examining the skin. If the skin feels thin and you can rub it off with your fingers, you are holding a new potato. New potatoes have a lot of moisture, and their flesh is almost juicy when cut.

BAKED POTATOES

IN THE WORLD OF JUNE CLEAVER, potatoes were baked at 350 degrees because they were put into the oven along with the roast, which cooked at 350 degrees. The world has changed a lot since Wally and Beav sat down to dinner. We wondered if there was a quicker or better route to perfect baked potatoes.

We baked all-purpose potatoes, Yukon Golds, and Idaho-grown russets. We tried baking them poked and unpoked, greased and ungreased, with ends dipped in salt, microwaved all the way, microwaved and finished in the oven, baked with gadgets that are supposed to decrease cooking time, and baked at various temperatures. And, against the wishes of all the potato experts we spoke with, we also tried baking them in foil.

After all this experimentation, we discovered that the traditional slow-baking method is best, mainly because of the effect it had on the skin. The skin of a potato baked at 350 degrees for an hour and 15 minutes simply has no peer. Just under the skin, a well-baked potato will develop a substantial brown layer. This is because the dark skin absorbs heat during cooking, and the starch just inside the skin is broken down into sugar and starts to brown. If you love baked potato skin, this is definitely the best method.

Potatoes cooked at 400 and 450 degrees will indeed cook faster—at 450 degrees they may even cook in 45 minutes—but because they cook for a shorter time, the inner browned layer isn't as even or as flavorful as it is with the slower-roast method. In addition, the skin isn't quite as thick and chewy. Cooked long enough at these higher temperatures to develop chewy skin, the potato's inner, browned layer becomes thick and unpleasant and somewhat overbrowned.

We also tried starting potatoes at 500 degrees for 10 minutes and then lowering the oven to 350 degrees, but again this method failed to promote even browning. The microwave does a decent job of shortening the overall cooking time and yields decent flesh. What's missing is the delicious browned layer under the skin and the chewy, dry skin that skin lovers covet. We found that cooking the potatoes for half the recommended microwave time and then finishing them in a 450-degree oven produced fluffy,

---

SCIENCE: Starch in Potatoes

Potatoes are composed mostly of starch and water. The starch is in the form of granules, which in turn are contained in starch cells. The higher the starch content of the potato, the more packed the cells. In high-starch potatoes (russets are a good example), the cells are completely full—they look like plump little beach balls. In medium-starch (Yukon Golds) and low-starch potatoes (Red Bliss), the cells look more like underinflated beach balls. The space between these less-than-full cells is taken up mostly by water.

In our tests, we found that the full starch cells of high-starch potatoes are most likely to maintain their integrity and stay separate when mashed, giving the potatoes a delightfully fluffy texture. In addition, the low water content of these potatoes allows them to absorb milk, cream, and/or butter without becoming wet or gummy. Starch cells in lower-starch potatoes, on the other hand, tend to clump when cooked and break more easily, allowing the starch to dissolve into whatever liquid is present. The broken cells and dissolved starch tend to produce sticky, gummy mashed potatoes.

However, the high moisture content of red potatoes makes them an excellent choice for dishes such as potato salad, where you want the potatoes to hold their shape. Because they contain a fair amount of moisture, they don't absorb much water as they boil. In contrast, low-moisture russets suck up water when boiled and fall apart. The resulting potato salad tastes starchy and looks sloppy.

---

dry flesh, some browning, and pretty good skin. If you're in a hurry, this half-and-half method works best.

As for some of our more unusual tests: Oiling the skin caused a potato to cook somewhat more quickly, but frankly the skin was not as good. We found that the expensive metal pokers that you stick into potatoes to decrease cooking time did not seem to have that effect. Cutting the ends off a potato and dipping them in salt made for crusty, salty ends but didn't measurably alter baking time. Finally, poking the potato before baking did not measurably affect the amount of moisture retained after baking. The flesh of a potato that had not been poked was just as dry as one that had been poked. However, it is a good idea to poke a hole or two in any potato you are going to microwave, since unpoked potatoes can explode when microwaved.

If slow baking is essential to good skin, the consistency of the flesh also requires some attention. Letting the potato sit awhile after baking without opening it up will steam the potato and cause the flesh to become more dense. For fluffy potatoes, create a wide opening as soon as the potatoes come out of the oven to let steam escape.

And what about foil-wrapped potatoes? They are a notion perpetuated by mediocre steakhouses that want to keep potatoes warm indefinitely. Foil is an insult to potatoes; it holds the steam in, causing limp, damp skins and dense flesh.

Master Recipe for Baked Potatoes

SERVES 4

We found no benefit or harm was done to the potatoes by poking them with the tines of a fork before putting them into the oven. Do use a fork to open the skin as soon as the potatoes come out of the oven.

4   medium russet potatoes
     (7 to 8 ounces each), scrubbed
     Butter
     Salt

OPENING A BAKED POTATO

To ensure that the flesh does not steam and become dense, it's imperative to open a baked potato (or sweet potato) as soon as it comes out of the oven. This technique maximizes the amount of steam released and keeps the potato fluffy and light.

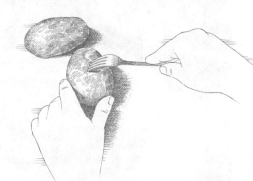

1. Use the tines of a fork to make a dotted X on top of each potato.

2. Press in at the ends of the potato to push the flesh up and out. Besides releasing steam quickly, this method helps trap and hold on to bits of butter.

217

Adjust an oven rack to the middle position and heat the oven to 350 degrees. Place the potatoes directly on the middle rack and bake for 1 hour and 15 minutes. Remove the potatoes from the oven and pierce them with a fork to create a dotted X on top of each potato (see illustration 1 on page 217). Press in at the ends of each potato to push the flesh up and out (see illustration 2 on page 217). Serve immediately with butter and salt.

➤ VARIATION

Faster Baked Potatoes

This half-and-half method (which takes 35 minutes, start to finish) produces far superior results than straight microwaving. By the time you have scrubbed and microwaved the potatoes, the oven will be preheated. To cook fewer potatoes by this method, plan on 2 minutes total cooking in the microwave for each potato.

> 4   medium russet potatoes
>   (7 to 8 ounces each), scrubbed
>   Butter
>   Salt

1. Adjust an oven rack to the middle position and heat the oven to 450 degrees.

2. Microwave the potatoes on high power for 4 minutes. Turn the potatoes over and microwave them on high power for another 4 minutes.

3. Transfer the potatoes to the hot oven and cook until a skewer glides easily through the flesh, about 20 minutes. Remove the potatoes from the oven and pierce them with a fork to create a dotted X on top of each potato (see illustration 1 on page 217). Press in at the ends of each potato to push the flesh up and out (see illustration 2 on page 217). Serve immediately with butter and salt.

TWICE-BAKED POTATOES

THIS SIMPLE DISH—ESSENTIALLY BAKED russet potatoes from which the flesh has been removed, mashed with dairy ingredients and seasonings, mounded back into the shells, and baked again—offers a good range of both texture and flavor in a single morsel. Done well, the skin is chewy and substantial without being tough, with just a hint of crispness to play off the smooth, creamy filling. In terms of flavor, cheese and other dairy ingredients make the filling rich and tangy, a contrast with the mild, slightly sweet potato shell.

Because twice-baked potatoes are put into the oven twice, we found it best to bake them for just an hour, rather than the usual 75 minutes we bake plain potatoes. Oiling the skins before baking promotes crispness, not something you necessarily want in plain baked potatoes but a trait we came to admire in creamy twice-baked potatoes.

Our favorite baked potato recipe under-

scores the importance of opening the potatoes right after baking to release as much steam as possible. For twice-baked potatoes, it's advisable to wait a few minutes for the potatoes to cool before slicing them apart and emptying out the flesh; cooled potatoes are much easier to handle, and because the flesh is mixed with wet ingredients, any compromise to the texture from unreleased moisture is negligible.

Once we had emptied the potato halves of their flesh, we noticed they got a little flabby sitting on the counter waiting to be stuffed. Because the oven was still on and waiting for the return of the stuffed halves, we decided to put the skins back in while we prepared the filling. This worked beautifully, giving the shells an extra dimension of crispness.

Pleased with our chewy, slightly crunchy skins, we now had to develop a smooth, lush, flavorful filling that would hold up its end of the bargain. (Lumpy, sodden, and dull-tasting would not do.) Twice-baked potatoes usually are filled with a mixture of well-mashed potato, shredded cheese, and other dairy ingredients, including one or more of the usual suspects: butter, sour cream, cream cheese, yogurt, ricotta, cottage cheese, milk, cream, and buttermilk. Various herbs and spices also often show up, as well as diced meats and sautéed vegetables.

To get an idea how we wanted to flavor our filling, we prepared 10 different recipes with various ingredient combinations. In a rare display of accord, all our tasters agreed on a few general observations. First, everyone preferred tangy dairy products, such as sour cream, yogurt, and buttermilk, to sweet ones, such as milk, cream, and ricotta. Second, the use of only one dairy ingredient produced a rather dull, one-dimensional filling. A second ingredient added depth of flavor and complexity. Third, nobody

favored too fatty a mouthfeel, a preference that left the addition of large amounts of butter (some recipes use up to a full stick for four potatoes) and cream cheese out of the running. Dozens of further tests helped us refine our filling to a rich, but not killer, combination of sharp cheddar, sour cream, buttermilk, and just 2 tablespoons of butter. We learned to season the filling aggressively with salt and pepper; for herbs, the slightly sharp flavor of scallions was best.

With the filling mixed and mounded back into the shells, our last tests centered on the final baking. We wanted to do more than just heat the filling through; we were intent of forming an attractive brown crust on it as well. Broiling turned out to be the easiest and most effective method. After about 10 minutes, the potatoes emerged browned, crusted, and ready for the table.

Master Recipe for Twice-Baked Potatoes
SERVES 6 TO 8

To vary the flavor a bit, try substituting other types of cheese, such as Gruyère, fontina, or feta, for the cheddar. Yukon Gold potatoes, though slightly more moist than our ideal, gave our twice-baked potatoes a buttery flavor and mouthfeel that everyone liked, so we recommend them as a substitution for the russets.

4	medium russet potatoes (7 to 8 ounces each), scrubbed, dried, and rubbed lightly with vegetable oil
4	ounces sharp cheddar cheese, shredded (about 1 cup)
1/2	cup sour cream
1/2	cup buttermilk
2	tablespoons unsalted butter, softened
3	medium scallions, sliced thin
1/2	teaspoon salt
	Ground black pepper

1. Adjust an oven rack to the upper-middle position and heat the oven to 400 degrees. Bake the potatoes on a foil-lined baking sheet until the skin is crisp and deep brown and a skewer easily pierces the flesh, about 1 hour. Setting the baking sheet aside, transfer the potatoes to a wire rack, and let cool slightly, about 10 minutes.

2. Using an oven mitt or a folded kitchen towel to handle the hot potatoes, cut each potato in half so that the long, blunt sides rest on a work surface (see the photograph at right). Using a small spoon, scoop the flesh from each half into a medium bowl, leaving ⅛ to ¼ inch thickness of flesh in each shell. Arrange the shells on the lined baking sheet and return them to the oven until dry and slightly crisped, about 10 minutes. Meanwhile, mash the potato flesh with a fork until smooth. Stir in the remaining ingredients, including pepper to taste, until well combined.

3. Remove the shells from the oven and increase the oven setting to broil. Holding the shells steady on the pan with an oven mitt or towel-protected hand, spoon the mixture into the crisped shells, mounding it slightly at the center, and return the potatoes to the oven. Broil until spotty brown and crisp on top, 10 to 15 minutes. Allow to cool for 10 minutes. Serve warm.

➤ VARIATIONS

Twice-Baked Potatoes with Blue Cheese and Thyme

Follow the master recipe, substituting 3 ounces crumbled blue cheese (about ½ cup) for the cheddar and 1 teaspoon finely minced fresh thyme for the scallions.

Twice-Baked Potatoes with Smoked Salmon and Chives

Follow the master recipe, omitting the cheese and scallions and stirring 4 ounces

SLICING BAKED POTATOES

Most potatoes have two relatively flat, blunt sides and two curved sides. Halve the baked potatoes lengthwise so the blunt sides are down once the shells are stuffed, making them much more stable on the pan during the final baking.

smoked salmon, cut into ½-inch pieces, and 3 tablespoons minced fresh chives into the filling mixture.

Twice-Baked Potatoes with Chipotle Chile and Onion

For a slightly smoky aftertaste with just a hint of heat, limit the chipotle to 1 tablespoon. For more heat, increase the chipotle to 1 ½ tablespoons.
Heat 2 tablespoons butter in a medium skillet over medium heat. Add 1 medium onion, chopped fine, and cook until soft, 3 to 4 minutes. Follow the master recipe, omitting the butter and adding 1 to 1 ½ tablespoons minced canned chipotle chiles in adobo sauce, the reserved sautéed onion, and 2 tablespoons chopped fresh cilantro leaves to the filling mixture in step 2.

Twice-Baked Potatoes with Indian Spices and Peas

Heat 2 tablespoons butter in a medium skillet over medium heat. Add 1 medium onion chopped fine and cook until soft, 3 to 4 minutes. Add 1 teaspoon finely grated fresh ginger, 3 medium minced garlic cloves, 1 teaspoon *each* ground cumin and ground coriander, and ¼ teaspoon *each* ground cinnamon, ground turmeric, and ground cloves; cook until fragrant, about 30 seconds more, taking care not to brown the garlic or ginger. Off the heat, stir in 1 cup thawed frozen peas; set aside. Follow the master recipe, omitting the cheese and butter and stirring the spiced peas into the filling mixture.

ROASTED POTATOES

THE PERFECT ROASTED POTATO IS crisp and deep golden brown on the outside, with moist, velvety, dense interior flesh. The potato's slightly bitter skin is intact, providing a contrast to the sweet, caramelized flavor that the flesh develops during the roasting process. It is rich but never greasy, and it is accompanied by the heady taste of garlic and herbs.

To start, we roasted several kinds of potatoes. We liked high-starch/low-moisture potatoes (we used russets) the least. They did not brown well; their dry, fluffy texture was more like baked than roasted potatoes; and their flavor reminded us of raw potatoes. The medium-starch all-purpose potatoes (we used Yukon Golds) produced a beautiful golden crust, but the interior flesh was still rather dry. The best roasting potatoes came from the low-starch/high-moisture category (we used Red Bliss). These potatoes emerged from the oven with a light, delicate crust and a moist, dense interior that had a more complex, nutty flavor than the others, with hints of bitterness and tang.

After choosing the Red Bliss potatoes, we began to test oven temperatures. At 425 degrees, the result was an even-colored, golden-brown potato with a thin, crisp crust and an interior that was soft and dense, although still slightly dry.

While researching, we came across some recipes that called for parboiling the potatoes before roasting them. Hoping that this approach would produce a texturally superior potato that retained more of its moisture after cooking, we tried boiling the potatoes for seven minutes prior to roasting. This produced a potato closer to our ideal, but preparation required considerable attention owing to the additional step.

We then tried covering the potatoes for a portion of their roasting time. We were especially drawn to this technique because it provided a way to steam the potatoes in their own moisture that required little extra effort on the cook's part. The results were perfect. The crisp, deep golden-brown crust was perfectly balanced by a creamy, moist interior. These potatoes had a sweet and nutty caramelized flavor, with just a hint of tang from the skin. This simplest of methods produced the very best roasted potatoes.

The next step in the process was figuring out how to add garlic flavor, which makes

SCRUBBING POTATOES

Buy a rough-textured bathing or exfoliating bath glove especially for use in the kitchen. The glove cleans dirt away from potatoes and other root vegetables, but it's relatively gentle and won't scrub away the skin.

a good variation on the standard roasted potatoes. If we added minced garlic during the last five minutes of cooking, it burned almost instantly; coating the potatoes with garlic-infused oil failed to produce the strong garlic flavor that we were after; and roasting whole, unpeeled garlic cloves alongside the potatoes and squeezing the pulp out afterward to add to the potatoes was too tedious. The best method turned out to be both simple and flavorful. Mash raw garlic into a paste, place it in a large stainless-steel bowl, put the hot roasted potatoes in the bowl, and toss. This method yields potatoes with a strong garlic flavor yet without the raw spiciness of uncooked garlic.

Master Recipe for Roasted Potatoes

SERVES 4

To roast more than 2 pounds of potatoes at once, use a second pan rather than crowding the first. If your potatoes are small, such as new potatoes, cut them in half instead of into wedges and turn them cut-side up during the final 10 minutes of roasting.

> 2   pounds Red Bliss or
>   other low-starch potatoes,
>   scrubbed, halved, and
>   cut into 3/4-inch wedges
> 3   tablespoons extra-virgin olive oil
>   Salt and ground black pepper

1. Adjust the oven rack to the middle position and heat the oven to 425 degrees. Toss the potatoes and oil in a medium bowl to coat; season generously with salt and pepper and toss again to blend.

2. Place the potatoes flesh-side down in a single layer in a shallow roasting pan. Cover tightly with aluminum foil and cook for 20 minutes. Remove the foil and roast until the side of the potato touching the pan is crusty golden brown, about 15 minutes more. Remove the pan from the oven and, with a metal spatula, carefully turn over the potatoes. (Press the spatula against the pan as it slides under the potatoes to protect the crusts; see the illustration on page 223.) Return the pan to the oven and roast until the side of the potato now touching the pan is crusty golden brown and the skins have raisin-like wrinkles, 5 to 10 minutes more. Transfer the potatoes to a serving dish (again, using a metal spatula and extra care not to rip the crusts) and serve hot or warm.

➤ VARIATIONS

Roasted Potatoes with Garlic and Rosemary

See the illustrations on page 127 for tips on mincing the garlic to a paste.

Follow the master recipe. While the potatoes roast, mince 2 medium garlic cloves. Sprinkle them with 1/8 teaspoon salt and mash with the flat side of a chef's knife blade until a paste forms. Transfer the garlic paste to a large bowl; set aside. In the last 3 minutes of roasting time, sprinkle 2 tablespoons chopped fresh rosemary evenly over the potatoes. Immediately transfer the finished potatoes to the bowl with the garlic, toss to distribute, and serve warm.

Roasted Potatoes with Lemon-Chive Butter

Lemon and chives are a classic combination. Chives should be added at the end of cooking to preserve their delicate flavor.

Follow the master recipe. While the potatoes roast, combine 2 tablespoons melted unsalted butter, 1 tablespoon minced fresh chives, 1 teaspoon grated lemon zest, and 2 tablespoons lemon juice in a large bowl.

Transfer the roasted potatoes to the bowl with the butter mixture, toss to distribute, and serve immediately.

Roasted Potatoes with Southwestern Spices

Serve these potatoes with barbecued ribs and grilled corn.

Follow the master recipe. While the potatoes roast, melt 2 tablespoons unsalted butter in a small skillet over medium heat. When the butter starts to sizzle, add 1 teaspoon ground cumin, 1 teaspoon chili powder, 1 teaspoon dry mustard, ⅛ teaspoon cayenne pepper, and 1 medium minced garlic clove and cook until fragrant, 30 seconds to 1 minute. Transfer the roasted potatoes to a serving bowl. Pour the spiced butter mixture over the potatoes, toss to distribute, and serve immediately.

FLIPPING ROASTED POTATOES

Press the metal spatula against the roasting pan as you slide it under the potatoes to protect the crisp crust. Flip the potatoes so that the other cut sides come into contact with the hot pan.

FRENCH FRIES

THE IDEAL FRENCH FRY IS LONG AND crisp, with right-angle sides, a nice crunch on the outside, and an earthy potato taste. Its bass flavor note should be rustic, like a mushroom, and its high note should hint of the oil in which it was created. It should definitely not droop, and its coloring should be two-tone: blond with hints of brown.

Obviously, a good french fry requires the right potato. Would it be starchy or waxy? We tested two of the most popular waxy (low-starch/high-moisture) potatoes, and neither was even close to ideal, both being too watery. During the frying, water evaporated inside the potato, leaving hollows that would fill with oil, so the finished fries were greasy. Next, we tested the starchy potato most readily available nationwide, the russet. This potato turned out to be ideal, frying up with all the qualities that we were looking for.

Because these are starchy potatoes, it is important to rinse the starch off the surface after you cut the potato into fries. To do this, simply put the cut fries into a bowl, place the bowl in the sink, and run cold water into it, swirling with your fingers until the water runs clear. This might seem like an unimportant step, but it makes a real difference. When we skipped the starch rinse, the fries weren't quite right, and the oil clouded.

At this point, you take the second crucial step: Fill the bowl with clear water, add ice, and refrigerate the potatoes for at least 30 minutes. That way, when the potatoes first enter the hot oil, they are nearly frozen; this allows a slow, thorough cooking of the inner potato pulp. When we tried making fries without this chilling, the outsides started to brown well before the insides were fully cooked.

Our preference is to peel potatoes for french fries. A skin-on fry keeps the potato

CUTTING POTATOES FOR FRYING

REGULAR FRIES

Slice the peeled potatoes lengthwise into ovals about ¼ inch thick. Stack several ovals on top of each other and slice them into ¼-inch-thick lengths.

STEAK FRIES

1. Cut each potato in half lengthwise. Place the potato half flat-side down and cut into thirds lengthwise.

2. Cut each piece of potato in half lengthwise to yield 12 wedges that measure about ¾ inch across on the skin side.

from forming those little airy blisters that we prefer. Peeling the potato also allows home cooks to see—and remove, if they want to—any imperfections and greenish coloring.

What is the right fat for making perfect french fries?

To find out, we experimented with lard, vegetable shortening, canola oil, corn oil, and peanut oil. Lard and shortening make great fries, but we figured that many cooks won't want to use these products. We moved on to canola oil, the ballyhooed oil of the '90s, now used in a blend with safflower oil by McDonald's, which produces 4 million pounds of finished fries a day. But we were unhappy with the results: bland, almost watery fries.

Corn oil was the most forgiving oil in the test kitchen. It rebounded well from temperature fluctuations and held up very well in subsequent frying, and the fries tasted marvelous. A potato fried in peanut oil is light, and the flavor is rich but not dense. The earthy flavor of the potato is there, as with corn oil, but is not overbearing. At this point, we were very close, and yet there

was still something missing. The high flavor note, which is supplied by the animal fat in lard, was lacking.

We tried a dollop of strained bacon grease in peanut oil, about two generous tablespoons per quart of oil. The meaty flavor came through but without its nasty baggage.

So bacon grease appeared to be the fat of choice. To be certain of this, we added bacon grease to each of the oils, with these results: canola oil—extra body but still short on flavor; corn oil—more body, more flavor, nearly perfect; peanut oil—flavor, bite, body, bass notes, high notes galore. At last, an equivalent to lard.

So now it was time to get down to the frying, which actually means double frying. First, we parfried the potatoes at a relatively low temperature to release their rich and earthy flavor. The potatoes were then quick-fried at a higher temperature until nicely browned and immediately served.

The garden-variety cookbook recipe calls for parfrying at 350 degrees and final frying at 375 to 400 degrees. But we found these temperatures to be far too aggressive. We prefer an initial frying at 325 degrees, with the final frying at 350 degrees. Lower temperatures allowed for easier monitoring; with higher temperatures, the fries can get away from the cook.

For the sake of convenience, we also attempted a single, longer frying. Like many cooks before us, we found that with standard french fries (as opposed to the much thinner shoestring fries), we could not both sear the outside and properly cook the inside with a single visit to the hot fat. When we left them in long enough to sear the outside, we wound up with wooden, overcooked fries.

Master Recipe for French Fries

SERVES 4

For those who like it, flavoring the oil with a few tablespoons of bacon grease adds a subtle, meaty flavor to the fries. Their texture, however, is not affected if the bacon grease is omitted. See the illustrations on page 208 for tips on cutting the potatoes.

4	large russet potatoes (about 10 ounces each), peeled and cut into ¼ by ¼ -inch lengths
2	quarts peanut oil
4	tablespoons strained bacon grease (optional)
	Salt and ground black pepper

1. Rinse the cut fries in a large bowl under cold running water until the water turns from milky colored to clear. Cover with at least 1 inch of water and then cover with ice. Refrigerate at least 30 minutes. (The potatoes can be refrigerated up to 3 days ahead.)

2. In a 5-quart pot or Dutch oven fitted with a clip-on candy thermometer, or in a large electric fryer, heat the oil over medium-low heat to 325 degrees. As the oil heats, add the bacon grease (if using). The oil will bubble up when you add the fries, so be sure you have at least 3 inches of room at the top of the cooking pot.

3. Pour off the ice and water, quickly wrap the potatoes in a clean kitchen towel, and thoroughly pat dry. Increase the heat to medium-high and add the fries, a handful at a time, to the hot oil. Fry, stirring with a Chinese skimmer or large-hole slotted spoon, until the potatoes are limp and soft and start to turn from white to blond, 6 to 8 minutes. (The oil temperature will drop 50 to 60 degrees during this frying.) Use a skimmer or slotted spoon to transfer the fries to a triple thickness of paper towels to drain; let rest at least 10 minutes. (The fries can stand at room temperature up to 2 hours or be wrapped in paper towels, sealed in a zipper-lock bag, and frozen up to 1 month.)

4. When ready to serve the fries, reheat the oil to 350 degrees. Using the paper towels as a funnel, carefully pour the potatoes into the hot oil. Discard the paper towels and line a wire rack with another triple thickness of paper towels. Fry the potatoes, stirring fairly constantly, until golden brown and puffed, about 1 minute. Transfer the fries to another triple thickness of paper towels and drain again. Season to taste with salt and pepper or other seasoned salt. Serve immediately.

➤ VARIATION
Spicy Fries

Combine 1 teaspoon chili powder, 1 teaspoon paprika, ½ teaspoon ground cumin, and ⅛ to ¼ teaspoon cayenne pepper in a small bowl. Follow the master recipe, using this mixture in place of the black pepper (and with the salt) in step 4.

INGREDIENTS: Salt

The food press has exalted exotic sea salts. We wondered if a pinch here or a smidgen there is really worth as much as $36 a pound. Will your steamed broccoli or mashed potatoes taste better if you spend more money on salt?

Salt is either mined from ancient seas that dried up millions of years ago or obtained by evaporating seawater. In their pure form, sodium chloride, salts from both locations taste the same. What distinguishes one salt from another in color and flavor is the type and amount of minerals (such as magnesium, calcium, and potassium) and/or clays attached to the crystals of sodium chloride. The size and texture of the crystals—whether big flakes, irregularly shaped large grains, or regularly shaped small grains—are largely determined by the way the salt is processed.

Unlike kosher salt and sea salt, most table salts contain additives. Iodized table salt contains potassium iodide, which protects against thyroid disease. Dextrose may be added to help stabilize the iodine, and calcium silicate or one of several other drying agents are often added to prevent caking. Many experts claim these additives can impart an off flavor.

To make sense of all these claims, we tasted two kinds of table salt (one iodized, one not), two brands of kosher salt, and five widely available sea salts. The price per pound ranged from 36 cents to $36. Tests were divided into three categories: salt used at the table (we sprinkled each sample on roast beef), salt used in baking (we used a plain biscuit recipe), and salt dissolved in liquids (we tested each salt in spring water, chicken stock, and pasta cooking water).

Of the five tests run, we uncovered the most profound differences in our beef tenderloin test. Tasters loved the crunch of the large sea salt flakes or crystals when sprinkled over slices of roast tenderloin. Here, Maldon Sea Salt was the clear winner, followed by Fleur de Sel de Camargue and Light Grey Celtic Sea Salt.

Why did the sea salts win this test? According to Dr. Gary Beauchamp, director of the Monell Chemical Senses Center in Philadelphia and a leading expert on the science of taste and smell, flat crystals or crystals with holes cause a taste sensation different from that of regularly shaped small crystals. And, based on our test results, it's clear that large crystals provided a more pleasing sensory stimulation than fine table salt. In fact, tasters really objected to fine salts sprinkled on the beef, calling them "harsh" and "sharp." Tasters did like kosher salt on meat but not as much as sea salt, which has larger crystals.

Does this mean that our tasters were reacting to the additives in table salt that the chefs had warned us about? It's possible, but given the results in our other tests, we are not convinced. In fact, the one fine sea salt in our tasting (La Baleine) finished next to last in this test, and it does not contain any additives. It's hard to sprinkle fine sea or table salt evenly over meat, and we think tasters may have been hitting pockets with a lot of salt and reacting negatively.

In the biscuit tests, Morton table salt was the winner, and most of the sea salts landed at the bottom of the ratings. The explanation here is simple. Small salt crystals are more evenly distributed in baked goods than large crystals, and tasters didn't like getting a big hit of crunchy salt as they nibbled on biscuits.

In the spring water, chicken stock, and pasta cooking water, all nine salts tasted pretty much the same. Why didn't the fancy sea salts beat the pants off plain table salt in these tests? The main reason is dilution. Yes, sea salts sampled right from the box (or sprinkled on meat at the table) did taste better than table salt. And while crystal size did undoubtedly affect flavor perception in the tenderloin test, we suspect that our tasters were also responding favorably to some of the trace minerals in these salts. But mineral content is so low in sea salt (by weight, less than 1 percent in all brands tested) that any effect these minerals might have on flavor was lost when a teaspoon of salt was stirred into a big pot of chicken stock or pasta cooking water.

What, then, can we conclude from the results of these tests? For one, expensive sea salts are best saved for the table, where their delicate flavor and great crunch can be appreciated. Don't waste $36-a-pound sea salt when blanching vegetables. If you like to keep coarse salt in a ramekin next to the stove, choose a kosher salt, which costs just pennies per pound. If you measure salt by the teaspoon when cooking, you might as well use table salt, which is also the best choice for baking.

STEAK FRIES

STEAK FRIES ARE THE RUSTIC, COUNTRY cousin to french fries. With their skin left on and their shape determined largely by the shape of the potato, these wedge-shaped fries are easier to prepare and less wasteful than the typical french fry, where much effort is expended to obtain ruler-perfect consistency. Much like good french fries, however, good steak fries should be crisp on the outside and tender on the inside. They should not be oily, dry, mealy, or soggy.

As with regular french fries, we found that starchy russets fried up beautifully. Their dense, starchy texture cooked to a consistently tender interior, while the thick skin fried up good and crisp. Russets we bought in 5-pound bags, however, came in various sizes and were difficult to cut into uniformly sized wedges. We found russets that are sold loosely are more consistent in size and are easier to cut into same-size wedges for more consistent cooking times. After cooking up fries of various thicknesses, we preferred wedges with an outside edge that measures ¾ inch wide—this works out to one large potato cut into 12 wedges. Any thicker or thinner and the ratio of tender interior to crisp exterior was thrown off.

Many recipes for deep-fried potatoes suggest refrigerating the raw wedges before frying them, and we found this step to be crucial. Cooling the potatoes down before plunging them into the hot oil allows them to cook more slowly and evenly. By soaking the wedges in a refrigerated bowl of ice water for at least 30 minutes, we were able to ensure that the inner pulp was fully cooked before the outside turned overly brown.

Like most who've fried potatoes before us, we found that simply dunking the chilled, raw fries into hot oil and cooking them until they are done will not produce a good fry. By the time the inside of the fry is cooked and the outside is well browned, the fry itself is wooden and overcooked. We first parfried them at a relatively low temperature to help them cook through without much browning. We then gave them a brief repose to cool off before refrying them quickly in oil at a higher temperature until nicely browned. In combination with the ice water bath, this technique worked like a dream. The thick wedges of potato were evenly cooked, with tender middles and crisp, browned exteriors.

Master Recipe for Steak Fries

SERVES 4

See the illustrations on page 224 for tips on cutting potatoes into wedges.

4   large russet potatoes (about 10 ounces each), scrubbed and cut lengthwise into ¾-inch-thick wedges (about 12 wedges per potato)
2   quarts peanut oil
    Salt and ground black pepper

1. Place the cut fries in a large bowl, cover with cold water by at least 1 inch, and then cover with ice cubes. Refrigerate at least 30 minutes or up to 3 days.

2. In a 5-quart pot or Dutch oven fitted with a clip-on candy thermometer, or in a large electric fryer, heat the oil over medium-low heat to 325 degrees. (The oil will bubble up when you add fries, so be sure you have at least 3 inches of room at the top of the pot.)

3. Pour off the ice and water, quickly wrap the potatoes in a clean kitchen towel, and thoroughly pat them dry. Increase the heat to medium-high and add the fries, one

handful at a time, to the hot oil. Fry, stirring with a Chinese skimmer or large-holed slotted spoon, until the potatoes are limp and soft and have turned from white to gold, about 10 minutes. (The oil temperature will drop 50 to 60 degrees during this frying.) Use a skimmer or slotted spoon to transfer the fries to a triple thickness of paper towels to drain; let rest at least 10 minutes. (The fries can stand at room temperature up to 2 hours or be wrapped in paper towels, sealed in a zipper-lock bag, and frozen up to 1 month.)

4. When ready to serve the fries, reheat the oil to 350 degrees. Using the paper towels as a funnel, carefully pour the potatoes into the hot oil. Discard the paper towels and line a wire rack with another triple thickness of paper towels. Fry the potatoes, stirring fairly constantly, until medium brown and puffed, 8 to 10 minutes. Transfer to the paper towels to drain. Season to taste with salt and pepper. Serve immediately.

OVEN FRIES

OVEN FRIES MAY HAVE THE SAME ingredients as regular fries (potatoes, oil, and salt), but they are a completely different animal. This recipe was "invented" about 20 years ago by cooks who didn't want the bother (and fat) associated with deep-frying. Although almost every modern all-purpose cookbook now contains a recipe for oven-fried potatoes, we have found that most are a pale imitation of the real thing. We wanted fries that were crisp and golden brown, not soggy and pale. In addition, the insides of the fries had to be fluffy and taste intensely of potatoes.

As with regular fries, it was immediately clear that russets are the best choice for oven fries. We then experimented with different ways of cutting the potatoes. We assumed that wedges of some sort would work best.

However, because the thickness varies (the ends are thinner, the middle quite thick), we found that wedges cook and color unevenly. We had far better luck when we cut the fries into uniform ½-inch-thick lengths.

As with fries cooked in oil, many sources suggest refrigerating or chilling the raw, cut potatoes in ice water to get oven fries to brown nicely. We found that chilled fries emerged from the oven with a mushy interior. Chilled fries were also less crisp than potatoes that were cut, rinsed to remove excess starch, and then cooked right away.

At this point, we wondered if the double-cooking method used with french fries could be adapted to oven fries. We tried steaming the potatoes first, hoping this would set the starches in the fries and help the exterior to crisp up. The potatoes emerged from the steamer quite sticky, because of the starches that had been released. We carefully dried the potatoes with a clean kitchen towel (they stuck to paper towels) and spread them out in a single layer on a preheated pan. (Earlier tests had demonstrated the benefits of starting the potatoes on a hot rather than a cold baking sheet.) The fries emerged from the oven crisp and delicious. By releasing some of their starch during steaming, the potatoes release less starch in the oven, which allows the exterior to become especially crisp and golden.

We fiddled around with the oven temperature and found that 450 degrees delivered the best results—maximum crispness without any risk of burning. At this high heat, we found we could skip turning the potatoes, a step in many other recipes that led to tearing the crisp skin. Although no one will mistake oven fries for french fries, these oven fries are very, very good.

Master Recipe for Oven Fries

SERVES 4

Like french fries, oven fries are twice-cooked for the best texture. First, they are steamed to cook the interior partially and set the starch. Next, they are baked in a hot oven until the exterior is crisp. Make sure to preheat the greased baking sheets as directed. Adding the steamed potatoes to a hot pan makes a difference. There's no need to turn the fries. The bottoms become especially crisp, while the other sides turn golden brown. See the illustrations on page 224 for tips on cutting the fries, but cut them ½ inch thick rather than ¼ inch as needed for regular fries.

4	large russet potatoes (about 10 ounces each), scrubbed and cut into $\frac{1}{2}$ by $\frac{1}{2}$-inch lengths
5	teaspoons peanut oil
	Salt and ground black pepper

1. Rinse the cut fries in a large bowl under cold running water until the water turns from milky colored to clear.

2. Put ½ teaspoon of the oil on each of two rimmed baking sheets. Use a paper towel to spread the oil evenly over the entire surface. Place both sheets in the oven (on the lower-middle and upper-middle racks) and heat the oven to 450 degrees.

3. Fit a large pot or Dutch oven with a steamer basket and fill the pot with enough water to reach just below the bottom of the basket. Bring the water to a boil over high heat and add the potatoes to the basket. Cover and steam until the potatoes are glistening but still very firm, about 5 minutes. Remove the potatoes from the pot and spread them out in a single layer on two clean kitchen towels. Pat the potatoes dry using a third kitchen towel.

4. Toss the potatoes and the remaining 4 teaspoons oil in a large bowl to coat. Season the potatoes generously with salt and pepper to taste and toss again to blend. Carefully remove one baking sheet from the oven and place half of the potatoes on the baking sheet so they are spread out and not touching each other. Place the baking sheet back in the oven and repeat the process using the second baking sheet and the remaining potatoes.

5. Bake until the potatoes are golden brown and have begun to puff, 25 to 30 minutes, reversing the baking sheets (from top to bottom) halfway through the baking time. Serve immediately.

➤ VARIATIONS

Oven Fries with Indian Spices

Combine 1 ½ teaspoons curry powder, 1 teaspoon ground turmeric, 1 teaspoon ground coriander, and ½ teaspoon ground cumin in a small bowl. Follow the master recipe, adding the spice mixture to the steamed potatoes along with the salt and pepper in step 4.

Oven Fries with Cheese

Follow the master recipe, replacing the pepper in step 4 with 1 teaspoon paprika. When the potatoes are done, pull all the fries close together on one baking sheet, sprinkle evenly with ¼ cup grated Parmesan cheese, and return to the oven until the cheese melts, about 1 minute. Serve immediately.

Oven Fries with Southwestern Spices

If you like, sprinkle the finished fries with additional hot pepper sauce along with lime wedges.

4	large russet potatoes (about 10 ounces each), scrubbed and cut into $\frac{1}{2}$ by $\frac{1}{2}$-inch lengths
5	teaspoons peanut oil
$\frac{1}{2}$	teaspoon chili powder

¼   teaspoon garlic powder
I   teaspoon hot pepper sauce,
       such as Tabasco
       Salt and ground black pepper
I   tablespoon minced fresh cilantro leaves
I   lime, cut into wedges

1. Rinse the cut fries in a large bowl under cold running water until the water turns from milky colored to clear.

2. Put ½ teaspoon of the oil on each of two rimmed baking sheets. Use a paper towel to spread the oil evenly over the entire surface. Place both sheets in the oven (on the lower-middle and upper-middle racks) and heat the oven to 450 degrees.

3. Fit a large pot or Dutch oven with a steamer basket and fill the pot with enough water to reach just below the bottom of the basket. Bring the water to a boil over high heat and add the potatoes to the basket. Cover and steam until the potatoes are glistening but still very firm, about 5 minutes. Remove the potatoes from the pot and spread them out in a single layer on two clean kitchen towels. Pat the potatoes dry using a third kitchen towel.

4. Combine the remaining 4 teaspoons oil, chili powder, garlic powder, and hot sauce in a large bowl. Add the potatoes and toss to coat. Season the potatoes generously with salt and pepper to taste and toss again to blend. Carefully remove one baking sheet from the oven and place half of the potatoes on the baking sheet so they are spread out and not touching each other. Place the baking sheet back in the oven and repeat the process using the second baking sheet and the remaining potatoes.

5. Bake until the potatoes are deep golden brown and have begun to puff, 25 to 30 minutes. Sprinkle with the cilantro and serve immediately with lime wedges.

GREEK-STYLE POTATOES

AS SURE AS YOU'LL FIND A HUGE picture of the Parthenon on the wall at your local Greek diner, you'll also find Greek-style garlic-lemon potatoes on the menu. Often cut into small cubes and either baked in the oven or sautéed on a huge griddle, these popular potatoes are at once tangy with lemon, sharp with garlic, and earthy with oregano. Served alongside every meal from breakfast through dinner, they can accompany an omelet or a simple roast chicken with authority. Done well, the potatoes are crusty, well browned, and accented by a full (but not overpowering) lemon flavor and plenty of garlic bite. If things go wrong, though, they turn out soggy and sour.

Most of the recipes we found revealed that the standard home-cooking technique for Greek potatoes is to cube raw potatoes; toss them into a baking dish with a mixture of lemon juice, garlic, oregano, and oil; add a little water; and then bake them until the water has evaporated and the potatoes have absorbed the flavors of the seasoning mixture. A number of recipes demanded what seemed to us an unreasonably long baking time of 90 minutes as well as constant monitoring and stirring of the potatoes near the end of cooking. As we discovered when we made the potatoes according to this traditional method, they didn't turn out even close to perfect anyway. The texture was downright soggy, and most tasters felt that the lemon flavor was harsh and acidic. Worse yet was the total absence of the crisp, browned crust we wanted on the potatoes. We decided our first task would be reducing the cooking time.

More research turned up two possible solutions: oven-roasting without the seasonings and stovetop cooking in a skillet.

Oven-roasting the potatoes and then adding a lemon-garlic-herb mixture when they emerged from the oven made for a huge improvement. These simple steps cut the cooking time in half, to 45 minutes, while also producing a flavorful, caramelized crust. The results we got from the skillet method were even better. With the intense heat of the hot pan over a medium-high flame, the potatoes developed a gorgeous, flavorful, mahogany brown crust in just 11 minutes. Although perfect on the outside, the potatoes were not completely cooked on the inside. After a number of tests, we found that simply covering the skillet and allowing the browned potatoes to cook for an additional six minutes gave them a tender and velvety interior. Now we had cut the time down from 90 minutes to less than 20, and the results were crisp and flavorful rather than soggy and acidic.

We tested different skillets and found a heavy-bottomed, 12-inch nonstick model best suited to the task. The heavy construction translates into even heat distribution, which reduces the risk of burning and maximizes browning. And don't skimp on size: The large diameter provided enough space to arrange the potatoes in a single layer for optimal browning. Finally, while the nonstick finish made cleanup a breeze, it is not essential. We successfully cooked the potatoes in a conventional pan (without a nonstick coating), but the pan required a fair amount of elbow grease to clean. In the course of testing, we learned to use only four potatoes, so as not to compromise the browning by crowding the pan, and to make sure the potatoes were evenly sized, so all the pieces would cook at the same rate.

In terms of the cooking medium, we liked the flavor of extra-virgin olive oil, but using it over high heat destroyed its delicate fruitiness. Next, we tried pure olive oil and then vegetable oil, and tasters found the flavor differences to be minimal (we chose vegetable oil since it is a pantry staple). Some butter was necessary to boost the flavor of the oil. Finally, because we wanted the flavor of extra-virgin olive oil, we decided to add some to the cooked potatoes along with the seasonings.

We were surprised that few recipes specified what type of potato to use. Surely there would be differences between high-starch/low-moisture potatoes such as russets (commonly used for baking), medium-starch potatoes such as all-purpose or Yukon Gold, and low-starch/high-moisture potatoes such

JUICING LEMONS

Everyone has a trick for juicing lemons. We found that this method extracts the most juice and works well for limes, too.

1. Start by rolling the lemon on a hard surface, pressing down firmly with the palm of your hand to break the membranes inside the fruit.

2. Cut the lemon in half. Use a wooden reamer to extract the juice into a bowl. To catch the seeds, place a mesh strainer over the bowl.

231

as Red Bliss, which are often used for roasting and boiling. After testing representatives from the three categories, our tasters consistently favored Yukon Golds for their appealing blend of smooth, velvety texture, rich yellow hue, and buttery flavor. Red Bliss potatoes took a close second for their supple, creamy texture. Russets were rejected because the pieces broke apart easily and were mealy. With regard to preparing the Yukon Golds, tasters preferred peeled potatoes cut into wedges ¾ inch thick as opposed to thicker wedges, slices, or cubes.

Lemon, garlic, and oregano give this dish its character. Most of the recipes we consulted called for lemon juice, some as little as 2 tablespoons and others as much as ½ cup. Throughout our testing, tasters agreed that potatoes flavored with lemon juice alone tasted sharp, shallow, and acidic. So we tried adding some grated lemon zest to impart a deeper lemon flavor. Indeed it did; tasters responded well to batches made with a full tablespoon of grated zest per 2 pounds of potatoes, along with a modest 2 tablespoons of juice for brightness and moderate acidity.

At first, we thought that raw garlic might have too much bite for the dish, but tasters dismissed our attempts to tame the garlic flavor by toasting the whole cloves or cooking the minced garlic in oil until it was sweet and mellow. Judging the flavor of these batches too "docile" and "wimpy," they agreed that raw garlic was the way to go. One clove, two cloves, and even three cloves were deemed too weak. We were shocked when tasters chose the batch of potatoes with four cloves of minced raw garlic, describing it as "bright, fresh, and gutsy." Last, we replaced the dusty-tasting dried oregano used in so many recipes with fresh, and all the tasters approved.

The only thing left was to determine the optimum amount of time for the potatoes and seasonings to get acquainted. Testing showed that adding the lemon, garlic, and herbs to the pan midway through the potatoes' cooking time (or any earlier) not only diminished their flavor but also increased the risk of burning the garlic. Instead, we mixed the seasonings into the potatoes once they were fully cooked, which provided the strong hits of flavor that our tasters demanded.

Now that these classic potatoes are so quick and easy to make, chances are you can get them on the table at home in less time than it would take you to drive to the nearest diner. Even better, the technique of sautéing potato wedges in a skillet can be used with any kind of seasonings—even something you might never see in a diner.

POTATOES DONE RIGHT

Don't cut the potatoes into haphazardly shaped pieces or crowd the pan (top). For even cooking and proper browning, the potatoes should be sliced evenly and cooked in a single layer (bottom).

Master Recipe for Greek-Style Potatoes

SERVES 4

This recipe could really be called Skillet Potatoes, because that's the technique employed. Although garlic, lemon, and oregano are traditional Greek flavors, other combinations are possible, as demonstrated in the variations. If your potatoes are larger than the size we recommend, you may have to increase the covered cooking time by up to 4 minutes. Though a nonstick pan makes cleanup easier, it is not essential.

I	tablespoon vegetable oil
I	tablespoon unsalted butter
4	medium Yukon Gold potatoes (7 to 8 ounces each), peeled and cut lengthwise into 8 wedges (see the illustration below)
4	medium cloves garlic, minced or pressed through a garlic press (about I heaping tablespoon)
I	tablespoon extra-virgin olive oil
I	tablespoon grated zest and 2 tablespoons juice from 2 lemons
2	tablespoons minced fresh oregano leaves
I	teaspoon salt
1/2	teaspoon ground black pepper
2	tablespoons minced fresh parsley leaves

1. Heat the oil and butter in a 12-inch heavy-bottomed nonstick skillet over medium-high heat until the butter melts and the foaming subsides, swirling the pan occasionally. Add the potatoes in a single layer and cook until golden brown (the pan should sizzle but not smoke), about 6 minutes. Using tongs, turn the potatoes so the second cut sides are down. Cook until deep golden brown on the second side, about 5 minutes longer. Reduce the heat to medium-low, cover tightly, and cook until the potatoes are tender when pierced with the tip of a paring knife, about 6 minutes.

2. While the potatoes cook, combine the garlic, oil, lemon zest and juice, and oregano in a small bowl. When the potatoes are tender, add the garlic-lemon mixture, salt, and pepper. Stir carefully (so as not to break the potato wedges) to distribute. Cook, uncovered, until the seasoning mixture is heated through and fragrant, 1 to 2 minutes. Sprinkle the potatoes with the parsley and stir gently to distribute it. Serve immediately.

➤ VARIATIONS

Greek-Style Potatoes with Olives and Feta

Follow the master recipe, adding 3 ounces crumbled feta cheese (about 1/3 cup) and 8 pitted and sliced Kalamata (or other black, brine-cured) olives (about 1/4 cup) along with the parsley.

CUTTING POTATO WEDGES

Halve the potato lengthwise and, holding the knife perpendicular to the board, cut each half in half lengthwise to make quarters. Holding the knife at 45 degrees to the board, cut each quarter in half lengthwise, dividing the potato into a total of eight equal-size wedges.

233

Greek-Style Potatoes with Spinach and Anchovies

If you don't fancy anchovies, this dish can be made without them.

Follow the master recipe, adding 1 teaspoon minced anchovies (about 3 fillets) to the garlic-lemon mixture. Stir the mixture into the potatoes, add 2½ ounces clean baby spinach leaves (about 3 cups), and gently stir the mixture again to distribute. Omit the parsley.

Spicy Greek-Style Potatoes

In keeping with the bold flavors of the dish, this variation is very spicy.

Follow the master recipe, adding 2 small jalapeño chiles cut into ¼-inch slices (with seeds and membranes) to the pan just before covering the skillet in step 1.

Greek-Style Garlic-Lemon Potatoes with Sun-Dried Tomatoes and Scallions

Follow the master recipe, adding 1 ounce sliced oil-packed sun-dried tomatoes (about ¼ cup) and 2 medium sliced scallions (about ¼ cup) to the garlic-lemon mixture.

Skillet Potatoes with Scallions and Curry

This variation takes the basic technique for Greek-Style Potatoes but uses Indian seasonings. Curry powder is actually a blend of spices that usually includes turmeric, coriander, cumin, cardamom, cloves, pepper, nutmeg, mace, tamarind, and fenugreek, among other spices. In authentic Indian cooking, this mixture is freshly ground and mixed as needed. The two kinds available in grocery stores are the basic curry powder and the hotter Madras curry powder. Either works in this recipe.

I	tablespoon vegetable oil
I	tablespoon unsalted butter
I	teaspoon curry powder
4	medium Yukon Gold potatoes (7 to 8 ounces each), peeled and cut lengthwise into 8 wedges (see the illustration on page 233)
2	medium scallions, sliced thin Salt and ground black pepper

Heat the oil and butter in a 12-inch heavy-bottomed nonstick skillet over medium-high heat until the butter melts and the foaming subsides, swirling the pan occasionally. Add the curry powder and cook until fragrant, about 30 seconds. Add the potatoes in a single layer and cook until golden brown (the pan should sizzle but not smoke), about 6 minutes. Using tongs, turn the potatoes so the second cut sides are down. Cook until deep golden brown on the second side, about 5 minutes longer. Reduce the heat to medium-low, cover tightly, and cook until the potatoes are tender when pierced with the tip of a paring knife, about 6 minutes. Gently stir in the scallions and season with salt and pepper to taste. Serve immediately.

HOME FRIES

WHEN WE BEGAN TRYING TO UNCOVER the secret of the ultimate home fries, we went right to the source—diners. But soon we learned that the problems with this dish are often the same, no matter where they are cooked and consumed. Frequently, the potatoes are not crisp; they are greasy, and the flavorings are either too bland or too spicy.

Our first step was to define home fries: individual pieces of potato cooked in fat in a frying pan on top of the stove and mixed with caramelized onions. We also knew what they should look and taste like. They should have a deep golden-brown crust and a tender interior with a full potato flavor. The potatoes should not be greasy but instead feel crisp and moist in your mouth.

Although there are dozens of varieties, potatoes can be divided into three major categories based on their relative starch content. Experience has taught us that high-starch potatoes (like russets) make the best baked potatoes and french fries, while low-starch potatoes (all red-skinned potatoes) are the top choice for boiling, making salads, and roasting. Medium-starch potatoes (like all-purpose and Yukon Golds) have a combination of these traits and can be roasted, baked, or mashed. Because the cooking method and the type of potato used are so intimately connected, we decided it made sense to try each cooking method with all three types of potatoes.

We knew the potatoes would end up in a skillet with fat, but would it be necessary to precook them, as our research suggested? We began testing with the simplest approach: Dice the potatoes raw and cook them in a hot skillet with fat. But in test after test, no matter how small we cut them, it proved challenging to cook raw potatoes all the way through and obtain a crisp brown crust at the same time. Low temperatures helped cook the inside, but the outside didn't crisp. High temperatures crisped the outside, but the potatoes had to be taken off the heat so early to prevent scorching that the insides were left raw. We decided to precook the potatoes before frying them in a skillet.

Because a common approach to home fries is to use leftover baked potatoes, we baked some of each type, stored them in the refrigerator overnight, diced them, and put them into a skillet with fat. These tests were disappointing. None of the resulting home fries had great potato flavor. They all tasted like leftovers, and their texture was somewhat gummy. The exterior of the red potatoes was not crisp, although they looked very good, and the starchier russet potatoes fell apart.

Next, we tried starting with freshly boiled potatoes. Potatoes that were boiled until tender broke down in the skillet, and the inside was overcooked by the time the exterior was crisp. So we tried dicing and then braising the potatoes, figuring we could cook them through in a covered pan with some water and fat, remove the cover, let the water evaporate, and then crisp up the potatoes in the remaining fat. Although this sounded like a good idea, the potatoes stuck horribly to the skillet.

Finally, we considered a technique we found in Lydie Marshall's book *Passion for Potatoes* (HarperPerennial, 1992). Marshall instructs the cook to cover diced raw potatoes with water, bring the water to a boil, immediately drain the potatoes well, and then sauté them. This treatment allows the potatoes to cook briefly without absorbing too much water, which is what makes them susceptible to overcooking and breaking down.

We tested this technique with russets, Red Bliss potatoes, and Yukon Golds. Eureka! It worked better with all three varieties of potato than any of the other methods we had tried. The Yukon Golds, though, were the clear favorite. Each individual piece of potato had a crisp exterior, and the inner flesh was tender, moist, and rich in potato flavor. The appearance of each was superior as well, the golden yellow color of the flesh complementing the crispy brown exterior. The russets were drier and not as full flavored but were preferred over the Red Bliss, which all tasters found to be somewhat mushy and disappointingly bland.

We decided to test another medium-starch potato. All-purpose potatoes also browned well and were tender and moist on the inside, but they lacked the rich buttery flavor and appealing yellow color of the Yukon Golds, which remained the favorite.

Having discovered the ideal cooking

method and the preferred potato variety, we moved on to the best way to cut the potatoes. We found sliced potatoes much harder to cook than diced ones. A pound of sliced potatoes stacks up three or four layers deep in a large skillet. The result is uneven cooking, with some slices burning and others remaining undercooked. Countless tests had convinced us that one of the keys to success in cooking home fries is to cook the potatoes in a single layer. When a pound of potatoes is diced, one cut side of each potato piece can have contact with the skillet at all times. We tested dices of various size and found the ½-inch cube to be ideal: easy to turn and to eat, characterized by that pleasing combination of crispy outside and soft fleshy inside.

Deciding whether or not to peel the potatoes was easy. All tasters preferred the texture and flavor contributed by the skin. Leaving it on also saved time and effort.

Thus far, we had determined that letting the potatoes sit undisturbed in hot fat to brown each side was critical to a crisp exterior. We found it best to let the potatoes brown undisturbed for four to five minutes before the first turn and then to turn them a total of three or four times. Three tablespoons turned out to be the ideal amount of fat for 1 pound of potatoes. When sampling potatoes cooked in different frying mediums, we found that a 50-50 combination of butter and oil offered the best of both worlds, providing a buttery flavor with a decreased risk of burning (butter burns more easily than vegetable oils). Refined corn and peanut oils, with their nutty overtones, were our first choices.

Soft, sweet, and moist, onions are the perfect counterpoint to crispy potatoes, but we had to determine the best way to include them. Tests showed the easiest and most

SCIENCE:
Out of Hot Water and into the Frying Pan

So what happens to the starch and moisture content of diced potatoes when they are cooked first in water and then in fat? The potato starch granules are composed of layer upon layer of tightly packed starch molecules. When the potatoes are first put into cold water, nothing happens to the starch molecules. As the water heats, it warms the molecules and starts seeping in between the layers. The hotter the water gets, the more rapidly it works its way into the softer areas of the granules, causing them to expand. Finally, near the boiling point, the starch molecules swell so much that they burst. By removing the diced potatoes just as the water begins to boil, the water absorption is stopped before the granules have a chance to explode.

When the just-boiled potatoes come into contact with hot fat, the starch granules on the surface expand immediately and absorb water from the inside of the potato. The moisture rushing to the surface creates the sizzling sound, and the expanding granules begin to seal the surface. If the surface is sealed and too much moisture remains stuck inside, the texture of the potato will be mushy; if there is not enough moisture on the inside, the texture will be dry and mealy; if there is no moisture left on the inside and the surface has not sealed, the starch granules will begin to absorb fat and the potatoes will be greasy. Medium-starch potatoes such as Yukon Golds have an ideal moisture content in that when a crisp crust has formed, just enough water is left to create a moist, tender inside.

STARCH...

IN COLD WATER

IN HEATED WATER

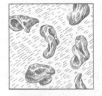

IN BOILING WATER

efficient way also produced the best results: Dice the onions and cook them before cooking the potatoes. More flavor can be added with help from parsley, red or green bell peppers (sautéed with the onion), or cayenne pepper, as you wish. Whatever your choice, these are home fries worth staying home for.

Master Recipe for Home Fries

SERVES 2 TO 3

If you need to double this recipe, instead of crowding the skillet, cook two batches of home fries separately. While making the second batch, you can keep the first batch hot and crisp by spreading the potatoes on a rimmed baking sheet placed in a 300-degree oven. The paprika adds a warm, deep color, but it can be omitted. An alternative is to toss in 1 tablespoon minced parsley just before serving the potatoes.

2 1/2	tablespoons corn or peanut oil
1	medium onion, chopped small
1	pound (2 medium) Yukon Gold or all-purpose potatoes, cut into 1/2-inch cubes (see the illustrations on page 238)
1 1/4	teaspoons salt
1	tablespoon unsalted butter
1	teaspoon paprika
	Ground black pepper

1. Heat 1 tablespoon of the oil in a 12-inch heavy-bottomed skillet over medium-high heat until hot but not smoking. Add the onion and cook, stirring frequently, until browned, 8 to 10 minutes. Transfer the onion to a small bowl and set aside.

2. Meanwhile, place the diced potatoes in a large saucepan, cover with 1/2 inch water, add 1 teaspoon of the salt, and place over high heat. As soon as the water begins to boil, after about 6 minutes, drain the potatoes thoroughly in a colander.

3. Heat the butter and the remaining 1 1/2 tablespoons oil in the empty skillet over medium-high heat until the butter foams. Add the potatoes and shake the skillet to evenly distribute the potatoes in a single layer; make sure that one side of each piece is touching the surface of the skillet. Cook without stirring until one side of the potatoes is golden brown, 4 to 5 minutes, and then carefully turn the potatoes with a wooden or heatproof plastic spatula. Spread the potatoes in a single layer in the skillet again and repeat the process until the potatoes are tender and browned on most sides, turning three to four times, 10 to 15 minutes longer. Add the onions, paprika, the remaining 1/4 teaspoon salt, and pepper to taste; stir to blend and serve immediately.

➤ VARIATIONS

Spicy Home Fries

Follow the master recipe, adding a pinch or two of cayenne pepper to the potatoes along with the paprika.

Home Fries with Bell Pepper and Cumin

Follow the master recipe, cooking 1 finely chopped red or green bell pepper with the onion. Remove the pepper with the onion and add both back to the pan along with the paprika and 1 teaspoon ground cumin.

Sautéed Potatoes with Rosemary and Garlic

This variation takes its cue from Italian cooking. Although it looks like regular home fries, it doesn't taste like any version you might find in a diner.

1	pound (2 medium) Yukon Gold or all-purpose potatoes, cut

into 1/2-inch cubes (see the
illustrations below)
1 1/4   teaspoons salt
3   tablespoons extra-virgin olive oil
2   teaspoons chopped fresh rosemary
1   medium clove garlic, minced or
pressed through a garlic press
Ground black pepper

1. Place the potatoes in a large saucepan, cover with ½ inch water, add 1 teaspoon of the salt, and place over high heat. As soon as the water begins to boil, after about 6 minutes, drain the potatoes thoroughly in a colander.

2. Heat the oil in a 12-inch heavy-bottomed skillet over medium-high heat until shimmering. Add the potatoes and shake the skillet to evenly distribute the potatoes in a single layer; make sure that one side of each piece is touching the surface of the skillet. Cook without stirring until one side of the potatoes is golden brown, 4 to 5 minutes, and then carefully turn the potatoes with a wooden or heatproof plastic spatula. Spread the potatoes in a single layer in the skillet again and repeat

the process until the potatoes are tender and browned on most sides, turning three to four times, 10 to 15 minutes longer.

3. Reduce the heat to low and add the rosemary and garlic. Cook, shaking the pan frequently to coat the potatoes with the rosemary and garlic, until the garlic is fragrant, about 2 minutes. Add the remaining ¼ teaspoon salt and pepper to taste, stir to blend, and serve immediately.

HASH BROWNS

MANY PEOPLE LIKE HOME FRIES— sautéed chunks of potato that retain their shape and individuality when cooked. Others prefer hash browns, which are thin, crisply sautéed potato cakes made with grated or chopped potatoes, raw or pre-cooked. Unlike other potato cakes (such as latkes; see page 242), hash browns do not contain eggs. The starch from the grated or finely chopped potatoes provides the binder needed to hold the cake together. With just salt and pepper added for seasoning, the focus remains on the potato flavor. They

ROUGH DICING

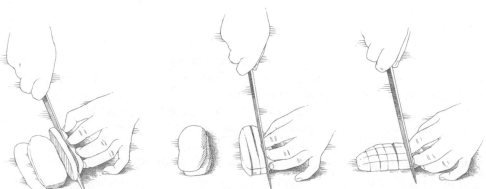

1. Slice the potato lengthwise into quarters.

2. Make two stacks and cut each stack lengthwise into quarters.

3. Turn the stacks 90 degrees and cut horizontally to complete the dice.

are probably most closely related to roesti (a Swiss potato pancake), although the latter are thicker and usually served as a dinner accompaniment while hash browns can be served for breakfast, lunch, or dinner.

Even though we assumed that a starchier potato would be best suited for this assignment, we began by testing all the major varieties. After thorough testing, the only type we completely eliminated was the waxy or low-starch variety, such as Red Bliss, which did not stay together or brown well and also lacked flavor in this recipe. The all-purpose potatoes sold in plastic bags in the supermarket, which have a medium starch content, worked well enough to be considered an adequate choice. We also liked the buttery color, as well as the taste, of Yukon Golds, another medium-starch potato. However, we found that the high-starch russets yielded the best overall results. They adhered well, browned beautifully, and had the most pronounced potato flavor.

Our next challenge was to decide between raw and precooked potatoes. Precooked potatoes tasted good, but when cut into chunks, they did not stay together in a cohesive cake. When grated, they needed to be pressed very hard to form a cake. Unfortunately, this meant they ended up having the mouthfeel of fried mashed potatoes. Although this is an acceptable alternative if you have leftover cooked potatoes, we preferred using raw, grated potatoes. We also liked the more textured interior, the pronounced potato taste, and the way the raw shreds of potatoes formed an attractive, deeply browned crust.

Choosing the best method for cutting the potatoes was easy. Grating on the large-hole side of a box grater or with the shredding disk on a food processor yielded hash browns that formed a coherent cake when cooked. Chopped potatoes, even when finely chopped, did not hold together as well. To peel or not to peel the potatoes is a matter of personal preference. The presence of the grated peel altered the taste a bit, but it did not negatively affect the overall cooking method or desired outcome.

After cooking countless batches of hash browns, we found that the pan itself was an important factor. A skillet with sloping sides made it considerably easier to press the potatoes into a flattened shape, invert them, and slide them from the pan. All these tasks were more difficult in a straight-sided frying pan. As for browning, properly seasoned cast-iron pans and uncoated stainless steel pans produced the best exterior, with potatoes that were evenly colored and crusty; however, nonstick pans browned adequately and, obviously, were easier to use and clean.

We found that cooking hash browns with butter provided good color and a very rich flavor. We tested bacon fat (figuring that many cooks might have some in the kitchen at breakfast time) and were disappointed. The color was a bit anemic, and the potato flavor was lacking. Vegetable oil could not produce the same rich, golden-brown color that butter did, and the flavor was lacking. Butter is clearly the best choice.

Our last cooking-method test was to cover the potatoes during cooking. What we found was that the cover trapped steam in the pan, which reduced the crispness of the crust. Since we began with a thin layer of potatoes in the pan anyway, we didn't need to steam the potatoes to help cook them through. Cooking the hash browns without the cover is the way to go.

While testing, we used only salt and pepper for seasonings, planning to experiment with other ingredients at a later time. However, we became so fond of the buttery salt and pepper taste that we decided to keep the seasonings as is for the master recipe. Of course, adding grated onion or chopped scallions and parsley (or other fresh herbs) is an option. The onion or herbs can be either tossed with the grated potatoes before cooking or sprinkled over the potatoes in the pan before pressing them with the spatula.

Hash browns can be made into one or more individual servings or one large portion that can be cut into wedges. We also liked using hash browns as a base for toppings or folding them over fillings like omelets. No matter how you choose to present the hash browns, make sure you serve them steaming hot.

Master Recipe for Hash Browns

SERVES 4

To keep the potatoes from turning brown, grate them just before cooking. This recipe cooks the potatoes in one large cake. For individual servings, simply divide the raw grated potatoes into four equal-size patties and reduce the cooking time to 5 minutes per side. To vary flavor, add 2 tablespoons grated onion, 1 to 2 tablespoons of an herb of your choice, or roasted garlic to taste to the raw grated potatoes. You can also garnish the cooked hash browns with minced chives or scallion greens just before serving. For extra-crisp hash browns, see the illustration on page 242. See the illustration at right for tips on squeezing as much moisture as possible from the potatoes.

1	pound russet potatoes, peeled, washed, dried, grated coarse, and squeezed dry in a kitchen towel (1 1/2 cups loosely packed grated potatoes)
1/4	teaspoon salt
	Ground black pepper
1	tablespoon unsalted butter

1. Toss the fully dried grated potatoes with the salt and pepper to taste in a medium bowl.

2. Heat half of the butter in a 10-inch skillet over medium-high heat until it just starts to brown and then scatter the potatoes evenly over the entire pan bottom. Using a wide spatula, firmly press the potatoes to flatten. Reduce the heat to medium and continue cooking until dark golden brown and crisp, 7 to 8 minutes.

3. Invert the hash browns, browned-side up, onto a large plate. Add the remaining butter to the pan. Once the butter has melted, slide the hash browns back into the pan. Continue to cook over medium heat until the remaining side is dark golden brown and crisp, 5 to 6 minutes longer.

4. Slide the hash browns onto a plate or cutting board, cut into wedges, and serve immediately.

> VARIATIONS

Hash Brown "Omelet" with Cheddar, Tomato, and Basil

Crisp potatoes offer a nice contrast to many filling ingredients. Fill with 1/4 cup chopped ham, cooked bacon, or cooked sausage and/or 1/4 cup cooked vegetables, such as mushrooms, peppers, or onions. Cheese is another option, as in this recipe.

DRYING GRATED POTATOES

To release the water from the grated potatoes, place them in a clean kitchen towel and, using two hands, twist the towel tightly to squeeze out as much moisture as possible.

Follow the master recipe, topping the potatoes with 1 medium tomato cut into small dice, 1 tablespoon chopped fresh basil leaves, and ¼ cup grated cheddar cheese once the potatoes have been returned to the skillet in step 3. Proceed as directed until the underside is crisp. Fold the hash browns (see the illustration on page 242) and cook just until the cheese melts, about 1 minute. Serve immediately.

Open-Faced Hash Browns with Ham, Tomato, and Swiss Cheese

You can still add fillings without folding the hash browns. Instead of the ingredients used here, try adding slices of smoked salmon and a dollop of sour cream just before serving the hash browns.
Follow the master recipe through step 3. Top the hash browns with 1 slice deli-style ham, 1 small tomato sliced thin, and ¼ cup grated Swiss cheese. Cover the pan and cook over medium heat just until the cheese melts, 1 to 2 minutes. Serve immediately.

Spicy Hash Browns with Cheddar and Red Bell Pepper

In this variation, the potatoes themselves are flavored before they go into the pan. If you want your hash browns to be really spicy, include some of the jalapeño seeds. See page 224 for tips on squeezing as much moisture as possible from the potatoes.

2   tablespoons unsalted butter
I   small red bell pepper, stemmed, seeded, and chopped fine
I   small jalapeño chile, stemmed, seeded, and minced
I   pound russet potatoes, peeled, washed, dried, grated coarse, and squeezed dry In a kitchen towel (I ½ cups loosely packed grated potatoes)

2   ounces cheddar cheese, shredded (about ½ cup)
I   tablespoon minced fresh parsley leaves
¼   teaspoon salt
   Ground black pepper

1. Heat 1 tablespoon of the butter in a 10-inch skillet over medium-high heat. When the foaming subsides, add the bell pepper and chile and cook, stirring occasionally, until they soften, about 4 minutes. Transfer the cooked peppers to a medium bowl; set the skillet aside. Add the fully dried grated potatoes, cheese, parsley, salt, and pepper to taste to the bowl with the peppers and toss to combine.

SCIENCE: Why Do Onions Prevent Browning?

Traditional cooks have always sworn that alternating the grating of potatoes with onions helped to prevent the potatoes from darkening. This was one theory that proved true: Potatoes grated alone darkened much more quickly than those grated with onions. According to Dr. Alfred Bushway, a food science professor at the University of Maine, browning occurs because, as potato cells are exposed to air after slicing, certain enzymes add oxygen to phenol compounds found in the potato cells. This process creates an unsightly but harmless brown pigment known as melanin.

There are a number of ways to retard this browning, including cooking, coating the cut surfaces with acid such as lemon juice, or covering the cut food with an airtight coating of plastic wrap. Commercial processing plants often use certain sulfur compounds to prevent browning, says Dr. Ralph R. Price, associate professor of nutrition at the University of Arizona in Tucson, because these compounds inhibit the action of the enzymes that cause browning. Onions contain several of these sulfur compounds, which not only lend onions their distinct odor but also act to prevent browning of any cut fruits or vegetables that the onions come into contact with.

2. Heat ½ tablespoon of the remaining butter in the empty skillet over medium-high heat until it just starts to brown and then scatter the potatoes evenly over the entire pan bottom. Using a wide spatula, firmly press the potatoes to flatten. Reduce the heat to medium and continue cooking until dark golden brown and crisp, 7 to 8 minutes.

3. Invert the hash browns, browned-side up, onto a large plate. Add the remaining ½ tablespoon butter to the pan. Once the butter has melted, slide the hash browns back into the pan. Continue to cook over medium heat until the remaining side is dark golden brown and crisp, 5 to 6 minutes longer.

4. Slide the hash browns onto a plate or cutting board, cut into wedges, and serve immediately.

EXTRA-CRISP HASH BROWNS

Folding the hash browns ensures that every bite has maximum crunch. Once the potatoes have been browned on both sides, fold the cake over, omelet style, with a spatula. When cut into wedges, each piece will now have four crisp surfaces—two inside and two outside.

LATKES

LATKES ARE THICK GRATED POTATO pancakes that are flavored with onion, bound with eggs and usually matzo meal, and pan-fried in vegetable oil. They should be golden and very crisp on the exterior, creamy and moist on the interior. To figure out how to make these ideal latkes, we had to find the best potato, the best grating method, and the best frying technique.

We began with the potatoes. We tested russets, which are high starch; Yukon Golds, which have a medium starch content; and red potatoes, which are low starch. The russet potato pancakes had a pleasantly pronounced potato flavor and a dry texture. The red potatoes were at the other end of the spectrum: very creamy, almost gluey on the inside. The Yukon Golds were the biggest surprise; the pancakes made with these potatoes were an attractive deep yellow-gold color, tasted somewhat sweet and mild, and were creamy in texture but not gluey or sticky. Everyone who tried the Yukon Gold latkes judged them superior in taste.

Some experts feel that latkes made with potatoes grated by hand on a box grater are superior to those made with potatoes grated in a food processor. We tried both methods and found a negligible difference in texture between the two. We did, however, discover a very useful two-step grating procedure.

For the first step, we put the peeled potatoes through the feed tube of the food processor, using the coarse shredding disk. We then removed about half to two thirds of the shreds and placed them in a separate mixing bowl. Next, we inserted the metal blade, added chunks of onion to the shreds left in the processor bowl, and processed the mixture in spurts until we had a very coarse puree, each piece being no larger than ⅛ inch. Then we combined the pureed potatoes and onions with the shredded potatoes.

This two-step procedure gave us latkes that had some larger shreds that cooked up quite crisp along the outside perimeters while the inside center portion was thicker and chewier, like a traditional pancake. This, we discovered, was the best of both latke worlds: crispy and lacy along the edges but still thick and chewy in the middle.

A similar result can be obtained without a food processor. First, grate the potatoes on the largest holes of a box grater and place half of them in a sieve set over a bowl. Then, using a chef's knife, chop the other half of the grated potatoes and all of the onions into a fine 1/8-inch dice. Mix this with the larger shreds and proceed with the recipe.

After we pressed the potatoes in a fine sieve to remove their moisture, we set them aside. We allowed the mixing bowl with the potato water to sit for a minute and then very slowly poured off the potato water that had accumulated. At the bottom of the bowl, there was a layer of thick, white potato starch. In all of our tests that were successful, this starch proved helpful in binding the latkes, whether or not flour or matzo meal was added.

Now we began to test the most crucial part of the whole process—frying. First, we tested three different frying mediums: a combination of chicken fat (schmaltz) and vegetable oil; solid vegetable shortening (Crisco); and vegetable oil.

The chicken fat and vegetable oil combination was impractical; chicken fat is just not readily available. We thought solid vegetable shortening might work well. But it reached its smoking point much more quickly than the liquid vegetable oil, and it was difficult to add more solid shortening to the frying pan to maintain a consistent depth as several batches of latkes were cooking. Vegetable oil, such as corn, peanut, safflower, or a combination,

proved to be the perfect oil for frying latkes.

We tried cooking latkes in several depths of oil, from 1/2 inch to only 1/16 inch, and we found that more oil does not necessarily result in oilier pancakes, if the oil is at the right temperature. It is much easier to regulate the temperature of the oil if you have at least 1/8 inch of oil in the pan, and that was the minimum amount for very thin pancakes. Also, if the oil is deep enough from the start, you don't have to add oil in between batches as frequently.

The temperature of the oil is crucial to frying the perfect latke. However, this is the one category that defies absolute analysis, because it is really difficult to accurately measure the temperature of oil that is only 1/4 inch deep. The key is to have the oil really hot, but not smoking, when the latkes go in. The temperature of the oil will reduce with the addition of more batter, but it should be kept at a constant lively bubble throughout the cooking of all the pancakes. When the oil is hot enough to start frying, it begins to shimmer on the surface and appears kind of wavy. If it is smoking, it's too hot, and the heat should be turned down. We tested the oil initially by dropping in about a teaspoon of batter and observing how quickly it cooked. If it browned in under a minute, the oil was too hot. Two minutes was just about right.

With every batch of latkes we made, we held some in a 200-degree oven and tried a bite every five to 10 minutes. With every bite after the first one, the latkes tasted progressively older and chewier. We concluded that you cannot hold latkes for more than 10 minutes at the most. They may still be hot, but the taste diminishes and the texture deteriorates so much that after all the trouble you have gone to preparing them, you might as well have chosen something else to cook.

We did discover, however, that latkes that

have been left to cool at room temperature for a few hours and then reheated in a 375-degree oven for about five minutes are the next-best thing to freshly fried.

We also reserved some of the latkes for the freezer. We placed them on a parchment-lined baking sheet and allowed them to freeze for about 15 minutes before we placed them in zipper-lock freezer bags. When we were ready to serve the latkes, we reheated them on a baking sheet in the middle of a 375-degree oven for about eight minutes per side. All our tasters agreed that there was only a slight difference in quality compared with the freshly fried.

Master Recipe for Latkes

MAKES APPROXIMATELY FOURTEEN 3-INCH PANCAKES

Matzo meal is a traditional binder, though we found that the pancake's texture does not suffer without it. Applesauce and sour cream are classic accompaniments for potato latkes.

2	pounds Yukon Gold or russet potatoes, peeled
1	medium yellow onion, peeled and cut into eighths
1	large egg
4	medium scallions, white and green parts, minced
3	tablespoons minced fresh parsley leaves
2	tablespoons matzo meal (optional)
1 1/2	teaspoons salt
	Ground black pepper
1	cup vegetable oil for frying

1. Grate the potatoes in a food processor fitted with the coarse shredding blade. Place half the potatoes in a fine-mesh sieve set over a medium bowl and reserve. Fit the food processor with the steel blade, add the onion, and pulse with the remaining potatoes until all pieces measure roughly ⅛ inch and look coarsely chopped, five to six 1-second pulses. Mix with the reserved potato shreds in the sieve and press against the sieve to drain as much liquid as possible into the bowl below. Let the potato liquid stand until the thick, white starch settles to the bottom, about 1 minute. Pour off the liquid, leaving the starch in the bowl. Beat the egg and then the potato mixture, scallions, parsley, matzo meal (if using), salt, and pepper to taste into the starch.

2. Meanwhile, heat ¼-inch depth of oil in a 12-inch skillet over medium-high heat until almost smoking. Working 1 latke at a time, place ¼ cup of the potato mixture, squeezed of excess liquid and pressed into a ½-inch-thick disk, in the oil. Press gently with a nonstick spatula; repeat until 5 latkes are in the pan.

3. Maintaining the heat so the fat bubbles around latke edges, fry until golden brown on the bottom and edges, about 3 minutes. Turn with a spatula and continue frying until golden brown all over, about 3 minutes more. Drain on a triple thickness of paper towels set on a wire rack over a rimmed baking sheet. Repeat with the remaining potato mixture, returning the oil to the proper temperature between batches and replacing the oil after every second batch. (Cooled latkes can be covered loosely with plastic wrap, held at room temperature for up to 4 hours, transferred to a heated baking sheet, and baked in a 375-degree oven until crisp and hot, about 5 minutes per side. Or they can be frozen on a cookie sheet, transferred to a zipper-lock freezer bag, frozen, and reheated in a 375-degree oven until crisp and hot, about 8 minutes per side.) Season with salt and pepper to taste and serve immediately.

➤ VARIATION

Potato Pancakes with Pepper Jack Cheese and Cilantro

These nontraditional pancakes are great with sour cream, freshly made salsa, and a splash of hot pepper sauce.

Follow the master recipe, replacing the parsley with an equal amount of cilantro, omitting the matzo meal, and adding ½ cup shredded Pepper Jack cheese with the scallions and other ingredients in step 1.

MASHED POTATOES

MOST OF US WHO MAKE MASHED POTA-toes would never consider consulting a recipe. We customarily make them by adding chunks of butter and spurts of cream until our conscience—or a backseat cook—tells us to stop. Not surprisingly, we produce batches of mashed potatoes that are consistent only in their mediocrity.

For us, the consummate mashed potatoes are creamy, soft, and supple, yet with enough body to stand up to sauce or gravy from an accompanying dish. As for flavor, the sweet, earthy, humble potato comes first, then the buttery richness that keeps you coming back for more.

We quickly determined that high-starch potatoes, such as russets, are best for mashing. Next, we needed to address the simple matter of the best way to cook the potatoes. We started by peeling and cutting some potatoes into chunks to expedite their cooking while cooking others unpeeled and whole. Even when mashed with identical amounts of butter, half-and-half (recommended by a number of trustworthy cookbooks), and salt, the two batches were wildly different. The potatoes that had been peeled and cut made mashed potatoes that were thin in taste and texture and devoid of potato flavor, while those cooked whole and peeled after cooking yielded mashed potatoes that were rich, earthy, and sweet.

We talked to several food scientists, who explained that peeling and cutting the potatoes before simmering increases the surface area through which they lose soluble substances, such as starch, proteins, and flavor compounds, to the cooking water. The greater surface area also enables lots of water molecules to bind with the potatoes' starch molecules. Combine these two effects and you've got bland, thin, watery mashed potatoes.

Next were the matters of butter and other dairy. Working with 2 pounds of potatoes, which serve four to six, we stooped so low as to add only 2 tablespoons of butter. The potatoes ultimately deemed best in flavor by tasters contained 8 tablespoons. They were rich and full and splendid.

When considering dairy, we investigated both the kind and the quantity. Heavy cream made heavy mashed potatoes that were sodden and unpalatably rich, even when we scaled back the amount of butter. On the other hand, mashed potatoes made with whole milk were watery, wimpy, and washed out. When we tried adding more butter to compensate for the milk's lack of richness, the mixture turned into potato soup. Half-and-half, which we'd used in our original tests, was just what was needed, and 1 cup was just the right amount. The mashed potatoes now had a lovely light suppleness and a full, rich flavor that edged toward decadent.

The issues attending butter and dairy did not end there. We had heard that the order in which they are added to the potatoes can affect texture and that melted butter makes better mashed potatoes than softened butter. Determined to leave no spud unturned, we threw several more pounds into the pot. As it turns out, when the butter goes in before the dairy, the result is a silkier, creamier, smoother texture than when the dairy goes first; by comparison, the dairy-first potatoes were pasty and thick. Using melted rather than softened butter made the potatoes even more creamy, smooth, and light.

With our curiosity piqued by the significant textural differences effected by minor differences in procedure, we again contacted several food scientists, who explained that when the half-and-half is stirred into the potatoes before the butter, the water in it works with the starch in the potatoes to make the mashed potatoes gluey and heavy. When the butter is added before the half-and-half, the fat coats the starch molecules, inhibiting their interaction with the water in the half-and-half added later and thereby yielding silkier, creamier mashed potatoes. The benefit of using melted butter results from its liquid form, which enables it to coat the starch molecules quickly and easily. This buttery coating not only affects the interaction of the starch molecules with the half-and-half but also affects the starch molecules' interaction with each other. All in all, it makes for smoother, more velvety mashed potatoes. (Melting the butter, as well as warming the half-and-half, also serves to keep the potatoes warm.)

There is more than one way to mash potatoes. In our testing, we had been using either a ricer or a food mill. We preferred the food mill because its large hopper accommodated half of the potatoes at a time. A ricer, which resembles an oversized garlic press, required processing in several batches. Both, however, produced smooth, light, fine-textured mashed potatoes.

A potato masher is the tool of choice for making chunky mashed potatoes, but it cannot produce smooth mashed potatoes on a par with those processed through a food mill or ricer. With a masher, potatoes mashed within an inch of their lives could

MAKING MASHED POTATOES

WITH A FOOD MILL

1. Hold the drained potato with a dinner fork and peel off the skin with a paring knife.
2. Cut the peeled potato into rough chunks and drop the chunks into the food mill.

WITH A RICER

Cut each potato in half and place it cut-side down in the ricer. Press down with the handle of the ricer to force the flesh through the holes. The skin will remain in the hopper. Discard the skin and repeat with the next potato half.

not achieve anything better than a namby-pamby texture that was neither chunky nor perfectly smooth. Since the sentiment among our tasters was that mashed potatoes should be either smooth or coarse and craggy, a masher is best left to make the latter.

There are two styles of potato mashers—one is a disk with large holes in it, the other a curvy wire loop (see page 289 for more details). We found the disk to be more efficient for reducing both mashing time and the number of lumps in the finished product.

EQUIPMENT: Food Mills

A food mill is no longer a fixture in American kitchens, but it is a terrific tool to have on hand. Think of it as part food processor, because it refines soft foods to a puree, and part sieve, because it separates waste such as peels, seeds, cores, and fiber from the puree. And it accomplishes all of this with the simple turn of a crank, which rotates a gently angled, curved blade. The blade catches the food and forces it down through the holes of a perforated disk at the bottom of the mill. The separation of unwanted material from the puree is the food mill's raison d'être, but another benefit is that it does not aerate the food as it purees, as do food processors and blenders, so you are able to avoid an overly whipped, lightened texture. (In the case of mashed potatoes, a food processor or blender creates a gummy texture.)

Since you can spend as little as $15 and as much as $100 on a food mill, we wondered if some were better than others. We gathered five models and used them to make mashed potatoes and applesauce. Honestly, there was very little difference in the resulting purees—they were all fine, smooth, and free of unwanted material. Thus, we evaluated the mills more on design factors, such as how easy it was to turn the crank, how efficiently the food was processed, and whether the mills offered adjustments in the texture of the puree produced.

The best mills in the group were the beautiful stainless-steel Cuisipro, the VEV Vigano, and the white plastic Moulinex. Each one was easy to crank and efficient, and they all came with fine, medium, and coarse disks. The top performer of the three was the Cuisipro, but at $90, it was also the most expensive. The $15 Moulinex did nearly as well, so it became the pick of the pack for its combination of low price and high performance. The

plastic is surely not as strong as the Cuisipro's stainless steel, but for occasional use, it is just fine.

Both the Foley and the Norpro mills were noticeably less efficient; their blades pushed the food around instead of forcing it through the perforated disk. In addition, neither one offered additional disks for different textures. There was just one medium disk, fixed in place.

THE BEST FOOD MILLS

The Cuisipro (top) took top honors in our testing of five food mills. The Moulinex (bottom) did nearly as well in our tests.

Master Recipe for Mashed Potatoes

SERVES 4 TO 6

Russet potatoes make slightly fluffier mashed potatoes, but Yukon Golds have an appealing buttery flavor and can be used if you prefer. Mashed potatoes stiffen and become gluey as they cool, so they are best served piping hot. If you must hold mashed potatoes before serving, place them in a heatproof bowl, cover the bowl tightly with plastic wrap, and set the bowl over a pot of simmering water. The potatoes will remain hot and soft-textured for 1 hour. This recipe yields smooth mashed potatoes. If you don't mind (or prefer) lumps, use a potato masher.

2	pounds russet potatoes, scrubbed
8	tablespoons unsalted butter, melted
1	cup half-and-half, warmed
1 ½	teaspoons salt
	Ground black pepper

1. Place the potatoes in a large saucepan with cold water to cover by about 1 inch. Bring to a boil over high heat, reduce the heat to medium-low, and simmer until the potatoes are just tender when pricked with a thin-bladed knife, 20 to 30 minutes. Drain the potatoes.

2. Set the food mill or ricer over the now empty but still warm saucepan. Spear a potato with a dinner fork and peel back the skin with a paring knife (see the illustrations on page 246). Repeat with the remaining potatoes. Working in batches, cut the peeled potatoes into rough chunks and drop into the hopper of the food mill or ricer (see the illustrations on page 246). Process or rice the potatoes into the saucepan.

3. Stir in the butter with a wooden spoon until incorporated. Gently whisk in the half-and-half, salt, and pepper to taste. Serve immediately.

VARIATIONS

Lumpy Mashed Potatoes

We prefer silky, smooth mashed potatoes and therefore recommend using a food mill or ricer. If you like chunky mashed potatoes, a potato masher can be used. (See page 289 for details about our testing of various potato mashers.) Use this technique in combination with any of the flavor variations that follow.

Follow the master recipe, dropping the peeled potato chunks back into the warm saucepan and mashing them with a potato masher until fairly smooth. Proceed as directed, reducing the half-and-half to ¾ cup.

Garlic Mashed Potatoes

Toasted garlic contributes the truest, purest garlic flavor imaginable to mashed potatoes. Best of all, the garlic can be peeled after toasting, when the skins will slip right off. Just make sure to keep the heat low and to let the garlic stand off heat until fully softened.

Toast 22 small to medium-large garlic cloves (about ⅔ cup), skins left on, in a small covered skillet over the lowest possible heat, shaking the pan frequently, until the cloves are a dark spotty brown and slightly softened, about 22 minutes. Remove the pan from the heat and let stand, covered, until the cloves are fully softened, 15 to 20 minutes. Peel the cloves and, using a paring knife, cut off the woody root end. Follow the master recipe, dropping the peeled garlic cloves into the food mill or ricer with the peeled potatoes.

Mashed Potatoes with Brie and Tarragon

The Brie adds a subtle, slightly nutty flavor to the potatoes. If you like the flavor of the rind, chop it finely and add it to the potatoes along with the Brie and tarragon.

Follow the master recipe, adding 6 ounces Brie with the rind removed (about ½ cup) and 1 tablespoon minced fresh tarragon along with the salt and pepper.

Mashed Potatoes with Wasabi and Scallions

Wasabi is a fiery condiment made from a type of Japanese horseradish. It can be found in the Asian section of most large grocery stores. Prepared wasabi comes in a tube; canned powdered wasabi is also available. If you have the powdered kind, follow the instructions on the can to make a smooth paste and proceed with the following recipe.

Follow the master recipe, whisking 2 teaspoons prepared wasabi paste into the warmed half-and-half. Add the half-and-half as directed along with 2 medium scallions, sliced thin. Season with salt and pepper as directed and taste, adding more wasabi paste (up to 1 teaspoon) if desired.

Colcannon

SERVES 4 TO 6

Colcannon is a traditional Irish mashed potato dish made with onions and cabbage or kale. Some recipes call for the potatoes and kale to be boiled together, but we found that doing so transferred some of the kale's bitterness to the potatoes.

2 ½	teaspoons salt
1	pound kale, stemmed (see the illustration on page 138), thoroughly washed, and roughly chopped
2	pounds russet potatoes, scrubbed
9	tablespoons unsalted butter (with 7 tablespoons melted)
1	medium onion, diced
1	cup half-and-half, warmed
	Ground black pepper

1. Bring 2 quarts of water to a boil in a large saucepan. Add 1 teaspoon of the salt and the kale, stir, cover, and cook until the greens are just tender, about 6 minutes. Drain the greens and plunge them into a large bowl of cold water to halt the cooking process. Drain the greens again and squeeze them dry. Chop finely and set aside.

2. Meanwhile, place the potatoes in a large saucepan with cold water to cover by about 1 inch. Bring to a boil over high heat, reduce the heat to medium-low, and simmer until the potatoes are just tender when pricked with a thin-bladed knife, 20 to 30 minutes. Drain the potatoes well.

3. As the potatoes cook, place the 2 tablespoons unmelted butter in a small skillet over medium heat. When the foaming subsides, add the onion and cook, stirring occasionally, until light golden brown, 7 to 10 minutes. Set the onion aside.

4. Set a food mill or ricer over the now empty but still warm saucepan. Spear a potato with a dinner fork and peel back the skin with a paring knife (see the illustration on page 246). Repeat with the remaining potatoes. Working in batches, cut the peeled potatoes into rough chunks and drop into

the hopper of the food mill or ricer (see the illustrations on page 246). Process or rice the potatoes into the saucepan.

5. Stir in the onions and the 7 tablespoons melted butter with a wooden spoon until incorporated. Gently whisk in the half-and-half, kale, the remaining 1 ½ teaspoons salt, and pepper to taste. Serve immediately.

BOILED POTATOES

MOST OFTEN, WE BOIL POTATOES FOR salad. However, freshly dug baby or new potatoes can be boiled, buttered, and served hot as a side dish. In many ways, this simple preparation is the best way to highlight the flavor of really good potatoes. That said, much can go wrong with this dish. The potatoes can split open and become soggy. The key is to cook the potatoes until they are just tender and then drain and butter them immediately.

From our initial tests, we concluded that having potatoes of varying sizes in the pot was problematic. The small potatoes overcooked and their skins split open while we waited for the larger potatoes to cook through. (The best test for doneness is a paring knife or skewer; it should glide easily through the potato without causing it to fall apart.)

While larger potatoes are fine for salad, we found that the best potatoes for boiling and buttering are small—less than 2 ½ inches in diameter and preferably smaller. These potatoes cooked more evenly. Larger potatoes tended to get a bit mushy right under the skin by the time the center was cooked through.

From previous tests, we knew that you must boil potatoes with their skins on to prevent them from becoming watery. However, we found that the flesh on a boiled potato must be exposed at some point so that it can soak up the butter and seasonings. When we tossed drained, whole, skin-on potatoes with butter, the butter just stayed in the bowl—it could not penetrate the skin.

We tried peeling a thin band around the center of each potato before boiling to eliminate the need to cut them after cooking. This test failed. Once the potatoes were cooked, the skin that had been left on started to break away from the flesh, and the flesh, too, was breaking apart.

For the best results, we found it necessary to cut the potatoes in half after boiling. Although a bit tedious, holding the hot potatoes one at a time with a pair of tongs and then slicing them with a knife worked well. Once all of the potatoes were cut in half, we immediately added them to the bowl with the butter. As soon as the potatoes are coated with fat, the seasonings can be added.

Cutting the boiled potatoes in half improves texture as well as flavor. When

HANDLING HOT BOILED POTATOES

Potatoes should be boiled whole and unpeeled so that they don't become soggy. After boiling, however, the potatoes should be cut in half because the fleshy portion of the potato absorbs butter and seasonings far better than the skin. To halve a hot potato, steady it with a pair of tongs while cutting with a sharp knife.

left whole, the potatoes were dry and bland, no doubt because little butter had penetrated the skin. When halved and buttered, the potatoes developed a rich flavor and a pleasantly moist mouthfeel.

Master Recipe for Boiled Potatoes with Butter

SERVES 4

The cooking time will vary depending on the size of the potatoes. For potatoes that measure 2 to 2 ½ inches in diameter (you will need 12 to 17 potatoes to make 2 pounds), plan on 15 to 18 minutes of cooking time. For potatoes that measure 1 ½ to 2 inches in diameter (you will need 18 to 24 potatoes to make 2 pounds), plan on 12 to 15 minutes of cooking time. For potatoes that measure 1 to 1 ½ inches in diameter (you will need 25 to 31 potatoes to make 2 pounds), plan on 10 to 12 minutes of cooking time. For potatoes that measure less than 1 inch in diameter (you will need 32 or more potatoes to make 2 pounds), plan on 8 to 10 minutes of cooking time.

3   tablespoons unsalted butter
2   pounds small Red Bliss or new potatoes, scrubbed
      Salt and ground black pepper

1. Place the butter in a medium serving bowl and set it aside to soften while you prepare and cook the potatoes.

2. Place the potatoes and 1 tablespoon salt in a Dutch oven and fill with enough cold water to cover the potatoes by about 1 inch. Bring to a boil over high heat, cover, reduce the heat to medium-low, and simmer, stirring once or twice, until the potatoes are just tender when pierced with a thin-bladed knife or skewer, 8 to 18 minutes depending on the size of the potatoes. Drain the potatoes.

3. Cut the potatoes in half (see the illustration on page 250). Place the halved potatoes in the bowl with the butter and toss to coat. Season with salt and pepper to taste and toss again to blend. Serve immediately.

➤ VARIATIONS
Boiled Potatoes with Butter and Chives

Follow the master recipe, adding 3 tablespoons minced fresh chives along with the salt and pepper in step 3.

Boiled Potatoes with Lemon, Parsley, and Olive Oil

Follow the master recipe, replacing the butter with 3 tablespoons extra-virgin olive oil. Add the minced zest from 1 lemon and 3 tablespoons chopped fresh parsley leaves along with the salt and pepper in step 3.

Boiled Potatoes with Shallots and Sage

Melt 3 tablespoons butter in a small skillet over medium-high heat. When the foaming subsides, add 1 medium shallot, minced, and cook until golden, 2 to 3 minutes. Add 1 tablespoon minced fresh sage leaves and cook until fragrant, about 1 minute. Scrape this mixture into a medium serving bowl and proceed with the master recipe from step 2.

AMERICAN POTATO SALAD

WHAT'S A SUMMER PICNIC OR BACK-yard barbecue without potato salad? This dish should be easy to assemble, but all too often, the potatoes are bland, and they fall apart under the weight of the dressing.

Potato salads come in numerous styles. Though recipes may seem dramatically different, most have four things in common: potatoes (of course), fat (usually bacon, olive oil,

INGREDIENTS: Mayonnaise

Mayonnaise might not be the most exciting item in the refrigerator, but given that it is a $1 billion industry, one thing is for certain: Americans buy the creamy, white condiment on a regular basis. And chances are that the jar in most refrigerators is either Hellmann's (sold under the Best Foods label west of the Rockies) or Kraft mayonnaise. Together, they account for 78 percent of mayonnaise sales. But a product that dominates the market isn't necessarily the best product. With the surge in popularity of preservative-free, unsweetened, and healthier mayos, we were curious to see if any of these newer spreads could challenge the favorites.

Our taste test included seven nationally available brands of mayonnaise along with Kraft Miracle Whip. Even though the U.S. Food and Drug Administration does not recognize Miracle Whip as a real mayonnaise, we included it in our tasting because of its resounding popularity (Kraft sells more Miracle Whip than it does regular mayonnaise). Why is Miracle Whip considered a salad dressing and not a mayonnaise? The FDA defines mayonnaise as an emulsified semisolid food that is at least 65 percent vegetable oil by weight, is at least 2.5 percent acidifying ingredient (vinegar and/or lemon juice) by weight, and contains whole eggs or egg yolks. Miracle Whip, which is also sweeter than regular mayo, weighs in with only 40 percent soybean oil. (Water makes up the difference.)

When you make mayonnaise at home, you whisk together egg yolks and seasonings (lemon juice, salt, mustard, etc.) and then slowly whisk in oil until the mixture is emulsified. The ingredients for commercial mayonnaise are premixed and then processed through a colloid mill, a machine that breaks the mixture down into tiny, uniform droplets and creates a stable emulsion with a light consistency. The biggest variations in brands of commercial mayonnaise concern the amount and type of oil, the amount and type of egg (both whole eggs and yolks are used in most products), and flavorings.

The results of our tasting mirrored the sales in America's grocery aisles. Hellmann's placed first, and Kraft finished second. No other brand was even close.

What explains such a strong showing by Hellmann's and Kraft, given that there are few ingredients in mayonnaise and that most commercial mayonnaises are manufactured in similar fashion? We sent the mayonnaises off to our food lab to test for oil, egg content (both whole eggs and yolks), acidity, and total fat.

The first suspect that we thought might explain our tasting results also happens to be the first item on the list of ingredients: oil. The oil content for the group ranged from 78.5 percent to 85.3 percent, well above the minimum 65 percent required by the FDA. The only exception, of course, was Kraft Miracle Whip, which has about half the oil of commercial mayonnaise. Oil level alone didn't yield any revealing information (Whole Foods had the most oil and 365 had the least oil, and they both scored poorly).

The past 15 years have been the halcyon era for canola oil as nutritionists have raved about its low saturated fat content. It was only a matter of time before canola oil made its way into commercial mayonnaise. Of the brands we tested, 365, Whole Foods, and Spectrum are all made with canola oil, but judges gave those three brands the lowest scores. Hellmann's, Kraft, and Trader Joe's, our top three finishers, respectively, are made with soybean oil. It would stand to reason then that superior commercial mayonnaise is made with soybean oil.

Not so fast. At least one thing the two oils are considered to have in common is their bland taste. "Canola oil and soybean oil are both highly refined oils," according to Earl Hammond, a professor in Iowa State University's food sciences and human nutrition department and a subcontractor for the United Soybean Board. "I am uncertain about attributing the poor showing by the canola-based mayonnaises to canola oil alone," he said. Robert Reeves, president of the Institute of Shortening and Edible Oils, agreed: "What people taste when eating food made with canola and soybean oils is usually the other ingredients."

With that in mind, we went back to the lab results to see if we could find another trend, but the information was ambiguous. Acidity levels were similar (with the exception of tangy Miracle Whip), and total fat did not vary much. As we pored over the data, we noticed that Hellmann's and Kraft both had a very low egg yolk content, but Trader Joe's, our third-place finisher, had the highest egg yolk content (making it the most similar of all the contestants to the test kitchen recipe for homemade mayonnaise).

At this point, we turned to tasters' comments on their tasting sheets. A good mayonnaise will have clear egg flavor and a touch of acidity to offset the significant amount of fat from the added oil. Hellmann's was liked for having that balance, and Kraft was thought to be "flavorful but not overpowering." Still, what tasters seemed to like most about these products was that they tasted like "what mayonnaise should taste like." Paul Rozin, a noted food psychologist from the University of Pennsylvania, wasn't surprised by our findings. "A blind taste test isn't blind to your past," he said. "The participant's first exposure to a food will usually become their standard to judge all others against. In the case of mayonnaise, many people grew up eating Hellmann's and Kraft. People like familiar tastes."

Well, if it's all about Hellmann's and Kraft, which one should you buy? In the bread tasting, Kraft beat out Hellmann's by a negligible margin, but in the macaroni salad trials, Hellmann's placed second (behind Trader Joe's), while Kraft came in fifth. We recommend Hellmann's, but the difference between the two contenders is not overwhelming. If you are interested in a preservative-free, unsweetened brand, try Trader Joe's. Our tasters liked its bold egg flavor, and what's more, it's the least expensive brand we tested.

Finally, is it possible for a light mayo to be as flavorful as the full-fat original? We put five brands to the test: Kraft Light Mayonnaise, Hellmann's Light Mayonnaise, Miracle Whip Light Salad Dressing, Spectrum Light Canola Mayonnaise, and Nayonaise (a soy-based sandwich spread), all with a fat content of between 3 and 5 grams per serving. To see if our tasters could tell the difference, we also threw the winner of the full-fat tasting into the mix (Hellmann's Real Mayonnaise, 11 grams of fat per serving). As in the mayonnaise tasting, we sampled these products spread on bread and tossed into macaroni salad.

The results? Last place went to Nayonaise. Tasters were unanimous in thinking it bore no resemblance to mayonnaise. One taster said it tasted like "a cross between pureed cottage cheese and tofu." Miracle Whip ("overly sweet" and "pasty") and Spectrum ("bland" and "artificial") didn't fare much better. Tasters thought Kraft was too sweet but made a fairly decent macaroni salad. Hellmann's Light came in second place, very nearly beating out the winner, Hellmann's Real Mayonnaise. Although the light version had a pastier texture than regular Hellmann's, the bright, balanced flavors were similar when tasted on bread, and the two products were virtually identical in the macaroni salad. Even our most finicky taster admitted that the salad made with Hellmann's Light was "not bad."

THE BEST MAYONNAISES

Hellmann's (top left), which is known as Best Foods west of the Rockies, took top honors in our tasting, followed by Kraft (bottom left) and Trader Joe's (bottom right). Among the five brands of reduced-fat mayonnaise tested, Hellmann's Light (top right) was the clear winner and rated nearly as well as its full-fat cousin.

or mayonnaise), an acidic ingredient to perk things up, and flavorings for distinction.

Classic American potato salad is dressed with mayonnaise. We decided to pursue a recipe that also contained hard-cooked eggs, pickles, and celery. We also planned on developing some variations that included alternative ingredients.

We first wanted to know what type of potato should be used and how it should be cooked. Recipe writers seemed split down the middle between starchy potatoes (like russets) and waxy potatoes (like Red Bliss), with starchy praised for being more absorbent and waxy admired for their sturdiness. We have always just boiled potatoes with the skin on, but steaming, microwaving, roasting, and baking are all options.

Next, should the potatoes be peeled? If so, when? Some recipes called for cooking potatoes with the skin on and then peeling and seasoning them immediately, working on the assumption that hot potatoes absorb more flavor than cold ones. We wondered if the extra step of seasoning the potatoes with vinegar, salt, and pepper first made any difference. Could we instead just toss all the ingredients together at the same time?

After boiling, steaming, baking/roasting, and microwaving four different varieties of potatoes—Red Bliss, russets, all-purpose, and Yukon Golds—we found Red Bliss to be the potato of choice and boiling to be the cooking method of choice. Higher-starch potatoes—all-purpose and Yukon Golds as well as russets—are not sturdy enough for salad making. They fall apart when cut and look sloppy in salad form.

Next, we wanted to see if we could boost flavor at the cooking stage by boiling the potatoes in chicken broth or in water heavily seasoned with bay leaves and garlic cloves. The chicken broth might just as well have

been water—there wasn't a hint of evidence that the potatoes had been cooked in broth. The bay leaves and garlic smelled wonderful as the potatoes cooked, but the potatoes were still bland.

The fact that nothing seemed to penetrate the potatoes got us wondering: Does the potato skin act as a barrier? We performed yet another experiment by cooking two batches of unpeeled potatoes, the first in heavily salted water and the second in unsalted water. We rinsed them quickly under cold running water and tasted. Sure enough, both batches of potatoes tasted exactly the same. We tried boiling potatoes without the skin, but they were waterlogged compared with their skin-on counterparts.

We found the paper-thin skin of the boiled red potato not unpleasant to taste and certainly pleasant to look at in what is often a monochromatic salad. Although this saved the peeling step, we found the skin tended to rip when cutting the potato. Because the skin was particularly susceptible to ripping when the potatoes were very hot, we solved the problem in two ways. First, we cut the potatoes with a serrated knife, which minimized ripping, and second, we found it isn't necessary to cut them when they are hot; warm ones are just as absorbent.

To find out if there was any benefit to preseasoning the potatoes, we made two salads. In the first, we drizzled the vinegar on the warm potatoes as soon as they were sliced and seasoned them with salt and pepper. In the second, we let the potatoes cool and then added the vinegar, salt, pepper, and mayonnaise dressing. The results were clear. The salad made with potatoes seasoned when still warm was zesty and delicious. The other salad was bland in comparison.

So here's how you make great potato salad: Boil unpeeled, low-starch, red-skinned potatoes in unsalted water, cool slightly, and then cut with a serrated knife to minimize tearing of the skin. While the potatoes are still warm, drizzle them with vinegar and season with salt and pepper. When cool, add the mayonnaise and other seasonings.

Master Recipe for American Potato Salad

SERVES 4 TO 6

Use sweet pickles, not relish, for the best results in this salad. Relish lacks the crunchy texture of freshly chopped pickles.

2	pounds Red Bliss potatoes (about 6 medium or 18 small), scrubbed
1/4	cup red wine vinegar
	Salt and ground black pepper
1/2	cup mayonnaise
1	medium celery rib, minced (about 1/2 cup)
2	tablespoons minced red onion
3	hard-cooked eggs (see page 20), peeled and cut into 1/2-inch dice
1/4	cup minced sweet pickles
2	teaspoons Dijon mustard
2	tablespoons minced fresh parsley leaves

1. Place the potatoes in a Dutch oven and fill with enough cold water to cover the potatoes by about 1 inch. Bring to a simmer over medium–high heat. Reduce the heat to medium and simmer, stirring once or twice to ensure even cooking, until the potatoes are tender (a thin-bladed paring knife or metal skewer can be slipped into and out of the center of the potatoes with no resistance), 25 to 30 minutes for medium potatoes or 15 to 20 minutes for small potatoes.

2. Drain; cool the potatoes slightly and peel if you like. Cut the potatoes into ¾-inch cubes (use a serrated knife if they have skins)

while still warm, rinsing the knife occasionally in warm water to remove starch.

3. Place the warm potato cubes in a large bowl. Add the vinegar, ½ teaspoon salt, and ¼ teaspoon pepper and toss gently. Cover the bowl with plastic wrap and refrigerate until cooled, about 20 minutes.

4. When the potatoes are cooled, toss with the remaining ingredients and season with salt and pepper to taste. Serve immediately or cover and refrigerate for up to 1 day.

> VARIATION

Potato Salad with Black Beans and Chipotle Chiles

Chipotle chiles are dried, smoked jalapeños that are sold canned in adobo sauce, a vinegary tomato sauce. They can be found in the Mexican food section of most large grocery stores.

2	pounds Red Bliss potatoes (about 6 medium or 18 small), scrubbed
1/4	cup red wine vinegar
	Salt and ground black pepper
1/2	cup mayonnaise
1	medium celery rib, minced (about 1/2 cup)
2	tablespoons minced red onion
1	(15-ounce) can black beans, rinsed and drained
1	canned chipotle chile in adobo sauce, seeded and minced, with 2 teaspoons sauce
2	tablespoons minced fresh cilantro leaves
1	teaspoon grated zest and 1 tablespoon juice from 1 lime

1. Place the potatoes in a Dutch oven and fill with enough cold water to cover the potatoes by about 1 inch. Bring to a simmer over medium–high heat. Reduce the heat to medium and simmer, stirring once or twice to ensure even cooking, until the potatoes

are tender (a thin-bladed paring knife or metal skewer can be slipped into and out of the center of the potatoes with no resistance), 25 to 30 minutes for medium potatoes or 15 to 20 minutes for small potatoes.

2. Drain; cool the potatoes slightly and peel if you like. Cut the potatoes into ¾-inch cubes (use a serrated knife if they have skins) while still warm, rinsing the knife occasionally in warm water to remove starch.

3. Place the warm potato cubes in a large bowl. Add the vinegar, ½ teaspoon salt, and ¼ teaspoon pepper and toss gently. Cover the bowl with plastic wrap and refrigerate until cooled, about 20 minutes.

4. When the potatoes are cooled, toss with the remaining ingredients and season with salt and pepper to taste. Serve immediately or cover and refrigerate for up to 1 day.

FRENCH POTATO SALAD

AMERICAN-STYLE POTATO SALAD, THICKLY dressed with mayonnaise and sweet pickle relish, is archetypal picnic fare and will always have a place on summer tables. We've cooked (and eaten) piles of it over the years, but sometimes we have a yearning for something lighter and fresher to serve with grilled fish, chicken, and even meat. In our minds, French potato salad is just the ticket. Having little in common with its American counterpart, French potato salad is served warm or at room temperature and is composed of sliced potatoes glistening with olive oil, white wine vinegar, and plenty of fresh herbs.

We expected quick success with this seemingly simple recipe—how hard could it be to boil a few potatoes and toss them in vinaigrette? We sliced the potatoes and dressed them while they were still warm (warm potatoes are more absorbent than

cool ones), and then we served them up to our tasters. The salad looked mangled, as the warm potatoes consistently broke apart upon slicing. We chose not to peel the potatoes for the sake of convenience and beauty, but the potato skins inevitably tore, leaving unsightly streaks. And the salad didn't taste much better than it looked. Despite an assertively seasoned vinaigrette, the potatoes themselves were uniformly bland. Another irksome point was that it was hard to tell when the potatoes were done. Unevenly sized potatoes made it difficult to avoid some over- or undercooked potatoes in the finished dish. This wasn't going to be as easy as we thought.

Our first task was to put a stop to homely salads with jagged, broken potatoes with ripped skins. We tried shocking the whole potatoes after cooking (reasoning that the ice-cold water might somehow set the skin—it didn't), slicing the potatoes with a serrated knife (this helped a little bit, but the results were inconsistent), and starting the potatoes in boiling instead of cold water (this made absolutely no difference). It was proving impossible to slice a just-cooked potato without having it fall apart.

We reevaluated our cooking technique: Boil the potatoes whole—generally the standard in the test kitchen, the idea being that the skins prevent potato starch from leaching out into the water—and then slice while warm. On a whim, we boiled some potatoes that we sliced *before* cooking. This, surprisingly, did the trick. The potato slices emerged from the water unbroken and with their skins intact. They had a clean (not starchy) taste, were evenly cooked, and held together perfectly, unlike those that had been cooked whole before slicing. (We still prefer boiling potatoes in their skins for American potato salad. French potato salad is served warm, so the potatoes must be dressed as soon as they

INGREDIENTS: Red Wine Vinegar

The source of that notable edge you taste when sampling any red wine vinegar is acetic acid, the chief flavor component in all vinegar and the by-product of the bacterium *Acetobacter aceti*, which feeds on the alcohol in wine. The process of converting red wine to vinegar once took months, if not years, but now, with the help of an acetator (a machine that speeds the metabolism of the *Acetobacter aceti*), red wine vinegar can be made in less than 24 hours.

Does this faster, cheaper method—the one used to make most supermarket brands—produce inferior red wine vinegar? Or is this a case in which modern technology trumps Old World craftsmanship, which is still employed by makers of the more expensive red wine vinegars? To find out, we included in our tasting vinegars made using the fast process (acetator) and the slow process (often called the Orleans method, after the city in France where it was developed).

We first tasted 10 nationally available supermarket brands in two ways: by dipping sugar cubes in each brand and sucking out the vinegar and by making a simple vinaigrette with each. We then pitted the winners of the supermarket tasting against four high-end red wine vinegars.

Although no single grape variety is thought to make the best red wine vinegar, we were curious to find out if our tasters were unwittingly fond of vinegars made from the same grape. We sent the vinegars to a food lab for an anthocyanin pigment profile, a test that can detect the 10 common pigments found in red grapes. Although the lab was unable to distinguish specific grape varieties (Cabernet, Merlot, Pinot Noir, Zinfandel, and the like), it did provide us with an interesting piece of information: Some of the vinegars weren't made with wine grapes (known as *Vitus vinifera*) but with less expensive Concord-type grapes, the kind used to make Welch's grape juice.

Did the vinegars made with grape juice fare poorly, as might be expected? Far from it. The taste-test results were both shocking and unambiguous: Concord-type grapes not only do just fine when it comes to making vinegar but may also be a key element in the success of the top-rated brands in our tasting. Spectrum, our overall winner, is made from a mix of wine grapes and Concord grapes. Pompeian, which came in second among the supermarket brands, is made entirely of Concord-type grapes.

What else might contribute to the flavor of these vinegars? One possibility, we thought, was the way in which the acetic acid is developed. Manufacturers that mass-produce vinegar generally prefer not to use the Orleans method, because it's slow and expensive. Spectrum red wine vinegar is produced with the Orleans method, but Pompeian is made in an acetator in less than 24 hours.

What, then, can explain why Spectrum and Pompeian won the supermarket tasting and beat the gourmet vinegars? Oddly enough, for a food that defines *sourness*, the answer seems to lie in its *sweetness*. It turns out that Americans like their vinegar sweet (think balsamic vinegar).

The production of Spectrum is outsourced to a small manufacturer in Modena, Italy, that makes generous use of the Trebbiano grape, the same grape used to make balsamic vinegar. The Trebbiano, which is a white wine grape, gives Spectrum the sweetness our tasters admired. Pompeian vinegar is finished with a touch of sherry vinegar, added to give the red vinegar a more fruity, well-rounded flavor. Also significant to our results may be that both Spectrum and Pompeian start with wines containing Concord grapes, which are sweet enough to be a common choice when making jams and jellies.

When pitted against gourmet vinegars, Spectrum and Pompeian still came out on top. Which red wine vinegar should you buy? Skip the specialty shop and head to the supermarket.

THE BEST RED WINE VINEGARS

Pompeian vinegar (left) and Spectrum vinegar (right) are available in supermarkets and bested gourmet brands costing 8 times as much.

are cooked. American potato salad is served chilled, so you can let the potatoes cool before cutting them. Also, although it is difficult to thinly slice hot potatoes for French potato salad, cooler potatoes are easily cut into large cubes for American-style potato salad.)

This one simple change in technique offered multiple benefits. First, the frustrating (and sometimes painful) task of slicing hot potatoes was eliminated. Second, we now had no need to find uniformly sized potatoes to assure even cooking. (We just needed to cut the potatoes into slices of uniform thickness.) Third, we found we could perfectly season the cut potatoes while they cooked by adding a hefty 2 tablespoons of salt to the cooking water.

We now shifted our focus to the vinaigrette and its usual suspects: olive oil, white wine vinegar, herbs, mustard, minced onion, chicken broth, and white wine. Because our initial tests had produced relatively dull salads, we decided to experiment with each component until we found a surefire way to pump up the flavor. The first improvement came by using slightly more vinegar than the test kitchen standard of 4 parts oil to 1 part vinegar. These bland potatoes could handle extra acid. We loved the sharp flavor notes added by champagne vinegar but found that white wine vinegar works well, too. As for the olive oil, extra-virgin and pure olive oil make an equally good base for the dressing; tasters found little distinction between the two (the former being more flavorful than the latter), presumably because of the other potent ingredients in the vinaigrette. However, expensive fruity olive oils were rejected for their overpowering nature.

We liked the extra moisture and layer of complexity that wine and chicken broth added (salads made strictly with oil and vinegar were a tad dry), but it seemed wasteful

to uncork a bottle or open a can only to use a few tablespoons. We found a solution to this problem and a revelation when we consulted Julia Child's *The Way to Cook* (Knopf, 1989). She suggests adding some of the potato cooking water to the vinaigrette, a quick and frugal solution that also added plenty of potato flavor and a nice touch of saltiness. Two teaspoonfuls of Dijon mustard and a sprinkle of freshly ground black pepper perked things up, while the gentle assertiveness of minced shallots and a blanched garlic clove (raw garlic was too harsh) added even more depth. As for the fresh herbs, we made salads with all manner of them, including chives, dill, basil, parsley, tarragon, and chervil. But an inherently French *fines herbes* mixture seemed appropriate in theory and was heavenly in reality. Chives, parsley, tarragon, and chervil make up this classic quartet, with its anise undertones.

The last problem was how to toss the cooked, warm potatoes with the vinaigrette without damaging the slices. The solution

SCIENCE: Keeping Potato Salad Safe

Mayonnaise has gotten a bad reputation, being blamed for spoiled potato salads and upset stomachs after many summer picnics and barbecues. You may think that switching from a mayonnaise-based dressing to a vinaigrette will protect your potato salad (and your family) from food poisoning. Think again.

The main ingredients in mayonnaise are raw eggs, vegetable oil, and an acid (usually vinegar or lemon juice). The eggs used in commercially made mayonnaise have been pasteurized to kill salmonella and other bacteria. The acid is another safeguard; because bacteria do not fare well in acidic environments, the lemon juice or vinegar inhibits bacterial growth. Mayonnaise, even when homemade, is rarely the problem. It's the potatoes that are more likely to go bad.

The bacteria usually responsible for spoiled potato salad are *Bacillus cereus* and *Staphylococcus aureus* (commonly known as staph). Both are found in soil and dust,

and they thrive on starchy foods like rice, pasta, and potatoes. If they find their way to your potato salad via an unwashed cutting board or contaminated hands, they can wreak havoc on your digestive system.

Most food-borne bacteria grow well at temperatures between 40 and 140 degrees Fahrenheit. This is known as the temperature danger zone, and if contaminated food remains in this zone for too long, the bacteria can produce enough toxins to make you sick. The U.S. Food and Drug Administration recommends refrigerating food within two hours of its preparation, or one hour if the room temperature is above 90 degrees.

Although the high acid content of the vinaigrette for our French potato salad might slow bacteria growth, it's best to play it safe and follow the FDA's guidelines. Don't leave the potato salad out for more than two hours and promptly refrigerate any leftovers.

---

was simple. We carefully laid the potatoes in a single layer on a sheet pan and poured the vinaigrette over them. Spreading out the potatoes in this way also allowed them to cool off a bit, preventing residual cooking and potential mushiness. While we let the vinaigrette soak into the potatoes, we had just enough time to chop the herbs and shallots before sprinkling them on the finished salad. Adding the herbs just before serving guards against wilting and darkening.

Master Recipe for French Potato Salad

SERVES 6

If fresh chervil isn't available, substitute an additional ½ tablespoon of minced parsley and an additional ½ teaspoon of tarragon. For best flavor, serve the salad warm, but to make ahead, follow the recipe through step 2, cover with plastic wrap, and refrigerate. Before serving, bring the

salad to room temperature and then add the shallots and herbs.

- 2 pounds Red Bliss potatoes (about 18 small), scrubbed and cut into ¼-inch-thick slices
- 2 tablespoons salt
- 1 medium clove garlic, peeled and threaded onto a skewer
- 1 ½ tablespoons champagne vinegar or white wine vinegar
- 2 teaspoons Dijon mustard
- ¼ cup olive oil
- ½ teaspoon ground black pepper
- 1 small shallot, minced
- 1 tablespoon minced fresh chervil leaves
- 1 tablespoon minced fresh parsley leaves
- 1 tablespoon minced fresh chives
- 1 teaspoon minced fresh tarragon leaves

1. Place the potatoes, 6 cups of cold water, and the salt in a large saucepan. Bring

to a boil over high heat and then reduce the heat to medium. Lower the skewered garlic into the simmering water and partially blanch, about 45 seconds. Immediately run the garlic under cold tap water to stop cooking; remove the garlic from the skewer and set aside. Simmer the potatoes, uncovered, until tender but still firm (a thin-bladed paring knife can be slipped into and out of the center of a potato slice with no resistance), about 5 minutes. Drain the potatoes, reserving ¼ cup cooking water. Arrange the hot potatoes close together in a single layer on a rimmed baking sheet.

2. Press the garlic through a garlic press or mince by hand. Whisk the garlic, reserved potato cooking water, vinegar, mustard, oil, and pepper together in a small bowl until combined. Drizzle the dressing evenly over the warm potatoes; let stand 10 minutes.

3. Toss the shallot and herbs together in a small bowl. Transfer the potatoes to a large serving bowl. Add the shallot/herb mixture and mix gently with a rubber spatula to combine. Serve immediately.

➤ VARIATIONS

French Potato Salad with Arugula, Roquefort, and Walnuts

Follow the master recipe, omitting the herbs and tossing the dressed potatoes with ½ cup toasted and coarsely chopped walnuts, 4 ounces crumbled Roquefort cheese, and 1 small bunch arugula, washed, dried, and torn into bite-size pieces (about 2 ½ cups) along with the shallots in step 3.

French Potato Salad with Hard Salami and Gruyère

Follow the master recipe, omitting the herbs and substituting 2 teaspoons grainy mustard for the Dijon mustard and 2 tablespoons minced red onion for the shallot.

Toss the dressed potatoes with 3 ounces hard salami cut into ¼-inch matchsticks, 2 ounces Gruyère very thinly sliced or shaved with a vegetable peeler, and 1 tablespoon minced fresh thyme leaves along with the red onion in step 3.

SCIENCE:
Stress-Free Spud Storage

Since potatoes seem almost indestructible compared with other vegetables, little thought is generally given to their storage. But because various problems can result from inadequate storage conditions, we decided to find out how much difference storage really makes. We stored all-purpose potatoes in five environments: in a cool (50 to 60 degrees), dark place; in the refrigerator; in a basket near a sunlit window; in a warm (70 to 80 degrees), dark place; and in a drawer with some onions at room temperature. We checked all the potatoes after four weeks.

As expected, the potatoes stored in the cool, dark place were firm, had not sprouted, and were crisp and moist when cut. There were no negative marks on the potatoes stored in the refrigerator, either; although some experts say that the sugar level dramatically increases in some potato varieties under these conditions, we could not see or taste any difference between these potatoes and the ones stored in the cool, dark but unrefrigerated environment.

Our last three storage tests produced unfavorable results. The potatoes stored in sunlight, in warm storage, and with onions ended up with a greenish tinge along the edges. When potatoes are stressed by improper storage, the level of naturally occurring toxins increases, causing the greenish tinge known as solanine. Because solanine is not destroyed by cooking, any part of the potato with this greenish coloring should be completely cut away before cooking.

The skin of the potatoes stored in sunlight became gray and mottled, while the potatoes stored in a warm place and those stored with onions sprouted and became soft and wrinkled. Sprouts also contain increased levels of solanine and should be cut away before cooking.

French Potato Salad with Radishes, Cornichons, and Capers

Follow the master recipe, omitting the herbs and substituting 2 tablespoons minced red onion for the shallot. Toss the dressed potatoes with 2 thinly sliced medium red radishes (about ⅓ cup), ¼ cup rinsed and drained capers, and ¼ cup thinly sliced cornichons along with the red onion in step 3.

GRILLED POTATO SALAD

GRILLED POTATO SALAD IS THE PERFECT backyard-barbecue dish. But grilling potatoes can be a challenge, requiring a deft hand and a good dose of patience on the part of the grill master. If the fire is too hot, all you're going to get is a raw-on-the-inside, burnt-on-the-outside spud. But if you're nursing a modest, low-fire grill, your potatoes are more likely to be served alongside tomorrow's bacon and eggs than with your burger.

When researching different ways to grill potatoes, we were confronted time and time again with the order to blanch the potatoes in boiling water first and then transfer them to the grill just long enough to char slightly. The advantage to this is that the potatoes finish cooking on the grill in the same time it takes for the skin to color. We wondered if it would be possible to cook the potatoes entirely on the grill.

We grilled two different types of potatoes—russets and Yukon Golds—in three different ways: diced and then skewered, cut into rounds, and diced and grilled on a grill pan (a perforated pan that allows you to grill small items without risk of their falling through the grill grate). We used a medium-hot grill. After we took the potatoes off the grill, we immediately dressed each with a simple vinaigrette. To our dismay, all of the potatoes were starchy, mealy, and dry.

These findings led us to trade in the russets and Yukon Golds for Red Bliss potatoes. We repeated the tests. Even though red potatoes are known for their high-moisture, low-starch content, they, too, turned out dry. While they're smaller than russets, they still had to be cut into smaller segments that exposed too much flesh to the fire. We tried new red potatoes—smaller still—which seemed to have it all: the high-moisture, low-starch characteristics of their larger cousins plus a higher skin to flesh ratio. We hoped the skin would protect the potatoes from being bullied by the flame.

We slid the cut potatoes onto skewers, figuring this would allow us to rotate them more easily when it came time to turn them for browning. While our assumption proved correct and the potatoes were much more moist, by the time the insides were tender, the skins were charred and ashy. We tried wrapping the skewered spuds in foil, and while this kept the skins from turning to carbon, the potatoes didn't pick up enough smoky flavor.

After these setbacks, we had to admit that the solution was only to be found in a pot of boiling water. We dropped a platoon of cut potatoes into boiling water, cooking them until slightly underdone. Now we faced another problem: Many of the parboiled chunks split as we tried to thread them onto skewers. A test cook came up with a brilliant solution—skewer the potatoes first, boil them on the skewers, and then transfer them to the hot grill. So we threaded the raw potatoes onto skewers and submerged them in boiling water until they were just tender. With tongs, we easily transferred the skewers from pot to baking sheet to grill. About five minutes later, we had perfectly browned potatoes that were tender, moist, and really smoky. But they still needed a bit of spunk. For the next round, we brushed the skewered potatoes with some olive oil and sprinkled them with salt and pepper before putting them on the fire. When these potatoes came off the grill, we had to hide them from the rest of the kitchen staff if we wanted to save any for a salad—they were just too tempting to eat on their own as a snack.

Now that we had finally found a grilling method for the potatoes, we tried a few with mayonnaise-based dressings. Horrid! Dressing the potatoes with mayonnaise required us to chill them first, which added more time to the salad preparation. While chilling, the potatoes became tough and rubbery. Even worse, the delicate smoky nuance we had worked so hard to get was overpowered by the tanginess of the mayonnaise. We concluded that grilled potatoes were much better suited to a simple oil and vinegar dressing. Still, the smoky flavor of these potatoes is so satisfying that one taster remarked, "Why dress them at all? I'd serve them plain."

Grilled Potatoes for Salad

SERVES 4 TO 6

When buying potatoes for these salads, the color is less important than the size; make sure they are no longer than 3 inches. You will need about fifteen 10-inch metal or bamboo skewers. Prepare the other salad ingredients while the water heats so that the salad can be made with potatoes that are hot off the grill. Because the potatoes are precooked, they need only brown on the grill; you can grill them alongside your main dish over a grill fire of any intensity.

1 ½	teaspoons salt
1 ½	pounds new potatoes, 2 to 3 inches long, scrubbed and cut into eighths
2	tablespoons olive oil
¼	teaspoon ground black pepper

1. Bring 4 quarts of water to a boil in a Dutch oven or stockpot over high heat. Add 1 teaspoon of the salt.

2. Meanwhile, if using wooden skewers, trim them to lengths that can be submerged in the Dutch oven or stockpot. Skewer each piece of potato through the center with the skin facing out. Place 8 or 9 potato pieces on each skewer.

3. Drop the skewers into the boiling water and boil until a paring knife slips in and out of a potato easily, about 10 minutes.

4. While the potatoes boil, line a rimmed baking sheet with paper towels. With tongs, transfer the skewers to the baking sheet. Pat the potatoes dry with additional paper towels. Discard the paper towels. (The potatoes can be cooled to room temperature, covered with plastic wrap, and kept at room temperature for up to 2 hours.) Brush all sides of the potatoes with the oil and sprinkle with the remaining ½ teaspoon salt and the pepper.

5. Place the skewers on the hot grill. Cook, turning the skewers twice with tongs, until all sides are browned, 2 to 3 minutes

per side over hot or medium-hot heat (you should be able to hold your hand 5 inches above the cooking grate for 2 seconds for hot heat and 3 to 4 seconds for medium-hot heat) or 4 to 5 minutes per side over medium or medium-low heat (you should be able to hold your hand 5 inches above the cooking grate for 5 to 6 seconds for medium heat and 7 seconds for medium-low heat).

6. Slide the hot potatoes off the skewers and into a medium bowl. Use immediately in one of the following recipes.

Grilled Potato and Arugula Salad with Dijon Mustard Vinaigrette

SERVES 4 TO 6

If you prefer, watercress can be substituted for the arugula.

I	recipe Grilled Potatoes for Salad
I ½	teaspoons rice vinegar
	Salt
½	teaspoon ground black pepper
3	tablespoons minced fresh chives
I	large bunch arugula, washed, dried, and stems trimmed (about 3 cups)
I	medium yellow bell pepper, stemmed, seeded, and cut into thin strips
I	teaspoon Dijon mustard
I	small shallot, minced (about 2 tablespoons)
2	tablespoons olive oil

1. Toss the hot potatoes with 1 teaspoon of the vinegar, ¼ teaspoon salt, and the pepper. Add the chives, arugula, and bell pepper and toss to combine.

2. Combine the mustard, shallot, remaining ½ teaspoon vinegar, oil, and salt to taste in a small bowl. Pour the dressing over the potatoes and toss to combine. Serve immediately.

Spicy Grilled Potato Salad with Corn and Poblano Chiles

SERVES 4 TO 6

We prefer to use corn kernels cut from grilled corn on the cob, but boiled corn works, too. See page 81 for tips on grilling corn. Poblano chiles are relatively mild; to alter the spiciness in this salad, decrease or increase the quantity of jalapeños. You can roast the poblano chiles right on the grill.

I	recipe Grilled Potatoes for Salad
I	teaspoon white wine vinegar
	Salt
¼	teaspoon ground black pepper
I	cup cooked corn kernels cut from 2 ears grilled or boiled corn
2	medium poblano chiles, roasted, peeled, seeded, and cut into ½-inch pieces
2	jalapeño chiles, stemmed, seeded, and minced
3	tablespoons juice from 2 limes
½	teaspoon sugar
4	tablespoons olive oil
3	medium scallions, white parts only, sliced thin
3	tablespoons minced fresh cilantro leaves

1. Toss the hot potatoes with the vinegar, ¼ teaspoon salt, and the pepper. Add the corn, poblanos, and jalapeños and toss to combine.

2. Whisk the lime juice and sugar together in a small bowl until the sugar dissolves. Whisk in the oil and salt to taste. Pour the dressing over the potatoes and add the scallions and cilantro. Toss to combine. Serve. (The salad can be covered with plastic wrap and kept at room temperature for up to 30 minutes; toss before serving.)

German-Style Grilled Potato Salad

SERVES 4 TO 6

For this recipe, toast the mustard seeds in a small dry skillet (with the cover on to keep the seeds in place) until lightly browned (this will take several minutes). Add the hot seeds to the vinegar and let them steep while you prepare the rest of the ingredients.

1	recipe Grilled Potatoes for Salad
1	tablespoon yellow mustard seeds, toasted and added to the red wine vinegar
3	tablespoons red wine vinegar
	Salt
1/2	teaspoon ground black pepper
4	ounces (about 4 slices) bacon, cut crosswise into 1/4-inch strips
1	medium shallot, minced (about 3 tablespoons)
1/3	cup low-sodium chicken broth
1	small celery rib, chopped fine (about 1/4 cup)
2	tablespoons minced fresh parsley leaves

1. Toss the hot potatoes with 2 tablespoons of the vinegar (with all the mustard seeds), 1/4 teaspoon salt, and the pepper.

2. Fry the bacon in a medium skillet over medium-high heat until brown and crisp, about 6 minutes. With a slotted spoon, transfer the bacon to the bowl with the potatoes. Reduce the heat to medium, add the shallot to the fat in the skillet, and cook, stirring occasionally, until softened, about 3 minutes. Add the broth and bring to a boil. Stir in the remaining 1 tablespoon vinegar. Pour the mixture over the potatoes and add the celery, parsley, and salt to taste; toss to combine. Serve. (The salad can be covered with plastic wrap and kept at room temperature for up to 30 minutes; toss before serving.)

SCALLOPED POTATOES

TRADITIONALLY RESERVED FOR HOLIdays and special events, scalloped potatoes are luxuriously waist defying. Cooked in fantastic amounts of heavy cream, butter, and cheese, their richness is hardly suitable for your average supper (or diet). But more and more versions of both frozen and boxed scalloped potatoes have been showing up in the supermarket, claiming to be an easy addition to weekday dinners. Although these quick products taste horrible, they are more convenient and lighter than traditional scalloped potatoes, which makes them more suitable for weeknight cooking. We wanted a lighter, more convenient recipe, but we also wanted a recipe that would taste good.

To begin, we made several standard scalloped potato recipes. We rubbed shallow dishes with garlic, sliced potatoes and laid them in rows, topped them with heavy cream and cheese, and baked them off. The ingredient lists were similar in their inclusion of garlic, cream, and sliced russets, but some also called for half-and-half or milk, while others called for butter and flour. All of the recipes were unabashedly rich and took as long as 1 1/2 hours to make from start to finish. Several tasted pasty from the flour (used as a thickener for the sauce), and nearly all were a bit dull from the sheer lack of aromatics beyond garlic. These stodgy potato dishes not only needed to be lightened up considerably but also begged for more flavor, as well as a realistic midweek cooking time.

Starting with the potatoes, we cooked russet, all-purpose, and Yukon Gold varieties side by side in basic scalloped fashion. While Yukon Gold and all-purpose potatoes weren't bad, tasters found them a bit waxy. The traditional russets, with their tender bite and earthy flavor, were the unanimous favorite. The russets also formed tighter,

EQUIPMENT: Mandolines and V-Slicers

What's cheaper than a food processor and faster (if not also sharper) than a chef's knife? A mandoline. This hand-operated slicing machine comes in two basic styles—the classic stainless-steel model, supported by legs, and the plastic hand-held model, often called a V-slicer. We put both types of machines—ranging in price from $8.99 to $169—to the test. To determine the winners, we sliced melons, cut carrots into julienne (matchstick pieces), cut potatoes into batonettes (long, skinny french fry pieces), and sliced potatoes into thin rounds. Then we evaluated three aspects of the mandolines: ease of use, including degree of effort, adjustment ease, grip/handle comfort, and safety; quality, including sturdiness and uniformity/cleanliness of the slices; and cleanup.

The Progressive Mandoline Multi Slicer ($8.99) and the Target Mandoline Slicer ($9.99) are plastic V-slicers with similar designs. Testers gave these models high marks for safety, handle comfort, and blade sharpness, which helped them whip through melon and potato slices. Interchangeable blade platforms cut respectable batonette and julienne pieces, though these cuts required more effort on the part of testers.

The two other V-slicers tested were the Börner V-Slicer Plus ($34.95) and the Joyce Chen Asian Mandoline Plus ($49.95). The latter produced flawless melon slices, carrot julienne, and potato batonettes but got low marks for its small, ineffective safety mechanism and tricky blade adjustment. Testers also downgraded the poorly designed and not very sturdy base. The Börner unit sliced melons and carrots with little effort, but the potato slices were inconsistent and required more effort to produce. The Börner's well-designed safety guard, however, kept hands away from blades, and its adjustments were quick and easy to make. In the end, testers preferred the cheaper V-slicers made by Progressive and Target to either of these more expensive options.

We also tested two classic stainless-steel mandolines. The de Buyer mandoline from Williams-Sonoma ($169) was controversial. Shorter testers had difficulty gaining leverage to cut consistently; some melon slices were $1/8$ inch thicker on one side. However, the safety mechanism, sturdiness, and adjustment mechanism were lauded by taller testers. With some practice, all testers were able to produce perfect slices, julienne, and batonettes with the Bron-Coucke mandoline ($99). This machine has fewer parts to clean and switch out than its plastic counterparts and requires less effort to operate once the user becomes familiar with it. Still, the quality comes at an awfully high price.

THE BEST V-SLICERS
Plastic mandolines (also called V-slicers) may not be as sturdy as stainless-steel versions, but their quality far exceeds the minimal dollar investment. Among the four models tested, we liked the Progressive and Target slicers, which are similar in design.

THE BEST CLASSIC MANDOLINE
Of the two stainless-steel mandolines tested, we preferred this model made by Bron-Coucke. Note, however, that it costs 10 times more than a good V-slicer.

more cohesive layers owing to their higher starch content.

Heavy cream is the obvious diet-crushing ingredient in traditional scalloped potatoes, so we figured it was probably to blame for their usual heft. To relieve some of the heaviness, we tried replacing the heavy cream with a number of less fatty liquids. We tried half-and-half, but the sauce curdled as it bubbled away in the oven. Half-and-half, as it turns out, doesn't have enough fat to keep the dairy proteins from coagulating under high heat. Supplementing some of the heavy cream with whole milk worked well (no curdling), but the potatoes still tasted a bit heavy and dairy rich for an everyday meal. Next, we tried replacing some of the heavy cream with canned chicken broth. The broth effectively mitigated some of the cream's heaviness. After trying a variety of broth-to-cream ratios, we landed on a 50-50 split.

With the sauce lightened up, it was time to tweak its flavor. While the delicate flavor of shallots was easily overpowered, a little sautéed onion and garlic worked wonders. Throwing in leaves of fresh thyme and dried bay also helped to spruce up the sauce.

Up until now, we had been using the tiresome technique of layering the raw potatoes and sauce in a shallow dish and baking them in the oven for 1½ hours. To speed things up, we tried parboiling the potatoes in water first, combining them with a sauce (thickened with flour to achieve a saucy consistency in less time), and finishing them in the oven. Although this did shave nearly 45 minutes off the cooking time, the potatoes had a hollow flavor, the sauce tasted gummy and flat, and we spent much of the time we had saved washing dirty pots.

Next, we tried parcooking the sliced potatoes in the chicken broth and cream in a covered pot on top of the stove before dumping it all into a shallow casserole dish and finishing it in the oven. Here was our solution. This technique gave the potatoes a head start on the stovetop, where they released some of their starch into the sauce. This starch, a natural thickening agent, transformed the consistency of the cooking liquid into a rightful sauce, negating the need for flour.

When slowly simmered on the stovetop for 10 minutes, at which time the potatoes were about halfway cooked, the casserole required only 15 minutes in a 425-degree oven to finish. We sprinkled a handful of cheddar over the top, and the potatoes emerged from the oven as a bubbling inferno with a golden crown. Although the ripping hot potatoes and sauce make for a sloppy casserole straight out of the oven, a rest of 10 minutes is all that's needed for them to cool off a bit and cohere.

Master Recipe for Scalloped Potatoes
SERVES 4 TO 6

The quickest way to slice the potatoes is in a food processor fitted with a ⅛-inch slicing blade. If the potatoes are too long to fit into the feed tube, halve them crosswise and put them in the feed tube cut-side down so that they sit on a flat surface. If the potato slices discolor as they stand, put them in a bowl and cover with the cream and chicken broth. A mandoline or V-slicer (see page 265) is the other option. Don't try to slice the potatoes with a knife; you won't get them thin enough. If you like, use Parmesan instead of cheddar.

2   tablespoons unsalted butter
1   medium onion, minced
2   medium cloves garlic, minced or
     pressed through a garlic press
1   tablespoon chopped fresh thyme leaves
1 ¼ teaspoons salt

1/4	teaspoon ground black pepper
2 1/2	pounds (about 5 medium) russet potatoes, peeled and sliced 1/8 inch thick
I	cup low-sodium chicken broth
I	cup heavy cream
2	bay leaves
4	ounces cheddar cheese, shredded (I cup)

1. Adjust an oven rack to the middle position and heat the oven to 425 degrees.

2. Melt the butter in a Dutch oven over medium-high heat. When the foaming subsides, add the onion and cook, stirring occasionally, until soft and lightly browned, about 4 minutes. Add the garlic, thyme, salt, and pepper and cook until fragrant, about 30 seconds. Add the potatoes, chicken broth, heavy cream, and bay leaves and bring to a simmer. Cover, reduce the heat to medium-low, and simmer until the potatoes are almost tender (a paring knife can be slipped into and out of a potato slice with some resistance), about 10 minutes. Discard the bay leaves.

3. Transfer the mixture to an 8 by 8-inch baking dish (or other 1 1/2-quart gratin dish). Sprinkle evenly with the cheese. Bake until the cream is bubbling around the edges and the top is golden brown, about 15 minutes. Cool 10 minutes before serving.

➤ VARIATIONS

Scalloped Potatoes with Mushrooms

Slice 8 ounces cremini mushrooms 1/4 inch thick; trim the stems off 4 ounces fresh shiitake mushrooms and slice the caps 1/4 inch thick. Follow the master recipe, adding the mushrooms to the butter along with the onion. Cook until the moisture released by the mushrooms has evaporated, about 5 minutes. Proceed as directed.

Scalloped Potatoes with Fontina and Artichokes

Fontina is a semisoft cheese with a nutty flavor. Thoroughly drain 4 ounces jarred or canned artichoke hearts and cut them into 1/2-inch pieces. (You should have about 1 cup.) Follow the master recipe, adding the artichokes with the potatoes in step 2. Proceed as directed, replacing the cheddar with an equal amount of shredded fontina cheese.

POMMES ANNA

IMAGINE THIN POTATO SLICES LAYERED meticulously in a skillet with nothing but butter, salt, pepper, and more butter, left to cook until the inverted dish reveals a potato cake with a lovely crisp, deep brown, glassine

PROPERLY SLICED POTATOES

When the potatoes were cut thicker than 1/8 inch (left), they slid apart when served. Yet when cut much thinner (right), the layers melted together, producing a mashed potato–like texture. At exactly 1/8 inch (center), the potatoes held their shape yet remained flexible enough to form tight, cohesive layers. Although it is possible to cut 1/8-inch slices by hand, it is far easier when using a food processor or mandoline.

crust belying the soft, creamy potato layers within. This is pommes Anna, the queen of potato cookery.

Legend has it that Anna was a fashionable woman who lived during the reign of Napoleon III. Whoever Anna was, the creator of this dish was, to be sure, a chef with an inordinate amount of time on his hands, as the recipe requires painstaking procedures and the patience of Job. Given the amount of effort required to make just one dish of pommes Anna, it was particularly irritating when, in our preliminary recipe testing, those we made suffered a 50 percent rate of failure to cleanly release from the pan. It's no surprise, then, that pommes Anna is rarely seen on menus or home dinner tables and that recipes for it are sequestered in only the staunchest of French cookbooks.

We hoped to find a means of simplifying and foolproofing this classic. If we could do away with some of the maddening work and guarantee more than a crapshoot's chance of perfect unmolding, pommes Anna could find her way back onto the culinary map . . . and certainly onto the dining room table.

First, we needed a pan for the perilous pommes. Of the four different cooking vessels we employed in tests—a cast-iron skillet, a copper pommes Anna pan, a heavy-bottomed skillet with a stainless-steel cooking surface, and a heavy-bottomed nonstick skillet—only the nonstick effortlessly released the potatoes onto the serving platter. As reluctant as we were to make such specific equipment requisite for pommes Anna, a nonstick skillet is essential to the dish's success. After all, once having expended the effort of slicing and arranging the potatoes, we found it both enraging and mortifying to later witness them clinging stubbornly to the pan.

Most, if not all, recipes for pommes Anna begin with clarified butter. To make it, butter is melted, the foamy whey is spooned off the top, and the pure butterfat is poured or spooned off of the milky casein at the bottom. Since it lacks solids and proteins, clarified butter has a higher smoking point (and so is more resistant to burning) than whole butter, but it also lacks the full, buttery flavor that those solids and proteins provide. We have always been annoyed by clarified butter because of the time required to make it, the waste involved (typically, about 30 percent of the butter is lost with clarifying), and the loss of flavor. But pommes Anna, which spends a substantial amount of time cooking at moderately high temperatures, is always made with clarified butter. Our big coup, we thought, would be to circumvent its necessity, so we made a pommes Anna with whole butter to see if we couldn't prove false the centuries-old maxim that says clarified butter is a must. Sure enough, the surface of the potatoes was dotted with unappealing black flecks. Still, as a few tasters noticed, the whole butter gave the potatoes a richer, fuller flavor that we missed in the versions made with clarified butter.

We thought to replace the butter in the bottom of the skillet with oil and then drizzle melted whole butter between potato layers. This worked better than we could have hoped. Our newfangled pommes Anna had a lovely crisp brown crust rivaling that of any made with clarified butter.

Thinly sliced potatoes (russets are traditional, but our tasters also liked Yukon Golds) are a defining characteristic of pommes Anna, as is the overlapping arrangement of the slices in concentric circles. In the early stages of our testing, we preferred to slice the potatoes by hand (for no good reason), but as numbers increased, we took to a food processor fitted with a fine slicing disk that could get the job done with effortless speed. If you own and are adept with a mandoline, it offers another quick means of slicing the potatoes.

Slicing wasn't the only obstacle presented by the potatoes. Because they will discolor if peeled and sliced and then kept waiting to be arranged in the skillet, they must be soaked in water, which in turn means that the slices must be dried before being layered. To avoid this incredible inconvenience, we opted to slice and arrange the potatoes in batches, making sure each group of slices was arranged in the skillet before slicing the next batch. This method prevented discoloration, but it was also awkward and inefficient. Someone suggested tossing the sliced potatoes in the melted butter to prevent them from discoloring (see page 271 for details). We tried this, and though the butter did not prevent the discoloration, it did slow it down to the extent that all slices could be layered in the skillet before severe discoloration set in. That the butter no longer required drizzling between layers was a bonus.

PREPARING POMMES ANNA

1. Using the nicest slices to form the bottom layer, place one slice in the center of the skillet. Overlap more slices in a circle around the center slice.

2. Use more slices to form an outer circle of overlapping slices in the bottom of the pan. Continue layering, alternating the direction of the slices in each layer.

3. To drain off excess fat before unmolding, press a cake pan against the potatoes while tilting the skillet. Be sure to use oven mitts or heavy potholders to hold the hot skillet.

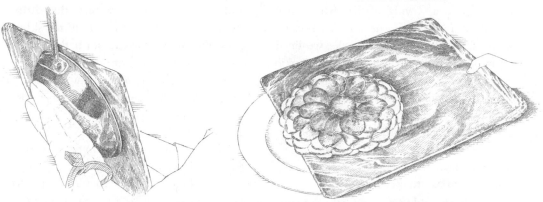

4. To invert, set a prepared baking sheet flat on top of the skillet. Invert the skillet and baking sheet together. Lift the skillet off the potatoes.

5. Carefully slide the pommes Anna from the baking sheet onto a serving platter.

Most pommes Anna recipes have the cook start layering potato slices in the skillet as it heats on the stovetop. It may sound dangerous, but it isn't, really, and it saves much time. After all the slices are in, the skillet is transferred to a hot oven or left on the stovetop to complete cooking. After many tests, we determined that the potatoes—started in a cold skillet—require 30 minutes on the stovetop at medium-low heat and then—after a firm pressing with the bottom of a cake pan to compact the potatoes into a cohesive cake—25 minutes more in a 450-degree oven. The time on the stovetop gets the browning going on the bottom, and the oven time cooks through the potatoes' thickness while completing the bottom browning. Now, we needed not only a nonstick skillet but a nonstick *ovenproof* one to do the job.

The final step of pommes Anna is, of course, unmolding. If only it could be so easy as inverting a layer cake onto a cooling rack, but with a heavy, hot-handled skillet, the process is awkward and clumsy and can make an experienced cook feel like a bumbling one. Rather than trying to invert the potatoes directly onto a serving platter, where they cannot be unmolded in dead center because of the skillet's protruding handle, we lined the back of a baking sheet (a rimless cookie sheet will do) with lightly greased foil. We inverted the potatoes onto this surface, much as we would invert a cake onto a cooling rack, and then slid them onto the serving platter. We found this technique a little less dangerous and much less complicated than going straight from pan to serving dish.

A last word on pommes Anna: Even simplified and streamlined, this recipe requires a good amount of patience, but it is no less a tour de force of culinary art and engineering than the classic rendition.

Pommes Anna

SERVES 6 TO 8

Do not slice the potatoes until you are ready to start assembling. Remember to start timing when you begin arranging the potatoes in the skillet—no matter how quickly you arrange them, they will need 30 minutes on the stovetop to brown properly. Use a mandoline or V-slicer (see page 265) or a food processor to slice the potatoes; a chef's knife may not get them thin enough. See the illustrations on page 269 for tips on preparing this recipe.

3 pounds russet or Yukon Gold potatoes, peeled and sliced $1/16$ to $1/8$ inch thick
5 tablespoons unsalted butter, melted
$1/4$ cup vegetable or peanut oil, plus additional for greasing the cookie sheet
   Salt and ground black pepper

1. Toss the potato slices with the melted butter in a large bowl until the potatoes are evenly coated. Adjust an oven rack to the lower-middle position and heat the oven to 450 degrees.

2. Pour the oil into a 10-inch heavy-bottomed ovenproof nonstick skillet. Swirl to coat the pan bottom with oil and set the skillet over medium-low heat. Begin timing. Arrange the potato slices in the skillet, using the nicest slices to form the bottom layer. To start, place one slice in the center of the skillet. Overlap more slices in a circle around the center slice and then form another circle of overlapping slices to cover the pan bottom. Sprinkle evenly with a scant ¼ teaspoon salt and pepper to taste. Arrange a second layer of potatoes, working in the opposite direction of the first layer; sprinkle evenly with a scant ¼ teaspoon salt and pepper to taste. Repeat, layering the potatoes in opposite directions and sprinkling with salt and pepper, until no slices remain (broken or uneven slices can be pieced together to form

SCIENCE:
Why Potatoes Turn Brown

As many of us find out the hard way, peeled and sliced potatoes take on a brick-red hue when left to sit out for several minutes before cooking. This was of particular concern in our pommes Anna recipe, because the peeled, sliced potatoes must wait to be layered in the skillet. We consulted spud expert Dr. Alfred Bushway, professor of food science at the University of Maine, to find out what causes potatoes to turn color. He explained that with slicing and peeling, potato cells are broken down and the enzyme polyphenol oxidase (PPO) is released. Two major substrates, chlorogenic acid and tyrosine, are also released.

The enzyme and substrates combine with oxygen, and they are then oxidized into a compound called orthoquinone. The orthoquinone quickly polymerizes (a process in which many molecules link up to form a chain of more complex material with different physical properties) and creates the dark pink-red color that we see in the potatoes.

Tossing the potatoes with butter, as in the pommes Anna recipe, helps limit oxygen exposure and therefore retards discoloration. We had also noted that certain potatoes discolor more rapidly than others. Bushway said that from cultivar to cultivar and over the storage season, potatoes vary in their enzyme and/or substrate concentrations and enzyme activity, so differences in discoloration rates can be expected. In our experience, russet potatoes seem to discolor most rapidly, so if you're a slow hand, opt for Yukon Golds for pommes Anna.

single slices; the potatoes will mound in the center of the skillet). Continue to cook over medium-low heat until 30 minutes elapse from the time you began arranging the potatoes in the skillet.

3. Using the bottom of a 9-inch cake pan, press the potatoes down firmly to compact them. Cover the skillet and place it in the oven. Bake until the potatoes begin to soften, about 15 minutes. Uncover and continue to bake until the potatoes are tender when a paring knife is inserted in the center and the edge of the potatoes near the skillet is browned, about 10 minutes longer. Meanwhile, line a rimless cookie sheet or the back of a rimmed baking sheet with foil and coat very lightly with oil. Drain off excess fat from the potatoes by pressing the bottom of the cake pan against the potatoes while tilting the skillet. (Be sure to use oven mitts or heavy potholders.)

4. Set the foil-lined cookie sheet on top of the skillet. With your hands protected by the oven mitts or potholders, hold the cookie sheet in place with one hand and carefully invert the skillet and cookie sheet together. Lift the skillet off the potatoes. Carefully slide the potatoes from the baking sheet onto a platter. Cut into wedges and serve immediately.

RADICCHIO

RADICCHIO MAY RESEMBLE RED CABBAGE IN APPEARANCE, BUT IT HAS more in common with Belgian endive. Like endive, radicchio has a bitter flavor that fades with cooking. Grilling is a popular way of cooking radicchio. The purple leaves become lightly crisp and smoky tasting. To keep the radicchio from falling apart on the grill, cut the radicchio through the core end into thick wedges. We found that radicchio needs to be brushed liberally with oil before it goes onto the grill. When we tried to skimp on the oil, the leaves singed. Also, for maximum browning, we found it best to turn each wedge of radicchio twice so that each flat side of the wedges could rest directly against the grill grate.

Braising is another easy way to cook radicchio. In this case, the radicchio is treated more like cabbage: shredded and then cooked. Slicing the head into thin strips ensures a short cooking time, and braising mellows the bitter flavors more than grilling. Both broth and cream proved to be great braising liquids. After about five minutes in a covered pan, the radicchio was wilted and tender. We then removed the cover and allowed the excess liquid to evaporate as the radicchio continued to simmer for another minute or so.

PREPARING RADICCHIO FOR GRILLING

Remove any brown leaves. Cut the radicchio in half through the core. Cut each half again through the core so that you end up with four wedges. Since each piece has a bit of the core, the layers of leaves will remain together on the grill.

Master Recipe for Grilled Radicchio

SERVES 4

This dish is delicious with grilled meat or poultry. The heads of radicchio are cut into wedges and lightly grilled, bringing out the sweetness of the vegetable while also letting it retain a pleasantly crisp texture.

3 medium heads radicchio (about 1 ¼ pounds), cut into quarters with core intact (see the illustration at left)
4 tablespoons extra-virgin olive oil
   Salt and ground black pepper

1. Place the radicchio wedges on a large baking sheet and brush all sides with the oil. Season with salt and pepper to taste.

2. Grill the radicchio over a medium-hot fire (you should be able to hold your hand 5 inches above the cooking grate for 3 to 4 seconds), turning every 1 ½ minutes, until the edges are browned and wilted but the centers remain slightly firm, about 4 ½ minutes total. Serve immediately.

➤ VARIATION

Grilled Radicchio with Garlic and Rosemary–Infused Oil

If you like, drizzle the grilled radicchio with some balsamic vinegar just before serving.

6	tablespoons extra-virgin olive oil
I	medium clove garlic, minced or pressed through a garlic press
I	teaspoon minced fresh rosemary
3	medium heads radicchio (about I ¼ pounds), cut into quarters with core intact (see the illustration on page 272)
	Salt and ground black pepper

1. Heat the oil, garlic, and rosemary in a small saucepan until hot. Remove the pan from the heat and cool the oil to room temperature.

2. Place the radicchio wedges on a large baking sheet and brush all sides with about 4 tablespoons of the oil. Season with salt and pepper to taste.

3. Grill the radicchio over a medium-hot fire (you should be able to hold your hand 5 inches above the cooking grate for 3 to 4 seconds), turning every 1 ½ minutes, until the edges are browned and wilted but the centers remain slightly firm, about 4 ½ minutes total. Transfer the radicchio to a serving platter and drizzle with the remaining oil. Serve immediately.

Master Recipe for Braised Radicchio

SERVES 4

Braised radicchio goes well with roast chicken or pork.

3	medium heads radicchio (about I ¼ pounds)
2	tablespoons unsalted butter
I	small onion, chopped fine
½	cup low-sodium chicken broth
I	tablespoon sugar
I	tablespoon minced fresh parsley leaves
	Salt and ground black pepper

1. Cut the radicchio in half through the core. Using a paring knife, remove and discard the white core. Lay the halves cut-side down on the cutting board and slice the radicchio crosswise into ½-inch strips.

2. Heat the butter in a Dutch oven or large saucepan over medium-high heat. When the foaming subsides, add the onion and cook, stirring occasionally, until golden, 5 to 6 minutes, adjusting the heat as necessary to prevent burning. Stir in the radicchio, broth, and sugar. Cover and cook until the radicchio is tender, about 5 minutes. Remove the cover and simmer to reduce the liquid slightly, about 1 minute. Stir in the parsley and season with salt and pepper to taste. Serve immediately.

➤ VARIATION

Braised Radicchio with Apple and Cream

The cream mellows the bitterness of the radicchio considerably. Don't be alarmed if the cream turns purple. This dish is especially good with pork.

3	medium heads radicchio (about I ¼ pounds)
2	tablespoons unsalted butter

1   small onion, chopped fine

1   medium Granny Smith apple, peeled, cored, and cut into ¹/₂-inch dice

¹/₂   cup heavy cream

1   tablespoon sugar

1   tablespoon cider vinegar

   Salt and ground black pepper

1. Cut the radicchio in half through the core. Using a paring knife, remove and discard the white core. Lay the halves cut-side down on the cutting board and slice the radicchio crosswise into ½–inch strips.

2. Heat the butter in a Dutch oven or large saucepan over medium–high heat. When the foaming subsides, add the onion and apple and cook, stirring occasionally, until golden, 5 to 6 minutes. Stir in the radicchio, cream, and sugar. Cover and cook until the radicchio is tender, about 5 minutes. Remove the cover and simmer to reduce the liquid slightly, about 1 minute. Stir in the vinegar and season with salt and pepper to taste. Serve immediately.

INGREDIENTS: Black Pepper

For a spice that we use just about every day, and with a wide variety of foods, it's hard not to wonder if we have taken pepper too much for granted. Although most of us tend to think that one jar of black pepper is the same as another, several varieties exist. The most readily available include Vietnamese pepper, Lampong (from the island of Sumatra), and Malabar and Tellicherry (both from India).

Or, at the other end of the spectrum, perhaps all this fuss over grinding fresh whole peppercorns is nonsense, not really providing any improved flavor. We decided to hold a blind tasting to sort it all out. We included in our tasting the two preeminent national supermarket brands as well as the above-mentioned varieties, which were ordered from specialty spice and gourmet stores.

All of the peppers were offered plain but with the option of being tasted on plain white rice. Overall, our tasting confirmed that freshly ground pepper is far superior to pepper purchased already ground. The latter carried minimal aroma and tended to taste sharp and dull, lacking in complexity. Those whole peppercorns that were fresh ground just before the tasting contained bold as well as subtle flavors and aromas that were both lively and complex.

As for differences among the varieties of whole peppercorns, we found them to be distinct yet subtle. All the peppercorns were appreciated for their particular characteristics, receiving high scores within a close range of one another. We concluded that what is important is not so much which variety of pepper you buy but how you buy it.

Why did we find the most noticeable differences in pepper to be between fresh-ground whole pepper and commercially ground pepper? When a peppercorn is cracked, the volatile chemical components that give pepper its bold aroma as well as its subtle characteristics immediately begin to disperse. These more subtle flavors often include pine and citrus. So with time (and cracking), what remains is the predominant nonvolatile compound in black pepper, piperine. Piperine is the source of black pepper's renowned pungency and is what gives it its characteristic hot, sharp, and stinging qualities.

Knowing this, a home cook can easily improve his or her cooking simply by buying whole peppercorns and grinding them fresh with each meal. That way, instead of merely experiencing the sharp sensation that ground pepper has to offer, you will unleash a spectrum of flavors from earthy to exotic.

THE BEST BLACK PEPPER

McCormick Whole Black Peppercorns beat out the rest of the supermarket competition as well as several mail-order brands. Note that this "premium" product fared better than McCormick peppercorns sold in plastic bottles. This brand is sold under the Schilling label on the West Coast.

RADISHES

FOR THOSE OF US WHO HAVE ONLY HAD RADISHES RAW AND IN SALADS, braised radishes come as a surprise. Cooking changes the radishes completely. The pungent flavor so characteristic of raw radishes disappears (along with the bright pink color) and is replaced by a mild, turnip-like sweetness.

To find the best braising liquid, we tried braising the radishes in water, chicken broth, and wine. Radishes braised in water were bland, and wine turned the radishes harsh and acidic. Chicken broth was the best choice, yielding mild but not bland radishes with a hint of richness. We also tried sautéing radishes in cream, and everyone in the test kitchen responded favorably. All cream was too rich, but a mixture of broth and cream created a lightly clinging, slightly rich sauce for the radishes.

We found that sautéing the radishes briefly in butter (before adding the liquid to the pan) helped to bring out their mellow, sweet flavor. Some minced shallot or garlic lent even more depth to the radishes. As for herbs, we found that chives and thyme complemented the radishes the best.

When shopping for radishes, try to find bunches with the greens still attached. If the greens are crisp and healthy looking, you can be assured that the radishes were freshly dug. We had mixed results when using the trimmed radishes sold in plastic bags in most supermarkets. Many of the radishes were tough and woody or soft and spongy.

MINCING SHALLOTS

1. Place the peeled bulb flat-side down on a work surface and slice crosswise almost to (but not through) the root end.

2. Make a number of parallel cuts through the top of the shallot down to the work surface.

3. Finally, make very thin slices perpendicular to the lengthwise cuts made in step 2.

Master Recipe for Braised Radishes

SERVES 4

The sweet flavor of the chives goes well with the radishes, which themselves are surprisingly sweet when braised. See below for a tip about mincing chives. Serve with chicken, pork, or fish.

I   tablespoon unsalted butter

I   medium shallot, minced

20   medium or 16 large radishes, leaves and stems removed (about I pound after trimming), halved if small and quartered if large

⅓   cup low-sodium chicken broth

2   teaspoons minced fresh chives
   Salt and ground black pepper

1. Place the butter in a large skillet over medium-high heat. When the butter begins to sizzle, add the shallot and cook until

softened, 2 to 3 minutes. Stir in the radishes and cook for 1 minute longer.

2. Add the broth, cover, and cook, stirring once or twice, until the radishes are tender, about 10 minutes. Remove the cover and simmer until the liquid thickens slightly, about 1 minute. Add the chives and season with salt and pepper to taste. Serve immediately.

➤ VARIATION

Radishes Braised in Cream with Garlic and Thyme

The bright pink color will transfer from the radishes to the sauce as they are cooked together.

I   tablespoon unsalted butter

3   medium cloves garlic, minced or pressed through a garlic press

20   medium or 16 large radishes, leaves and stems removed (about I pound after trimming), halved if small and quartered if large

¼   cup low-sodium chicken broth

2   tablespoons heavy cream

I   teaspoon minced fresh thyme leaves
   Salt and ground black pepper

1. Place the butter in a large skillet over medium-high heat. When the butter begins to sizzle, add the garlic and cook until fragrant, about 30 seconds. Stir in the radishes and cook 1 minute longer.

2. Add the broth, cream, and thyme. Cover and cook, stirring once or twice, until the radishes are tender, about 10 minutes. Remove the cover and simmer until the liquid thickens slightly, about 1 minute. Season with salt and pepper to taste and serve immediately.

MINCING CHIVES

Although many recipes call for snipped chives, we find scissors useful only for harvesting. To cut chives finely, gather them tightly in one hand and mince finely with the other, turning your fingertips under to shield your fingers from the knife blade.

RUTABAGAS & TURNIPS

MANY COOKS CONFUSE RUTABAGAS AND TURNIPS, A CONFUSION THAT NO doubt arises from the fact that many markets label rutabagas as "yellow turnips." Although these root vegetables are related (both are members of the brassica family, which also includes kale, cauliflower, and broccoli), their flavors and appearance are quite distinct.

Rutabagas are quite large, often weighing 2 pounds each. They are covered with a tan skin (sometimes streaked with purple) and are often waxed to prolong their shelf life. (For this reason, rutabagas are almost always peeled.) The flesh is pale yellow and has a mild, mellow, even sweet flavor.

Turnips range in size from quite small (no larger than a new potato) to fairly large (the size of a russet potato). The most common variety has white skin (often tinged with purple) and white flesh. The flavor is peppery, almost like horseradish, to which it is also related.

Our research identified two main ways to prepare these root vegetables—mashing and roasting. We decided to tackle mashing first. Similar to mashed potatoes, mashed rutabagas are smooth and creamy, with an added edge of tangy, sweet turnip flavor. When cooked poorly, they are fibrous and watery. When cooked well, their light, fluffy texture and unique flavor, accented with a little butter and fresh cream, make a welcome break from the same old dish of potatoes.

To start, we tested both white turnips and yellow rutabagas. The white turnips were harsh and overpowering, but the mashed rutabagas had a mild, mellow flavor that

tasters liked. You can mash white turnips, but we find that they are best tempered with some potatoes or another root vegetable. We decided to stick with rutabagas and create a 100-percent rutabaga puree.

Our first tests yielded purees that were unacceptably starchy—they almost resembled loose polenta. Wanting a tighter, smoother consistency, we focused on the cooking method. While many recipes simply peel, dice, and boil the rutabagas before mashing them with cream and butter, we had little success with this technique. Even when the boiled rutabagas were thoroughly cooked, dried, and forced through a food mill or ricer, the texture of the puree was mealy and loose.

Next, we tried microwaving the rutabagas whole, a method we often use for stringy sweet potatoes. While this method made a tighter puree, it still had a mealy, tapioca-like quality, and the turnips were easy to overcook. Finally, we tried steaming, and although the resulting puree was still slightly mealy, it was not loose, and the cooking process was easy to control. To combat the mealy starchiness, we put the steamed rutabagas into the food processor. Unlike potatoes, which turn to glue when cooked and processed, the steamed rutabagas suddenly became a smooth and silky puree.

With a smooth puree in hand, we were ready to add the butter and other dairy component. Testing heavy cream, half-and-half, and whole milk, tasters preferred the full rich flavor of heavy cream. Because mashed rutabagas are not nearly as starchy as mashed potatoes, much less cream is required to loosen their texture and add flavor. After testing various amounts of heavy cream and butter, we found 2 pounds of rutabagas (enough for four people) had the best consistency and flavor when mixed with 4 tablespoons of butter and ½ cup of heavy cream.

Wondering if the order in which the butter and heavy cream are added to the mixture would make a difference (as it does with potatoes), we tasted three batches side by side: one in which the butter was added before the cream, another in which the cream was added before the butter, and the last in which the butter and cream were tossed into the food processor right along with the cooked rutabagas. As is the case with mashed potatoes, the butter-first batch turned out far lighter and creamier than the other batches. By comparison, the cream-first rutabagas were pasty and thick, while the all-ingredients-at-once batch was stiff and starchy tasting.

What process was at work here? We learned that when butter is added before cream, the fat coats the starch molecules, inhibiting their interaction with the water in the cream once it is added, yielding a silkier, creamier puree. Melted butter works better than solid butter, because the liquid can coat the starch molecules more quickly and easily. This buttery coating also affects the starch molecules' interaction with each other. All in all, it makes for smoother, more velvety mashed rutabagas.

Our final task was to see if any flavorings or spices would benefit the mix. We tried nutmeg, allspice, and cinnamon and found the flavor of each to be overpowering, marring the clean rutabaga flavor. Instead, tasters preferred the simple, straightforward flavor of rutabagas seasoned with salt, pepper, and a pinch of sugar (to bring out their natural sweetness), plus the gentle flavor of fresh thyme when quickly steeped in the heavy cream.

With our mashing method developed, it was time to turn our attention to roasting. After the first few tests, it was apparent that tasters preferred roasted white turnips to roasted rutabagas. The potent, harsh turnip flavor that had bothered some tasters when turnips were mashed was gone when the turnips were roasted. Instead, the turnips became a bit sweet, and their texture was creamy and moist. In contrast, rutabagas became a bit dry and mealy when roasted. Not bad, but the white turnips were better.

We had the best results with smaller turnips—those no more than 2 inches in diameter. Larger turnips occasionally were woody or spongy—no doubt because of their age. Our roasting tests proceeded quickly. Tasters found that 1-inch pieces achieved a golden crust by the time the interior was cooked through. An oven temperature of 425 degrees delivered the best results (at higher temperatures, burning was a risk), and the turnips required some oiling to prevent sticking. Although canola and vegetable oil were fine, everyone agreed that turnips benefited from olive oil and plenty of salt and pepper.

Master Recipe for Mashed Rutabagas

SERVES 4

The hot cream should be ready just as the rutaba-gas go into the food processor. If you prepare the cream too far ahead of time, a skin will form on the surface. If you start step 2 when the rutabagas have been steaming for 25 minutes, the timing should work out perfectly.

2   pounds rutabagas (yellow turnips),
    peeled and cut into $1/2$-inch pieces
$1/2$ cup heavy cream
2   sprigs fresh thyme (optional)
    Salt and ground black pepper
    Pinch sugar
4   tablespoons unsalted butter,
    melted

1 Bring about 1 inch of water to a boil over high heat in a large saucepan or Dutch oven set up with a wire rack, steamer, or pasta insert. Add the rutabagas, cover, and return the water to a boil. Reduce the heat to medium-high and steam until the rutaba-gas are tender, about 30 minutes.

2. Meanwhile, bring the cream, thyme (if using), ¾ teaspoon salt, ¼ teaspoon pepper, and sugar to a simmer in a small saucepan over medium heat. Remove the pan from the heat and discard the thyme.

3. Remove the rutabagas from the steamer and place them in the workbowl of a food processor. Process the hot rutabagas until smooth, scraping down the sides of the workbowl as necessary, about 1 minute. Transfer the puree to a clean bowl.

4. Stir the melted butter into the puree and gently incorporate with a rubber spat-ula. Gently stir in the hot cream. Adjust the seasonings, adding salt and pepper to taste. Serve immediately.

VARIATION

Mashed Rutabagas with Apples, Sage, and Bacon

For this recipe, start frying the bacon after the ruta-baga has been steaming for 15 minutes. To give this dish some texture, the apples are cooked until soft and added to the rutabaga puree.

2   pounds rutabagas (yellow turnips),
    peeled and cut into $1/2$-inch pieces
3   ounces (about 3 slices) bacon,
    cut crosswise into $1/2$-inch strips
1   medium shallot, minced
1   medium McIntosh apple, peeled,
    cored, and cut into $1/4$-inch dice
$1/2$ cup heavy cream
1   tablespoon finely chopped
    fresh sage leaves
1   tablespoon light or dark brown sugar
4   tablespoons unsalted butter, melted
    Salt and ground black pepper

1. Bring about 1 inch of water to a boil over high heat in a large saucepan or Dutch oven set up with a wire rack, steamer, or pasta insert. Add the rutabagas, cover, and return the water to a boil. Reduce the heat to medium-high and steam until tender, about 30 minutes.

2. Meanwhile, cook the bacon in a medium skillet over medium heat until crisp, about 5 minutes. Using a slotted spoon, transfer the bacon to a plate lined with paper towels. Add the shallot and apple to the bacon drippings in the pan. Cook, stirring occasionally, until the apples are very soft, about 7 minutes. Add the cream, sage, and brown sugar and simmer for 1 minute. Remove the pan from the heat.

3. Remove the rutabagas from the steamer and place them in the workbowl of a food processor. Process the hot rutabagas until smooth, scraping down the sides of

the workbowl as necessary, about 1 minute. Transfer the puree to a clean bowl.

4. Stir the melted butter into the puree and gently incorporate with a rubber spatula. Stir in the hot cream mixture. Adjust the seasonings, adding salt and pepper to taste. Garnish with the reserved bacon and serve immediately.

Master Recipe for Roasted Turnips

SERVES 4

This simple dish goes well with any roasted meat. For the best results, make sure the turnip pieces are not crowding each other in the roasting pan. Choose smaller turnips (less than 2 inches in diameter), if possible.

2	pounds white turnips, peeled and cut into 1-inch cubes
2	tablespoons extra-virgin olive oil
	Salt and ground black pepper
1	tablespoon minced fresh parsley leaves

1. Adjust an oven rack to the lower-middle position and heat the oven to 425 degrees.

2. Toss the turnips and oil in a large bowl until the turnips are coated with the oil. Season with salt and pepper to taste. Spread the turnips in a single layer over a large rimmed baking sheet. Roast until the bottom of the turnip pieces is golden, 10 to 12 minutes. Using a metal spatula, turn the turnips and continue to roast until they are tender and golden, another 10 to 12 minutes. Sprinkle with the parsley and adjust the seasonings, adding salt and pepper to taste. Serve immediately.

➤ VARIATION

Ginger-Roasted Turnips with Maple
The smoky, sweet flavor of maple syrup complements the turnips well.

Follow the master recipe, tossing the turnips and oil with 1 teaspoon minced or grated fresh ginger in step 1. Proceed as directed, tossing the roasted turnips with 2 tablespoons maple syrup just before serving.

GRATING GINGER

Most cooks who use fresh ginger have scraped their fingers on the grater when the piece of ginger gets down to a tiny nub. Instead of cutting a small chunk of ginger off a larger piece and then grating it, try this method. Peel a small section of the large piece of ginger. Grate the peeled portion, using the rest of the ginger as a handle to keep fingers safely away from the grater.

SPINACH

SPINACH CAN BE COOKED AND SERVED AS A SIDE DISH. (FOR MORE information, see the section on greens that begins on page 137.) However, spinach is also used as a salad green. Our favorite kind of spinach salad uses a warm dressing to wilt the leaves slightly.

Many cooks consider wilted spinach salad—in which a warm, fragrant dressing gently wilts fresh spinach leaves—to be a restaurant indulgence. While these elegant salads are surprisingly easy to make at home, there are potential problems. After sampling several recipes in the test kitchen, tasters concurred that these salads can disappoint in two major ways: with greasy, dull-tasting dressings and with spinach reduced to mush in puddles of dressing as deep as a fish pond.

The first hurdle—having to wash, dry, and trim mature curly spinach—was easily overcome. Kitchen tests determined that prewashed, bagged baby spinach works well in this salad, as it is both more tender and more sweet than the mature variety.

Next, we wanted to identify the best type of oil to use in these salads. Though dressings made with pure olive oil were fine—use it if that's what you have on hand—the flavor nuances of extra-virgin oil gave the dressings more depth and dimension.

When it came to the acidic component, tasters favored fresh lemon juice for its bright, tangy flavor. We discovered that dressings in which the lemon juice was added early and heated through lacked brightness. The punch was restored when we swirled in the lemon juice after the oil and other ingredients had been heated.

We also tested the ratio of oil to acid. The ratio we use for most vinaigrettes, 4 parts oil to 1 part acid, produced greasy dressings. Mindful that we didn't want too much oil overpowering the tender spinach, we scaled back the ratio to 3 parts oil and 1 part acid. A little extra acid made the dressings sharp and fresh tasting.

Several of us in the test kitchen had in the past encountered wilted salads swimming in dressing, which gave the greens a decidedly drowned, slimy texture. After tasting salads tossed with various quantities of dressing, our tasters settled on just ¼ cup of dressing for 6 cups of greens. The ¼ cup coated the greens generously yet allowed them to retain enough structural integrity to leave these wilted salads with a slight but satisfying crunch. Serve these salads without delay to enjoy the best of their singular texture.

Wilted Spinach Salad with Feta, Olives, and Lemon Vinaigrette

SERVES 4 AS A FIRST COURSE

If you prefer, use goat cheese in place of the feta.

5 ounces baby spinach, about 6 cups

3 tablespoons extra-virgin olive oil

1 medium shallot, minced (about 2 tablespoons)

1 medium clove garlic, minced or pressed through a garlic press (about 1 teaspoon)

1 teaspoon minced fresh oregano leaves

1/4 teaspoon salt

1/8 teaspoon ground black pepper

1/8 teaspoon sugar

1 tablespoon juice from 1 lemon

2 ounces feta cheese, crumbled (about 1/4 cup)

6 black olives, sliced thin

Place the spinach in a large bowl. Cook the oil, shallot, garlic, oregano, salt, pepper, and sugar in a small skillet over medium heat until the shallot is slightly softened, 2 to 3 minutes. Add the lemon juice and swirl to incorporate. Pour the warm dressing over the spinach, add the feta and olives, and toss gently with tongs to wilt. Serve immediately.

Wilted Spinach Salad with Oranges, Radishes, and Citrus Vinaigrette

SERVES 4 AS A FIRST COURSE

See page 117 for tips on segmenting the oranges.

5 ounces baby spinach, about 6 cups

3 tablespoons extra-virgin olive oil

1 medium shallot, minced about 2 tablespoons)

1/4 teaspoon grated zest and segments from 2 medium oranges

1/4 teaspoon salt

1/8 teaspoon ground black pepper

1/8 teaspoon sugar

1 tablespoon juice from 1 lemon

4 medium radishes, grated on the large holes of a box grater (about 1/3 cup)

Place the spinach in a large bowl. Cook the oil, shallot, orange zest, salt, pepper, and sugar in a small skillet over medium heat until the shallot is slightly softened, 2 to 3 minutes. Add the lemon juice and swirl to incorporate. Pour the warm dressing over the spinach. Add the orange segments and grated radishes and toss gently with tongs to wilt. Serve immediately.

WILTED SPINACH SALAD WITH BACON DRESSING

WE CAN'T THINK OF A BETTER WAY to enjoy fresh spinach than to toss it with a rich, warm, sweet-tart dressing and then cover the lot with plenty of crisp bacon. Yet ordering a wilted spinach salad in a restaurant is a move we usually regret. The spinach, which is often drowned in an oily, bland dressing and sprinkled with minuscule bacon bits, leaves us perplexed—and still hungry. This salad can be made with a simple method and a short list of ingredients. Why, then, was a good one so hard to find?

Aside from the spinach, bacon is the central ingredient, with the potential to provide plenty of smoky, salty flavor. We chose thick-cut bacon, finding that it offered more presence and textural interest than thin-cut. (Slab bacon can also be used, but it fries up chewy, not crispy.) The easiest way to achieve substantial, uniform pieces (and avoid tiny Bac-O–style bacon bits) was to cut the strips before frying them rather than crumbling them afterward. At this point, we also confirmed that hard-cooked egg wedges (a common ingredient) belonged in this salad. Their creamy yolks and cool whites formed a natural partnership with the bacon.

With plenty of mouth-watering bacon fat at the ready, we were loath to use another type of oil in the dressing, though some recipes call for either vegetable or olive oil. Happily, tests bolstered our conviction that dressing made solely with bacon grease had not only a lush mouthfeel but also a hearty flavor; oil-based dressings tasted flat.

We found eight types of vinegar in the test kitchen cabinets and tested all of them, as well as lemon juice. Tasters criticized many of the choices, calling them boring and one-dimensional. Rice vinegar showed promise—its sweetness played well against

STORING BACON

Roll up the bacon in tight cylinders, each with two to four slices of bacon. Place the cylinders in a zipper-lock plastic bag and place the bag flat in the freezer. (Once the slices are frozen, the bag can be stored as you like.) When bacon is needed, simply pull out the desired number of slices and defrost.

the rich bacon fat—but it wasn't acidic enough and seemed a bit out of place for such an American recipe. More traditional cider vinegar, which is quite sharp, brightened the dressing considerably. A little sugar added a pleasing sweet element.

Most recipes for this salad call for a generous amount of fat (or oil) and a small amount of acid (vinegar). Typical ratios are 2, 3, or even 4 parts fat to 1 part acid, a standard formula for vinaigrette. We mixed up bacon fat and cider vinegar dressings using each proportion and were disappointed with all of them. To avoid being saddled with a fatty, lifeless mixture, we'd have to throw convention by the wayside. This meant cutting back on the bacon fat and elevating the vinegar level to counterbalance the fat and richness contributed by the fried bacon and egg yolks. After fiddling with the ratio, we settled on a dressing made with 3 tablespoons each of fat and vinegar.

We now had a great-tasting salad, but tasters asserted that it wasn't wilted enough. Because adding more dressing would only result in an overdressed, swampy salad, we weren't sure how to proceed. Luckily, the issue resolved itself when we sautéed a half-cup of onions

and mixed them into the dressing. They added enough volume and heat to wilt the spinach perfectly after a few tosses. Wondering if yellow onions were the best choice, we also tested sautéed scallions, shallots, red onions, and garlic. Tasters preferred red onions and garlic, so we opted to use both.

Wilted Spinach Salad with Warm Bacon Dressing

SERVES 4 TO 6 AS A FIRST COURSE

This salad comes together quickly, so have the ingredients ready before you begin cooking. When adding the vinegar mixture to the skillet, step back from the stovetop—the aroma is quite potent.

6	ounces baby spinach (about 8 cups)
3	tablespoons cider vinegar
1/2	teaspoon sugar
1/4	teaspoon ground black pepper
	Pinch salt
10	ounces (about 8 slices) thick-cut bacon, cut into 1/2-inch pieces
1/2	medium red onion, chopped medium (about 1/2 cup)
1	small clove garlic, minced or

pressed through a garlic press (about 1/2 teaspoon)

3   hard-cooked eggs (page 20), peeled and quartered lengthwise

1. Place the spinach in a large bowl. Stir the vinegar, sugar, pepper, and salt together in a small bowl until the sugar dissolves; set aside.

2. Fry the bacon in a medium skillet over medium-high heat, stirring occasionally, until crisp, about 10 minutes. Using a slotted spoon, transfer the bacon to a plate lined with paper towels. Pour the bacon fat into a heatproof bowl and then return 3 tablespoons of the fat to the skillet. Add the onion to the skillet and cook over medium heat, stirring frequently, until slightly softened, about 3 minutes. Stir in the garlic and cook until fragrant, about 15 seconds. Add the vinegar mixture and remove the skillet from the heat. Working quickly, scrape the bottom of the skillet with a wooden spoon to loosen the browned bits.

3. Pour the hot dressing over the spinach, add the bacon, and toss gently with tongs until the spinach is slightly wilted. Divide the salad among individual plates, arrange the egg quarters over each, and serve immediately.

WILTING GONE WRONG

If you use too much dressing, the spinach will overwilt and appear lifeless (left). If you don't use enough dressing, or if you let the dressing cool, the spinach barely wilts and remains chewy (right). When the spinach is properly wilted, some of the leaves will soften, while others remain crisp (see the color photograph on page 210).

OVERWILTED SPINACH: LIFELESS

UNDERWILTED SPINACH: CHEWY

SWEET POTATOES

IT'S AN AGE-OLD CULINARY QUESTION: WHAT IS THE DIFFERENCE BETWEEN a yam and a sweet potato? Answer: It depends on where you live. In U.S. markets, a "yam" is actually a mislabeled sweet potato. If you can get a glimpse of the box it's shipped in, you'll see the words *sweet potato* printed somewhere, as mandated by the U.S. Department of Agriculture. In other parts of the world, *yam* refers to a true yam, a vegetable having no relation to the sweet potato. Sold under the label "ñame" (ny-AH-may) or "igname" here in the United States, a true yam has a hairy, off-white or brown skin and white, light yellow, or pink flesh. This tuber is usually sold in log-shaped chunks that weigh several pounds

each. Unlike a sweet potato, a true yam tastes bland and has an ultra-starchy texture. It cannot be used as a substitute for sweet potatoes.

Even if you purchase sweet potatoes rather than yams, not all sweet potatoes are the same. Sweet potatoes come in two very distinct types, dry and moist. Endless varieties allow for confusion with sizes and shapes, but the most basic rule is that dry sweet potatoes have white to yellow flesh, while moist ones have varying deep shades of orange. Dry sweet potatoes are slightly sweet and, because they have a relatively high starch content, also somewhat mealy. Moist sweet potatoes have a higher sugar content and are dense, watery, and more easily caramelized.

We sampled six different sweet potatoes and found a wide range of flavors and textures. Among the moist orange varieties, Beauregard (the variety most supermarkets stock) was favored for its "standard sweet

potato flavor" and perfect texture. Jewel and Red Garnet sweet potatoes (often mislabeled as yams) were less sweet and wetter. Among the dry white varieties, the Japanese Sweet was the clear favorite, with tasters praising its "buttery," "chestnut" flavor. The White Sweets were similar but less potent. The Batatas were very mild tasting, and their texture was very dry.

Whatever the variety, most commercially grown sweet potatoes are harvested in the fall. They are then transferred to ventilated curing rooms where, for a period of days, high heat and humidity levels allow cuts and bruises from harvesting to heal. In this controlled environment, starches begin converting to sugar, so that a cured sweet potato is literally sweeter than a freshly harvested one.

Once you get the sweet potatoes home, do not wash them until you are ready to use them, because this exposes the vulnerable skin and causes them to go bad more quickly. Refrigeration is also a no-no; it causes the core of the potato to gradually change texture until it resembles a soft, damp cork. The best storage is a dark, well-ventilated spot, out of plastic bags.

Baked Sweet Potatoes

SWEET POTATOES HAVE BEEN HIDING under the bushel basket of holiday meals long enough. They have wonderful flavor and they're available all year, so why not bake and eat one anytime, just like a potato?

We believe we should do just that, so we set out to find the best way to bake sweet potatoes. We were looking for evenly cooked, moist flesh and softened, slightly caramelized, delicious skin. In trying to reach this goal, we considered and tested 23 individual variables.

Oven variables included temperature, rack level, and whether a baking sheet worked better than just laying the potatoes on the oven rack. We found that the best oven temperature was 400 degrees. Lower temperatures took longer with no improvement, while higher temperatures left burned spots on the bottom of the potatoes. Similarly, the best rack position was the center. Placing the rack either higher or lower resulted in blackening of the potatoes' thin skins. When we placed the potatoes directly on the rack, sticky juice oozed straight down and burned, so we use a baking sheet lined with foil.

We also tested oven tricks like placing the potatoes on unglazed oven tiles and beds of rock salt, but neither proved productive. We even tried cooking the potatoes halfway in the microwave and then transferring them to the oven, but the skin did not soften and there was no caramelization. We also tried

baking the potatoes wrapped in foil, which turned out to be just what we suspected: a school cafeteria abomination that holds heat in soggy, overbaked potatoes.

We also did a number of tests to find the best way to deal with the skin, which is thin and very delicious when cooked properly. Uncoated skin stayed tough and unappealing, but coating it with butter tended to cause burning. Lightly rubbing it with vegetable or olive oil, though, softened the skin just the right amount.

Piercing the skin, we found, was essential to prevent the infamous exploding potato. But our big payoff in the search for tasty skin was the discovery that you should not turn the potatoes during baking. This method resulted in perfectly browned bottom skin that was beautifully caramelized.

Master Recipe for Baked Sweet Potatoes

SERVES 4

This recipe is for the moist, orange-fleshed varieties of sweet potatoes that generally show up in supermarkets. If you have white-fleshed sweet potatoes, increase the baking time by 10 minutes and use plenty of butter after baking to moisten their drier flesh. You can cook up to six potatoes at one time without altering the cooking time. Buying potatoes of the same size is a good idea, because it standardizes cooking time. As with regular baked potatoes, we find it best to open the baked sweet potatoes as wide as possible so that steam can quickly escape; this ensures that the flesh is fluffy rather than dense.

4   small sweet potatoes (about 2 pounds), scrubbed and lightly pricked with a fork

2   tablespoons vegetable or olive oil
     Salt and ground black pepper
     Unsalted butter

1. Adjust an oven rack to the center position and heat the oven to 400 degrees. Rub the potatoes with the oil and arrange them on a foil-lined baking sheet as far apart from each other as possible.

2. Bake until a knife tip slips easily into the potato center, 40 to 50 minutes. Remove the sweet potatoes from the oven and pierce with a fork to create a dotted X (see illustration 1 on page 217). Press in at the ends of the sweet potatoes to push the flesh up and out (see illustration 2 on page 217). Season to taste with salt and pepper. Dot with butter to taste and serve immediately.

MASHED SWEET POTATOES

MASHED SWEET POTATOES ARE OFTEN overdressed in a Willy Wonka–style casserole topped with marshmallows and whipped cream, but when it comes to flavor, this candied concoction doesn't hold a candle to an honest sweet potato mash. With a deep, natural sweetness that requires little assistance, the humble sweet potato, we thought, would taste far better if prepared with a minimum of ingredients.

Yet even with a simple recipe, mashed sweet potatoes can pose problems. Nailing a fork-friendly puree every time is a form of cooking roulette. Mashed sweet potatoes often turn out thick and gluey or, at the other extreme, sloppy and loose. We also found that most recipes overload the dish with pumpkin pie seasonings that obscure the potato's natural flavor. We wanted a recipe that pushed that deep, earthy sweetness to the fore and that reliably produced a silky puree with enough body to hold its shape on a fork. We decided to focus first on the cooking method, then test the remaining ingredients,

and, finally, fiddle with the seasonings.

To determine the best cooking method, we tested a variety of techniques: baking potatoes unpeeled, boiling them whole and unpeeled, boiling them peeled and diced, steaming them peeled and diced, and microwaving them whole and unpeeled. Adding a little butter and salt to the potatoes after mashing, we found, yields a huge improvement in texture, flavor, and ease of preparation.

The baked sweet potatoes produced a mash with a deep flavor and bright color, but the potatoes took more than an hour to bake through, and handling them hot from the oven was risky. Boiling whole sweet potatoes in their skins yielded a wet puree with a mild flavor. When we used a fork to monitor the potatoes as they cooked, we made holes that apparently let the flavor seep out and excess water seep in. Steaming and boiling pieces of peeled potato produced the worst purees, with zero flavor and loose, applesauce-like textures. The microwave, although fast and easy, was also a disappointment. The rate of cooking was difficult to

control, and the difference between under-cooked and overdone was only about 30 seconds. Overmicrowaving the potatoes, even slightly, produced a pasty mouthfeel and an odd plastic flavor. By all accounts, this first round of testing bombed. Yet, it did end up pointing us in a promising direction.

We had certainly learned a few facts about cooking sweet potatoes. First, their deep, hearty flavor is surprisingly fleeting and easily washed out. Second, the tough, dense flesh reacts much like winter squash when it's cooked, turning wet and sloppy. We also found it safer to peel the sweet potatoes when raw and cold rather than cooked and hot. Taking all of this into account, we wondered if braising the sweet potatoes might work. If cut into uniform pieces and cooked over low heat in a covered pan, the sweet potatoes might release their own moisture slowly and braise themselves.

Adding a little water to the pan to get the process going, we found the sweet potatoes were tender in about 40 minutes. We then simply removed the lid and mashed them right in the pot. To our delight, they were full of flavor because they cooked, essentially, in their own liquid. We tried various pots and heat levels and found that a medium-size pot (accommodating two or three layers of potatoes) in combination with low heat worked best.

Up to this point, we had been adding only butter to the mash; we wondered what the typical additions of cream, milk, or half-and-half would do. Making four batches side by side, we tasted mashes made with only butter, with butter and milk, with butter and half-and-half, and with butter and heavy cream. Tasters found the butter-only batch tasted boring, while milk turned the mash bland and watery. The batch made with half-and-half came in second, with heartier flavor and fuller body, but the heavy cream stole the show.

As we had now made this recipe many times, a glaring oversight became obvious. Why didn't we replace the small amount of water used to cook the potatoes with the butter and heavy cream? Curious about how the recipe would react without the water, we were gratified when this streamlined technique produced the ultimate mash. The puree stood up on a fork, with a luxurious texture that was neither loose nor gluey. Further, with the water out of the picture, the sweet potato flavor was more intense than ever.

Master Recipe for Mashed Sweet Potatoes

SERVES 4

Cutting the sweet potatoes into slices of even thickness is important in getting them to cook at the same rate. The potatoes are best served immediately, but they can be covered tightly with plastic wrap and kept relatively hot for 30 minutes. This recipe can be doubled and prepared in a Dutch oven; the cooking time must be doubled as well.

- 4   tablespoons unsalted butter, cut into 4 pieces
- 2   tablespoons heavy cream
- 1/2   teaspoon salt
- 1   teaspoon sugar
- 2   pounds sweet potatoes (about 2 large or 3 medium), peeled, quartered lengthwise, and cut crosswise into 1/4-inch-thick slices
    Pinch ground black pepper

1. Combine the butter, cream, salt, sugar, and sweet potatoes in a 3- to 4-quart saucepan. Cover and cook over low heat, stirring occasionally, until the potatoes fall apart when poked with a fork, 35 to 45 minutes.

2. Off the heat, mash the sweet potatoes in the saucepan with a potato masher. Stir in the pepper and serve immediately.

➤ VARIATIONS

Mashed Sweet Potatoes with Ginger and Brown Sugar

If you like, garnish these potatoes with chopped crystallized ginger.

Follow the master recipe, replacing the sugar with 1 ½ tablespoons light or dark brown sugar and adding 2 teaspoons minced or grated fresh ginger along with the sweet potatoes in step 1.

Mashed Sweet Potatoes with Sesame and Scallions

The tahini gives these potatoes a wonderful, nutty flavor. Black sesame seeds can be used for color variation, but white sesame seeds are fine, too.

EQUIPMENT: Potato Mashers

The two classic styles of potato masher are the wire-looped masher with a zigzag presser and the disk masher with a perforated round or oval plate. Modern mashers, as it turns out, are simply variations of these two original designs. We tested eight mashers to see which had the most comfortable grip and the most effective mashing mechanism.

When we wrapped up our mash-fest, we concluded that the wire-looped mashers were second-rate. The space between the loops made it hard to achieve a good, fast mash, and most of the potato pieces escaped between the loops unscathed. One model, the Exeter Double Masher ($9.99), is worth mentioning, however, as it is spring loaded and uses a double-tiered set of wire loops for mashing. It took some muscle to use this masher, but it was the fastest of all the mashers tested, turning a pot of cooked potatoes into a smooth puree in just 20 strokes.

In general, the disk mashers outperformed the wire-looped models, and the Profi Plus ($15.99) was our favorite. With its small holes, this oval-based masher turned out soft and silky spuds with a reasonable 40 thrusts. Its rounded edges snuggled right into the curves of the saucepan, enhancing its efficacy, and its round handle was easy to grip. The runner-up, the Oxo Smooth Masher ($9.99), has an oval metal base and rectangular perforations. The larger perforations allowed a bit more potato through, so it took 50 mashes to get the job done; still, this squat device with its cushiony handle was easy to use. We did not like the all-plastic Oxo Good Grips Masher—it has an awkward grip and ineffective mash—so shop carefully if buying this brand.

THE BEST POTATO MASHERS

The Profi Plus Masher (left) yielded silky spuds with little effort and was testers' top choice. The Oxo Smooth Masher (center) was comfortable but slower than the winner, making it our runner-up. The spring-loaded Exeter Double Masher (right) was the best of the wire-loop mashers. Although fast, it was a bit awkward to use.

Toast the sesame seeds in a small skillet until fragrant, which should take 4 or 5 minutes.

Follow the master recipe, adding ½ teaspoon toasted sesame oil along with the sweet potatoes in step 1. Proceed as directed, stirring in 2 tablespoons toasted sesame seeds, 1 tablespoon tahini, and 1 medium scallion, sliced thin, along with the pepper in step 2.

OVEN-FRIED SWEET POTATOES

WITH AN EXCELLENT RECIPE FOR OVEN-fried potatoes already developed (see page 229), we figured that we could follow the same formula to cook sweet potatoes. As we soon found out, parts of our recipe for regular oven fries would work with sweet potatoes, but other parts of the recipe needed to be eliminated.

For regular oven fries, we found it best to cut the potatoes into ½-inch-thick lengths. The potatoes were steamed (to help cook the interior) and then oiled and baked at 450 degrees on oiled and preheated baking sheets. When we followed this method with sweet potatoes, we encountered some problems. Sweet potatoes are already very moist, so steaming them made the oven fries soggy. Clearly, this step was not necessary—oven roasting for the entire cooking time would be better. However, when we cooked sweet potato oven fries at 450 degrees, they scorched. A more moderate oven (set at 400 degrees) proved more successful.

Tasters also wanted thicker wedges rather than skinny lengths. This request was easy to accommodate—we simply cut each sweet potato lengthwise into 8 thick wedges. Oiling the baking sheets and preheating them did make the sweet potatoes brown better, so we retained these parts of the original potato recipe.

Oven-fried sweet potatoes will always be moist on the interior. They contain too much moisture to turn fluffy like russet potatoes. However, when prepared by this method (which is simpler than our technique for handling russet potatoes), they become crisp and nicely browned on the exterior and tender on the inside.

Master Recipe for Oven-Fried Sweet Potatoes
SERVES 4

Make sure to handle the potatoes with a thin metal spatula in the oven. You need to loosen them carefully from the baking sheet so that the crusty exterior does not rip or stick to the pan. These oven fries are pretty simple; see the variation that follows or any of the variations for oven fries made with regular potatoes for flavoring options.

I	teaspoon plus I tablespoon peanut oil
2	pounds sweet potatoes (about 3 medium), scrubbed
	Salt and ground black pepper

1. Adjust the oven racks to the upper-middle and lower-middle positions and heat the oven to 400 degrees. Place ½ teaspoon of the oil on each of two rimmed baking sheets. Use a paper towel to spread the oil evenly over the entire surface and place both sheets in the oven.

2. Cut each sweet potato from end to end into eight thick wedges. Toss the sweet potatoes and the remaining tablespoon of oil in a large bowl to coat. Season generously with salt and pepper and toss again to blend. Carefully remove one baking sheet from the oven and place half of the sweet potatoes on the baking sheet cut-side down. Spread

them out so that they do not touch each other. Return the baking sheet to the oven and repeat the process using the second baking sheet and the remaining sweet potatoes.

3. Bake until the cut side of the sweet potatoes touching the baking sheet is crusty and golden brown, 15 to 20 minutes. Remove each baking sheet from the oven and carefully turn the sweet potatoes, using a thin metal spatula. Bake until the second cut side of the sweet potatoes now touching the pan is crusty and golden brown, 10 to 15 minutes. Use the metal spatula to transfer the sweet potatoes to a platter and serve the oven-fried potatoes immediately.

➤ VARIATION

Garlicky Oven-Fried Sweet Potatoes with Chipotle Mayonnaise

The chipotle mayonnaise makes a great dipping sauce for these sweet potato fries.

1/2	cup mayonnaise
1	canned chipotle chile in adobo sauce, minced, plus 2 teaspoons adobo sauce
1	tablespoon juice from 1 lime
1	tablespoon minced fresh cilantro leaves
	Salt and ground black pepper
4	teaspoons peanut oil
2	pounds sweet potatoes (about 3 medium), scrubbed
2	medium cloves garlic, minced or pressed through a garlic press

1. Mix the mayonnaise, minced chipotle, adobo sauce, lime juice, and cilantro together in a small bowl. Season to taste with salt and pepper; let stand to blend flavors.

2. Follow the master recipe as directed, tossing the minced garlic with the oil and sweet potatoes in step 2. Serve the oven-fried sweet potatoes with the chipotle mayonnaise.

CANDIED SWEET POTATOES

CANDIED SWEET POTATOES ARE A TRA-ditional side dish served alongside a roast ham or Thanksgiving turkey. All too often, however, they turn out watery, overseasoned, and overly sweet, tasting more like a loose, crustless pumpkin pie than a savory side dish. We wanted lightly seasoned and perfectly cooked sweet potatoes soft enough to slice with a fork yet resilient enough not to fall through the fork tines while being eaten.

To start, we followed the method touted in many cookbooks and boiled peeled pieces of sweet potato before tossing them with a brown sugar and butter sauce. Despite the popularity of the method, we found these sweet potatoes to be watery and lacking in flavor. Boiling the sweet potatoes washed away vital flavors and added moisture that was difficult to get rid of. We tried partially cooking the sweet potatoes in the microwave before mixing them with the sauce but found that they overcooked easily, and the sauce still lacked substantial flavor. Next, we tossed raw, peeled pieces of sweet potato with brown sugar and butter and baked them in a covered casserole dish. This method also produced a watery sauce as well as unevenly cooked sweet potatoes. As the brown sugar and butter began to melt, the potatoes leached some of their liquid, making a watery cooking solution in which the potatoes began to float. It was difficult to keep these floating sweet potatoes completely submerged, and any unsubmerged parts of potato dried out.

We had better luck once we tried cooking the sweet potatoes on the stovetop. By cooking the potatoes in a Dutch oven with butter and brown sugar, the flavors of the potatoes and the sauce melded. Lubricated with a little water and covered, the sweet potatoes cooked perfectly in about 50 minutes, resulting in the ultimate candied sweet potatoes, with a rich and complex sauce. Although the sauce was still a bit watery when we removed the lid, it was easy to crank up the heat and reduce the sauce quickly to a thicker consistency.

We then tested adding chicken broth, wine, and cider, but tasters preferred the clean taste of the sweet potatoes on their own, seasoned with only a little salt and pepper. While a few tasters preferred the flavor of dark brown sugar to light brown, most found it overpowering. White sugar, on the other hand, was unanimously deemed too bland. We also tried all sorts of spices and herbs, but tasters once again preferred the simple flavors of sweet potatoes seasoned only with salt and pepper.

Master Recipe for Candied Sweet Potatoes

SERVES 8 TO 10

For a more intense molasses flavor, use dark brown sugar in place of light brown sugar.

8	tablespoons unsalted butter, cut into 1-inch pieces
6	medium sweet potatoes (about 3 ¾ pounds), peeled, cut lengthwise into quarters, and then cut crosswise into 1-inch pieces
1	cup packed light brown sugar
1	teaspoon salt
¼	teaspoon ground black pepper

1. Melt the butter in a large saucepan or Dutch oven over medium-high heat. When the foaming subsides, add the sweet potatoes, brown sugar, salt, pepper, and ½ cup water and bring to a simmer. Reduce the heat to medium-low and cover. Cook until the sweet potatoes are tender (a paring knife can be slipped into and out of the center of the potatoes with very little resistance), 45 to 55 minutes, stirring often (every 5 minutes or so).

2. When the sweet potatoes are tender, remove the lid and bring the sauce to a rapid simmer over medium-high heat. Simmer until the sauce has reduced to a glaze, about 10 minutes. Remove the pot from the heat and serve immediately.

➤ VARIATIONS

Candied Sweet Potatoes with Marshmallows

Follow the master recipe through step 1. While the sauce is reducing in step 2, adjust one oven rack so it is 6 inches from the broiler element and heat the broiler. Transfer the finished potatoes and sauce to an ovenproof casserole dish and top with 4 cups mini marshmallows. Place the casserole under the broiler until the marshmallows are brown and have melted slightly, 3 to 4 minutes. Serve immediately.

Candied Sweet Potatoes with Cranberries and Pecans

Currants or chopped dried apricots can be substituted for the cranberries, and walnuts or cashews can be used instead of pecans.

Follow the master recipe, replacing the water in step 1 with ½ cup orange juice and adding ⅓ cup dried cranberries. Just before serving, sprinkle the candied sweet potatoes with ½ cup toasted and coarsely chopped pecans.

TOMATOES

TOMATOES COME IN ALL SHAPES, COLORS, AND SIZES. SUPERMARKET SHOP-pers are most likely to see three varieties: cherry tomatoes, round beefsteak tomatoes, and oblong plum tomatoes. At farmers' markets, you will see heirloom varieties—old-fashioned varieties grown more for their flavor than appearance.

Fresh and canned tomatoes are used in countless recipes and many vegetable preparations. (For more information on canned tomatoes, see page 163.) This chapter focuses on dishes where the tomatoes are the focal point.

SAUTÉED CHERRY TOMATOES

MOST COOKS DON'T THINK ABOUT cooking cherry tomatoes. They use them for salads, but when it comes to heating toma-toes, they turn to plum or round beefsteak varieties. However, cherry tomatoes can be sautéed in minutes to make a quick side dish. In addition, they generally taste pretty good, even in the dead of winter, making them even more appealing.

We did want to explore the ins and outs of this simple technique. We knew it was important to cook the tomatoes as quickly as possible so they wouldn't fall apart. We found that a large skillet (which allows the tomatoes to cook in a single layer) and medium-high heat are essential.

In our testing, we discovered that some batches of cherry tomatoes were bitter. We liked the results when we sprinkled a little sugar over the tomatoes before they went into the pan. The sugar helped with caramelization and balanced the acidity in the tomatoes. Olive oil was our tasters' favorite choice for fat, but butter was a close second. Sautéed cherry tomatoes can be seasoned in numerous ways; fresh herbs, however, are a must.

Sautéed Cherry Tomatoes
SERVES 4

If the cherry tomatoes are especially sweet, you may want to reduce or omit the sugar. Serve this juicy side dish with fish or chicken (especially a dish that could use extra moisture) or with beef.

1	tablespoon extra-virgin olive oil
4	cups (2 pints) cherry tomatoes, halved unless very small
2	teaspoons sugar
1	medium clove garlic, minced or pressed through a garlic press
2	tablespoons thinly sliced fresh basil leaves
	Salt and ground black pepper

Heat the oil in a large skillet over medium-high heat until almost smoking. Mix the tomatoes and sugar in a medium bowl and add them to the hot oil. (Do not mix the tomatoes ahead of time or you will draw out their juices.) Cook for 1 minute, tossing frequently. Stir in the garlic and cook for another 30 seconds. Remove the pan from the heat, add the basil, and season with salt and pepper to taste. Serve immediately.

➤ VARIATION
Sautéed Cherry Tomatoes with Capers and Anchovy

These tomatoes work well with any Mediterranean dish and are especially good with mild, white fish, including swordfish and red snapper.

- 1 tablespoon extra-virgin olive oil
- 2 medium anchovy fillets, minced
- 4 cups (2 pints) cherry tomatoes, halved unless very small
- 2 teaspoons sugar
- 2 tablespoons capers
- 2 medium cloves garlic, minced or pressed through a garlic press
- 2 tablespoons minced fresh parsley leaves
  Salt and ground black pepper

Heat the oil and anchovies in a large skillet over medium-high heat until the anchovies begin to sizzle. Mix the tomatoes and sugar in a medium bowl and add them to the hot oil along with the capers. (Do not mix the tomatoes ahead of time or you will draw out their juices.) Cook for 1 minute, tossing frequently. Stir in the garlic and cook for another 30 seconds. Remove the pan from the heat, add the parsley, and season with salt and pepper to taste. Serve immediately.

STUFFED TOMATOES
OUR PAST EXPERIENCES WITH OVEN-baked stuffed tomatoes have not exactly been great. Still, when we are presented

SEEDING TOMATOES
The seeds are watery and sometimes bitter and are often removed before chopping a tomato. These techniques work for both peeled and unpeeled tomatoes. Because of their different shapes, round and plum (also called Roma) tomatoes are seeded differently.

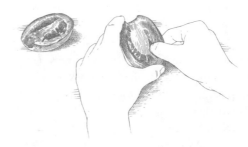

ROUND TOMATOES

Halve the cored tomato along its equator. If the tomato is ripe and juicy, gently give it a squeeze and shake out the seeds and gelatinous material. If not, scoop them out with your finger or a small spoon.

PLUM TOMATOES

Halve the cored tomato lengthwise, cutting through the core end. Break through the inner membrane with your finger and scoop out the seeds and gelatinous material.

CORING TOMATOES

Place the tomato on its side on a work surface. Holding the tomato stable with one hand, insert the tip of a paring knife about 1 inch into the tomato at an angle just outside the core. Move the paring knife with a sawing motion, at the same time rotating the tomato toward you until the core is cut free.

with one, the thought of its potential juicy tenderness and warmth is too tempting to pass up. We succumb to the hope that maybe this time the stuffed tomato will live up to its potential, only to be let down by the first bite into sodden mediocrity.

What irks us is that the stuffed tomato's singular components hold forth the promise

of perfection. What could be better than a ripe, sun-drenched summer tomato, garden-fresh herbs, garlicky bread crumbs, and a sprightly bite of sharp cheese? When these elements are brought together into one vessel, however, their divinity dissipates. The once-buxom tomato becomes mealy and bland, and the flavor of the stuffing is drowned within the waterlogged texture of the bread. Determined to save this traditional dish from the bland and watery depths, we set out to prove that an oven-baked stuffed tomato can taste as good as we've always imagined.

We began testing by following the directions called for in most cookbook recipes: stuff a hollowed-out, raw beefsteak tomato with a bread crumb filling and bake it at 375 degrees for 30 minutes. The outcome was a soggy mess. The tomato was bland and watery, and the stuffing tasted dull and overly moist. What's more, the tomato seemed to lack the structural strength to keep the filling intact. We concluded that perhaps the same element

PEELING TOMATOES

Many recipes call for peeling fresh tomatoes. If left on, the peels can separate from the flesh and roll up into hard, unappetizing bits when the tomatoes are cooked. Here's how we peel tomatoes in the test kitchen.

1. Place cored tomatoes in a pot of boiling water, no more than 5 at a time. Boil until the skins split and begin to curl around the core area of the tomato, 15 seconds for very ripe tomatoes or up to 30 seconds for firmer, underripe ones. Remove the tomatoes from the water with a slotted spoon or mesh skimmer and place them in a bowl of ice water to stop the cooking process and cool the tomatoes.

2. With a paring knife, peel the skins using the curled edges at the core as your point of departure. The bowl of ice water serves a helpful second function—the skins will slide right off the blade of the knife if you dip the blade into the water.

EQUIPMENT: Large Skillets

Have you shopped for a skillet recently? The choices in material, weight, brand, and price—from $10 to $140—are dizzying. Preliminary tests on a lightweight discount store special selling for $10 confirmed our suspicions that cheap was not the way to go. But how much do you need to spend on this vital piece of kitchen equipment? To find out what more money buys, we zeroed in on a group of eight pans from well-known manufacturers, ranging in price from $60 to more than twice that, and sautéed our way to some pretty surprising conclusions.

All of the pans tested had flared sides, a design that makes it easier to flip foods in the pan (accomplished by jerking the pan sharply on the burner). Oddly, this design feature has created some confusion when it comes to nomenclature. Different manufacturers have different names for their flare-sided pans, including sauté pan, skillet, fry pan, chef's pan, and omelet pan. In the test kitchen, we refer to flare-sided pans as skillets and to pans with straight sides (and often lids as well) as sauté pans. All of the pans tested also fall into a category we refer to as traditional—that is, none of the pans were nonstick. Most had uncoated stainless-steel cooking surfaces, which we prize for promoting a fond (the brown, sticky bits that cling to the interior of the pan when food is sautéed and that help flavor sauces). We also included a Le Creuset model made from enameled cast iron.

The pans tested measured 12 inches in diameter (across the top) or as close to that as we could get from each manufacturer. We like this large size in a skillet because it can accommodate a big steak or all of the pieces cut from a typical 3½-pound chicken. Because the pan walls slope inward, the cooking surface of each pan measures considerably less than 12 inches. In fact, we found that even ¼ inch less cooking space could determine whether all of the chicken pieces fit without touching and therefore how well they would brown. (If a pan is too crowded, the food tends to steam rather than brown.) For instance, the All-Clad, with its 9¼-inch cooking surface, accommodated the chicken pieces without incident, whereas the 9-inch cooking surface of the Viking caused the pieces to touch.

Skillet construction also varies, and our group included the three most popular styles: clad, disk bottom, and cast. The All-Clad, Viking, Calphalon, Cuisinart, and KitchenAid units are clad, which means that the whole pan body, from the bottom up through the walls, is made from layers of the same metal that have been bonded under intense pressure and heat. These layers often form a sandwich, with the "filling" made of aluminum—which has the third highest thermal conductivity of all metals, behind silver and copper—and each slice of "bread" made of stainless steel—which is attractive, durable, and nonreactive with acidic foods but is a lousy heat conductor on its own.

In the disk-bottom construction style, only the pan bottom is layered, and the walls are thus thinner than the bottom. In our group, the Farberware has an aluminum sandwich base, and the Emerilware has disks of both aluminum and copper in its base.

Casting is the third construction style, represented here by Le Creuset, in which molten iron is molded to form the pan, body and handle alike. Cast-iron pans are known to be heavy, to heat up slowly, and to retain their heat well. The French Le Creuset pans are also enameled, which makes them nonreactive inside and out.

Did our testing uncover any significant differences in performance based on these three construction styles? Although some manufacturers tout the benefits of cladding, our kitchen testing did not support this. The two skillets with disk bottoms, the Farberware and the Emerilware, did heat up a little faster than the rest of the field, but it was easy to accommodate this difference by adjusting the stovetop burner. Both of these pans also performed well in cooking tests.

To get a more precise answer to our question, we set up an experiment. Around the perimeter of pans of each construction type (and in the lightweight $10 pan mentioned earlier), we placed rings of solder with a melting point of 361 degrees and heated them from dead center. Over the course of several trials, we averaged the time it took the pans to reach 361 degrees all around (that is, the time it took all of the solder beads to melt). The difference between the clad and disk-bottomed pans was less than 15 percent (they all reached 361 degrees in four to five minutes), with the disk-bottomed pans heating up a little faster than the clad pans. This difference was of little significance.

We checked our observations with an industry expert, who, after expressing the desire to remain anonymous, admitted to reaching the same conclusion about skillets after trying many different models over the years. Because you cook on the bottom of a skillet (not the sides), cladding is not that important. It may be more important in saucepans and Dutch ovens, in which it's common practice to cook liquids, which are of course in contact with the sides of the pan.

The weight of the pans turned out to be more important than construction, especially in our solder tests. The lightweight (1-pound, 1-ounce) aluminum budget pan was the quickest to reach 361 degrees, at an average of 2.8 minutes, while the heavy 6½-pound Le Creuset was the slowest, at an average of 10.1 minutes. The lightweight pan performed poorly in kitchen tests, while the Le Creuset did well. Still, cast iron does have its disadvantages. The heavy Le Creuset pan is difficult to lift on and off the burner and to handle while cleaning. If your strength is limited, these factors can mean a lot. In addition, the pan's iron handle gets just as hot as the rest of the pan, so it's necessary to use a potholder both during and just after use.

We concluded that a range of 3 to 4 pounds is ideal in a 12-inch skillet. The medium-weight pans (especially those from All-Clad, Viking, and Calphalon) brown foods beautifully, and most testers handled them comfortably. These pans have enough heft for heat retention and structural integrity but not so much that they are difficult to lift or manipulate.

Which skillet should you buy? For its combination of excellent performance, optimum weight and balance, and overall ease of use, the All-Clad was our favorite. But others, such as the Calphalon and Farberware, nearly matched the All-Clad in performance and good handling and did so for less than half the price, making these pans our two best buys.

THE BEST LARGE SKILLETS

The All-Clad Stainless 12-Inch Frypan (top) took top honors in our testing. The Calphalon Tri-Ply Stainless 12-Inch Omelette Pan (middle) and the Farberware Millennium 18/10 Stainless Steel 12-Inch Covered Skillet (bottom) were rated best buys, costing about half as much as the winning pan.

that lends majesty to a tomato—water—was the source of our failure.

Ridding the tomato of its excess liquid was our goal. At first, we tested oven drying, rationalizing that the slow, low heat would concentrate the tomato's sweetness and vaporize the water. The dried tomato was laden with rich flavor notes, but it was also shriveled and shrunken, a collapsed vessel that was in no condition to hold any stuffing.

We then decided that if we chose a tomato with a naturally lower water content, such as a plum tomato, we might eliminate the water issue altogether. While we did end up with a meaty and sweet stuffed tomato, it lacked the complexity of flavor that the

SLICING TOMATOES

Unless you have a very sharp knife, tomato skin can resist the knife edge, and the tomato becomes crushed. Here's a neat trick that starts with a cored tomato.

1. Use a paring knife to remove a strip of skin from the exposed core area down to the blossom end of the tomato.

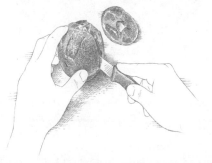

2. Slice the tomato along the skinned strip so that the knife does not have to cut through the skin before it can enter the tomato.

beefsteak possessed, and the effort required to stuff the smaller shell—coupled with the fact that we would have to make twice as many if we were substituting for beefsteak tomatoes—turned us off the plum variety.

Recalling how salt is used to sweat eggplant, we thought it might do the same for a tomato. We cored and seeded a beefsteak, rubbed salt into its interior, and placed it upside down on a stack of paper towels. Within 30 minutes, our dry paper towels had absorbed a tremendous amount of liquid. Dr. Bill Morris, professor in the University of Tennessee's department of food science and technology, explained that when we salted the interior of the tomato, water passed through the cells' semipermeable membranes, moving from the inside of the cells to the outside—in effect, draining the tomato of its excess juices. In addition, the salt brightened and enhanced the tomato's flavor.

Now that we had the moisture problem solved, we moved on to stuffing, baking times, and temperatures. For the stuffing, we tested store-bought bread crumbs, homemade bread crumbs made from stale French bread, and variations in the ratio of crumbs to cheese to herbs. The fine, store-bought crumbs were dry and gritty. Their homemade counterpart, on the other hand, absorbed the tomato's juices yet still provided an interesting chew and crunch, especially when paired with garlic, olive oil, and tangy Parmesan cheese.

Our previous oven-roasting experiment negated a low and long baking period, whereas experiments baking the tomato at an extremely high temperature (450 degrees) for a short time yielded burnt, crusty stuffing and a raw tomato. Baked at 375 degrees for 20 minutes, the tomatoes were tender and topped with a lovely golden crust. The result: a sweet—and savory—tomato triumph.

Master Recipe for Stuffed Tomatoes

SERVES 6 AS A SIDE DISH

To make homemade bread crumbs, grind any hunk of stale country, Italian, or French bread in the food processor. Use your fingers to gently pull the seeds from the cored tomatoes.

6	large (about 8 ounces each) firm, ripe tomatoes, $1/8$ inch sliced off the stem end, cored, and seeded
1	teaspoon kosher salt
$3/4$	cup coarse homemade bread crumbs
3	tablespoons plus 1 teaspoon olive oil
$1/3$	cup grated Parmesan cheese
$1/3$	cup chopped fresh basil leaves
2	medium cloves garlic, minced or pressed through a garlic press (about 2 teaspoons)
	Ground black pepper

1. Sprinkle the inside of each tomato with salt and place it upside down on several layers of paper towels. Let stand to remove any excess moisture, about 30 minutes.

2. Meanwhile, toss the bread crumbs with 1 tablespoon of the oil, Parmesan, basil, garlic, and pepper to taste in a small bowl; set aside. Adjust an oven rack to the upper-middle position and heat the oven to 375 degrees. Line the bottom of a 9 by 13-inch baking dish with foil.

3. Roll up several sheets of paper towels and pat the inside of each tomato dry. Arrange the tomatoes in a single layer in the baking dish. Brush the cut edges of the tomatoes with 1 teaspoon of the oil. Mound the stuffing into the tomatoes (about ¼ cup per tomato) and drizzle with the remaining 2 tablespoons oil. Bake until the tops are golden brown and crisp, about 20 minutes. Serve immediately.

➤ VARIATION

Stuffed Tomatoes with Pecorino Romano, Oregano, and Olives

Pecorino Romano is a hard grating cheese made from sheep's milk. Its pungent flavors complement the briny olives. If you like, substitute finely crumbled feta for the Pecorino.

Follow the master recipe, replacing the Parmesan and basil with ⅓ cup grated Pecorino Romano cheese, 2 tablespoons chopped fresh oregano leaves, and 12 black olives (such as Kalamatas), pitted and chopped.

SLOW-ROASTED TOMATOES

ROASTING FLAWLESS, VINE-RIPENED tomatoes with garlic and olive oil takes them to a new level of perfection; the tomato's juices are concentrated by the steady heat and become one with the garlic and herb-scented olive oil. As a relish for grilled meats or a topping for toasted bread, the dish is hard to beat. It is the distillation of summer in one easy-to-assemble and foolproof dish.

There are only five ingredients in this dish, and for the best results, each must be flawless. In other words, this is not a place to use pale, cardboardy supermarket tomatoes and cheap oil, as roasting merely magnifies their flaws. The tomatoes must be the best you can find, preferably from your local farmers' market—or your garden, if you are so lucky. In the heart of a New England winter, we used "vine-ripened" tomatoes from our gourmet market with some success, but we longed for the beauties of August, still warm from the sun's touch.

The oil should be the best you can find. We tried batches with varying oils, and the differences were profound; the best-quality oil was in a league of its own—heady with an herbaceous, peppery aroma and a taste that elevated the tomatoes beyond comparison. (For recommendations about brands of olive oil, see page 95.)

For flavoring the tomatoes, garlic and basil were the only choices, according to our tasters. Oregano, mint, thyme, and rosemary all seemed inappropriate in this circumstance. Slivered garlic fared better than minced and looked much more attractive, too. The fine slivers practically melted during the slow bake, reduced to sweet and slightly chewy tidbits.

As this is a rustic dish, hand-torn basil leaves were the logical choice. Because they shrivel to mere shadows of themselves in the oven, we left the pieces large and left small leaves whole. Layering the leaves on both top and bottom of the tomatoes guaranteed potent flavor.

For seasoning, coarse salt, like kosher or sea salt, was the unanimous choice of tasters, chosen for its crunchy texture and intense bursts of salinity. Regular table salt will do in a pinch, of course.

Preparation takes mere moments, but the roasting takes some time. These are not oven-dried tomatoes, which can take upward of eight hours in a tepid oven, but they are also not classic oven-roasted tomatoes, heat-shriveled to a near candy-like sweetness and intensity. Aiming for something in between, we set the baking temperature parameters between 300 and 400 degrees and began testing.

In a 400-degree oven, the garlic browned too quickly and turned acrid, ruining the dish. Erring on the side of caution, we lowered the temperature to 325 degrees and were pleased with the results. Within 1 ½ hours, the tomatoes were slightly wrinkled and touched with brown, but more important, their juices

had largely evaporated and been replaced by the olive oil. A lower temperature yielded no better-tasting results and took longer, so we stuck with 325 degrees.

Master Recipe for Slow-Roasted Tomatoes
SERVES 4 TO 6

For flavor and color contrast, feel free to mix and match varieties of tomatoes—Green Zebras, a relatively common heirloom variety, are stunning when interspersed with ruby-red beefsteaks. Use whatever tomatoes you can find, as long as they are flawlessly ripe. If you are left with a pool of olive oil in the pan, save it for flavoring a vinaigrette or brushing on bruschetta.

- ½ cup extra-virgin olive oil
- 4 medium cloves garlic, sliced thin
- 1 cup lightly packed fresh basil leaves, coarsely torn into large pieces
- 2 pounds vine-ripened tomatoes, cored and cut crosswise into ½-inch-thick slices
- 1 teaspoon coarse salt

1. Adjust an oven rack to the lower-middle position and heat the oven to 325 degrees. Lightly coat the bottom of a 9 by 13-inch baking dish with 2 tablespoons of the oil and evenly sprinkle half of the garlic and basil leaves across the bottom of the dish. Lay the tomato slices in the dish, overlapping the edges if necessary to fit. Cover the tomatoes with the remaining garlic, basil, and oil and sprinkle with the salt.

2. Roast until the tomatoes are slightly shriveled and their juices have been replaced with oil, about 1 ½ hours. Allow to cool at least 20 minutes or up to 1 hour before serving. Serve warm or at room temperature.

➤ VARIATION

Slow-Roasted Tomatoes with Parmesan and Balsamic Glaze

The sweet-tart flavors of the roasted tomatoes are highlighted by the balsamic glaze. Serve these as a side dish or as a topping for bruschetta.

Follow the master recipe, replacing the basil with 2 tablespoons chopped fresh oregano leaves. While the tomatoes are roasting, bring ⅓ cup balsamic vinegar to a boil in a small saucepan over medium-high heat. Reduce the heat and simmer until reduced to 3 tablespoons, about 7 minutes. Just before serving, drizzle the balsamic reduction over the tomatoes and sprinkle with ½ cup grated Parmesan cheese.

OVEN–DRIED TOMATOES

AS THE WAVE OF ITALIAN COOKING has swept over America, sun-dried tomatoes have become a staple in many kitchens. Although the original version of these flavorful, partially desiccated tomatoes was truly dried in the sun, these days most commercially dried tomatoes are prepared in dehydrators. We wanted to assess whether tomatoes could alternatively be dried in a home oven.

We also had a second goal for our testing. We were not interested in making a completely dry shelf-stable product. Rather, we wanted something plumper and moister. Although this partially dried tomato would have to be refrigerated and used quickly, it would have different uses—as a condiment and a sandwich ingredient.

When we began to research the subject, we found that the proper preparation of the tomatoes was a matter of some debate. Various authors claimed to have success with peeled and unpeeled, cored and uncored, seeded and unseeded, and sliced and halved tomatoes. Some sources even suggested stuffing with herbs and drizzling with olive oil. One of the only factors that everyone agreed on was that plum tomatoes are the best choice for drying, as they offer more meat and less moisture than round tomatoes. With that as a starting point, we began to test various drying methods.

Most home ovens cannot maintain temperatures below 150 degrees. We thought that this temperature would be best since dehydrators generally work at 125 to 135 degrees. We began with the easiest preparation procedure—halving the tomatoes lengthwise and placing them cut-side down on racks set on baking sheets. Unfortunately, this approach did not work. The combination of the very low oven temperature and the amount of moisture held within the tomatoes via the seeds and core prevented the tomatoes from giving off their moisture easily and evenly. As a result, it took nearly 12 hours to dry tomatoes.

We tried propping the oven door open for increased ventilation, cutting the tomatoes in slices, coring them, and cutting across the tomatoes rather than lengthwise. In most cases, the tomatoes dried fairly well up to a point, but there always seemed to be a pocket of moisture in the middle that never dried out. We tried peeling and seeding the tomatoes and finally got our first good results. But because peeling adds a step to this process, we pressed on.

Some helpful tips did surface as we played with preparation methods. Slicing the tomatoes in half lengthwise before coring them proved useful, as did scooping out all the seeds and gelatinous matter with a teaspoon. Piercing the skin with the tip of a sharp paring knife also yielded good results. Maybe we did not have to peel the tomatoes after all.

At this point, we started to reconsider our assumptions about oven temperature. Although higher temperatures seemed wrong, a couple of sources suggested 200 degrees. We also thought that placing a wire rack containing the tomatoes directly on the oven rack (with the baking sheet on the rack below) might increase air circulation.

We halved and seeded the tomatoes, pricked the skin, and then placed the tomatoes cut-side down on the rack. After three hours for smaller tomatoes and up to six hours for larger ones, they were perfect. The tomatoes were consistently dry with a nice texture and intense flavor. We tried higher temperatures to reduce the drying time, but this just cooked the tomatoes.

Master Recipe for Oven-Dried Tomatoes

MAKES ABOUT 1 1/4 OUNCES
DRIED TOMATOES

Because these tomatoes need at least several hours in the oven, dry as many as possible at one time. Depending on your oven size, you can multiply the recipe, keeping in mind that drying times may increase. See the illustrations on page 294 for tips on seeding the tomatoes. Use these tomatoes in antipasto spread, on sandwiches, or in pasta sauces.

2   pounds plum tomatoes (as uniform in size as possible), halved lengthwise, cored, thoroughly seeded, and skin pricked 6 to 8 times with the point of a sharp knife

1. Adjust the oven racks to the middle and low positions and heat the oven to 200 degrees. Line a large baking sheet with aluminum foil.

2. Place the tomatoes cut-side down on a large wire rack. Set the wire rack on the middle oven rack and place the foil-lined tray on the lower rack. Dry for 3 to 6 hours, depending on the tomatoes' size and the desired texture. When they're dry and cool, place the tomatoes in an airtight container and refrigerate for up to 1 week.

TOMATO TART

FALLING SOMEPLACE IN BETWEEN pizza and quiche, tomato and mozzarella tart shares the flavors of both but features problems unique unto itself. For starters, this is not fast food, as some sort of pastry crust is required. Second, the moisture in the tomatoes almost guarantees a soggy crust. Third, tomato tarts are often tasteless, their spectacular open faces offering false promises. We wanted a recipe we could easily make at home with a solid bottom crust and great vine-ripened flavor.

The first thing we learned is that tomato and mozzarella tarts come in all shapes and sizes: everything from overwrought custardy pies resembling quiche to stripped-down, minimalist models that are more like pizza. A test kitchen sampling of these various styles delivered dismal results—sodden bottoms and tired toppings across the board—but we did agree that one recipe stood out: a simple construction of tomatoes and cheese shingled across a plain, prebaked sheet of puff pastry. Unwilling to make puff pastry from scratch (who is?), we grabbed some store-bought puff pastry and started cooking.

The winning recipe from the taste test consisted of a flat sheet of puff pastry with a thin border to contain the topping (tomatoes easily slip off a flat sheet of anything) and a thick glaze of egg wash to seal the dough tight against the seeping tomatoes. From a single rectangular sheet of pastry dough (we found Pepperidge Farm to be the most available;

two pieces of dough come in a single box), we trimmed thin strips of dough from the edges and cemented them with egg wash to the top of the sheet to create a uniform 1-inch border. This single tart shell looked large enough for two to three servings. With scarcely any more effort, we found we could serve twice as many by joining the two pieces of dough that came in the box (we sealed the seam tightly with egg wash and rolled it flat) and making

ASSEMBLING THE TART SHELL

1. Brush the beaten egg along one edge of one sheet of puff pastry. Overlap with a second piece of dough by 1 inch and press down to seal the pieces together.

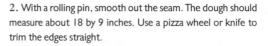

2. With a rolling pin, smooth out the seam. The dough should measure about 18 by 9 inches. Use a pizza wheel or knife to trim the edges straight.

3. With a pizza wheel or knife, cut a 1-inch strip from one long side of the dough. Cut another 1-inch strip from the same side.

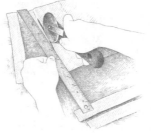

4. Cut a 1-inch strip from one short side of the dough. Cut another 1-inch strip from the same side. Transfer the large piece of dough to a parchment-lined baking sheet and brush with the beaten egg.

5. Gently press the long strips of dough onto each long edge of the dough and brush the strips with egg. Gently press the short strips of the dough onto each short edge and brush the strips with egg.

6. With a pizza wheel or knife, trim the excess dough from the corners.

GOOD TART, BAD TART

If you neglect to salt the tomatoes and brush the dough with egg wash, the baked tart will be soggy and limp (left). If you take both of these precautions (and add a layer of grated Parmesan), individual slices will be firm and dry and have enough structural integrity to hold their shape (right).

a long rectangular version (roughly 16 by 8 inches). Once assembled, the tart got a heavy brushing with beaten egg.

From the initial test results, we knew that prebaking the crust would be essential to give it a fighting chance against the moisture from the tomatoes. Following the recipe on the back of the Pepperidge Farm box, we baked the enlarged tart shell at 400 degrees until it was light, airy, and golden brown. Now we ran into our first problem. The shell was too frail to support a heavy, wet filling. Baked at 350 degrees, the shell was noticeably squatter and drier—and better suited to a heavy filling—but it was also unpleasantly tough and chewy. We wondered if a two-step baking method might be more successful: a high temperature for initial lift and browning and then a lower temperature to dry out the shell for maximum sturdiness. When started at 425 degrees (and held there until puffed and light golden, about 15 minutes) and finished at 350 degrees (and held there until well browned, 15 minutes longer), the crust was flaky yet rigid enough to hold it aloft while holding on to just one end.

Now we had half-solved the problem of the soggy crust, but there was still work to do. The egg wash coating had proven only

deflective, not impermeable. Liquid soaked through to the puff pastry, albeit at a slower rate than uncoated pastry. Egg wash was part of but not the whole solution.

Our next thought was that a layer of cheese might help. We gathered up a trio of mozzarellas for a tasting: fresh cow's milk, low-moisture part-skim cheese from the supermarket, and low-moisture whole-milk cheese, also shrink wrapped and from the supermarket. Fresh mozzarella won accolades for flavor, but its high moisture content rendered the crust mushy (even after pressing to extrude excess moisture). Part-skim mozzarella was deemed "a little bland," though its dry constitution fit the tart's needs. Whole-milk mozzarella packed a fuller, creamier flavor and most pleased tasters; it was clearly the best choice. A scant half pound of grated cheese melted into a smooth, seemingly watertight layer across the tart's bottom. When the entire tart was assembled and baked, the bottom crust was vastly improved, but the tomatoes still gave off too much water, which affected the texture of the crust and the overall flavor of the tart.

Our first thought was to use tomatoes with a relatively low water content. We limited our tests to standard beefsteak (round) and Roma (plum) tomatoes, as they are the two most readily available. A quick side-by-side test ruled out beefsteaks as excessively high in liquid. As we had suspected, Romas were the better choice for this recipe.

As for extracting the tomatoes' juices, roasting was an obvious choice, but we ruled it out as too time and labor intensive. Besides, we wanted the brighter flavor of lightly cooked tomatoes. Salting worked well but not perfectly. We sprinkled sliced tomatoes with salt and left them to drain on paper towels for 30 minutes. The underlying toweling was soaked through, but the tomatoes were still juicy to the touch. Increasing the amount of salt and time accomplished frustratingly little. A little gentle force, however, worked magic: We sandwiched the salted slices between paper towels and pressed down with enough force to extrude any remaining juices (and the seeds) but not enough to squish the slices flat. They were as dry as could be, yet still very flavorful.

Baked quick and hot to melt the cheese and preserve the tomatoes' meaty texture

(425 degrees turned out to be the best temperature), the tart looked ready for the cover of a magazine, especially when slicked with a garlic-infused olive oil and strewn with fresh basil leaves. But just a few minutes from the oven, the horrible truth revealed itself: The crust was soggy. Despite the egg wash, the melted mozzarella, and drained and pressed tomatoes, the tart continued to suffer the ills of moisture.

Discouraged but not undone, we kept turning the same image over in our minds: bits of hard-baked Parmesan cheese on bread sticks or those dreadful prebaked "pizza crusts." We wondered if a solid layer of crisply baked Parmesan, on top of the egg wash but beneath the mozzarella, would seal the base more permanently. We sprinkled finely grated Parmesan over the tart shell for the prebake and crossed our fingers. The cheese melted to such a solid (and deliciously nutty-tasting) layer that liquid rolled right off, like rain on a duck's back.

We assembled a whole tart and were stunned by the results: Slices could be lifted freely and consumed like pizza, even hours from the oven. Rich in flavor and sturdy in form, it had character to match its good looks—and it was quick, too. Ready-made dough and minimal ingredients kept preparation brief, and total cooking time was less than an hour and a half. This tart was not only better than we expected but also simpler.

Master Recipe for Tomato and Mozzarella Tart

SERVES 4 TO 6

The baked tart is best eaten warm within 2 hours of baking. If you prefer to do some advance preparation, the tart shell can be prebaked through step 1, cooled to room temperature, wrapped in plastic wrap, and kept at room temperature for up

to 2 days before being topped and baked with the mozzarella and tomatoes. Use a low-moisture, shrink-wrapped supermarket cheese rather than fresh mozzarella. To keep the frozen dough from cracking, it's best to let it thaw slowly in the refrigerator overnight.

Flour for the work surface

1   (1.1-pound) box frozen puff pastry (Pepperidge Farm), thawed in its box in the refrigerator overnight

1   large egg, beaten

½   cup finely grated Parmesan cheese

1   pound Roma tomatoes (about 3 to 4 medium), cored and cut crosswise into ¼-inch-thick slices
     Salt

2   medium cloves garlic, minced or pressed through a garlic press (about 2 teaspoons)

2   tablespoons extra-virgin olive oil
     Ground black pepper

8   ounces low-moisture whole-milk mozzarella, shredded (2 cups)

2   tablespoons coarsely chopped fresh basil leaves

1. Adjust an oven rack to the lower-middle position and heat the oven to 425 degrees. Dust the work surface with flour and unfold both pieces of puff pastry onto the work surface. Following the illustrations on page 303, form one large sheet with a border, using the beaten egg as directed. Sprinkle the Parmesan evenly over the bottom of the shell. Using a fork, uniformly and thoroughly poke holes in the bottom. Bake 15 minutes and then reduce the oven temperature to 350 degrees. Continue to bake until golden brown and crisp, 15 to 17 minutes longer. Transfer the baking sheet to a wire rack. Increase the oven temperature to 425 degrees.

2. While the shell bakes, place the tomato slices in a single layer on a double layer of paper towels and sprinkle evenly with ½ teaspoon salt; let stand 30 minutes. Place a second double layer of paper towels on top of the tomatoes and press firmly to dry the tomatoes. Combine the garlic, oil, and a pinch each of salt and pepper in a small bowl; set aside.

3. Sprinkle the mozzarella evenly over the bottom of the warm (or cool, if made ahead) baked shell. Shingle the tomato slices widthwise on top of the cheese (about 4 slices per row). Brush the tomatoes with the garlic oil.

4. Bake until the shell is deep golden brown and the cheese is melted, 15 to 17 minutes. Cool on a wire rack 5 minutes, sprinkle with the basil, slide onto a cutting board or serving platter, cut into pieces, and serve.

➤ VARIATIONS

Tomato and Mozzarella Tart with Prosciutto

Follow the master recipe, laying 2 ounces of thinly sliced prosciutto in a single layer on top of the mozzarella before arranging the tomato slices.

Tomato and Smoked Mozzarella Tart

Follow the master recipe, substituting 6 ounces smoked mozzarella for the whole-milk mozzarella.

Winter Squash

THERE ARE MANY WAYS TO COOK WINTER SQUASHES, BUT THE IDEAL method for one kind may not necessarily be best for another. We quickly discovered this when we set out to find the best way to cook the two most common winter squashes, acorn and butternut. After only a few tests, we found that they responded very differently. We figured that we should develop several basic cooking methods and recommend the best kinds of squash for each method.

One thing that all winter squashes have in common is that, counter to the current fashion for al dente vegetables, they must be cooked until well done to develop their sweetest flavor and smoothest texture. With this as the only given, we tried cooking various kinds of squash by microwaving, baking, roasting, steaming, and boiling to find what produced the best texture and flavor.

We began by microwaving a whole unpeeled butternut squash, on the off chance that ease of cooking and good taste would coincide. It worked—that is, the squash did cook—but it cooked unevenly, and we also found the taste too "seedy."

Next, we microwaved halved and seeded squashes, hoping this would produce a better result, but they did not fare well, either. The small end was always done before the large end, there were patches of raw squash in the center, and the flesh was watery. All in all, microwaving turned out to be a poor cooking method for squash.

So we tried a more traditional approach: baking squash halves. After some experimentation, we found that baking the unpeeled and seeded halves cut-side down gave a slightly better texture than cut-side up. We found it best to cook the squash on a foil-lined baking sheet that had been oiled. The oil promoted better browning and reduced the risk of sticking, and the foil made cleanup easy.

Although this method was a success, when we began thinking about serving the squash, we realized that a baked squash half was fine only if you could find relatively small squash. But what about those times when the market has only 3-pound butternut squash? Roasting chunks of peeled squash proved to be a much more successful way to cook such big squash.

We peeled the squash and cut it into 1-inch cubes, then we roasted it uncovered at varying oven temperatures. The squash became quite caramelized, with a good chewy texture and a much sweeter and more pronounced flavor. The ideal temperature turned out to be 425 degrees.

At lower temperatures, the squash was no better and took much longer to cook, and at higher temperatures, it burned on the outside before it was fully cooked inside. A few sources suggested parboiling the cubed squash in lightly salted water for five to six minutes until it was about half cooked and then roasting it. Squash cooked this way was rather bland, so we discarded this idea.

Since sautéing also caramelizes, we decided to try sautéing diced squash in butter and oil until it became lightly caramelized and tender. This process took about 20 minutes and produced very satisfactory squash. But we found the flavor not as deep as the roasted squash, and roasting also had the advantage of requiring less attention during cooking. Adding some liquid and seasonings to the pan, and thus turning the sauté into a braise, was an easy way to add more flavor to the squash. Braising became our third method for handling squash, along with roasting halves and roasting smaller peeled chunks of squash.

Finally, we tried pureeing squash. We prepared the squash for pureeing in two different ways: by boiling peeled cubes in lightly salted boiling water until they were tender and by steaming cubes over simmering water. Both methods took about the same amount of time, 15 minutes, and each method resulted in squash with good texture for pureeing, but steaming gave a somewhat stronger flavor. It seems that steaming concentrates the taste of squash, while boiling dilutes it. (We also tested putting slices of peeled fresh ginger in the water during steaming to see if it would flavor the squash, but the taste did not come through at all in the finished product.)

Once the squash was ready for pureeing, we tried mashing it with a food processor, an electric mixer, and a hand masher. Hand mashing produced a chunky puree that many tasters liked. The food processor gave the squash an ultrasmooth, silky consistency that was the test kitchen favorite.

CUTTING SQUASH

Winter squash are notoriously difficult to cut. Even the best chef's knives can struggle with their thick skins and odd shapes. We prefer to use a cleaver and mallet when trying to open a winter squash.

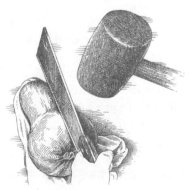

1. Set the squash on a damp kitchen towel to hold it in place. Position the cleaver on the skin of the squash.

2. Strike the back of the cleaver with a mallet to drive the cleaver deep into the squash. Continue to hit the cleaver with the mallet until the cleaver cuts through the squash and opens it up.

Master Recipe for Roasted Winter Squash Halves
SERVES 4

This recipe can be made with acorn, buttercup, butternut, kabocha, or delicata squash. The cooking time will vary depending on the kind of squash you use. Start checking for doneness after the first 30 minutes.

2   tablespoons extra-virgin olive oil
1   medium or 2 small winter squash
     (about 2 pounds total), halved
     lengthwise and seeded
     Salt and ground black pepper

1. Adjust an oven rack to the lower-middle position and heat the oven to 400 degrees. Line a rimmed baking sheet with aluminum foil. Brush the oil onto the foil and the cut sides of the squash. Place the squash, cut-side down, on the foil. Roast until a skewer inserted into the squash meets no resistance, 40 to 50 minutes.

2. Remove the squash from the oven and turn cut-sides up. If necessary, cut large pieces in half to yield four pieces. Season the squash with salt and pepper to taste and serve immediately.

➤ VARIATIONS
Roasted Winter Squash with Soy and Maple

Soy sauce and squash may sound like an unlikely combination, but the salty flavor of the soy sauce and the sweetness of the squash complement each other. This recipe works especially well with kabocha or acorn squash. Given the strong flavors of soy and maple, we find it best to brush the squash with vegetable oil, rather than olive oil, before it goes into the oven.

2   tablespoons vegetable oil
1   medium or 2 small winter squash
     (about 2 pounds total), halved
     lengthwise and seeded
3   tablespoons maple syrup
2   tablespoons soy sauce
1/2 teaspoon minced or
     grated fresh ginger
     Salt and ground black pepper

1. Adjust an oven rack to the lower-middle position and heat the oven to 400 degrees. Line a rimmed baking sheet with aluminum foil. Brush the oil onto the foil and the cut sides of the squash. Place the squash, cut-side down, on the foil. Roast until a skewer inserted into the squash meets no resistance, 40 to 50 minutes.

2. While the squash is in the oven, mix the maple syrup, soy sauce, and ginger together in a small bowl.

3. Remove the squash from the oven and turn cut-sides up. Brush the cut sides of the squash with the maple-soy mixture and return the squash to the oven. Roast

until the cut sides of the squash begin to caramelize, about 5 minutes. Remove the squash from the oven. If necessary, cut large pieces in half to yield four pieces. Season the squash with salt and pepper to taste and serve immediately.

Roasted Winter Squash with Brown Butter and Sage

The warm flavors of sage and winter squash complement each other beautifully. Serve with roast turkey or chicken.

2	tablespoons extra-virgin olive oil
1	medium or 2 small winter squash (about 2 pounds total), halved lengthwise and seeded
6	tablespoons unsalted butter
6	medium sage leaves, sliced thin
	Salt and ground black pepper

1. Adjust an oven rack to the lower-middle position and heat the oven to 400 degrees. Line a rimmed baking sheet with aluminum foil. Brush the oil onto the foil and the cut sides of the squash. Place the squash, cut-side down, on the foil. Roast until a skewer inserted into the squash meets no resistance, 40 to 50 minutes.

2. When the squash is almost done, place the butter in a small skillet over medium heat. When the butter melts, add the sage and cook, swirling the pan occasionally, until the butter is golden brown and the sage is crisp, 4 to 5 minutes. Remove the skillet from the heat.

3. Remove the squash from the oven and turn cut-sides up. If necessary, cut large pieces in half to yield four pieces. Season the squash with salt and pepper to taste, drizzle with the sage butter, and serve immediately.

Master Recipe for Braised Winter Squash
SERVES 4

This simple recipe is a great way to cook squash quickly. Braise the squash until it just begins to fall apart and absorb the juicy braising liquid. The recipe is best with butternut, buttercup, delicata, or kabocha squash. Cooking times may differ depending on the type of squash you are using.

2	tablespoons unsalted butter
1	medium shallot, minced
2	pounds winter squash, peeled, seeded, and cut into 1-inch cubes
1/2	cup low-sodium chicken broth
1	teaspoon minced fresh thyme leaves
	Salt and ground black pepper

Heat the butter in a Dutch oven or large saucepan over medium-high heat. When the foaming subsides, add the shallot and cook, stirring occasionally, until golden, about 4 minutes. Add the squash, broth, thyme, and salt and pepper to taste. Stir, cover, reduce the heat to medium, and cook until the squash is very tender, 16 to 20 minutes. Adjust the seasonings, adding salt and pepper to taste. Serve immediately.

➤ VARIATION
Braised Winter Squash with Asian Flavors

Kabocha is often used in braises and stews in Asian cooking and is the most traditional choice.

2	tablespoons vegetable oil
1	small onion, diced
2	pounds winter squash, peeled, seeded, and cut into 1-inch cubes
1/2	cup low-sodium chicken broth
1	tablespoon soy sauce

1   tablespoon mirin
    Salt and ground black pepper
1   medium scallion, sliced thin

Heat the oil in a Dutch oven or large sauce-pan over medium-high heat until almost smoking. Add the onion and cook, stirring occasionally, until golden, about 4 minutes. Add the squash, broth, soy sauce, mirin, and salt and pepper to taste. Bring to a simmer, cover, and reduce the heat to medium-low. Simmer until the squash is tender, 16 to 20 minutes. Remove the lid and simmer until the liquid thickens, 2 to 3 minutes. Adjust the seasonings, adding salt and pepper to taste. Sprinkle with the scallion and serve immediately.

Master Recipe for Roasted Winter Squash Pieces

SERVES 4

Peeled and cut squash pieces (usually butternut) are available in the produce section of most grocery stores. It is preferable to peel and cut your own, but if you are short on time, the bagged variety is an acceptable substitute. One whole 2-pound squash yields about 1½ pounds of trimmed pieces. This recipe is best with butternut, buttercup, or kabocha squash. If peeling the squash yourself, use a heavy-duty vegetable peeler that will remove a thick layer of the skin and the tough greenish flesh right below the skin (see page 93 for details on our testing of peelers). With most squash, it's easiest to cut the squash in half, remove the seeds, and then start peeling.

2   pounds winter squash, peeled, seeded, and cut into 1-inch cubes
1   medium shallot, minced
2   tablespoons extra-virgin olive oil
2   teaspoons minced fresh thyme leaves
    Salt and ground black pepper

REMOVING SQUASH SEEDS

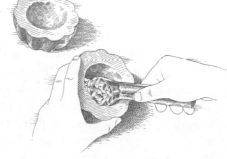

Use an ice cream scoop with a curved bowl to cut out all the seeds and strings without damaging the flesh. Because the edge on this kind of scoop is very sharp, it cuts easily, and because the scoop is larger than a spoon, it can remove more seeds in a single swipe.

Adjust an oven rack to the lower-middle position and heat the oven to 425 degrees. Toss the squash, shallot, oil, thyme, and salt and pepper to taste in a large bowl. Spread the squash pieces on a rimmed baking sheet large enough to hold them without crowding. Roast, shaking the pan every 10 minutes, until the squash is tender and evenly browned, 25 to 35 minutes. Adjust the seasonings, adding salt and pepper to taste. Serve immediately.

➤ VARIATION
Roasted Winter Squash Pieces with Parsley, Sage, Rosemary, and Thyme

This isn't just a great song, it's also a delicious combination of herbs. To preserve the parsley's fresh flavor, add it at the end of the recipe. Serve with roast chicken or turkey.

2   pounds winter squash, peeled, seeded, and cut into 1-inch cubes
2   tablespoons extra-virgin olive oil
1   teaspoon minced fresh thyme leaves
1   teaspoon minced fresh sage leaves
½   teaspoon minced fresh rosemary

Salt and ground black pepper

1 tablespoon minced fresh parsley leaves

Adjust an oven rack to the lower-middle position and heat the oven to 425 degrees. Toss the squash, oil, thyme, sage, rosemary, and salt and pepper to taste in a large bowl. Spread the squash pieces on a rimmed baking sheet large enough to hold them without crowding. Roast, shaking the pan every 10 minutes, until the squash is tender and evenly browned, 25 to 35 minutes. Stir in the parsley and adjust the seasonings, adding salt and pepper to taste. Serve immediately.

Master Recipe for Pureed Winter Squash

SERVES 4

This works best with butternut squash. If you prefer a chunkier puree, use a potato masher instead of a food processor.

STORING HARDY HERBS

In plastic containers with tight lids, stack the clean, dry herbs in loose layers separated by parchment paper or paper towels to allow for maximum air flow, then seal tightly. Smaller amounts of herbs can be placed in food storage bags.

2 pounds winter squash, peeled, seeded, and cut into 1-inch chunks

2 tablespoons unsalted butter, melted

2 tablespoons heavy cream

  Salt and ground black pepper

1. Bring about 1 inch of water to a boil over high heat in a large saucepan or Dutch oven set up with a wire rack, steamer, or pasta insert. Add the squash, cover, and return the water to a boil. Reduce the heat to medium-high and steam until the squash is tender, about 30 minutes.

2. Transfer the squash to the workbowl of a food processor. Pulse until the squash is smooth, about ten 1-second pulses, scraping down the sides of the workbowl as necessary. Add the melted butter and heavy cream and pulse 5 more times or until incorporated. Season to taste with salt and pepper and serve immediately.

VARIATION

Winter Squash Puree with Chinese Spices

Chinese five-spice powder is a combination of cinnamon, cloves, fennel seed, star anise, and Sichuan peppercorns. It can be found in the spice section or Asian food section of most large supermarkets.

Follow the master recipe, adding ¼ teaspoon Chinese five-spice powder along with the butter and cream.

ZUCCHINI & SUMMER SQUASH

GARDENS OVERFLOW WITH ZUCCHINI AND OTHER SUMMER SQUASH EVERY summer, but cooks are often at a loss for ideas for using this bounty. The biggest problem that confronts the cook when preparing zucchini is its wateriness. This vegetable is about 95 percent water and becomes soupy if just thrown into a hot pan. If zucchini cooks in its own juices, it won't brown—and because it is fairly bland, zucchini really benefits from browning. Clearly, some of the water must be removed before sautéing.

The first precautions against wateriness must take place in the supermarket. Size and firmness are the most important factors when purchasing zucchini.

After extensive testing, we found that smaller zucchini are more flavorful and less watery. Smaller zucchini also have fewer seeds. Look for zucchini no larger than 8 ounces and preferably just 6 ounces each. Mammoth zucchini may look impressive in the garden (or supermarket), but they will only cause problems in the kitchen.

Even if you've bought small zucchini, you still need to remove moisture before cooking them. Many sources recommend salting sliced zucchini before cooking. We tested salting to draw off some water and found that sliced and salted zucchini sheds about 20 percent of its weight after sitting for 30 minutes. One pound of sliced zucchini threw off almost 3 tablespoons of liquid, further confirmation that salting works. We tested longer periods and found that little additional moisture is extracted after 30 minutes.

Given that you don't always have 30 minutes, we wanted to develop quicker methods for cooking zucchini. We tried shredding the zucchini on the large holes of a box grater and then squeezing out excess water by hand. We were able to reduce the weight of shredded zucchini by 25 percent by wrapping it in paper towels and squeezing until dry. Because sliced zucchini has so much less surface area than shredded zucchini, the process works much more efficiently with the latter.

We also tried extracting moisture from shredded zucchini by placing it in batches in a potato ricer fitted with a very fine disk. This method was equally effective at removing moisture but tended to bruise the zucchini. Stick with paper towels.

Another quick-prep option is the grill. The intense heat quickly expels excess moisture in zucchini, and that moisture harmlessly drops down onto the coals rather than sitting in the pan. We found that so much evaporation occurs during grilling that neither salting nor shredding is necessary.

Pattypan squash (also known as custard squash or scallop squash) are characterized by their starburst shape and scalloped edges. While zucchini and other summer squash, such as the yellow crookneck, can be prepared and cooked in the same fashion, pattypan are meatier and require some different approaches. It seems a shame to finely chop or slice these squash. We wanted to cut them into larger pieces and thus retain their pretty shape.

We tried steaming and boiling the squash—

SHREDDING ZUCCHINI AND SUMMER SQUASH

1. For quick indoor cooking, shred trimmed zucchini or squash on the large holes of a box grater or in a food processor fitted with the shredding disk.

2. Wrap the shredded zucchini or squash in paper towels and squeeze out excess liquid. Proceed immediately with sautéing.

two common methods touted in many sources as the best way to preserve their flavor and shape—but we had poor results. Even though pattypan are not as watery as zucchini and other summer squash, they don't respond well to a moist-heat cooking. Grilling is out because of their odd shape (they can easily fall through the grate onto the coals), and sautéing also can be problematic unless you cut them into very small pieces. We had the best results with roasting. Coating the squash pieces with olive oil and roasting them at 425 degrees brought out their natural sweetness.

Master Recipe for Shredded Zucchini or Summer Squash

SERVES 4

This recipe is best when you're pressed for time and want to cook zucchini indoors. If you like, replace one of the zucchini with two medium carrots that have been peeled and shredded on the large holes of a box grater—there's no need to squeeze the carrots dry.

3   tablespoons extra-virgin olive oil

4   medium zucchini or summer squash (about 1 1/2 pounds), trimmed, shredded, and squeezed dry (see the illustrations at left)

3   medium cloves garlic, minced or pressed through a garlic press

2   tablespoons minced fresh parsley, basil, mint, tarragon, or chives
     Salt and ground black pepper

Heat the oil in a large nonstick skillet over medium-high heat until almost smoking. Add the zucchini and garlic and cook, stirring occasionally, until tender, about 7 minutes. Stir in the herb and salt and pepper to taste. Serve immediately.

✗ VARIATIONS

Sautéed Shredded Zucchini or Summer Squash with Sweet Corn and Chives

This recipe also works with frozen corn—just defrost the corn and add it during the last minute or two of the cooking time.

3	tablespoons unsalted butter
1	medium shallot, minced
4	medium zucchini or summer squash (about 1 ½ pounds), trimmed, shredded, and squeezed dry (see the illustrations on page 314)
2	medium ears sweet corn, kernels cut away with a knife (about 1 ¼ cups)
1	tablespoon minced fresh chives Salt and ground black pepper

Heat the butter in a large nonstick skillet over medium-high heat. When the foaming subsides, add the shallot and cook, stirring occasionally, until soft, 2 to 3 minutes. Add the zucchini and corn and cook, stirring occasionally, until tender, about 7 minutes. Stir in the chives and salt and pepper to taste. Serve immediately.

Spicy Sautéed Shredded Zucchini or Summer Squash with Anchovy

Anchovies (when used in moderation) add a deep, salty flavor without any hint of fishiness.

3	tablespoons extra-virgin olive oil
3	medium cloves garlic, minced or pressed through a garlic press
¼	teaspoon hot red pepper flakes
2	medium anchovy fillets
4	medium zucchini or summer squash (about 1 ½ pounds), trimmed, shredded, and squeezed dry (see the illustrations on page 314) Salt and ground black pepper

Heat the oil in a large nonstick skillet over medium-high heat until almost smoking. Add the garlic, pepper flakes, and anchovies and cook, mashing the anchovies into the oil, until fragrant, about 30 seconds. Add the zucchini and cook, stirring occasionally, until tender, about 7 minutes. Add salt and pepper to taste. Serve immediately.

✗ Sautéed Zucchini or Summer Squash
SERVES 4

If you want browned zucchini, you must salt it before cooking. Salting drives off excess water and helps the zucchini sauté rather than stew in its own juices. Coarse kosher salt does the best job of driving off liquid and can be wiped away without rinsing. Do not add more salt when cooking or the dish will be too salty.

4	medium zucchini or summer squash (about 1 ½ pounds), trimmed and sliced crosswise into ¼-inch-thick rounds
1	tablespoon kosher salt
3	tablespoons extra-virgin olive oil
1	small onion, minced
1	teaspoon grated zest and 1 tablespoon juice from 1 lemon
1–2	tablespoons minced fresh parsley, basil, mint, tarragon, or chives Ground black pepper

1. Place the zucchini slices in a colander and sprinkle with the salt. Set the colander over a bowl until about ⅓ cup water drains from the zucchini, about 30 minutes. Remove the zucchini from the colander and pat dry with a clean kitchen towel or several paper towels, wiping off any remaining crystals of salt.

2. Heat the oil in a large skillet over medium heat. Add the onion and cook until

almost softened, about 3 minutes. Increase the heat to medium-high and add the zucchini and lemon zest. Cook until the zucchini is golden brown, about 10 minutes. Stir in the lemon juice and herb and season with pepper to taste. Serve immediately.

> VARIATION

Sautéed Zucchini or Summer Squash with Olives and Oregano

Follow the master recipe, adding ¼ cup chopped Kalamata olives with the lemon juice and use 1 teaspoon minced fresh oregano leaves as the herb.

Master Recipe for Grilled Zucchini or Summer Squash

SERVES 4

Excess water evaporates over hot coals, so salting the zucchini before cooking is not necessary. If you like, drizzle the zucchini with a little balsamic vinegar just before serving.

4	medium zucchini or summer squash (about 1 ½ pounds), trimmed and sliced lengthwise into ½-inch-thick strips (see the illustrations on page 317)
2	tablespoons extra-virgin olive oil Salt and ground black pepper

1. Lay the zucchini slices on a large baking sheet and brush both sides with the oil. Sprinkle generously with salt and pepper to taste.

2. Grill the zucchini over a medium-hot fire (you should be able to hold your hand 5 inches above the cooking grate for 3 to 4 seconds), turning once, until marked with dark stripes, 8 to 10 minutes. Serve hot, warm, or at room temperature.

Master Recipe for Roasted Pattypan Squash

Choose squash that are 3 inches or smaller in diameter; as the squash gets larger, it will lose its buttery flavor.

1 ½	pounds pattypan squash, stem ends trimmed and halved (or quartered if large)
2	tablespoons extra-virgin olive oil
1	medium clove garlic, minced or pressed through a garlic press Salt and ground black pepper
1	tablespoon minced fresh parsley or chives

Adjust an oven rack to the lower-middle position and heat the oven to 425 degrees. Toss the squash, oil, garlic, and salt and pepper to taste together in a large bowl. Arrange the squash on a rimmed baking sheet and roast until lightly browned and tender, about 20 minutes. Sprinkle with the parsley or chives and adjust the seasonings, adding salt and pepper to taste. Serve immediately.

> VARIATION

Roasted Pattypan Squash with Shallot, Lemon, and Parmesan

Serve this preparation along with fish or pasta. Feel free to use basil, mint, chives, chervil, or tarragon in place of the parsley.

1 ½	pounds pattypan squash, stem ends trimmed and halved (or quartered if large)
3	tablespoons extra-virgin olive oil
1	medium shallot, minced Salt and ground black pepper
1	tablespoon minced fresh parsley leaves
1	teaspoon grated zest and 1 teaspoon juice from 1 lemon

2   teaspoons honey

¼   cup grated Parmesan cheese

1. Adjust an oven rack to the lower-middle position and heat the oven to 425 degrees. Toss the squash, 2 tablespoons of the oil, shallot, and salt and pepper to taste together in a large bowl. Arrange the squash on a rimmed baking sheet (save the bowl for later use) and roast until lightly browned and tender, about 20 minutes.

2. Mix the remaining 1 tablespoon oil, parsley, lemon zest and juice, and honey together in the reserved bowl. Add the roasted squash and toss to combine. Adjust the seasonings, adding salt and pepper to taste. Sprinkle with the cheese and serve immediately.

SUMMER SQUASH SAUCES FOR PASTA

THE PAIRING OF PASTA AND ZUCCHINI or summer squash sounds like the perfect marriage. This common recipe is light and healthy, and it's a great way to make use of the abundance of squash in your garden or at farmers' markets at this time of year. For most of us, however, this promise of ideal matrimony is likely to end in divorce. The pasta and the squash are bland, and the squash is often so watery that it quickly turns to mush. The resulting dish has no flavor and little texture.

From early tests, we realized that the squash would have to be salted before cooking in order to rid it of excess moisture. We salted a pound of sliced squash and let it sit in a colander nestled in a bowl. Thirty minutes later, the squash had released almost 3 tablespoons of liquid—a promising sign. We blotted the squash dry with paper towels and, not wanting to take up any method that would add back water, decided to sauté this batch. Bingo: Browned squash came out of the pan.

Extra-virgin olive oil was an obvious addition to this dish, as was garlic. The oil helped coat the pasta with sauce, and the garlic added a pungent bite. Tasters also gave a thumbs-up to fresh, halved grape tomatoes, added after cooking, for their sweetness and color. Fresh chopped herbs, in the form of basil or parsley or mint, were another winning ingredient, adding still more color as well as their clean and pungent flavors. Pepper flakes added a subtle dimension of heat and pine nuts a light, toasty crunch.

SLICING ZUCCHINI OR SUMMER SQUASH FOR THE GRILL

1. Cut a thin slice from each end of the zucchini or summer squash. Slice the trimmed squash lengthwise into ½-inch-thick strips.

2. You may want to trim the peel from the outer slices so they match the others. (You can do the same thing with outer eggplant slices.) Besides developing more attractive grill marks, the flesh cooks better when directly exposed to the heat.

Tasters also approved of a handful of grated Parmesan or crumbled goat cheese or feta cheese. But something was still lacking; the dish had yet to escape from the realm of bland. We tried a batch with a few tablespoons of balsamic vinegar. This was the ingredient that transformed the marriage of pasta and squash into something extraordinary. We experimented with other acidic ingredients and found that lemon juice and red wine vinegar succeeded as well.

As for the pasta, we found fresh too delicate and limp for the chunky squash and so focused on dried. Long noodles were not a good match; the squash sat on top of them like a cat on a pillow. Convinced that chunkier shapes would better suit the squash, providing more balanced mouthfuls, we tested fusilli, shells, orecchiette, mezze rigatoni, penne, cavatappi, and farfalle. Everyone in the test kitchen was surprised to learn that farfalle was the hands-down favorite. This delicate pasta, with its shape reminiscent of a bow tie or a butterfly, was ideal, trapping bits of the flavor-packed ingredients and adding lightness to the dish. Finally, a match made in heaven.

Pasta and Squash with Tomatoes, Basil, and Pine Nuts

SERVES 4 TO 6 AS A MAIN DISH

Make sure to use medium squash—larger ones have too many seeds for this recipe. Kosher salt works best for salting the squash, because residual grains are easily wiped away. Toast the nuts in a small dry skillet over medium-low heat until lightly browned and fragrant, about 4 minutes.

5	medium zucchini and/or summer squash (about 2 pounds), trimmed, halved lengthwise, and sliced crosswise into ½-inch-thick rounds
	Kosher salt
I	pound farfalle
5	tablespoons extra-virgin olive oil
3	medium cloves garlic, minced or pressed through a garlic press (about I tablespoon)
½	teaspoon hot red pepper flakes
I	pint grape tomatoes, each tomato halved
½	cup packed chopped fresh basil leaves
2	tablespoons balsamic vinegar
¼	cup pine nuts, toasted
	Grated Parmesan cheese

1. Place the squash slices in a colander and sprinkle with 1 tablespoon salt. Set the colander over a bowl until about ⅓ cup water drains from the slices, about 30 minutes. Remove the slices from the colander and pat dry with a clean kitchen towel or several paper towels, wiping off any remaining crystals of salt.

2. Bring 4 quarts of water to a boil, covered, in a stockpot. Add 2 tablespoons salt and the pasta, stir to separate, and cook until al dente. Drain and return the pasta to the stockpot.

3. While the pasta is cooking, heat 1 tablespoon of the oil in a 12-inch nonstick skillet over high heat until almost smoking; swirl to coat the pan. Add half of the squash and cook, stirring occasionally, until golden brown and slightly charred, 5 to 7 minutes; transfer to a baking sheet or large plate. Add 1 tablespoon of the oil to the skillet, swirl to coat the pan, and repeat with the remaining squash. Return the empty skillet to medium-high heat, add 1 tablespoon of the oil, and swirl to coat the pan. Add the garlic and pepper flakes and cook until fragrant, about 10 seconds. Return the squash to the skillet and stir well to combine and heat through, about 30 seconds.

4. Add the squash mixture, the remaining 2 tablespoons oil, tomatoes, basil, vinegar, and pine nuts to the pasta in the stockpot and toss to combine. Adjust the seasonings, adding salt and pepper flakes, if necessary. Serve immediately, passing the cheese separately.

INGREDIENTS: Dried Pasta

In the not-so-distant past, American pasta had a poor reputation, and rightly so. It cooked up gummy and starchy, and experts usually touted the superiority of Italian brands. We wondered if this was still the case.

To find out, we tasted eight leading brands of spaghetti four American and four Italian. American brands took two of the three top spots, while two Italian brands landed at the bottom of the rankings. It seems that American companies have mastered the art of making pasta.

American-made Ronzoni was the top finisher, with tasters praising its "nutty, buttery" flavor and superb texture. Mueller's, another American brand, took third place. Tasters liked its "clean," "wheaty" flavor.

DeCecco was the highest-scoring Italian brand, finishing second in the tasting. It cooked up "very al dente" (with a good bite) and was almost chewy. Other Italian brands did not fare quite so well. Martelli, an artisanal pasta that costs nearly $5 a pound, finished in next-to-last place, with comments like "gritty" and "mushy" predominating on tasters' score sheets. Another Italian brand, Delverde, sank to the bottom of the ratings.

Our conclusion: Save your money and don't bother with most imported pasta—American brands are just fine. If you must serve Italian pasta in your home, stick with DeCecco.

THE BEST PASTA

Ronzoni won tasters over with its firm texture and nutty, buttery flavor.

Pasta and Squash with Tomatoes, Capers, and Goat Cheese

SERVES 4

Given the large amount of capers in this recipe, it's best to rinse them to remove excess salt.

5	medium zucchini and/or summer squash (about 2 pounds), trimmed, halved lengthwise, and sliced crosswise into $1/2$-inch-thick rounds
	Kosher salt
1	pound farfalle
5	tablespoons extra-virgin olive oil
3–4	large shallots, chopped fine (about 1 cup)
$1/4$	cup capers, rinsed and coarsely chopped
2	teaspoons grated zest and 2 tablespoons juice from 1 lemon
$1/2$	teaspoon ground black pepper
1	pint grape tomatoes, each tomato halved
$1/4$	cup chopped fresh parsley leaves
4	ounces goat cheese, crumbled (about 1 cup)

1. Place the squash slices in a colander and sprinkle with 1 tablespoon salt. Set the colander over a bowl until about ⅓ cup water drains from the slices, about 30 minutes. Remove the slices from the colander and pat dry with a clean kitchen towel or several paper towels, wiping off any remaining crystals of salt.

2. Bring 4 quarts of water to a boil, covered, in a stockpot. Add 2 tablespoons salt and the pasta, stir to separate, and cook until al dente. Drain and return the pasta to the stockpot.

3. While the pasta is cooking, heat 1 tablespoon of the oil in a 12-inch nonstick skillet over high heat until almost smoking; swirl to coat the pan. Add half of the squash and cook, stirring occasionally, until golden brown and

319

slightly charred, 5 to 7 minutes; transfer to a baking sheet or large plate. Add 1 tablespoon of the oil to the skillet, swirl to coat the pan, and repeat with the remaining squash. Return the empty skillet to medium-high heat, add 1 tablespoon of the oil, and swirl to coat the pan. Add the shallots and cook, stirring frequently, until softened and browned, about 1 minute. Add the capers, lemon zest, pepper, and squash to the skillet and cook, stirring constantly, until combined and heated through, about 30 seconds.

4. Add the squash mixture, the remaining 2 tablespoons oil, lemon juice, tomatoes, and parsley to the pasta in the stockpot and toss to combine. Adjust the seasonings, adding salt and pepper, if necessary. Serve immediately, sprinkling individual bowls with a portion of the cheese.

Pasta and Squash with Tomatoes, Olives, and Feta

SERVES 4

Choose a feta that's not overly salty for this recipe.

5	medium zucchini and/or summer squash (about 2 pounds), trimmed, halved lengthwise, and sliced crosswise into 1/2-inch-thick rounds
	Kosher salt
1	pound farfalle
5	tablespoons extra-virgin olive oil
1	small red onion, chopped fine (about 1 cup)
3	medium cloves garlic, minced or pressed through a garlic press (about 1 tablespoon)
1	teaspoon grated zest and 1 tablespoon juice from 1 lemon
1/2	teaspoon ground black pepper
1	pint grape tomatoes, each tomato halved
1/4	cup chopped fresh mint leaves
2	teaspoons red wine vinegar
1/2	cup pitted and quartered Kalamata olives
4	ounces feta cheese, crumbled (about 3/4 cup)

1. Place the squash slices in a colander and sprinkle with 1 tablespoon salt. Set the colander over a bowl until about 1/3 cup water drains from the slices, about 30 minutes. Remove the slices from the colander and pat dry with a clean kitchen towel or several paper towels, wiping off any remaining crystals of salt.

2. Bring 4 quarts of water to a boil, covered, in a stockpot. Add 2 tablespoons salt and the pasta, stir to separate, and cook until al dente. Drain and return the pasta to the stockpot.

3. While the pasta is cooking, heat 1 tablespoon of the oil in a 12-inch nonstick skillet over high heat until almost smoking; swirl to coat the pan. Add half of the squash and cook, stirring occasionally, until golden brown and slightly charred, 5 to 7 minutes; transfer to a baking sheet or large plate. Add 1 tablespoon of the oil to the skillet, swirl to coat the pan, and repeat with the remaining squash. Return the empty skillet to medium-high heat, add 1 tablespoon of the oil, and swirl to coat the pan. Add the onion and cook, stirring frequently, until softened and browned, about 3 minutes. Add the garlic, lemon zest, and pepper and cook until fragrant, about 10 seconds. Return the squash to the skillet and cook, stirring constantly, until combined and heated through, about 30 seconds.

4. Add the squash mixture, the remaining 2 tablespoons oil, lemon juice, tomatoes, mint, vinegar, and olives to the pasta in the stockpot and toss to combine. Adjust the seasonings, adding salt and pepper, if necessary. Serve immediately, sprinkling individual bowls with a portion of the cheese.

Vegetable Soups

SOUPS ARE A GREAT WAY TO USE MANY VEGETABLES TOGETHER IN A single dish. Although you can make wonderful single-vegetable soups (such as cream of tomato or hearty mushroom), our goal here was to create two multiveg-etable soups—one lighter in style and appropriate for the spring; the other more substantial and better for fall and winter. For both recipes, we wanted to start with prepared broth rather than homemade stock—we did not want these soups to require so much effort. For the results of our taste-test of chicken broths, see page 325. For the results of our taste-test of vegetable broths, see page 328.

Spring Vegetable Soup

VEGETABLE SOUP IS A WELCOME SUPPER any time of year. But as warm weather arrives in spring, we find ourselves hungry for vegetable soup that, unlike the hearty stew-like soups of winter, offers a light broth filled with delicate vegetables.

Vegetable soup has many interpretations. Some consider it inherently vegetarian, while others depend on beef bones and meat for flavor. Many recipes go for something clear and brothy, while others aspire to a thickened puree. Some note the importance of cutting the vegetables into tiny, perfect cubes for the ultimate presentation.

As we began to research and cook up some of these recipes, problems arose. The purees turned out too heavy, and the lighter soups had the tinny taste of the canned broth we used to make them. The vegetarian soups were sweet and bland, while the addition of beef bones muscled all fresh flavors out of the way. As for the vegetables, most recipes simply packed in the standard, year-round varieties without paying much attention to fresh greens. What ultimately emerged from these many disappointments was a clear idea of the kind of soup we were after: It should be simple and clean tasting, and it should make use of tender greens. It should be light and fresh, yet substantial enough to serve as supper on a chilly night.

While most other soups rely on their main ingredients for flavor, character, and overall heft, we soon found that some veg-etables, including leeks, peas, and fresh spin-ach, are simply too delicate to carry this load alone. They are easily overcooked if sim-mered for too long, and their flavors can be overpowered at the drop of a hat. To make a good soup, these tender vegetables would need the support of a broth that was rich and multidimensional, not characterized by any single, distinctive flavor. To maintain the vegetables' delicate character, we focused on how to build a flavorful broth base that was not overly assertive.

We knew that one solution to this problem would be to make a rich, savory vegetable stock, but we couldn't justify the amount of time that would take. We tried using canned vegetable broths, but they were incredibly thin and sweet, with an overwhelming taste of celery. Beef stocks and broths gave the soup some heft, but they also imparted an unwanted meaty flavor that couldn't be quieted. Canned chicken broth, while not perfect, was promising, with a mellow and sturdy character. On its own, it wasn't nearly balanced or flavorful enough, but we figured it would work well with a little doctoring. Looking for a quick way to give the chicken broth a rounder, fuller vegetable flavor, we decided to borrow some techniques from previous test kitchen recipes for stock.

To start, we looked at our recipe for quick homemade chicken soup, which begins by cooking onions and chicken pieces covered, over low heat, to encourage them to release their flavor. Not wanting any more chicken flavor, we tried adding onions alone. The resulting broth was better but still not there. Looking to our vegetable stock recipe, with its diverse selection of ingredients, we began to realize that it would take more than just onions to help out this canned broth. Not wanting to cut or cook anything unnecessarily, we worked our way one by one through a variety of other vegetables, from carrots and celery to dried mushrooms and cauliflower. In the end, we found a core group of vegetables to be key. The hallowed trio of carrot, celery, and onion, with some extra help from shallots, leeks, and garlic, turned the boring canned chicken broth into something rich and satisfying. Parsley stems, a sprig of thyme, and a bay leaf also helped to reinforce the

overall flavor change from canned to fresh.

Now that we had decided on the vegetables for the broth, we wanted to streamline the process of making it. We tried using a food processor to cut the vegetables, but it produced a wholly inferior broth. The processed vegetables had a harsher edge and rougher flavor than those cut by hand. The blades of the food processor made for battered and torn vegetables, eliciting an off,

INGREDIENTS: Cooking Spray

Cooking sprays, most often used in low-fat cooking or to coat bakeware, have been around since the late 1950s. The convenient sprays consist of oil, soy lecithin, propellants, and sometimes silicone or grain alcohol. Under pressure, this combination of ingredients creates a stick-resistant spray that evenly distributes a minuscule amount of fat on a surface. We found that a light mist of oil made all the difference when sweating vegetables for soup broth. Larger amounts of oil turned the broth cloudy, and smaller amounts were difficult to measure and work with. Although we were wary of food that comes packaged in an aerosol can, the convenient spray made quick work of coating vegetables with a negligible amount of fat.

There are several types of cooking spray on the market, as well as self-serve pumps like the Quick Mist that allow you to dispense your oil of choice. While all of the sprays we tried worked well with our vegetable soup, we recommend avoiding any that are "flavored."

OLIVE OIL   PAM   QUICK MIST   CANOLA

acidic flavor from the onions, leeks, and shallots. After going back to chopping by hand, we realized how important it is to cut these vegetables into small pieces so they can cook and release their flavors more quickly. It may take a couple minutes longer to cut the vegetables by hand into petite pieces, but the resulting flavor and speedy cooking time are worth the extra effort.

Taking a cue from our other stock recipes, we tried cooking the vegetables lightly on their own first, in a process known as sweating, before covering them with the canned broth. The difference in flavor between this sweated broth and a broth in which the vegetables were simply simmered was dramatic. Once strained, the sweated vegetable broth had a full, round flavor, while the simmered broth tasted thin and one-dimensional. Sweating allows the vegetable cells to break down and release their flavor into the pot before the broth is even added. This process is a good way to get flavor into the broth without taking the time for a long simmer.

At this point, we went back and reexamined our initial thoughts about not using canned vegetable broth. Our flavor-boosting treatment, which had worked so well with canned chicken broth, did improve vegetable broth and make it suitable for use in a soup. Tasters were evenly divided between chicken broth and vegetable broth in this application.

Now that we had a flavorful broth, we could focus on the main characters of this soup: the vegetables. Not wanting to clutter the soup with vegetables that were inessential, we steered toward a simple, clean soup with tender green vegetables. Leeks, green peas, and baby spinach all made the cut quickly. Their delicate flavors, different shapes, and varying shades of green made for a balanced and elegant lineup. Although

chard, arugula, and asparagus are brightly colored and flavorful, their spicy, overpowering flavors and sulfuric aroma took over the otherwise delicate soup. Small, new red potatoes were a nice addition, giving the soup some body and a little variety in color. Scallions, celery, and carrots, on the other hand, managed only to crowd and distract.

Cooking the four finalists—leeks, peas, baby spinach, and red potatoes—was easy enough. The broth, still warm after being doctored and strained, was at just about the perfect temperature to poach this somewhat fragile foursome. The leeks and potatoes went in first, the spinach, peas, and herbs just before serving. The vegetables took well to this gentle cooking process, as the simmering broth brought out and reinforced the flavor of each. Garnished only with some chopped parsley and tarragon, the soup's fresh flavor is unmistakable.

Spring Vegetable Soup
MAKES ABOUT 2 QUARTS,
SERVING 4 TO 6

This soup uses canned chicken or vegetable broth as its base, but the broth is first doctored with vegetables and herbs to brighten and improve its flavor.

BROTH
1   medium carrot, minced
1   small celery rib, minced
2   medium onions, minced
1   medium shallot, minced
1   medium leek, white and light green parts only, minced
3   medium cloves garlic, unpeeled and crushed
    Vegetable cooking spray
7   cups low-sodium chicken or vegetable broth
1/4 teaspoon black peppercorns, crushed

1 bay leaf

1 sprig fresh thyme

5 parsley stems

SOUP

2 medium leeks, white and light green parts only, halved lengthwise, cut into 1-inch lengths, washed, and drained thoroughly

6 small Red Bliss potatoes (about 9 ounces), unpeeled and cut into ¾-inch chunks

1 cup frozen peas (about 5 ounces)

2 cups packed baby spinach (about 3 ounces)

2 tablespoons chopped fresh parsley leaves

1 tablespoon chopped fresh tarragon leaves

Salt and ground black pepper

1. FOR THE BROTH: Combine the carrot, celery, onions, shallot, leek, and garlic in a large Dutch oven. Spray the vegetables lightly with cooking spray and toss to coat. Cover and cook the vegetables over medium heat, stirring frequently, until slightly softened and translucent, about 6 minutes. Add the broth, peppercorns, bay leaf, thyme, and parsley. Increase the heat to medium-high and bring to a simmer. Simmer until the broth is flavorful, about 20 minutes. Strain the broth through a fine-mesh sieve; discard the solids in the sieve. (The broth can be cooled to room temperature and refrigerated in an airtight container up to 3 days.)

2. FOR THE SOUP: Bring the broth to a simmer in a large saucepan over medium heat. Add the leeks and potatoes and simmer until the potatoes are tender, about 9 minutes. Stir in the peas, spinach, parsley, and tarragon. Season to taste with salt and pepper and serve immediately.

HEARTY VEGETABLE SOUP

IT WOULD BE NICE TO START BY SAYING THAT all of us in the test kitchen fondly remember the vegetable soups our mothers used to make. But the truth is that in most families, Mom made vegetable soup when the refrigerator crisper drawer was overflowing and the vegetables were a few days away from rotting. The recipe went something like this: Dissolve a few bouillon cubes in a pot of water, fill the pot with vegetables, and simmer away. Of course, that method yielded a bland, thin broth and dull, mismatched vegetables.

We wanted just the opposite—a rich, hearty, satisfying soup ideal for fall or winter. We wanted to develop a deeply flavored vegetable soup that could stand on its own for dinner.

Some primary tests helped us to outline what we didn't want: Pureed and cream soups were out; we wanted a chunky, brothy texture. Beef vegetable soups are common, but we sought a pure vegetable soup without

INGREDIENTS: Commercial Chicken Broth

Few of the commercial broths in our tasting came close to the full-bodied consistency of a successful homemade stock. Many lacked even a hint of chicken flavor. Interestingly, the four broths we rated best were all products of the Campbell Soup Company, of which Swanson is a subsidiary. In order, they were Swanson Chicken Broth, Campbell's Chicken Broth, Swanson Natural Goodness Chicken Broth (with 33 percent less sodium than regular Swanson chicken broth), and Campbell's Healthy Request Chicken Broth (with 30 percent less sodium than regular Campbell's chicken broth). The remaining broths were decidedly inferior and hard to recommend.

We tried to find out why Campbell's broths are superior to so many others, but the giant soup company declined to respond to questions, explaining that its recipes and cooking techniques are considered proprietary information. Many of the answers, however, could be found on the products' ingredient labels. As it turned out, the top two broths happened to contain the highest levels of sodium. Salt has been used for years in the food industry to make foods with less than optimum flavor tastier. The top two products also contained the controversial monosodium glutamate (MSG), an effective flavor enhancer.

Sadly, most of the products that had lower levels of salt and did not have the benefit of other food industry flavor enhancers simply tasted like dishwater. Their labels did indicate that their ingredients included "chicken broth" or "chicken stock," sometimes both. But calls to the U.S. Food and Drug Administration and the U.S. Department of Agriculture revealed that there are no standards that define chicken broth or stock, so an ingredient label indicating that the contents include chicken broth or chicken stock may mean anything as long as some chicken is used.

Ingredients aside, we found one more important explanation for why most commercial broths simply cannot replicate the full flavor and body of homemade stock. Most broths are sold canned, which entails an extended heating process carried out to ensure a sterilized product. The immediate disadvantage of this processing is that heat breaks down naturally present flavor enhancers found in chicken protein. Further, as it destroys other volatile flavors, the prolonged heating concentrates flavor components that are not volatile, such as salt.

A few national brands of chicken broth have begun to offer their products in aseptic packaging (cartons rather than cans). Compared with traditional canning, in which products are heated in the can for up to nearly an hour to ensure sterilization, the process of aseptic packaging entails a flash heating and cooling process that is said to help products better retain both their nutritional value and their flavor.

We decided to hold another tasting to see if we could detect more flavor in the products sold in aseptic packaging. Of the recommended broths in the tasting, only Swanson broths are available in aseptic packaging. We tasted Swanson's traditional and Natural Goodness chicken broths sold in cans and in aseptic packages. The results fell clearly in favor of the aseptically packaged broths, both tasted cleaner and more chickeny than their canned counterparts. So if you are truly seeking the best of the best in commercial broths, choose one of the two Swanson broths sold in aseptic packaging. An opened aseptic package is said to keep in the refrigerator for up to two weeks (broth from a can is said to keep, refrigerated, for only a few days).

THE BEST CHICKEN BROTHS

Swanson Chicken Broth (left) and its reduced-sodium counterpart, Swanson Natural Goodness Chicken Broth (center), are our top choices in the test kitchen. In testing, we've found that broth packaged in aseptic cartons (right) tastes better than canned broth.

chunks of meat. Finally, we wanted this to be a soup, not a stew. Stews have larger chunks of vegetables (or meat) and are generally less brothy than soups.

In the test kitchen, we often make soup bases by enhancing canned broth with additional ingredients. We decided to start testing using canned chicken broth; we'd try other options later. In the first of two batches, we simmered aromatics (carrots, celery, onions, and garlic) and herbs (parsley, thyme, and bay leaves) in the broth, strained out the solids, and finished by adding a basic mixture of vegetables—russet potatoes (we wanted a potato that would leach starch into the soup), carrots, and canned tomatoes. The second batch was identical except we sautéed the aromatic vegetables before simmering them in the broth. Tasters preferred the sautéed version—it was slightly heartier because of the added oil and caramelized vegetables—but both soups were far too light in taste and texture. We prepared a third pot of soup, sautéing the vegetables with a heaping spoonful of tomato paste. It was better, but we knew it wouldn't get accolades on a cold December evening.

We thought to roast the vegetables for the stock, hoping that caramelization would contribute the richness we were after. When we tried it, the resulting stock indeed had a much more concentrated flavor than the previous ones. Determined that roasting was the way to go, we experimented with the vegetables. We roasted fennel along with the whole head of garlic, carrots, celery, and onion we'd been using. Its contribution was minor, so we left it out. Shallots also proved to be too mild. Leeks were keepers, but they burned easily in the oven, so we decided to add the green parts raw to the stock and save the white parts for the soup. Mushrooms were a huge success—once roasted, they added meaty, deep notes

unlike any of the other vegetables we'd tried. We started out using earthy cremini mushrooms but soon switched to more intense (and quicker to clean) portobellos.

As for herbs, we made one batch of stock using dried thyme and one using fresh thyme (we dislike dried parsley in any application). Tasters had mixed opinions, but a few said the soup made with dried thyme had a strange aftertaste, so our recipe calls for fresh.

It was time to test different liquid options for the soup base. We made five pots of soup: one with water, one with canned beef broth, one using our recipe for homemade vegetable broth, one made with canned vegetable broth, and one with the usual canned chicken broth. The soup made with water was, well, watery. The canned beef broth soup was tinny, salty, and artificial tasting. Homemade vegetable stock takes several hours to make; we don't recommend it for this soup. Tasters were split when it came to canned chicken and canned vegetable broth; either may be used. Chicken broth produces a soup that has clean, balanced flavors, while soup made with vegetable broth has sweeter, tomatoey undertones.

We wanted to supplement the sparse combination of potatoes, carrots, leeks, and tomatoes we'd been using in the soup itself with some more interesting vegetables. Potent root vegetables like parsnips, turnips, and rutabagas were ruled out immediately for their tendency to overtake the soup. Cruciferous vegetables (broccoli, cauliflower, cabbage, and Brussels sprouts) met the same fate for their assertive nature. Eggplant seemed a weird addition to any soup, so we automatically eliminated it. Green beans and peas were too spring-like, but lima beans were just right. (Because some tasters dislike limas, we made them optional.) Celery was too unsubstantial, but its starchy, heartier cousin, celeriac, was perfect.

For visual and textural contrast, we wanted

to add leafy greens. Collard greens tasted too sharp, and spinach and chard are better saved for lighter soups. Kale turned the soup a murky green, but bitter, quick-cooking escarole did the trick, adding bright color and flavor.

Still in search of even more flavor, we turned our attention to technique—perhaps if we also roasted the vegetables for the soup (rather than simmering them), we could double the richness? We prepared some enhanced stock and then stirred in roasted vegetables. This was a mistake—the roasted flavor was overpowering, and the vegetables that had been first roasted and then simmered in the stock took on an odd, leftover consistency and taste. Next, we tried roasting only the tomatoes, but the payoff was minimal. We'd have to stick with simmering.

Our soup was getting really good, but we had several ideas for making it even better. First up was adding toasted walnuts to the stock; we'd seen this trick in several vegetarian cookbooks. Nearly every taster described the soup as lush and beefy tasting. But there was a hitch. The stock turned a disturbing purplish-brown color and was very cloudy, so we were forced to discard the idea. White wine turned the soup a little acidic. A Parmesan cheese rind brought nuttiness and richness to the soup, but it reminded us of Italian minestrone—we wanted an all-American recipe. We weren't surprised when the meatiness of pancetta was praised, but we wanted to leave the possibility of a vegetarian soup open. In search of ways to simulate pancetta's smoky flavor, we stirred two tablespoons of paprika into a pot of soup. This was a bomb. The soup tasted artificially smoky and had a neon red tint. Our last try, dried porcini mushrooms, put the soup over the top. Their meaty, mellow flavor created a soup with superior, intense flavor.

The last problem to tackle was that the soup stock was too thin. We pureed a few ladles of the soup in a blender and mixed it back into the soup pot—a successful thickening technique, but a hassle. Mashing some of the potatoes against the side of the soup pot with a spoon had the same effect. And instead of discarding the roasted garlic head used to flavor the stock, we borrowed an idea from a colleague and added the mashed cloves to the soup. As a final flourish, we added some chopped parsley and crostini (garlicky toasts). Now we had a soup with multidimensional flavor and a great texture—and it was substantial enough for dinner.

Hearty Vegetable Soup
MAKES ABOUT 2 QUARTS, SERVING 4 TO 6

The broth for the soup may be made ahead and frozen in an airtight container for up to 2 months. Use canned vegetable broth rather than chicken broth for a vegetarian soup. The recipe may be doubled. To keep the sand trapped in the dried mushrooms from marring the broth, place the porcini in a paper coffee filter and tie the filter closed with a piece of kitchen twine.

BROTH

1   large carrot, peeled and chopped medium
1   medium celery rib, chopped medium
1   medium onion, chopped medium
3   medium portobello mushrooms (about 6 ounces), cleaned and roughly chopped
1   head garlic, top third cut off and discarded, loose outer skins removed
3   tablespoons olive oil
1   heaping tablespoon tomato paste
9   cups low-sodium chicken or vegetable broth
2   leeks, cleaned, green parts roughly chopped, white parts sliced thin crosswise, separated into rings, and reserved for soup

INGREDIENTS: Commercial Vegetable Broth

We don't like canned vegetable broth. That was our assumption, at least, when we began this tasting. Usually thin, metallic, and overly sweet and/or salty, canned vegetable broth was a good idea in theory, we thought, but when it came time to prepare vegetable soups, sauces, and risottos, we instinctively reached for canned chicken broth.

But after one too many arguments around the editorial table about making vegetable dishes completely meat free, we decided to review our preconceptions. We gathered nine popular brands of packaged vegetable broth and tasted them in three different applications: warmed broth, in an enriched vegetable soup stock, and in asparagus risotto.

The winner of the straight broth tasting, Swanson, was praised for its "nice sweet-sour-salty balance," though some tasters noted the "barely perceptible vegetable flavor." Second-place Better than Bouillon was deemed "good, nicely flavored" and "very tasty," but many found it "very sour" with "strong metallic flavors." Coming in at the bottom of the tasting was Kitchen Basics, which lost points for a sweet molasses flavor that one taster described as "honey tea." It's no surprise that top-ranked Swanson had the highest sodium level, with 970 milligrams per cup, compared with 330 milligrams per cup of Kitchen Basics, which had the lowest sodium level. Salt is perceived as flavor, whereas the less salty broths were deemed bland and flavorless.

Our winning vegetable broth had a mean score of 5.3 out of 10—perfectly average but not exactly high praise. That's OK—we're not advocating drinking straight vegetable broth. But how would canned vegetable broth fare in a recipe where it was not the leading lady but instead a strong supporting character?

For the second test, we enriched the canned vegetable broth with roasted vegetables and garlic, like we would do for our Hearty Vegetable Soup (page 324). We pitted the winner, Swanson, and the loser, Kitchen Basics, of our straight broth tasting against each other. Swanson eked out a win, with a saltier flavor that most tasters preferred. Kitchen Basics was praised by some as "flowery," "earthy," and "more vegetal," though it was those same qualities that some tasters listed as negatives in the plain broth tasting. Neither soup was bad; each had different flavor characteristics that worked in this application.

In the asparagus risotto, the results were surprising. We threw in what we thought would be a ringer—Swanson reduced-sodium chicken broth, the winner of our canned chicken broth tasting—to compete against Swanson and Kitchen Basics vegetable broths. Swanson vegetable broth was the tasters' favorite, praised as "well-balanced" with "round, full flavors." The darkest colored of all the original broths in the tasting, Kitchen Basics, was liked by some for its "rich and hearty" flavor, though most tasters found the "muddy" color distracting, resulting in a last-place finish. The chicken broth finished a strong second.

Though there was a clear winner—and loser—in the straight broth tasting, the varied results in other applications lead us to believe that the differences between the broths are subtle. If you are using canned vegetable broth in a recipe with lots of other strong flavors, it probably doesn't matter which broth you use. If the flavors of the broth are going to be more up front, like in a simple brothy soup or risotto, you should probably use Swanson. And if you are sensitive to salt, you may want to check the sodium level before you buy.

One last thought. Chicken broth, not vegetable broth, is still the standard in the test kitchen, used in stir-fry sauces and braises. Many recipes in this book call for it. However, in each of these cases, vegetable broth can be substituted if you prefer to make the dish vegetarian.

**THE BEST
VEGETABLE BROTH**
Swanson Vegetable Broth had the most flavor of the nine brands we tested. It also contains the most sodium, which partly explains its strong showing in our tasting.

10   sprigs fresh parsley
4   sprigs fresh thyme
2   bay leaves
1/3   ounce dried porcini mushrooms,
     wrapped in a coffee filter
     (see note above)

SOUP

1   (14.5-ounce) can diced tomatoes,
     drained; tomato pieces slightly
     crushed with fingers
2   small russet potatoes, peeled and cut
     into 1/2-inch dice (about 1 1/2 cups)
2   medium carrots, peeled and cut into
     1/2-inch dice (about 1 cup)
1/2   medium celeriac, peeled and cut into
     1/2-inch dice (about 1 1/2 cups)
4   heaping cups escarole, stems discarded,
     leaves cut into 1-inch pieces
1   cup frozen baby lima beans,
     defrosted (optional)
2   tablespoons minced fresh parsley leaves
     Salt and ground black pepper

1   recipe Crostini for Soup (optional)

1. FOR THE BROTH: Adjust an oven rack to the middle position and heat the oven to 450 degrees. Place the carrot, celery, onion, portobellos, and garlic on a rimmed baking sheet. Toss the vegetables first with the oil and then with the tomato paste, making sure that the vegetables are evenly coated. Spread the vegetables out evenly on the pan (the garlic should be cut-side up). Roast until well browned, 25 to 30 minutes.

2. Transfer the roasted vegetables to a heavy-bottomed stockpot or Dutch oven. Add the broth, the green part of the leeks, parsley, thyme, bay leaves, and porcini. Cover, increase the heat to medium-high, and bring to a simmer. Reduce the heat to medium-low and simmer, partially covered,

for 30 minutes. Remove the garlic and, using tongs, squeeze the cloves out of their skin and into a small bowl. Mash the garlic to a paste with the back of a fork and set aside. Strain the stock through a fine-mesh strainer, pressing firmly on the solids to release the flavorful juices. Discard the remaining solids.

3. FOR THE SOUP: Transfer the stock to a large saucepan or Dutch oven and add the tomatoes, potatoes, carrots, celeriac, and the white part of the leeks. Bring to a simmer over medium-high heat. Reduce the heat to medium-low and simmer, partially covered, until the vegetables are tender, about 25 minutes.

4. Add the escarole and lima beans (if using). Simmer until the escarole is wilted and the limas are tender, about 5 minutes. Stir in the parsley and season with salt and pepper to taste. Serve immediately with crostini, if desired.

~>✦

Crostini for Soup
MAKES ENOUGH FOR 6 BOWLS OF SOUP

1/2   baguette or long Italian loaf (6 to 8
     ounces), cut into 1/2-inch-thick slices
1   large clove garlic, peeled
1/4   cup good-quality extra-virgin olive oil
     Salt and ground black pepper

Adjust an oven rack to the middle position and heat the oven to 400 degrees. Arrange the bread slices in a single layer on a baking sheet and bake until they are dry and crisp, about 10 minutes, turning them over halfway through the baking time. While still hot, rub each slice of bread with the raw garlic clove. Liberally drizzle the olive oil over the slices. Sprinkle with salt and pepper. (Crostini are best straight from the oven, but they can be set aside on a plate for several hours.)

INDEX

NOTE: Page numbers in *ITALICS* refer to color photographs.